ON SECULAR GOVERNANCE

To Sheldon,

with deep appreciation for your ministry, vision for the possibili[t]y for the future, and for your many fine sermons.

Ron Duty
4-4-16

On Secular Governance

Lutheran Perspectives
on Contemporary Legal Issues

Edited by

Ronald W. Duty and Marie A. Failinger

WILLIAM B. EERDMANS PUBLISHING COMPANY
GRAND RAPIDS, MICHIGAN / CAMBRIDGE, U.K.

Published 2016 by
Wm. B. Eerdmans Publishing Co.
2140 Oak Industrial Drive N.E., Grand Rapids, Michigan 49505 /
P.O. Box 163, Cambridge CB3 9PU U.K.

Printed in the United States of America

22 21 20 19 18 17 16   7 6 5 4 3 2 1

ISBN 978-0-8028-7228-9

www.eerdmans.com

In memory of my mother and father, Evelyn and William Duty. Her consistent respect and hunger for learning shaped my own, her deep Lutheran piety and sense of Christian vocation led her sons by example, and her own lifelong pursuit of an education was — tragically — affected by her obedience of the Fourth Commandment. His support, both for her educational pursuits and my own, was constant and generous.

RWD

To my parents, Joan and Conard Failinger, for the many sacrifices they made in taking their six children to weekly worship and sending us to Lutheran schools and colleges so that our lives could be informed by the Lutheran witness and conformed to our many diverse callings. And to my grandparents, Emma and Conard Failinger, and Nina and Harold Lang, for guiding us in the faith by word and example.

MAF

Contents

CONTENTS

viii

Contents

PART IV
LUTHERANS IN THEIR ROLE AS CITIZENS

Contributors

Svend Andersen is Professor of Ethics and Philosophy of Religion at Aarhus University, Aarhus, Denmark.

Robert Benne is the Jordan Trexler Professor Emeritus and a Research Associate at Roanoke College, Salem, Virginia.

Ibrahim Bitrus has been a lecturer at Bronnum Lutheran Seminary in Yola, Nigeria, and in 2015 received his Ph.D. in systematic theology from Luther Seminary, St. Paul, Minnesota.

James M. Childs Jr. is Joseph A. Sittler Professor Emeritus of Theology and Ethics at Trinity Lutheran Seminary, Columbus, Ohio.

Wanda Deifelt is Professor of Religion at Luther College in Decorah, Iowa.

Ronald W. Duty is the retired Assistant Director for Studies in Church and Society, Evangelical Lutheran Church, Chicago, Illinois.

Marie A. Failinger is Professor of Law at Mitchell Hamline School of Law, St. Paul, Minnesota.

Mary Gaebler is Associate Professor of Theological Ethics at Gustavus Adolphus College, St. Peter, Minnesota.

Patrick R. Keifert is the Olin S. and Amanda Fjelstad Reigstad Professor of Systematic Theology at Luther Seminary and President and Director of Research at Church Innovations Institute, St. Paul, Minnesota.

Morten Kjaer is a fellow in the Department of Law, University of Southern Denmark, Odense, Denmark.

Susan R. Martyn is the Stoepler Professor of Law and Values and Distinguished University Professor at University of Toledo College of Law, Toledo, Ohio.

Richard J. Perry Jr. is Professor of Church and Society and Urban Ministry at Lutheran School of Theology at Chicago, Illinois.

Leopoldo A. Sánchez M. is Associate Professor of Systematic Theology and Director of the Center for Hispanic Studies in the Werner R. H. Krause and Elizabeth Ringger Krause Endowed Chair for Hispanic Ministries at Concordia Seminary, St. Louis, Missouri.

Kirsi Stjerna is Professor of Reformation Church History and Director of the Institute for Luther Studies at the Lutheran Theological Seminary at Gettysburg, Pennsylvania.

John R. Stumme is the retired Director for Studies, Church in Society, Evangelical Lutheran Church in America, Chicago, Illinois.

Victor Thasiah is Assistant Professor of Religion at California Lutheran University, Thousand Oaks, California.

W. Bradley Wendel is Professor of Law at Cornell University School of Law, Ithaca, New York.

Acknowledgments

As editors, we would like to express our appreciation to our authors, Lutheran lawyers and theologians who stepped out of their disciplinary comfort zones to engage their faith and their learning to initiate a conversation about how Lutheran theology can be a voice in the debates within modern nation-states about secular law and legal institutions. We hope their work will stimulate other theologians and lawyers in the Lutheran tradition to add their insights to the field of law and religion.

After we decided that our book would benefit from a conversation among the authors, Valparaiso University School of Law provided valuable support by offering to fund and host an authors' conference for us and many other Lutheran theologians, law professors, lawyers, and clergy. We are grateful to Dean Ivan Bodensteiner for approving the funding for this project, and for Associate Dean Jeremy Telman and Melissa Mundt for the countless hours they put into organizing the details of that conference. The conference, held at Valparaiso University's Chicago location at the Lutheran School of Theology, on March 27-28, 2014, provided rich food for thought for our chapters, and we thank the additional speakers who made our book conference so rich: Dr. Per Anderson, Dr. Heath Carter, Edward Engelbrecht, Hon. Humes Franklin, Dr. Slavica Jakelić, Dr. Robert Kolb, Prof. Faisal Kutty, Dr. Martin Marty, Hon. David R. Minge, Hon. Christopher Nuechterlein, Hon. Rebecca Pallmeyer, Dr. Gary Simpson, and Dr. Christina Traina.

We would be remiss not to acknowledge our Hamline research assistants, Julianna Passe, who did excellent technical work on footnotes and proofreading, and Brittany Levine, who worked on the index to this book. Finally, we are so grateful to Dr. Norman Hjelm and Chairman William Eerdmans for seeing the value of bringing Lutheran insights into the ongoing interfaith conversation about religion and law, and to the entire staff at Eerdmans for their editorial work to help us make this a stronger work.

A Note on Citations of Legal Materials

Citations of articles from law journals in this volume vary from what is customary for legal scholars. Because this volume is intended for a general multidisciplinary audience, we have adopted a style frequently used by John Witte Jr. in his publications for a similar audience. Deviation from the usual custom is intended to help scholars outside the legal profession better understand where to find the source should they wish to read an article from a legal journal in its entirety. For example, the customary style of citation for legal journals is like the following:

Tamar Frankel, *Fiduciary Law,* 71 Cal. L. Rev. 795, 830 (1983).

In this volume, however, citations like this appear as follows:

Tamar Frankel, "Fiduciary Law," *California Law Review* 795 (1983): 830.

A later citation from this same source would appear as follows:

Frankel, "Fiduciary Law," p. 830.

We have maintained, however, the customary style used by the courts and legal scholars for citing decisions in law cases. These styles are necessary to locate cases decided by the courts and recorded in court records for those who wish to read and analyze them. Thus, a case decided by the U.S. Supreme Court appears as:

Reynolds v. United States, 98 U.S. 145 (1879).

An example of a case decided in a Federal District Court is:

City of El Paso v. Reynolds, 563 F. Supp. 379 (D.N.M. 1983).

A case decided by a state court, such as the Arizona Supreme Court, might appear similar to:

In re: The General Adjudication of All Rights to Use Water in the Gila River System and Source, 35 P.3d 68, 76 (Ariz. 2001).

We hope this will help scholars outside the legal professions locate these cases, either online or with the help of a law librarian.

Introduction

Ronald W. Duty and Marie A. Failinger

In the past thirty years, the worldwide conversation about the relationship between religion and law has taken firm root as an area of intellectual study, particularly in the legal academy in the United States and throughout the world. Theologians and scholars from other disciplines that intersect with law are also finding new interest in considering how their religious insights might inform both jurisprudence and practical lawmaking, both for local and nation-state governments and for international legal institutions and covenants. Over this period, numerous academic journals specializing in law and religion have been born, along with centers for law and religion at many of the great church-related law schools in many countries, as well as international organizations such as the International Consortium for Law and Religion Studies (ICLARS). Even beyond these centers, however, courses on law and religion have sprouted in many law schools and universities, helped along by textbooks by prominent legal scholars, such as Americans John Noonan and Edward McGlynn Gaffney, Thomas Berg, Cole Durham and Brett Scharffs, Leslie Griffin, Frank Ravitch, and Howard Lesnick.

In these conversations, Jewish, Muslim, Catholic, and Reformed perspectives have largely dominated. While Lutherans have weighed in on national public policy debates and produced important social ethics texts, in the United States and many English-speaking countries, at least, they have been largely absent from this conversation between the disciplines of law and religion. Our ambition is to bring more Lutheran voices to the pressing legal issues in these and other nations. Moreover, we hope that Lutherans throughout the world might begin to document the ways in which the Lutheran Church in their country has shaped and should shape the civic conversation about justice and civil law. We believe that Lutherans have important insights to offer fellow citizens from other religious and nonreligious traditions as they debate laws affecting immigration reform, human trafficking, property and the environment, social welfare law, and crime, just to name a few.

The Lutheran tradition might not seem an obvious resource for informing the values that should shape secular law. For one thing, the Lutheran witness has been almost single-mindedly focused on one key message, found in Luther's explanation to the Second Article of the Apostles' Creed, "I believe that Jesus Christ, true God, begotten of the Father from eternity, and also true man, born of the Virgin Mary, is my Lord, who has redeemed me, a lost and condemned creature, purchased and won me from all sins, from death and from the power of the devil, not with gold or silver, but with His holy, precious blood and with His innocent suffering and death. . . ."

Moreover, unlike some faith traditions, Lutherans have always carefully guarded the distinction between the two ways in which God governs the world, sometimes referring to the work of God's "left hand" in co-creating, with us, a just and trustworthy world in this earthly life for the sake of human community, and God's "right-hand" work of saving us from sin and evil for the life that is here and to come. In Luther's theology, all human persons, creatures of God, have been endowed with reason capable of discerning how we should order our common life. Christians, including Lutherans, possess neither a special endowment for doing this work nor any special exemption from the sin and self-justification that infects human reasoning about how we should live our lives together.

This twofold understanding of God's work in the world, however, strengthens the case for Lutheran participation in shaping secular law in governments around the world. Precisely because we recognize that we are equal partners with those from other faith-traditions in reasoning about what a trustworthy world that permits human flourishing should look like, we can debate these issues using accessible, often common, arguments and vocabularies. Indeed, precisely because Lutherans do not imagine secular law as a specific divine command, Lutherans can be politically divided, as our text demonstrates, without being theologically divided about what is at the heart of our faith.

Moreover, the Lutheran tradition has developed rich insights about human behavior and well-being that can inform attempts to create vibrant and responsive legal institutions. Lutheran insights into human nature, for example, the creative capacity of humans to reason about their situation always infected by their unacknowledged tendency toward self-interest and self-justification, can be important in framing the institutions of civic life as well as specific rules of law for matters ranging from environmental protection to domestic violence.

This collection by Lutheran theologians and legal academics illustrates some of the ways in which "Lutheran thinking" can be brought to bear on the diversity of problems that lawyers and those who shape the law encounter, from interpretive questions to specific rules of law. In Part I of this text, law professor Bradley Wendel and theologians John Stumme and Richard Perry deal with broad jurisprudential concerns that shape our conversations about legal rules. Wendel reviews parallel debates in theology and religion about interpretation and legitimate practical authority, arguments about whether texts such as the Bible and the Constitution should be interpreted as literal commands to humans, or understood as living documents and repositories of "constitutive political and moral ideals" and values. He suggests that as both citizens and Christians, we are part of an authentic narrative of people that must be discovered time and again. Describing the historical loss of "dual jurisdictions" theology as a part of modern secular public discourse, John Stumme surveys the arguments of prominent modern law and religion scholars to make the case that "secular orthodoxy" has jeopardized the rationale for religious freedom. He argues that reclaiming religious freedom as a special freedom in our democracies is vital to a thriving human community. Richard Perry, drawing on his own experience of racial profiling, makes the case that African Americans live out of a paradoxical relationship with both Christian theology and secular law, a relationship forged in a commitment to human rights and yet profound experiences of human rights violations. Grounded in Dr. Martin Luther King's theology of just and unjust laws, and its parallels in Lutheran theology, he proposes a prophetic challenge to racism and the violation of rights in our communities.

In Part II, authors Mary Gaebler and Ronald Duty engage the work of legal scholar Joseph Sax to consider how modern secular law can protect or destroy the wider creation. Gaebler draws on the Lutheran doctrine of *"finitum capax infiniti"* or "the finite can bear the infinite" to reflect on how environmental and property law might be very different if it were grounded in the reality that God is present "in, with, and under the created order," including in our own being and doing. She suggests, with Sax, that shaping law out of a flexible, adaptive, and creative response to changing conditions in the wider creation permits us to exercise our Lutheran calling of stewardship to that creation. Ronald Duty confronts the water crisis in the American Southwest through recent Supreme Court cases between contesting states over who will share dwindling natural water supplies in that region. Drawing on Sax's distinction between transformational economies and economies of nature, Duty employs Luther's explication of water as an example of daily bread and his description about theft in the Seventh Commandment to propose that national water policy can be constructively managed through principles of precaution, sufficiency, sustainability, participation, solidarity, and equity.

At the heart of Lutheran theology is the belief that we are created and called by God to serve the neighbor, a commitment that has important implications for legal institutions. In "Temporal Authority: The Extent to Which It Should Be Obeyed," Luther argued that the "first use" of the law, its temporal application, was to "instruct, constrain and compel" persons in the ways in which they should live with their fellow citizens; and in other writings, he described how this "first use" imposed responsibilities on secular governments to engage in many community-preservative tasks from educating children to caring for victims of epidemics.

In Part III, Kirsi Stjerna employs the Lutheran understanding that children are God's gift to our communities, which imposes a calling *coram homnibus* on us all to care for them under the Fifth Commandment. She targets sex trafficking as a case study in sin and human rights violation, requiring aggressive and diligent reform of existing laws on sex trafficking, describing some hopeful efforts against such transgressive behavior. Wanda Deifelt extensively documents the worldwide problem of human trafficking and the law's inadequate efforts to respond to it. She employs Lutheran theology to argue that secular laws against trafficking must be articulated from the perspective of global citizenship and grounded in values such as advocacy, solidarity, and empowerment, mutuality, and accountability.

Leopoldo A. Sánchez M. takes on the controversial and difficult topic of American immigration reform. Drawing from debates among Lutherans who have radically different political visions about immigration reform, he shows how these debates are grounded in different prioritization of the same themes Lutherans have employed for centuries in analyzing secular law: "love of neighbor (including the stranger), obedience to the law (including civil law), God's work in the two kingdoms (spiritual and temporal realms), and vocation." Marie Failinger and Patrick Keifert confront the United States Supreme Court's unwillingness to recognize a constitutional right to the means to live, and suggest that Christians might better make use of "first use of the law" arguments in crafting an understanding of the moral responsibilities of government to our most vulnerable citizens. Susan Martyn employs Luther's understanding of "usefulness," grounded in ancient fiduciary

4

law, and the biblical parallel of the unjust steward, to derive lawyers' chief fiduciary duties to their clients, involving client control, communication, resolving conflicts of interest, keeping confidences, and providing competent service.

In Part IV of the book, we turn to the ways in which the Lutheran Church and Lutheran citizens have fruitfully interacted with secular governments around the world, and how Lutherans might ethically consider their responsibilities as citizens. The political relationship between the state and traditional church institutions has been the subject of much law and religion literature. Svend Anderson and Morten Kjaer provide a historical introduction to how the Reformation changed the relationship between the ruler and the church in Lutheran countries. They show how Denmark has most closely adhered to the post-Reformation model and how other European countries have forged different models based on stronger separation and church autonomy principles. James Childs Jr. looks at a common trouble spot in defining the relationship between the church and the state: the role of military chaplains. He argues that the American Establishment Clause justifies an accommodation for the free exercise rights of military personnel that can serve their well-being while being true to the constitutional intentions.

The Lutheran Church in Africa can play an important role in the development of African nations. Victor Thasiah explores the work of Lutheran pastor John Rutsindintwarane in building and supporting the right to freedom of association through community empowerment, by building community organizations that deliberate and advocate for peaceful development. He describes how these institutions are grounded in the Lutheran doctrine of callings, as a strong form of civic democracy built on a theology of Christian love. Conversely, Ibrahim Bitrus critiques the Nigerian Christian churches for being complicit in the graft and terror visited upon Nigerian people, an "unjust peace" that has terrible implications for the rule of law and social development in Nigeria. He advocates for a church encounter with state officials that goes beyond public rebuke, to "use the *whole law and gospel* in the public sphere" to expose and publicly protest these injustices, employing Luther's vision of the rule of the world by the triune God.

Finally, Robert Benne looks at failed historical attempts by Lutherans to work out the two kingdoms doctrine on two extremes: on one hand, complete passivity in the face of government evil; and on the other, Americanist Lutheran attempts to build the kingdom of God in America and the "liberal Protestant" approach of the ELCA. He argues for a set of common Lutheran principles more authentically recognizing the Lutheran witness on the two kingdoms doctrine, one that embraces its embeddedness in the larger Christian witness to the state, indirect modes of influence on political life, and some common grounding principles on the protection of life, marriage, and the family.

We hope that these essays will initiate new conversations about the nature of just law and legal institutions with our brothers and sisters in Lutheran denominations through the world, in the wider Christian community, and in the world we inhabit with all of God's creation, and most especially those created in God's image. As Prof. Benne notes, "An authentic Lutheran voice of public witness needs to be heard."

PART I

Framing the Problems of Law and Theology

CHAPTER 1

Nomos and Narrative in Civil Law and Theological Ethics

W. Bradley Wendel

This essay on authority and interpretation seeks to establish a fruitful connection, or at least some instructive parallels, between the domains of civil law and Lutheran social ethics.[1] The practical authority of scripture is one of the foundations of Lutheran theology, but right away one can per-

---

1. Following Luther, theologians tend to use the term "civil law" to avoid confusion with the two realms or modes of divine activity through which God orders the universe, i.e., law and gospel. For lawyers the reference to civil law inevitably calls to mind either the distinction between civil and criminal law (e.g., the possibility of state-imposed punishment as opposed to liability to a private party) or the large-scale structure distinction between legal systems descended from the English common law, and those systems called "civil law" which are ultimately rooted in Roman law of antiquity but have their typical modern expression in the French or German civil codes. The term "civil law" in Lutheran theology is well established, however, and I will use it here. In any event I wish to avoid the complex issue of the relationship between God's law and state law, with the state understood as "a divine order endowed by God with certain creative tasks and quite independent from the church as an ecclesiastical institution." George Wolfgang Forell, *Faith Active in Love: An Investigation of the Principles Underlying Luther's Social Ethics* (Minneapolis: Augsburg Publishing House, 1954), p. 24. The discussion here of the analogy between interpreting scripture and interpreting state law is intended as suggestive only, not as staking out any theological ground.

I am grateful to Mary Lowe, Rick Bair, Mary Streufert, and Roger Willer for their patient guidance and suggestions for further readings in Lutheran theology and biblical hermeneutics. The standard disclaimer is that any remaining errors are mine alone, but in this case it is worth emphasizing that I am truly a babe in the woods of academic theology and it would be exceedingly unfair to share any blame with people who have tried diligently to set me on the right path.

ceive the problem of locating practical authority in a text.[2] For anything to be an authority (practical or theoretical) it must create new reasons for someone to do something. A person subject to a practical authority must not act on what she perceives to be the thing to do, all things considered; rather, she must follow the directive of an authority *because* that is what it says to do.[3]

That is the case whether the authority is an institution like the Roman Catholic Church, a complex set of institutions such as the political and legal system of the United States, or a set of books compiled into a canon of scriptures. For all but the most straightforward cases of personal authority — for instance, a parent saying to a child, "Put on a helmet before you ride your bicycle!" — those subject to the directives of an authority may encounter the problem of interpretation. One must work out exactly what the authority commands or forbids. As an example, does a criminal prohibition on "carrying" a firearm in connection with a drug transaction prohibit driving around with a gun in the glove compartment of a car?[4] The trunk? The U.S. Constitution prohibits cruel and unusual punishment and forbids state governments to deny citizens the equal protection of the law. Does this mean the death penalty is unconstitutional?[5] Or particular means of putting condemned prisoners to death? What about a mandatory sentence of life without parole? Are they prohibited for some defendants

2. On the authority of scripture and Lutheran theology, see, e.g., Carl E. Braaten, *Principles of Lutheran Theology* (Philadelphia: Fortress Press, 1983), chapter 1.

3. See generally Joseph Raz, *The Authority of Law,* 2nd ed. (Oxford: Oxford University Press, 2009), pp. 23, 26-27. See also Eric W. Gritsch and Robert W. Jenson, *Lutheranism: The Theological Movement and Its Confessional Writings* (Philadelphia: Fortress Press, 1976), p. 7 ("By your utterance you in some way determine my future. This determination is what we mean by 'authority.' "). Practical authorities should be distinguished from theoretical authorities. The former have only epistemic effect — that is, they inform their subjects about the reasons that exist independently of the authority. For example, the *Physicians' Desk Reference* is a theoretical authority with respect to the side effects associated with pharmaceuticals. Practical authorities, on the other hand, change the normative situation of their subjects; they create new reasons for action or block reasons that otherwise would have existed. For this distinction see Joseph Raz, "Authority, Law, and Morality," in *Ethics in the Public Domain* (Oxford: Clarendon Press, 1994), p. 211.

4. *Bailey v. United States,* 516 U.S. 137 (1995).

5. *Furman v. Georgia,* 408 U.S. 238 (1972) (holding that the death penalty violated the prohibition on cruel and unusual punishment, because the imposition of death sentences was often arbitrary). After states modified their capital punishment statutes to address the Supreme Court's concerns in *Furman,* the Court reversed course on the constitutionality of the death penalty. *Gregg v. Georgia,* 428 U.S. 153 (1976).

(e.g., juveniles) but not others?[6] Outside the context of the criminal law, consider the First Amendment to the Constitution, which says that Congress shall not abridge the freedom of speech. Do state (not Congressional) restrictions on the sale of violent video games to minors abridge the freedom of speech?[7] What about a state law prohibiting pharmaceutical companies from using information about the patterns of prescriptions written by doctors to make more effective marketing pitches — does the sale of information constitute the freedom of speech?[8] Even if no one seriously questions the power of the U.S. Constitution to create reasons, there can be considerable uncertainty about how a provision of the Constitution bears on a particular decision.

The issue is considerably more subtle for Christians in the Lutheran tradition for whom it is not really a text, per se, that is the authority. Luther was careful to assert the distinction between the scriptures and the Word of God.[9] The Bible is the written Word of God, but the Word of God is also proclaimed in the world, and present eternally as the second person of the Trinity, which became personally incarnate in the world in Jesus Christ.

Other Protestants, particularly of a fundamentalist orientation, tend to identify the Word of God with the Bible (generally in its original languages), and accordingly are drawn to an account of interpretation that emphasizes the perspicuity of the written text and the authority of the plain meaning of biblical language.[10] There is undoubtedly a strand of the Lutheran tradition that emphasizes the plain meaning of scripture.[11] Luther's critique of the Roman Church's ordering of tradition over scripture in the hierarchy of authority, and the resulting principle of *sola scriptura* seemed to imply that the *text* of the Bible *itself* was authoritative and, therefore, readily under-

---

6. *Miller v. Alabama,* 132 S. Ct. 2455 (2012) (holding that mandatory life without parole sentences for juveniles violated Eighth Amendment prohibition on cruel and unusual punishment).

7. *Brown v. Entertainment Merchants Association,* 131 S. Ct. 2729 (2011).

8. *Sorrell v. IMS Health, Inc.,* 131 S. Ct. 2653 (2011).

9. Braaten, *Principles of Lutheran Theology,* p. 5; William H. Lazareth, *Christians in Society: Luther, the Bible, and Social Ethics* (Minneapolis: Fortress Press, 2001), pp. 33-36; Erik M. Heen, "The Theological Interpretation of the Bible," *Lutheran Quarterly* 21, no. 4 (2007): 376.

10. See, e.g., Vincent Crapanzano, *Serving the Word: Literalism in America from the Pulpit to the Bench* (New York: New Press, 2000), p. 64.

11. Hans W. Frei, *The Eclipse of Biblical Narrative: A Study in Eighteenth and Nineteenth Century Hermeneutics* (New Haven: Yale University Press, 1974), pp. 37-40, 54-55.

standable without the intervening interpretive authority of the church and its teaching tradition.[12]

But *sola scriptura* does not entail literalism. One of the best-known principles of Lutheran hermeneutics is the christocentric principle: Scripture and the church's teaching tradition should both be tested by the criterion of, "Does it urge (or inculcate [*treiben*]) Christ?"[13] This principle is, in turn, generally elaborated in terms of the dualistic revelation of the reign of God in the world as both law and gospel.[14] God's Word conveys both judgment by God's law and salvation by God's grace. It is therefore not an authority in the simplistic command-sanction model that is sometimes used (incorrectly) to describe positive, civil law.[15] God is at work in the world through, among other things, the institutions of civil government, including the law of the state — this is one response to the presence of sin and evil in the world, one mode of governance within God's twofold rule.[16]

The division Luther described is not just between the realms of earth and heaven (as Reinhold Niebuhr wrongly believed), with God pretty much leaving earth to its own devices while God concentrates on redeeming fallen humanity in a world to come.[17] Rather, God works everywhere in two different, complementary ways, by telling us what to do and keeping us oriented toward God (law) and promising us the unconditional gift of grace wholly apart from whether we comply with the requirements of law (gospel).[18] The

12. Braaten, *Principles of Lutheran Theology*, p. 6.

13. Lazareth, *Christians in Society*, p. 35; Braaten, *Principles of Lutheran Theology*, pp. 2-5, 23. I like this way of stating it: "The hermeneutical principle necessarily involves squeezing the text until it proves christologically fruitful." Helmut Thielicke, *Theological Ethics*, vol. 1, *Foundations,* ed. William H. Lazareth (Grand Rapids: Eerdmans, 1979), p. 105.

14. See, e.g., Martin Luther, "Preface to the New Testament," in *Martin Luther: Selections from His Writings,* ed. John Dillenberger (New York: Anchor Books, 1962), pp. 14-19; James M. Childs Jr., "Ethics and the Promise of God: Moral Authority and the Church's Witness," in *The Promise of Lutheran Ethics,* ed. Karen L. Bloomquist and John R. Stumme (Minneapolis: Fortress Press, 1998), p. 106; Lazareth, *Christians in Society,* p. 53 (quoting Luther's first rule of translating scripture: "If some passage is obscure, I consider whether it treats of grace or of law . . . for God divides his teaching into law and gospel"); Gritsch and Jenson, *Lutheranism,* pp. 8-9.

15. For an overview of H. L. A. Hart's decisive refutation of John Austin's command-sanction theory of law, see W. Bradley Wendel, *Ethics and the Law* (Cambridge: Cambridge University Press, 2014).

16. Lazareth, *Christians in Society,* p. 110.

17. Braaten, *Principles of Lutheran Theology,* p. 133 ("This is not a 'God is in heaven and man is on earth' type of dualism . . .").

18. Steven D. Paulson, *Lutheran Theology* (London: Bloomsbury, 2011), pp. 119-21.

law protects us from the illusion that we are no longer in need of justification, and avoids the problem of "cheap grace," but it is essential never to believe that one can earn the possibility of communion with God by following God's law. The free gift of grace alone is the sole means of justification in the sight of God *(coram Deo)*.

Read with a law/gospel lens, the interpretation of scripture becomes a matter of organizing our understanding of the story around the revelation of God's promise. Interpretation is "normed by [its] truly redemptive fulfillment in the Christ-event."[19] The Word of God is the proclamation of a narrative of estrangement from God and from each other (confirmed in God's law), the recognition that we are powerless to attain communion with God through anything we are capable of doing on our own, the promise of God's grace and the gift of faith, and the orientation of all action toward an eschatological horizon — "Thy kingdom come."[20]

The authority of scripture is therefore not best understood on the model of parental authority ("wear your helmet!") or legal prescription ("no cruel and unusual punishment") but as freeing its subjects to possibilities that are not otherwise theirs, namely, moving toward the possibility of communion with God.[21] The law stands against the gospel as something that accuses us, against which we cannot stand, but the gospel frees us from this condemnation. Without the law there can be no gospel: "Who . . . may speak of 'grace' without . . . taking from grace the very thing which makes it grace, namely, the element of miracle, the inexplicable, that which conforms to no law."[22] But the deeply paradoxical observation that there can be no promise of grace apart from the condemnation of law, along with the characteristically Lutheran formulation of the "now . . . not yet" structure of God's saving activity, suggests a dynamic, narrative approach to interpreting scripture, not a static plain-meaning account of the meaning of biblical texts.[23]

The title of this essay is an allusion to a classic article by Robert Cover, which argues, with great subtlety and sophistication, that no *nomos,* no nor-

---

19. Lazareth, *Christians in Society,* p. 43.

20. Braaten, *Principles of Lutheran Theology,* p. 135; Reinhard Hütter, "The Twofold Center of Lutheran Ethics: Christian Freedom and God's Commandments," in Bloomquist and Stumme, *The Promise of Lutheran Ethics,* pp. 31-54.

21. Gritsch and Jenson, *Lutheranism,* p. 8; Hütter, "The Twofold Center of Lutheran Ethics," p. 32.

22. Thielicke, *Theological Ethics,* p. 99.

23. See Childs, "Ethics and the Promise of God," p. 105, on the "now . . . not yet" structure of God's saving activity.

mative universe, no scheme of legitimate authority, can exist apart from the narratives that constitute it.[24] The meaning of texts, understood as constituent elements of a narrative, is not a matter of picturing the world but of telling participants in the narrative they describe how to be.[25]

One property of narratives, however, is that it is not really up to those who conserve and proclaim them to alter their message. We are guided by narratives as we act in ways that elaborate them. As theologian Robert Jenson argues, "the story is not your story or my story . . . or some neat story someone read or made up. The story of the sermon and of the hymns and of the processions and of the sacramental acts and of the readings is to be God's story, the story of the Bible."[26] Legitimacy depends on getting the story right.

So right away we encounter a problem in Cover's account of the relationship between authority and narratives. If we are using a narrative to norm interpretation, but the story is the story of the Bible, how do we escape the circularity inherent in deriving principles of interpretation from the thing to be interpreted? Luther's famous statement that scripture interprets itself, and the nineteenth-century idea of the hermeneutic circle seem only to be ways of restating the problem.[27] The idea that the fundamental structure of biblical narratives is oriented toward freeing people from the domination of sin and the law is derived from the Bible, yet this interpretive principle is used to distinguish between true and false interpretations. "From the very outset in Genesis, it was God's Word that distinguished the true church from the false church."[28]

More generally, how do we know when we've got any story right? One tempting answer is that there are extra-narrative criteria to which one can appeal when trying to figure out which of several competing narratives is true, in the sense of providing the best account of text, tradition, reason,

24. Robert M. Cover, "Foreword: *Nomos* and Narrative," *Harvard Law Review* 97 (1983): 4-68.

25. See Stanley Hauerwas, "Story and Theology," in *Truthfulness and Tragedy: Further Investigations into Christian Ethics* (Notre Dame: University of Notre Dame Press, 1977): 71-81. See also Frei, *The Eclipse of Biblical Narrative,* pp. 288-89 (noting that, for Hegel, knowing or understanding is intelligible only in application).

26. Robert W. Jenson, "How the World Lost Its Story," *First Things* 36 (Oct. 1993): 22.

27. For a discussion of the hermeneutic circle, citing Luther's approach to scriptural interpretation, see Hans-Georg Gadamer, *Truth and Method,* 2nd rev. ed., trans. Joel Weinsheimer and Donald G. Marshall (New York: Continuum, 1994), pp. 174-75.

28. Lazareth, *Christians in Society,* p. 41.

and experience. But pluralism and the fragmentation of tradition give rise to the possibility of the loss of authority — as Martin Marty observes, quoting Yeats, the fear is that the center cannot hold.[29] Thus, a different possibility is that a narrative may be internally complex, and may consist of competing normative visions, so that there is an ongoing debate over the location of the center. The important thing is that this debate is always within a normative universe constituted by these plural stories. So, for example, one might observe that there are different accounts within scripture of what it means to live a godly life, from God's law in Exodus and Deuteronomy, to the Wisdom literature in the Old Testament, through to the Gospels, which have their own differences (particularly between the Synoptic Gospels and John).[30]

I am sensitive to the critique that mainline Protestant theological interpretation in the United States is squishy, unrigorous, not standing for anything, trendy, and politically correct.[31] For the center to hold there must be something to which we can look to determine whether we are getting the story right. There may not be a standpoint outside the normative world constituted by the community's narrative, from which it is possible to evaluate a narrative as true or false. But this does not mean anything goes, or that authority is always up for grabs. Narratives constrain while also enabling creativity, and interpreters of narratives are not perfectly free. They are always aiming toward the realization of the *telos* of the story — that aim toward which the action is moving, which constitutes the sense and purpose of the narrative. There is a way to be within a narrative and participate in its creation while still regarding it as a practical authority.

Because I am lawyer, I am drawn to analogize this dilemma to something quite familiar in my world, namely the way in which the U.S. Constitution functions as a practical authority for judges, political officials, and citizens. The resolution of questions of constitutional interpretation is often a matter of writing the next chapter in the narrative of our common political heritage, clarifying what is meant by values such as liberty and equality, and applying these meanings to the sorts of practical problems that present themselves to courts.

In the domain of civil law, and particularly the interpretation of the Constitution, arguments about hermeneutics are actually arguments about

---

29. Martin E. Marty, "The Widening Gyres of Religion and Law," *DePaul Law Review* 45 (1996): 669-70.

30. I am grateful to Ron Duty for raising this possibility.

31. Compare Hütter, "The Twofold Center of Lutheran Ethics," p. 40 (attacking the "widespread antinomianism of contemporary Protestant ethics").

legitimate practical authority, and for that reason about democracy. The text of the Constitution — its plain language, the intent of its drafters, or the then-accepted public meaning of terms used in it — has practical authority because the drafting, debate, signing, and ratification of the Constitution represent an act of popular sovereignty, of "we the people" coming together to form an enduring framework of government that is legitimate because it is the product of an act of collective self-determination, which is the hallmark of democracy. If the language and intentions of Hamilton, Madison, and other venerated Framers (often capitalized, to give quasi-religious signifi-cance to the Constitution) have authority for us today, it may be because we recognize either our participation in a collective subject persisting over time or else exhibit an attitude of attachment to the Constitution as *constituting* a narrative unity of ourselves as a people over time. We thus may share a political project that is rooted in a particular history and stretches forward into the future.[32]

One implication of the democratic account of legitimacy might be that the text of the Constitution should be interpreted in ways that enhance its capacity to serve as the basis for an ongoing process of democratic self-government.[33] Alternatively, a court interpreting the Constitution might take into account changes in the way "we the people" understand constitutive political and moral ideals such as equality, justice, and fairness; thus, the Constitution might be a living document, a repository of the community's values which evolve over time but are nevertheless rooted in the community's history.[34] Theories of popular constitutionalism emphasize the people themselves, not the courts, as the authoritative interpreters of constitutional meaning.[35]

In any case, the constraint on the interpreter's discretion is a commit-ment to the shared understanding that the Constitution is not the story of a

32. Jack M. Balkin, *Living Originalism* (Cambridge, MA: Belknap Press, 2011), pp. 60-63. As an aside, I will refer to the *framers* of the Constitution for convenience, but scholars working on constitutional originalism today generally are concerned with the generally accepted public meaning of words at the time the Constitution was drafted and ratified by state conventions. Thus, it is not really the intention of the constitutional framers that is important, but the way in which the words they used in the text of the Constitution would have been generally understood.

33. John Hart Ely, *Democracy and Distrust: A Theory of Judicial Review* (Cambridge, MA: Harvard University Press, 1980).

34. David A. Strauss, *The Living Constitution* (Oxford: Oxford University Press, 2010), chapter 2.

35. See, e.g., Larry D. Kramer, *The People Themselves: Popular Constitutionalism and Judicial Review* (New York: Oxford University Press, 2005).

litigant (even a famous one like Clarence Earl Gideon), a group (the NAACP or the African American parents who wanted desegregated schools for their children), a social movement (the struggle for civil rights for women, African Americans or, more recently, marriage equality), a lawyer (Thurgood Marshall), a judge (John Marshall Harlan or Earl Warren), or even the Supreme Court, but the nation's story.

As a lawyer I am acutely aware that theories of legal interpretation are pervaded by anxiety about the subjectivity of the interpreter, and hence the power of the interpreter to displace the law itself as the source of authority. "Whoever hath an absolute authority to interpret any written or spoken laws, it is He who is truly the Law-giver to all intents and purposes, and not the person who first wrote or spoke them."[36] Call this the anxiety of interpretation.

Literalism and other original-meaning hermeneutic approaches are a response to the anxiety of interpretation, shifting as they do the source of meaning from the interpreter to the text.[37] Ironically, however, the resort to plain-language or original-meaning approaches not only responds to the anxiety of interpretation, but also serves an empowering or democratizing function that threatens to undermine the authority of the texts being interpreted. Luther, of course, appealed to the Bible to criticize the institutional church's aggrandizement of power. For scripture to perform this role, and to underwrite Luther's doctrine of the priesthood, its meaning had to be available to ordinary people. Similarly, some of the drafters of the U.S. Constitution sought to make its meaning available to ordinary people as a means of checking the power of elites. Constitutional historian Jack Rakove quotes Oliver Ellsworth, who noted that if the Constitution had

been expressed in the scientific language of law, or those terms of art which we often find in political compositions, to the honourable gentleman it might have appeared more definite and less ambiguous; but to the great body of people altogether obscure. . . .[38]

36. Bishop Benjamin Hoadly, quoted in John Chipman Gray, *The Nature and Sources of the Law* (New York: Columbia University Press, 1909), p. 100.
37. "What then would prevent spiritual anarchy and as many readings of scriptural truth as there were readers to read them? . . . That authority, a phenomenon of a Protestantism carried to its logical conclusion, was not the authority of the individual reader but rather the authority of the literal text to which the reader submitted himself." Peter J. Gomes, *The Good Book: Reading the Bible with Mind and Heart* (New York: William Morrow, 1996), p. 42.
38. Jack N. Rakove, *Original Meanings: Politics and Ideas in the Making of the Constitution* (New York: Vintage Press, 1996), pp. 344-45.

If ordinary citizens, or at least ordinary lawyers (as opposed to professional historians or highly specialized constitutional lawyers), can understand the plain meaning of the Constitution, then citizens can serve as effective checks on state power, shoring up the rule of law in society.[39] This would locate the source of authority in the people, fulfilling the promise of the Constitution to establish a system of democratic self-government.

The claim to be tentatively explored here is that what rightly constrains subjectivity is not the literal words of a text, nor an institutional authority, but the community-bound practice of interpreting and putting the text into effect in the life of the community. At least since the eighteenth century, many theologians have denied that *understanding* is simply a one-way process of reading the plain meaning of language off a text; rather, it is a dialectical process of engagement between the speaker (or the text) and the interpreter, who is actively involved in the process of interpretation.[40]

I would argue, to modestly extend that claim, that the process of interpretation is also, necessarily, a process of discerning together as a community what should be done about some issue. In that way the community participates in the ongoing self-constitution of its *nomos*. Jack Rakove has argued that the drafters of the U.S. Constitution, including Madison, who is often cited as someone who believed the original understanding of the framers should provide a guide to ascertaining the meaning of the Constitution, expected that constitutional interpretation would be a two-stage process, beginning with understanding the words of the text but not fully commencing until the business of constitutional governance was up and running.[41] Authority begins with the text of the Constitution, but requires an ongoing elaboration through the process of applying constitutional principles to the quotidian work of governing. As our history shows, the significance of the Constitution may be highlighted in times of crisis, such as the Civil War and Reconstruction, and the civil rights movement, in which the extent of the power of the federal government to enforce constitutional guarantees of equality was directly and forcibly challenged.[42]

39. See H. Jefferson Powell, "On Not Being 'Not an Originalist,'" *University of St. Thomas Law Journal* 7, no. 2 (2010): 271.

40. See Frei, *The Eclipse of Biblical Narrative*, pp. 290-94 (discussing Schleiermacher).

41. Rakove, *Original Meanings*, pp. 340-42.

42. See, for example, *Cooper v. Aaron,* 358 U.S. 1 (1958), involving the refusal of the Governor of Arkansas, Orval Faubus, to enforce the Supreme Court's ruling that segregated schools violated the Constitution. Faubus called up the state National Guard unit and ordered them to prevent African American children from attending all-white schools. A

The plain meaning of words used in the text of the Constitution does not fully determine the application of the document, but the words are also not irrelevant. Interpretive debates pertaining to, for example, school desegregation revolve around the meaning of the words "equal protection of the laws," but there can be an open question whether equal protection of the laws is denied by, say, forced busing to integrate schools, affirmative action plans, redistricting for racial balance, and so on.[43] It may be the case, however, that it is possible to settle on a conception of a value such as equality by asking what it would mean, within the history of our political community, to treat people as equal with respect to some characteristic.

A judge seeking to determine what the Constitution requires or permits in any given case should, on this narrative approach to interpretation, understand him- or herself as part of a historically extended tradition of trying to work out what the words of the text mean not in the dictionary but *in practice,* in the life of the political community. In Robert Cover's terms a narrative links reality with visions of what the world might be like, which is to say the ideals expressed in the Constitution using language such as equality, freedom, and due process.[44] The subjectivity of the interpreter is constrained by the narrative itself, which permits some creativity but always reminds the interpreter that, at root, it is not *his* or *her* story to alter, but only to make a good-faith effort to continue.

The search for semantic meaning is thus a process of description; narrative integrates description and normativity, links the ought and the is, and expresses ideals and aspirations. Unlike plain-meaning or literalist approaches, which assume a conception of authority as a one-way process of understanding (the text tells interpreters what to do), the narrative approach envisions authority as a dialectical process, with judges expressing fidelity to the traditions handed down by prior interpreters, but with an awareness that the normativity of law depends on having some relationship with the constitutive political morality of the community.

The judge's dilemma was posed in a book, *The Tempting of America,*

---

group of African American schoolchildren, the so-called Little Rock Nine, were permitted to attend Little Rock Central High School only after President Eisenhower ordered the U.S. Army's 101st Airborne Division to enforce compliance with the Court's order.

43. See, for example, *Parents Involved in Community Schools v. Seattle School District No. 1,* 551 U.S. 701 (2007) (use of race-conscious factors for school assignment); *Swann v. Charlotte-Mecklenburg Board of Education,* 402 U.S. 1 (1970) (busing to achieve integration goals).

44. Cover, "*Nomos* and Narrative," p. 10.

written by U.S. Court of Appeals Judge Robert Bork after he failed to gain confirmation for a seat on the U.S. Supreme Court after highly contentious confirmation proceedings.[45] Bork's argument is that judges have a great deal of power to make decisions about what rights and duties individuals, corporations, and the state have with respect to one another; that at least federal judges, whose life tenure is guaranteed by Article III of the Constitution, face the prospect of very little democratic accountability for the decisions they make. Therefore, judges are naturally tempted to rely on their own views — call them policy preferences, ideologies, or political commitments — when deciding what the Constitution requires or permits. In the same vein, the earlier work of Alexander Bickel focused constitutional theory scholars for decades to come on the "counter-majoritarian difficulty" posed by judicial review of legislation.[46]

Anticipating such a problem years earlier, Herbert Wechsler insisted that the only legitimate considerations counting in favor of a judicial decision are those which are general, i.e., which transcend the result reached in a particular case.[47] The timing of this interest in judicial review is not coincidental. Bickel and Wechsler were reacting to the Supreme Court's 1954 decision in *Brown v. Board of Education,* holding that maintaining separate public schools for white and black children is unconstitutional.[48] Wechsler even dared to question whether the Court had indeed articulated a principled basis for its conclusion that segregated schools were unconstitutional.[49]

Bork rightly noticed that Wechsler's call for neutral principles of con-

---

45. For a flavor of the tone of the debate concerning Bork's confirmation, consider this speech by Senator Ted Kennedy:

> Robert Bork's America is a land in which women would be forced into back-alley abortions, blacks would sit at segregated lunch counters, rogue police could break down citizens' doors in midnight raids, school children could not be taught about evolution, writers and artists would be censored at the whim of government, and the doors of the Federal courts would be shut on the fingers of millions of citizens for whom the judiciary is — and is often the only — protector of the individual rights that are the heart of our democracy.

133rd vol. of the *Congressional Record,* 100th Congress, 1st session, 1987, p. 28851.

46. Alexander M. Bickel, *The Least Dangerous Branch: The Supreme Court at the Bar of Politics* (New York: Bobbs-Merrill, 1962).

47. Herbert Wechsler, "Toward Neutral Principles of Constitutional Law," *Harvard Law Review* 73 (1959): 1-35.

48. *Brown v. Board of Education of Topeka et al.,* 347 U.S. 483 (1954).

49. Wechsler, "Toward Neutral Principles of Constitutional Law," p. 34.

stitutional adjudication is intimately connected to the problem of legitimate practical authority.[50] We have a democratic government with limited powers which is not strictly majoritarian, because the Constitution places limits on what the majority can do to the minority (where "majority" and "minority" are defined here in terms of their share of the electorate). An institution deciding what those rights are, and what majoritarian actions they prohibit, must be able to appeal to something within democratic theory to justify the counter-majoritarian effect of enforcing rights. Bork's theory of adjudication depends on the distinction between making and implementing value choices.[51] If the Constitution is silent regarding the existence and scope of a right that is asserted as a basis for invalidating a statute, however, to what can a judge appeal, except his or her own values, to determine whether or not the statute is constitutional?

The originalist response, championed by Bork and many other, typically conservative constitutional scholars, is that the power of judges should be limited to enforcing rights that are provided for in the written Constitution. That is, the meaning of the Constitution at the time it was drafted or ratified is the solely legitimate authority for judges to follow when deciding whether action by other branches of government complies with the requirements of the Constitution. If there is some ambiguity in the meaning of the relevant provision of the Constitution, judges should fall back on a default rule for interpreting it, which is that the enactments of democratically accountable legislatures should be given effect and not invalidated by an unaccountable judiciary. Constitutional originalism now comes in a variety of flavors, some of which emphasize the original subjective *intentions* of the framers of the Constitution regarding its expected application, while others are focused more on the original shared, public *meanings* that the words used by the framers would generally be understood to have.[52]

---

50. Robert H. Bork, "Neutral Principles and Some First Amendment Problems," *Indiana Law Journal* 47 (1971): 1-35.

51. Bork, "Neutral Principles and Some First Amendment Problems," p. 6.

52. For an overview, see Keith E. Whittington, "Originalism: A Critical Introduction," *Fordham Law Review* 82 (2013): 375-409; Balkin, *Living Originalism,* chapter 6. The variety of originalism that seeks the original meaning of words used in the Constitution, as opposed to the intention of the drafters, is associated with Justice Scalia. See Antonin Scalia, *A Matter of Interpretation: Federal Courts and the Law* (Princeton: Princeton University Press, 1997). For a defense of intentionalism as a theory of meaning, from an unexpected quarter, see Stanley Fish, "Intention Is All There Is: A Critical Analysis of Aharon Barak's Purposive Interpretation in Law," *Cardozo Law Review* 29, no. 3 (2008): 1109-46.

In any case, originalism is a response to the anxiety of interpretation and the fear of the unbounded subjectivity of interpreters. Confronted by vague generalities such as "due process," "equal protection," "cruel and unusual punishment," or "abridging the freedom of speech," an interpreter can restrain her subjectivity and keep her own normative preferences in check by referring to the solid, determinate standard of "what the words of the Constitution mean" or "what the framers intended the Constitution to provide."[53]

Despite its promise to reduce the anxiety of interpretation, difficulties with originalism as a method of constitutional interpretation are well known.[54] First, it can be quite a difficult task to ascertain the intention of the authors of a text, and the difficulty of this task becomes greater with increasing temporal and cultural gaps between the moment of authorship of a document and its interpretation by a reader.

Not surprisingly, lawyers and judges may be content with evidence of original meaning that is good enough for their purposes.[55] Consider the litigation over the District of Columbia's ban on handguns, which turned on the original understanding of the framers with regard to the meaning of the Second Amendment's guarantee of the right to keep and bear arms.[56] Both sides in the litigation submitted briefs citing historical evidence for their claim that the framers of the Constitution would have understood that the Second Amendment either permitted or prohibited the handgun ban. Lo and behold, the members of the Court who might have been predisposed to favor one position or the other found historical support for their conclusions.

Even if it were possible to find a core of settled meaning, the descriptive project of pinning down the meaning of a term does not necessarily have the normative consequences sought by originalists. To put it bluntly, at the time

53. Many originalists are also proponents of judicial restraint and are content that if the text is silent, then the democratic theory underlying originalism instructs judges to defer to the rights and duties established by democratically accountable institutions. In this way, a hermeneutic approach — originalism — is connected with the underlying values of democratic political theory.

54. See generally Michael C. Dorf, "The Undead Constitution," *Harvard Law Review* 125, no. 8 (2012): 2018-36 (reviewing Balkin, *Living Originalism,* and Strauss, *The Living Constitution*); Paul Brest, "The Misconceived Quest for the Original Understanding," *Boston University Law Review* 60 (1980): 204-38.

55. A lawyer may give a different answer to a historical question than a historian, for the simple reason that a historian is concerned to understand a particular provision of the Constitution, while a lawyer is interested in persuading a court about its importance to a case at hand.

56. *District of Columbia v. Heller,* 554 U.S. 570 (2008).

of the drafting and ratification of the Constitution, flogging and branding were accepted as punishments and not considered cruel or unusual — well, so what? Times have changed, and the reference of the word "cruelty" has changed as well, to incorporate flogging and branding, so that we would now understand the meaning of the utterance "no cruel and unusual punishment" to mean "no flogging or branding."

H. Jefferson Powell has argued that the evidence is at best ambiguous regarding the issue of whether the constitutional framers had the original intent that their original intent would control future interpretation (or construction) of the Constitution at all.[57] It may be that Madison, Hamilton, Jay, and the many others whose understanding of the purpose of the Constitution we now believe is constitutive of the notion of "the intent of the framers" assumed that matters of constitutional interpretation would be settled in the way lawyers reasoned about the meaning of any other document, i.e., appealing to a variety of interpretive techniques such as semantic meaning, the syntax of sentences, the structure of the document, the background against which the document was drafted, suppositions about the problem it was meant to solve (what British lawyers call the "mischief rule"), considerations of institutional competence, and so on. The practice of the framers themselves lends support to non-originalist methods of interpretation — paradoxically, as Powell argues, a committed originalist should be a non-originalist. Or it may be that, whatever the framers thought about interpretation, they believed the application of the text would not be constrained by the original semantic meaning of the terms used in the document. Even if it were possible to determine the content of the framers' intent, or a shared public understanding of the meaning of a right to keep and bear arms, at the time of the drafting and adoption of the Bill of Rights, there is a further question of whether that meaning translates to our time.[58]

---

57. See H. Jefferson Powell, "The Original Understanding of Original Intent," *Harvard Law Review* 98, no. 5 (1985): 885-948.

58. While the language of a rule constrains its interpretation, a term (either understood with reference to the intent of the drafters or then-current semantic meaning) could be interpreted broadly or narrowly. Perhaps the framers sought to prohibit only those punishments then deemed cruel — e.g., boiling in oil but not death by hanging — but it may also be the case that they intended to recognize that social norms regarding cruelty may change, and at some subsequent point in time the political community may come to regard capital punishment, or a sentence of life without parole for minors, to be cruel. It also may be the case that the constitutional drafters could secure agreement only by stating certain limitations on the power of government at a high level of generality.

If not originalism, then what? In keeping with the theme of this paper, a different approach to constitutional interpretation relies on a narrative linking the language of the Constitution, the characteristics of the political community it establishes, and the history of the community's engagement with the Constitution both in humdrum cases and in times of crisis (such as the Civil War and the civil rights movement of the 1950s and '60s). One characteristic of a narrative is that it is always aiming at something counterfactual — an unrealized, perhaps unrealizable ideal. In Robert Cover's words,

> Law may be viewed as a system of tension or a bridge linking a concept of a reality to an imagined alternative — that is, as a connective between two states of affairs, both of which can be represented in their normative significance only through the devices of narrative. Thus, one constitutive element of a *nomos* is the phenomenon George Steiner has labeled "alternity": "the 'other than the case.' . . ."[59]

There is a parallel here with the eschatological horizon that provides the structure of the narrative of God's promise as revealed and as-yet-to-be fulfilled. Remember the problem of the anxiety of interpretation. A political actor cannot read the Constitution to mean any ol' thing, nor can the church simply follow popular whim when attempting to discern the meaning of a scriptural passage. If the text itself cannot serve as a norm to constrain interpretation, however, there must be something else — otherwise the process of interpretation is vulnerable to the unfettered subjectivity of the interpreter. Cover's answer is that the community's *nomos* is made up of the narratives that constitute it.

To make the idea of a narrative norming interpretation more concrete, however, we can consider a contribution to legal theory that has come in for severe criticism, is sometimes mocked,[60] but which I believe still contains one of the central insights concerning legal interpretation: Ronald Dworkin's analogy of the common law as a chain novel.[61] Dworkin's insight is that a judge is acting on behalf of the community when rendering an interpretation

---

59. Cover, "*Nomos* and Narrative," p. 9.

60. Stanley Fish, "Working on the Chain Gang: Interpretation in Law and Literature," *Texas Law Review* 60 (1982): 551-67; Stanley Fish, "Wrong Again," *Texas Law Review* 62 (1983): 299-316; Stanley Fish, "Still Wrong After All These Years," *Law & Philosophy* 6 (1987): 401-18.

61. See Ronald Dworkin, *Law's Empire* (Cambridge, MA: Belknap Press, 1986), pp. 225-54; Ronald Dworkin, "Law as Interpretation," *Texas Law Review* 60 (1982): 527-50.

of law. The judge is not radically free. His or her decision is normed by the background against which it is rendered, while the decision contributes to the ongoing elaboration of the tradition. The judge's decision is *our* decision; it speaks in our name. When a judge decides a case that establishes some legal right or duty, it must be *justified* on grounds that have an appropriate relationship with the community as a whole. Obviously the decision is not put up for a vote; not only would this be wildly impractical, but it would be contrary to the common law foundation of American law in which judges are entrusted with the authority to make decisions about the existence and content of the rights and duties of citizens.

But a judge also cannot simply make it up based on his or her own ideological commitments or policy preferences — again we encounter the anxiety of interpretation — but must render a faithful account of the community's stance with respect to this issue. Judges therefore should "identify legal rights and duties, so far as possible, on the assumption that they were all created by a single author — the community personified — expressing a coherent conception of justice and fairness."[62] The community has continuity through time, through the founding of the republic into the heritage of English common law, and also is comprised of citizens with a wide diversity of political commitments. The community's history and its current instantiation will therefore contain multitudes of competing views about what the judge ought to do.

Judging, as a practice, demands justification in terms of the common good, or the community's constitutive normative commitments (to allude again to Cover, the community's *nomos*). An underappreciated aspect of Dworkin's theory is his reliance on the third part of the French Revolution slogan — liberty, equality, fraternity. His argument for the political value of *integrity,* which is the basis of the obligation of judges to render principled decisions, is that a political community is (or ought to be — it is not always clear in Dworkin's theory) characterized by the mutual respect and concern that citizens have for one another. Only a "community of principle . . . can claim the authority of a genuine associative community and can therefore claim moral legitimacy — that its collective decisions are matters of obligation and not bare power — in the name of fraternity."[63] Although Dworkin's emphasis on fraternity is often overlooked by commentators, it is important in the comparative analysis of interpretation in civil law and theologi-

62. Dworkin, *Law's Empire,* p. 225.
63. Dworkin, *Law's Empire,* p. 214.

cal ethics because, whatever one thinks about fraternity in civil society, the principle that we are all one in Christ is clearly a constitutive commitment of Christian social ethics.

Returning to the problem of adjudication in civil law, how should a judge proceed in order to ensure the moral legitimacy of a decision? Here is the connection between *nomos* and narrative. Dworkin asks the judge to imagine herself or himself as writing the next chapter in a long chain novel, in which previous chapters were written by prior judges, each of whom was attentive to the will of electoral majorities, the common law tradition, and broader normative notions of justice, fairness, and due process.

Constitutional litigation tends to suggest that our national story is characterized by a clash of narratives, with some citizens favoring a return to what they believe to be an authentic tradition of limited government, while others contend that more than two centuries of history since the nation's founding have shown that the national government has grown in power in response to the changing needs of the people. Significantly, this clash of narratives is a debate *within* the political community, about *our* history, tradition, and values.

In selecting among these narratives, however, it would be problematical to read Dworkin as suggesting that the judge should aim to make the narrative *morally* the best it can be, because then he or she risks losing connection with the positivity of the law. Dworkin does argue that judges should sometimes act like philosophers, an aspect of his theory that gives conservative critics apoplexy.[64] In response, Dworkin claims that Hercules, Dworkin's ideal judge, is attempting to discover the community's morality, not simply read his own policy preferences into the law, but it is nevertheless clear that the standard for what makes one narrative better than the other is an evaluative one.[65]

64. A frequent target of conservative criticism is Justice Kennedy, who has a tendency to wax philosophical in the course of opinions finding fundamental rights in cases such as *Planned Parenthood of Southeastern Pennsylvania v. Casey,* 505 U.S. 833 (1992), and *Lawrence v. Texas,* 539 U.S. 558 (2003). See, e.g., Michael Stokes Paulsen, "The Worst Constitutional Decision of All Time," *Notre Dame Law Review* 78 (2003): 995-1043.

65. As he has an unfortunate tendency to do, Dworkin misstates the criticism leveled at his theory at this point. See Dworkin, *Law's Empire,* pp. 259-60. Critics like Bork who accuse liberal judges of playing politics, imposing their own preferences on the law, and engaging in judicial activism are not claiming that judging is a morally neutral activity, but that the value choices that go into adjudication have already been made, either by the framers of the Constitution or by democratically accountable institutions, and in both cases what a judge owes is *deference* to majoritarian processes.

The question is therefore how to constrain the evaluation to minimize the influence of the subjectivity of interpreters. The Constitution, precedent cases, legislation, and other bits and pieces of legal materials do not have their authority because, or only because, they reflect a morally attractive response to some problem that arose between people. Rather, their authority depends — again, at least to some extent — on the fact that they were enacted pursuant to social procedures for making valid law. There is a "positivity" to the law, reflecting that it is an artifact as well as something that aims to have practical authority. The law also belongs to a particular community. As much as I love New Zealand and believe it is a decent, well-ordered society, I am bound to concede that the Treaty of Waitangi is not part of *my* political tradition as an American citizen. The point of Dworkin's chain novel metaphor is that his ideal judge is not writing on a blank slate, but is seeking to remain faithful to our political tradition — seeking to make it the best it can be, but nevertheless always remaining within it.

As the church approaches any contested issue in social ethics, narrative theology suggests that the task of discernment resembles the labor of Hercules, Dworkin's ideal judge, who must write the next chapter in the story in a way that is faithful to tradition but also shows the tradition in its best light.

To get out of my comfort zone in law and philosophy and into the (for me) uncertain terrain of theological ethics, the comparison between legal and scriptural hermeneutics seems to demonstrate that plain-meaning, literalist, or original-intent approaches to interpretation are deeply unsatisfactory. People who take quite seriously their duty of fidelity to a written authority, whether the Bible or the U.S. Constitution, cannot avoid the anxiety of interpretation. That is, there is no way to making constructive ethical arguments based on more general values immanent in the text, such as democracy (in the case of the Constitution) or, in the Lutheran tradition, an understanding of scripture as "not primarily God's commands, but a treasure of promises."[66]

These are not the subjective values of the interpreter, but belong to the relevant political or theological tradition. As lawyers we are seeking to discover our authentic constitutional tradition, and as members of the church, we are part of God's story: "Neither you nor I nor all of us together can so shape the world that it can make narrative sense; if God does not invent the world's story, then it has none, then the world has no narrative that is

---

66. Paulson, *Lutheran Theology,* p. 14.

its own."[67] Neither the plain meaning of a text nor observed facts about the world can provide ground upon which to stand that is any more solid than this. But this is nothing to be anxious about; it is just the way ethics works. Perhaps this brief comparison with the relationship between *nomos* and narrative in constitutional law has shown that the alternative to literalism is not inviting judges to play politics, but is rather a grounded discourse aimed at understanding the practical authority of a text.

67. Jenson, "How the World Lost Its Story," p. 21.

CHAPTER 2

Why *Religious* Freedom?

John R. Stumme

Martin Luther speaks of dual jurisdictions: to protect the world from chaos, he writes, "God has ordained two governments: the spiritual, by which the Holy Spirit produces Christians and righteous people under Christ; and the temporal, which restrains the un-Christian and wicked so that — no thanks to them — they are obliged to keep still and to maintain an outward peace."[1] These divinely established authorities are separate. The spiritual authority operates only through the Word, and the temporal authority has definite limits: "The soul," Luther asserts, "is not under the authority of Caesar."[2] Lutherans continue to insist with other Christians that gospel and faith are outside of Caesar's jurisdiction. A theology of dual jurisdictions answers the "why" of religious freedom: because they belong to God's spiritual governance, both the individual in her relation with God and the church in its life and mission are immune from government control and coercion. If this theology is true, then *religious* freedom is a special freedom, not reducible to other freedoms.

Although such an approach was common in eighteenth-century America, today a theological rationale for religious freedom seems, to many, passé and out of place in a pluralistic society, unconstitutional or worse. Today's prevailing scholarly interpretations of the First Amendment and those by the Supreme Court operate with a different set of assumptions. Two conflicting fields of discourse concerning the basis of religious freedom are in play. One is theological, the other secular, that is, nonreligious. One requires discourse

1. Martin Luther, "Temporal Authority: To What Extent It Should Be Obeyed" (1523), in *Luther's Works,* vol. 45, *The Christian in Society II,* ed. Walter I. Brandt, trans. J. J. Schindel (Philadelphia: Muhlenberg Press, 1962), p. 91.
2. Luther, "Temporal Authority," p. 111.

about God; the other prohibits it. The one is "constitutional heresy" and the other "constitutional orthodoxy."[3] Insofar as the secular orthodoxy is hegemonic and determines legal meanings, justifications for *religious* freedom have become problematic, and there is a strong current that denies that religious freedom is a special freedom. When persuasive justifications are lacking, *religious* freedom is vulnerable.

Christianity's Novelty

The claim that God has established dual jurisdictions is critical and intrinsic to the church's faith. It belongs to the origins of the Christian church; it is hardly unique to Lutherans. Throughout the church's history, Christians have interpreted this claim in different ways, seeking to be guided by this duality in sorting out the relationship of "church and state" in their situation. Where the church has had a significant presence, as in the late Roman world, it has introduced a new understanding of temporal authority.[4]

Christianity originated in the Roman world where imperial power and the gods lived in harmony. "Greek and Roman religion lived only through and for the state and almost by necessity had the same objectives."[5] What was rendered to the gods was rendered to Caesar. There was one jurisdiction and only one. "Official religion existed chiefly to serve the state; private religion had little influence on politics."[6] A certain toleration existed with respect to private religions, a "toleration of indifference," since questions of truth, salvation, and inner faith were not at stake with them.[7]

3. The terms come from Steven D. Smith, *The Rise and Decline of American Religious Freedom* (Cambridge, MA: Harvard University Press, 2014), p. 124. "This deleterious effect on discourse is a natural consequence of the shift from a situation of open and legitimate contestation to a discourse structured in terms of constitutional orthodoxy (political secularism) versus constitutional heresy (political providentialism)." The situation is not readily acknowledged since "modern secular orthodoxies typically refuse to acknowledge their character as orthodoxies," as Smith argues. Smith, *Rise and Decline,* p. 137.

4. For a historical-theological discussion of "the doctrine of the Two," see Oliver O'Donovan, *The Desire of the Nations: Rediscovering the Roots of Political Theology* (New York: Cambridge University Press, 1996), pp. 193-226.

5. Joseph R. Strayer, "The State and Religion: An Exploratory Comparison in Different Cultures," *Medieval Statecraft and Perspectives of History: Essays by Joseph R. Strayer,* ed. Thomas N. Bisson and John F. Benton (Princeton: Princeton University Press, 1971), pp. 325-26.

6. Strayer, "The State and Religion," pp. 325-26.

7. Smith, *Rise and Decline,* p. 18.

Christianity disrupted this harmony. When Jesus said to Pilate, "My kingdom is not of this world" (John 18:36, KJV), he was telling Rome's representative that his kingdom or jurisdiction — in but not from the world — was beyond the emperor's authority and control. When Jesus said, "Render to Caesar the things that are Caesar's and to God the things that are God's" (Matt. 22:21, KJV), he was not calling for a private religion subservient to an all-powerful state, for God is the all-powerful one whom his followers are to love with their whole being while loving others in all of life (Luke 10:27). Rather, he was drawing a distinction between two independent jurisdictions, both to whom obligation is owed. Jesus' remark set terms for the church's subsequent approach to matters of "church and state." Similarly, Paul coupled a theological understanding of governing authority and a call to obey it (Romans 13) with knowledge that Christians belong to another jurisdiction, to the "commonwealth . . . in heaven" (Phil. 3:20).

"Unlike Islam, Christianity began as a community distinct from the body politic, and for the first several centuries it existed independent of political authority."[8] This initial experience of the church as a corporate body separate from government control continued to be a guiding or subversive memory in the church's history. "Only with the conversion of Constantine, the Roman emperor in the fourth century, did Christianity receive the blessing of the ruling powers."[9] While the emperor played a preeminent role in the church and the church came to enjoy toleration and later became the official religion of the empire, it remained an independent body, as Ambrose's humiliation of the emperor Theodosius demonstrates.[10]

8. Robert Louis Wilken, *The First Thousand Years: A Global History of Christianity* (New Haven: Yale University Press, 2012), p. 327.

9. Wilken, *The First Thousand Years,* p. 327. James Luther Adams comments: "Therefore it is asserted by contemporary, modern historians that one of the great innovations in the history of the West was the innovation provided by primitive Christianity in its assertion that we have the right to form a church that is not controlled by, not formed by, and does not serve directly Caesar." "Churches and Social Reform: By Their Groups Shall Ye Know Them" (Lecture, Waco, TX, 1969 or later; on file with author).

10. Hugo Rahner, *Church and State in Early Christianity* (San Francisco: Ignatius Press, 1992), pp. 39-79. Rahner titles his chapter on the fourth century, "The Struggle for the Church's Freedom under the Constantinian State." In commenting on Ambrose's confrontation with the emperor, David Bentley Hart captures the historical significance of dual jurisdictions: "Still, a principle had been established on the day of Theodosius's penance: the state could never again enjoy the unquestioned divine authority or legitimacy it had possessed before the rise of Christianity. . . . [I]t was . . . an irremediable blow to the ultimacy of the state; and this much, at least, the church bequeathed to the future." This "unhappy

This duality of two jurisdictions is a Christian novelty, and it "represented in the ancient world a revolution without precedent."[11] Peter Brown describes the change:

> The division between church and state had been unknown in the classical World. . . . It was a division that grew from a remarkable polarization of the social imagination, by which nonviolent pastoral power was pitted against mere "worldly" power. It was a development which, in the year 300, had

marriage of church and state also, quite unexpectedly, began to desacralize the state. Of course, from that point on it was inevitable that these two allied but essentially irreconcilable orders would continue to struggle for advantage, one over the other. And only in the early modern period would that struggle be decided, with the reduction of the church to a state cult, as part of the West's transition to late modernity's cult of the state." David Bentley Hart, *Atheist Delusions: The Christian Revolution and Its Fashionable Enemies* (New Haven: Yale University Press, 2009), p. 196.

11. Joseph Lecler, S.J., *The Two Sovereignties: A Study of the Relationship between Church and State* (New York: Philosophical Library, 1952), p. 8. Diverse scholars underscore Lecler's argument in their own way: Charles Taylor writes: "From the Christian side, the insistence on some distinction between church and state seemed to render impossible the kind of fusion between polis and religious community that was normal in the ancient world. . . . It is one of the legacies of Christendom that religion can neither be fully integrated in nor fully excluded from the state." "Religion in a Free Society," in *Articles of Faith, Articles of Peace: The Religious Liberty Clauses and the American Public Philosophy*, ed. James Davison Hunter and Os Guinness (Washington, DC: The Brookings Institution, 1990), p. 100. Jean Bethke Elshtain in discussing the spiritual and temporal authorities observes: "The saga of sorting this out gave the history of the Western half of Christendom a distinctive dynamic that channeled cultural energy, conflict, and contestation." *Sovereignty: God, State, and Self* (New York: Basic Books, 2008), p. 12. Hugh Heclo notes that the normal pattern in history was for religious and political authority to be united. Christianity introduced "a vast disruption" into this picture. First, Christianity is a threat to the established civil order because a Christian life is expected to extend its loyalty to God (and make other loyalties secondary) and to extend its fellowship to a universal humanity. Second, it does not withdraw from the world but makes demands on the powers-that-be. Hugh Heclo, *Christianity and American Democracy* (Cambridge, MA: Harvard University Press, 2007), p. 21. John Courtney Murray claims that "the essential political effect of Christianity was to destroy the classical view of society as a single homogeneous structure, within which the political power stood forth as the representative of society both in its religious and in its political aspects. . . . The new Christian view was based on a radical distinction between the order of the sacred and the order of the temporal." See Francis P. Canavan, S.J., "*Dignitatis Humanae*, the Catholic Conception of the State, and Public Morality," in *Catholicism and Religious Freedom: Contemporary Reflections on Vatican II's Declaration on Religious Liberty*, ed. Kenneth L. Grasso and Robert P. Hunt (New York: Rowman & Littlefield, 2006), pp. 71-72.

been unimaginable . . . to the overwhelming majority of the population of the Roman world who were not yet Christian.[12]

An early version of this duality can be found in Pope Gelasius's (492-496) influential two-power theory: "There are two powers, august Emperor, by which this world is chiefly ruled, namely, the sacred authority of the priests and the royal power."[13] Both powers were Christian institutions committed to building a Christian society.[14] "Religion," that is, the Christian faith, permeated all of society; everything had to do with God.[15] The two powers formed a pattern of "friendly mergers" in which the two lived in "mutual dependence, mutual distinction, and mutual deference."[16]

Religious freedom emerged from a history shaped by centuries of cooperation, competition, and conflict between the temporal and spiritual authorities. Particularly important was the struggle over "lay investiture" in

12. Peter Brown, *Through the Eye of a Needle: Wealth, the Fall of Rome, and the Making of Christianity in the West, 350-550 AD* (Princeton: Princeton University Press, 2012), p. 504.

13. "Gelasius I on Spiritual and Temporal Power, 494," *Internet Medieval Source Book, Fordham University,* accessed March 11, 2014, http://www.fordham.edu/halsall/source/gelasius1.asp. In his famous Bull Unam (1302) Boniface VIII spoke of "two swords" (replacing Gelasius's "two powers") and placed both swords "in the power of the Church." Lecler, *The Two Sovereignties,* p. 60.

14. Strayer, "The State and Religion," p. 323. John Courtney Murray notes the importance that the church was an institution. He writes that it was not von Harnack's "essence of Christianity" idea that began the liberal tradition of Western politics; such a "pale phantom" would not have been up to the task. "What appeared within history was not an 'idea' or an 'essence' but an existence, a Thing, a visible institution that occupied ground in this world at the same time that it asserted an astounding new freedom on a title not of this world." John Courtney Murray, S.J., *We Hold These Truths: Catholic Reflections on the American Proposition* (Garden City, NY: Image Books, 1964), p. 198.

15. Thomas Brady's characterization of how "religion" was integrated into "public life" for the period from 1400 to 1650 holds for earlier times: "The term 'political' covers here the entire realm of what may be called 'public life,' a world in which authority, power, belief, and behavior remained (from the modern point of view) fused and interwoven. Political and religious norms were public, because they generated and reproduced, bounded and informed the terms of governance in units great and small. 'Public life' is therefore not to be confused with the modern concept of a 'public sphere,' which is a creation of bourgeois society in the age of capitalism. The latter's hallmarks are separation of public from private, centralization of power, uniformity of legal status, and a degree of secularization at least in principle." Thomas A. Brady Jr., *German Histories in the Age of Reformations, 1400-1650* (Cambridge: Cambridge University Press, 2009), p. 5.

16. Monica Duffy Toft, Daniel Philpott, and Timothy Samuel Shah, *God's Century: Resurgent Religion and Global Politics* (New York: W. W. Norton, 2011), p. 57.

the eleventh century when Gregory VII forbade the appointment of bishops by secular rulers. This marked a beginning of a movement to free the church from outside political interference, the movement for *libertas ecclesiae*, for the freedom of the church.[17] "The most obvious way in which the leaders of the medieval church contributed (unintentionally of course) to the emergence of modern religious liberty was by their insistence on the freedom of the church from control by temporal rulers."[18]

Luther's Impact

If the "Papal Revolution" of the eleventh and twelfth centuries is important for the freedom of the church, the "Protestant Revolutions" in the sixteenth century are significant for contributing to the development of religious freedom for the individual, or, as it is also called, "the freedom of conscience" in religious matters.

Luther's understanding of God's dual jurisdictions means, as we have seen, that government has no authority in the God-human relationship. Since in his spiritual governance God creates faith through noncoercive means, government is also both incompetent and ineffective when it interferes in this relationship. "For faith is a free act," writes Luther, "to which no one can be forced. Indeed, it is a work of God in the spirit, not something which outward authority should compel or create. Hence arises the common saying, found also in Augustine, 'No one can or ought to be forced to believe.'"[19] Luther in this essay also rejected the idea that heresy should be a matter of the sword.[20]

---

17. Smith, *Rise and Decline,* p. 32. For more on the "Papal Revolution," see Harold J. Berman, *Law and Revolution: The Formation of the Western Legal Tradition* (Cambridge, MA: Harvard University Press, 1983), pp. 94-119.

18. Brian Tierney, "Religious Rights: A Historical Perspective," in *Religious Liberty in Western Thought,* ed. Noel B. Reynolds and W. Cole Durham Jr. (Atlanta: Scholars Press, 1996), p. 34. See Berman: "The separation, concurrence, and interaction of the spiritual and secular jurisdictions was a principal source of the Western legal tradition." Berman, *Law and Revolution,* p. 99.

19. Luther, "Temporal Authority," p. 108. James M. Estes argues that the proper translation of Luther's term *weltlich* is not "temporal" but "secular" or "worldly." Estes also notes that the distinction between the spiritual and the secular realm is not the same as between church and state since "the earthly, physical church" is in both realms. James M. Estes, "Luther on the Role of Secular Authority in the Reformation," in *The Pastoral Luther: Essays on Martin Luther's Practical Theology,* ed. Timothy J. Wengert (Grand Rapids: Eerdmans, 2009), pp. 355, 367.

20. Luther, "Temporal Authority," p. 114.

This line of theological thinking coupled with Luther's example at the Diet of Worms ("Here I stand") and other elements of his theology had a strong positive influence in the development of religious freedom. Nicholas P. Miller, in his recent study, *The Religious Roots of the First Amendment*, begins with Luther and describes "a continuous strand of this religious thought" emanating from his work:

> The argument . . . is quite simple. It is that Protestant commitments, at least as maintained by some dissenting Protestants, to the right of private judgment in matters of biblical interpretation — a corollary of the Protestant doctrine of the priesthood of believers — led to a respect for individual conscience that propelled ideas of religious liberty and disestablishment in the early modern West.[21]

Nevertheless, Luther's and early Lutheranism's understanding of the relationship between the dual jurisdictions separates them from what Lutherans today do and should support. In early Lutheranism, temporal authority came to dominate spiritual authority. The pattern of relationships in early modern Europe (1450-1750), including governments holding to other confessions, was one of "friendly takeover" in which the two authorities forged a tight integrated relationship with the secular rulers firmly in control.[22] This "takeover" was not antireligious or antichurch but, as in the Lutheran case, it was encouraged by the reformers. In commenting on the significance of Luther's 1520 appeal to the Christian nobility, the historian Thomas Brady writes that Luther's "most radical innovation" was "in conferring the duty of ecclesiastical reform on the German princes." This "opened the way to . . . the assumption by princes and magistrates of authority over the local churches."[23] In the late 1520s, Luther called upon his prince, the Elector John, to authorize visitations to congregations. "This was the beginning of a questionable and originally unintended development toward a church government under the temporal sovereign."[24] "Emergency bishops" became permanent.[25]

21. Nicholas P. Miller, *The Religious Roots of the First Amendment: Dissenting Protestants and the Separation of Church and State* (New York: Oxford University Press, 2012), p. 1.

22. Toft, *God's Century*, pp. 58-63.

23. Brady, *German Histories*, p. 152.

24. Martin Brecht, *Martin Luther: Shaping and Defining the Reformation, 1521-1532,* trans. James L. Schaaf (Minneapolis: Fortress Press, 1990), p. 267.

25. Both Luther and Melanchthon "viewed the Christian prince as someone burdened

Luther criticized the church of his day for carrying out responsibilities that belonged to the temporal authority, as did *The Augsburg Confession:* "Some people improperly mixed the power of the church and the power of the sword," so the reformers were compelled "to show the difference between" them so that both might be honored as God's gifts. "Some people" referred to the church as the body that usurped the power of civil government.[26] For Lutherans, the church did not bear the sword. The "church's jurisdiction" according to God's Word was "to forgive sins, to reject teaching that opposes the gospel, and to exclude from the communion of the church the ungodly whose ungodliness is known."[27] Another confessional document extended the authority of secular agents to the church: "It is especially necessary for the most eminent members of the church, the kings and princes, to attend to the church and take care that errors are removed and consciences restored to health."[28]

Luther, particularly in his essay on "Temporal Authority," emphasized its limits, and the reformer could sharply criticize princes and rulers. *The*

---

with obligations to the church rather than endowed with power over it, and as someone subject to the Word of God as interpreted by the theologians rather than free to impose his own version of the truth. Above all, the rights of the pastors in the exercise of their ministry were not to be trampled by princes and their officials." After Napoleon, reforms turned the German churches into the useful instruments of the state that the Enlightenment believed they should be. In later years Luther referred to secular rulers as "emergency bishops *(Notbischofe).*" Estes, "Role of Secular Authority," pp. 379-80.

26. "The Augsburg Confession: Concerning the Church's Power, art. XXVII," in *The Book of Concord: The Confessions of the Evangelical Lutheran Church,* ed. Robert Kolb and Timothy J. Wengert, trans. Charles Arand et al. (Minneapolis: Fortress, 2000), pp. 91 and 93.

27. "Concerning the Church's Power," p. 95.

28. "Treatise on the Power and Primacy of the Pope," *The Book of Concord,* p. 335. Luther's views were more complex than Melanchthon's but he could make the same point: The first virtue of rulers "is that they can secure justice for those who fear God and repress those who are godless. . . . For if God's Word is protected and supported so that it can be freely taught and learned, and if the sects and false teachers are given no opportunity and are not defended against the teachers who fear God, what greater treasure can there be in a land?" "Commentary on Psalm 82" (1530), in *Luther's Works,* vol. 13, *Selected Psalms II,* ed. Jaroslav Pelikan, trans. C. M. Jacobs (St. Louis and Philadelphia: Concordia and Fortress, 1956), p. 52. Estes claims that in this psalm there was no longer the distinction between ruler and Christian that there was earlier. Estes, "Role of Secular Authority," pp. 377-78. Luther arrives "at a somewhat long-winded and convoluted affirmation of the *cura religionis* of secular magistrates that later generations of Lutheran court preachers and theologians would perceive to be essentially the same as that in Philip Melanchthon's contemporary second edition of the Loci communes." Estes, "Role of Secular Authority," p. 379. This strain of Luther's thought clearly did not contribute to the development of religious freedom.

Augsburg Confession similarly referred to Acts 5:29 to insist that Christians owe greater obedience to God than to magistrates.[29] The Lutheran Reformation also gave a new theological legitimation to secular authority, viewing rulers as responsible to God's law and their calling to be caring fathers of their subjects.[30] It exhibited creative collaboration of theologians and jurists in shaping civil law.[31]

Nevertheless, what came to be in Lutheran lands for centuries was an Erastian arrangement of church and state relations that supported centralized power and the emergence of the modern state. Lutherans believed that the spiritual government was not an institution like the papacy but the power of Christ's Word and Sacrament, a power that was independent of temporal power.[32] Since the spiritual government was not the same as the empirical church, the existing, visible church was understood to belong to the temporal realm and therefore must submit to the ruler.[33] This understanding led to an increase in the scope and power of secular authority in churchly

29. "The Augsburg Confession: Concerning Civic Affairs, art. XVI," in *The Book of Concord*, p. 51.

30. For more on how Lutherans limited princes' arbitrary power, see Harold J. Berman, *Law and Revolution II: The Impact of the Protestant Reformations on the Western Legal Tradition* (Cambridge, MA: Harvard University Press, 2003), pp. 43-45, 65-67.

31. See John Witte Jr., *Law and Protestantism: The Legal Teachings of the Lutheran Reformation* (New York: Cambridge University Press, 2002), and Berman, *Law and Revolution II.*

32. Berman understands that Luther and his followers proclaimed "in effect, the abolition of the ecclesiastical jurisdiction. The church, Luther said, is not a lawmaking institution; the church is the invisible community of the faithful, in which all believers are priests. . . . The secular political authority must undertake the lawmaking responsibilities that previously were within the jurisdiction of the Roman Catholic Church." Berman, *Law and Revolution II*, p. 6.

33. Brady, *German Histories*, p. 262. Historical Lutheran orthodoxy, for example, ascribes to Lutheran magistrates a long list of responsibilities in sacred affairs: "The appointing of suitable ministers of the Church; the erection and preservation of schools and houses of worship, as well as the providing for the honorable support of ministers; the appointing of visitations and councils; the framing and maintenance of the laws of the Church; the controlling of the revenues of the Church, and the preservation of Church discipline; the trial of heretical ministers, as also of those of bad character. . . ." Still the spiritual authority, at least in theory, has its independence: "The inner economy and government of sacred things, consisting in the doctrine of the Word, in absolution from sins, and the lawful administration of the Sacraments, are peculiar to the ministers of the Church. The magistrate cannot claim them for himself without committing crime." David Hollaz, quoted in Heinrich Schmid, *Doctrinal Theology of the Evangelical Lutheran Church* (Minneapolis: Augsburg, 1961), p. 619. The Erastian or caesaropapist control of the church also characterized Catholic, Anglican, and Reformed territories. Smith, *Rise and Decline*, p. 35.

matters and a weakening of the church's institutional independence. Still to-day, Lutheran questions concerning the institutional character of the church remain unresolved.[34]

Brady effectively captures Luther's impact on matters of church and state:

> With one hand, Luther conveyed to Christian rulers authority over the church in this world and removed the foundation of the Catholic Church's power, the priesthood, by universalizing it. With the other hand, he denied to the Christian rulers the possibility of ultimate and exclusive authority over the world, including the soul, without which, as Hobbes taught and Rousseau confirmed, a new seamless fusion of spiritual author-ity and material power could not be formed.[35]

Even under Erastian Lutheranism, the spiritual authority claimed in-dependence in gospel matters. It was not a Hobbesian single-jurisdiction state. Yet it and other European Erastian states were not able to resist "the hostile takeover" of churches by states, a pattern that after 1750 left churches subservient, most clearly seen in the French and Russian revolutions.[36]

Western church history exhibits different understandings of what each authority means and what their relationship is, yet this same history reveals how pervasive this duality has been in the church. A theology of dual juris-dictions in its various forms differs profoundly from ancient and modern philosophies that claim that there is only one authority. Unlike Luther's perception of his situation, the church today is not about to usurp secular power and claim supremacy. Today the powerful secular state is supreme and creates the framework for the relationship.

---

34. According to Hans Barth, "Luther had no primary interest in the church as institu-tion." This meant "that the orders then in existence or in the process of development were adopted." One of the new trends was "the rise of absolutism in the organization of state church regimes.... It took World War I and the collapse of the German empire to finally set the Lutheran churches in Germany on their own institutional feet." *The Theology of Martin Luther: A Critical Assessment* (Minneapolis: Fortress Press, 2013), pp. 300, 302. Lutherans do well to ask with O'Donovan: "Does the authority of the Gospel word confer no social structure on the community which bears it? Does that community have no 'social space' determined by the truth?" *Desire of the Nations*, p. 208.

35. Brady, *German Histories*, p. 235.

36. Toft, *God's Century*, pp. 65-75. The authors of *God's Century* see a resurgence of religion independent of the state since the 1960s.

A Modern Invention

With the rise of the nation-state, the church's position changed. "When the church eventually became, in the secular mind, *an association within the state, as contrasted with an association beyond and against the state,* then the plural jurisdictions in each country of the West were swallowed up by the one national jurisdiction, and the plural legal systems were absorbed more and more by the one national legal system."[37] How then did the emerging nation-state deal with the church's belief that God rules the world through two authorities?

The tendency was to replace, marginalize, or obscure the Christian claims about dual jurisdictions with a new framework. The key category in this framework was "religion" contrasted with "secular." While used earlier in the church, "religion" was not a central category in the Bible or in the first sixteen hundred years of Christianity. The King James Version (1611), for example, "uses 'religion' or 'religious' only five times in its rendering of the New Testament from Greek, and for three different Greek terms."[38] Augustine, for example, could use *religio* to mean the "public and communal worship" of the one true God with the understanding that worship and love of God meant a person's love was rightly ordered in all of life. Yet Augustine also questioned whether *religio* captured the uniqueness of Christian worship since "the word applies to the observance of duties in human relationships."[39]

With the rise of the nation-state, the meaning of "religion" changed, and it became a category for talking about private beliefs that were different and separate from all else in civil society. In this sense, "religion is a modern invention" that came into being in "a certain range of time and a particular historical context."[40] Sometime in the seventeenth century, "religion" and

---

37. Berman, *Law and Revolution*, p. 269 (italics added).

38. Paul J. Griffiths, "The Very Idea of Religion," *First Things* 103 (May 2000): 31.

39. Augustine, *The City of God against the Pagans,* ed. and trans. R. W. Dyson (New York: Cambridge University Press, 2007), p. 392.

40. Brent Nongbri, *Before Religion: A History of a Modern Concept* (New Haven: Yale University Press, 2013), p. 5. Nongbri charts "the emergence of the conception of religions as apolitical paths to individual salvation." *Before Religion,* p. 6. He finds a similar understanding in Supreme Court decisions, as in a 1963 decision that states: "The place of religion in our society is an exalted one, achieved through a long tradition of reliance on the home, the church and the inviolable citadel of the individual heart and mind." Nongbri, *Before Religion,* p. 20. William Cavanaugh and Paul J. Griffiths also use the same language of "invention."

the rest of reality began to become unfused. "What was new in the early modern period were the distinctions between religion and politics and between religious and secular."[41] For William Cavanaugh, the religious/secular divide "is an invention that facilitated the rise of the sovereign state by making it appear obvious and natural that the civil authorities should enjoy a monopoly of power over worldly concerns."[42]

At the same time, "religion" came to be understood as a single, universal phenomenon with many expressions, as "a genus of which there are many species."[43] Having abandoned an Augustinian type of definition, modern scholars and the courts have failed to agree upon an accepted concept of religion. "Philosophically [religion] is 'essentially contested.'"[44] Substantivists (for whom God or Transcendence is an essential part of a definition) and functionalists (who ask what subjectively functions as one's ultimate concern) argue over what really is a religion and what is not. Constructivists see "religious" and "secular" as "constructed categories that are used in different times and places for different purposes, sometimes benign, sometimes not."[45] They make the case that "religion" and "the

41. William Cavanaugh, "Rejecting the Religion of Secularism," *ABC Religion and Ethics,* February 13, 2012, http://www.abc.net.au/religion/articles/2012/02/13/3429329.htm. One consequence of this view of religion is that "some sets of convictions about human nature and human flourishing would be called 'religious' and others 'political,' though without any very clear idea, then or now, of what differentiated the one set from the other." Griffiths, "Cheerleader, Lapdog, Hobbyist? 'Religion' and Its Relation to the State," *ABC Religion and Ethics,* Oct. 19, 2012, http://www.abc.net.au/religion/articles/2012/10/19/3614200.htm.

42. Cavanaugh, "Rejecting the Religion." He continues: "And it was the aggrandizement of state power which was the primary cause of the violence of the sixteenth and seventeenth centuries." This last point is a primary thesis of Cavanaugh's important book, *The Myth of Religious Violence* (New York: Oxford University Press, 2009). In it, he debunks "the myth" of "the wars of religion," and shows how this myth has influenced Supreme Court decisions.

43. Griffiths, "Very Idea," p. 32. Griffiths is commenting favorably on Timothy Fitzgerald's *The Ideology of Religious Studies:* "Fitzgerald's view, in summary form, is that when theological assumptions about religion are jettisoned, the category ceases to be either believable . . . or analytically useful. . . ." Griffiths thinks Fitzgerald's argument "affirms . . . only what theologians ought already to think, which is that an attempt to make sense and use of an idea of religion that systematically rejects theological assumptions will fail." "Very Idea," pp. 33-34. What Griffiths says about religious studies also illuminates discussions about the meaning of religion in constitutional law, particularly why secular rationales have difficulty in showing that *religious* freedom is a special freedom.

44. David Martin, *The Future of Christianity: Reflections on Violence and Democracy, Religion and Secularization* (Burlington, VT: Ashgate, 2011), p. 13.

45. William T. Cavanaugh, "Are We Free Not to Be a Religion? The Ambivalence of

secular" are not neutral, universally valid descriptors of the way things are but are historical constructs with their own background beliefs that are reflective of interests and power relations. "Religion itself is a historically conditioned category."[46]

The modern dichotomy of "religion" and "secular" is not the same as the distinction between God's dual authorities, although the influence and elements of the original distinction may be present in the modern understanding. "Church" is not the same as "religion," and "church" may find itself protected and also unprotected by law when it is considered as "religion." The pressure exists — both in the church and in the law — to define the church's mission to fit what is "religious," that is, as restricted to private belief and acts. "The idea that the church's responsibility was for something called 'religion,' which is essentially otherworldly . . . is [also] an invention of the early modern period."[47] When "religion" defines the church, the communal, corporate reality of the church may suffer or its social or educational mission may be divorced from the church.[48]

Christians have ample reason to view use of the terms "religion" and "religious" in constitutional discourse critically. Yet Christians will also recognize that this language can be a means, inadequate and malleable, for protecting a special human freedom for all people in a pluralistic society. Therefore they will point to the influence of the theology of God's dual governance in the religious language of the First Amendment.

Religious Freedom," *Pro Ecclesia* 23, no. 3 (Winter 2014): 11. Cavanaugh, "Rejecting the Religion."

46. Martin, *The Future of Christianity*, p. 13.

47. William Cavanaugh, "Rejecting the Religion."

48. Cavanaugh, "Are We Free Not to Be a Religion?" pp. 18-21. The title poses an important question. When religion is defined individualistically and as a separate part of life divorced from "secular" concerns, the church does not fit, since it is a corporate body called to care for the whole of life. An important Lutheran social statement, "The Nature of the Church and Its Relationship with Government," in protesting a government regulation, declared: "The heart of the issue is that the regulation relative to 'integrated auxiliaries' seeks to impose on the churches a definition of 'religious' and 'church' which the churches cannot accept theologically, one which constitutes an unwarranted intrusion by the government into the affairs of the churches. . . . But the churches object on principle to having any of their ministries, including their agencies and institutions, be treated as 'not religious.'" This social statement was adopted by the Lutheran Council in the USA on May 16, 1979. The American Lutheran Church also adopted it as a social statement in 1979. The social statement develops the principle of "institutional separation and functional interaction." See John R. Stumme and Robert W. Tuttle, *Church and State: Lutheran Perspectives* (Minneapolis: Fortress Press, 2003), pp. 51-73.

JOHN R. STUMME

Dual Jurisdictions in Early America

Dual jurisdiction theology was alive and well in eighteenth-century America, often making itself present under the cover of "religion." This theology carried by the churches in different forms mixed with Enlightenment ideas to shape early America's commitment to religious freedom as a special freedom. This commitment was both discontinuous and continuous of the Christian tradition.

"Religion" in this context referred principally (but not exclusively) to Protestant churches. These churches were not experiencing the state's "hostile takeover" as churches did in Europe in the eighteenth century and later. Many rejected "friendly takeovers" (established churches) and insisted on their independence from government. "Unlike the French enlightenment and the French Revolution, the American Revolution involved a cordial working relationship between the dominant religious groups and most enlightened ways of thinking. In fact, a distinctive feature of the American experience was the synthesis of Protestant and enlightenment principles that one finds widely in the early republic."[49]

George M. Marsden is not alone among scholars who speak about "the significant place of Protestant Christianity in the American enlightenment."[50] As we have seen, Nicholas Miller looks to "Protestant dissenters" whose churches were free from government support for the religious roots of religious freedom. Thomas Kidd shows how the alliance of evangelicals and Enlightenment thinkers was vital for securing religious freedom.[51] Charles Taylor observes that "[r]eligion and democratic self-rule were at the outset all but indissolubly linked."[52] Hugo Heclo uses an image to describe the relationship: "In America, for the first time, Christianity and democratic self-government launched themselves together in a kind

49. George M. Marsden, *The Twilight of the American Enlightenment: The 1950s and the Crisis of Liberal Belief* (New York: Basic Books, 2014), p. xxiii.

50. Marsden, *The Twilight of the American Enlightenment*, p. xxiii. This of course was a major theme in Alexis de Tocqueville's *Democracy in America*, ed. J. P. Mayer (New York: Harper Perennial, 1969).

51. Thomas S. Kidd, *God of Liberty: A Religious History of the American Revolution* (New York: Basic Books, 2012). Kidd documents the role evangelicals played in the Revolution, in the formation of the Constitution, and in the election of Jefferson in 1800. He writes that there were five beliefs that evangelicals and the deists shared: religious freedom, God as the guarantor of human rights or common creation, the threat of sin, the need for virtue, and providence moving in and through nations.

52. Taylor, "Religion in a Free Society," p. 93.

of double-stranded helix spiraling through time . . . moving together, each affecting the other."[53]

Already in his 1965 classic *The Garden and the Wilderness,* Mark DeWolfe Howe argued that the Court has made too much of Jefferson's "political" metaphor of "wall of separation" and has not done justice to Roger Williams's "theological" wall metaphor whose purpose was to keep the world and government out of the garden of the church.[54] The rights recognized by the religious provisions of the Constitution "are, in their essence, liberties or immunities, not claims."[55] These prohibitions were based on "the deep conviction that the realm of the spirit lay beyond the reach of government." They were more an expression of Williams's philosophy than of Jefferson's because "by and large, American opinion in 1790 accepted the view that religious truth is identifiable and beneficent."[56]

Faith not skepticism was decisive in James Madison's defense of religious freedom in his "Memorial and Remonstrance against Religious Assessments" (1785). His defense incorporated a theistic and theological understanding of religion: it is "the duty which we owe to our Creator and the Manner of discharging it," which "can be directed only by reason and conviction, not by force or violence."[57] Like Luther, Madison understood religion to be outside of Caesar's jurisdiction: every person's duty to the Creator "is prec-

---

53. Heclo, *Christianity and American Democracy,* p. 35.

54. Mark DeWolfe Howe, *The Garden and the Wilderness: Religion and Government in American Constitutional History* (Chicago: University of Chicago Press, 1965), pp. 5-6.

55. Howe, *The Garden and the Wilderness,* p. 17. Avery Cardinal Dulles also understands religious freedom as immunity. "Religious freedom, strictly speaking, is not a right to *do* anything. In technical terms, it is not a *ius agendi* but a kind of *ius exigendi* — a right to make a demand on the state. Negatively, it is a right not to be coerced in one's religious life unless one is jeopardizing public order. Positively, it is a right to be supported in one's quest to know religious truth and live accordingly. This twofold right, rooted in the dignity of the person, is not a merely 'civil' right — one that could be conferred or abrogated by the state — but a natural right that may and should be protected by civil law." Avery Cardinal Dulles, S.J., "*Dignitatis Humanae* and the Development of Catholic Doctrine," in Grasso and Hunt, *Catholicism and Religious Freedom,* p. 58. The understanding of immunity in Howe and in Dulles corresponds with the theology of dual jurisdictions.

56. Howe, *The Garden and the Wilderness,* pp. 18, 19.

57. Quoted in Steven D. Smith, "The Places and Functions of Freedom of Conscience," *Religion and Human Rights: An Introduction,* ed. John Witte Jr. and M. Christian Green (New York: Oxford University Press, 2012), p. 157. See also James Madison, "Memorial and Remonstrance against Religious Assessments (Virginia), 1785," in *Church and State in the Modern Age: A Documentary History,* ed. J. F. Maclear (New York: Oxford University Press, 1995), pp. 59-63, p. 60.

edent both in order of time and degree of obligation, to the claims of Civil Society. . . . We maintain therefore that in matters of Religion, no man's right is abridged by the institution of Civil Society, and that Religion is wholly exempt from its cognizance."[58]

In eighteenth-century America, there was unanimity on one subject, according to the historian James Hutson: "Government must not interfere in the spiritual realm of religion, in men's beliefs and modes of worship. . . . Everyone agreed that the spiritual realm must be walled off from government."[59] Dual-jurisdiction theology gave substance to this ethos. This eighteenth-century commitment is an example of what Reinhard Hütter calls *"genuine liberalism,"* one "that is enlightened about its limits and its dependency upon what transcends its very limits."[60]

Lutherans coming from Europe had to learn how to be church without depending on an Erastian state. Henry Melchior Muhlenberg, the "founder" of Lutheranism in America, recognized the challenge and worked "toward the ideal of a united, independent, self-sustaining church."[61] He shared the country's unanimous conviction that government should not interfere in the church and affirmed a much broader understanding of the freedom of the church than did early Lutheranism. More than forty years before the adoption of the First Amendment, in 1747, Muhlenberg used the language of that amendment in his journal: "[T]he subjects of His Majesty, George, in this country enjoy the free exercise of religion. . . ."[62] This meant for him that people had the freedom to form congregations and to worship God and that

58. Madison, "Memorial and Remonstrance," p. 60. Smith notes that Madison is stating a dual-jurisdiction rationale for the freedom of conscience. The other two traditional rationales — the incompetence rationale and the voluntariness/futility rationale — are also in Madison's "Memorial." Today the dual-jurisdiction rationale is bound to "seem implausible or inadmissible" within a secular framework. Smith wonders if conscience is being "dissolved" into personal autonomy and thereby trivializing conscience. Smith, "The Places and Functions of Freedom of Conscience," pp. 157-58. Marie Failinger writes that freedom of conscience "has come to mean very little beyond the notion of personal existential decision-making." Quoted in Steven D. Smith, *The Disenchantment of Secular Discourse* (Cambridge, MA: Harvard University Press, 2010), p. 144.

59. James H. Hutson, *Church and State in America: The First Two Centuries* (New York: Cambridge University Press, 2008), p. 137.

60. Reinhard Hütter, *Dust Bound for Heaven: Explorations in the Theology of Thomas Aquinas* (Grand Rapids: Eerdmans, 2012), p. 104.

61. Sydney E. Ahlstrom, *A Religious History of the American People* (New Haven: Yale University Press, 1972), p. 255.

62. Quoted in Ahlstrom, *A Religious History*, p. 257.

persons had the freedom to become part of them. "Free exercise" included both freedom of belief and freedom of practice, such as sacramental action and church organization and discipline.[63]

The significance of the churches' influence on the early American republic's commitment to religious freedom is often downplayed in favor of a narrative that sees Enlightenment thinking as the key agent. According to Steven Smith, "the standard story" about the origin of religious freedom in the United States emphasizes its radical break with a religious past " 'filled with turmoil, civil strife, and persecutions,' " in the words of Justice Hugo Black in *Everson v. Board of Education.*[64] In this story, the founders, shaped by the Enlightenment, separated church and state, thus protecting the freedom of the religious conscience, thereby inaugurating a new period in human history.

Smith wants to revise this story. Yes, the embrace of separation of church and state "was a break from the immediately preceding Erastian pattern." Yes, the embrace of the freedom of conscience repudiated practices that violated conscience — the Inquisition being the most vivid example. Yet, he claims, the standard depiction is "incomplete . . . [and causes] it to be badly misleading." What it fails to acknowledge is that the major components of the American position were not new ideas; rather, they represented a retrieval and consolidation, under the circumstances of the new American republic, of distinctively Christian themes that had been defended and sometimes practiced for centuries. The commitment to separation of church and state manifests the family features of a descendant of the ancient Christian ideal of dual jurisdictions — an ideal that had driven the centuries-long medieval struggle for "freedom of the church" from secular control. And the American commitment to freedom of conscience was a modern embodiment of another longstanding Christian commitment; this commitment was grounded in the convergence of the idea of inner, sincere religion as the prerequisite for salvation with the more Protestant development in which "freedom of the church" came to be extended to the "inner church" of conscience.[65] This

---

63. Ahlstrom, *A Religious History,* p. 257. Michael J. Sandel confirms Muhlenberg's understanding of "free exercise": "For Madison and Jefferson, freedom of conscience meant the freedom to exercise religious liberty — to worship or not, to support a church or not, to profess belief or disbelief — without suffering civil penalties or incapacities. It had nothing to do with a right to choose one's beliefs." In his "Memorial," Madison never mentions "autonomy" or "choice." Michael J. Sandel, "Freedom of Conscience or Freedom of Choice?" in Hunter and Guinness, eds., *Articles of Faith,* p. 87.

64. Smith, *Rise and Decline,* p. 14; *Everson v. Board of Education,* 330 U.S. 1, 8 (1947).

65. Smith, *Rise and Decline,* p. 46.

revised narrative rightly highlights the theological background and presuppositions of the early republic's commitment to religious freedom. The commitment to the separation of church and state draws from dual-jurisdiction theology to protect the freedom of the church; the commitment to the free exercise of religion has roots in the Christian understanding of faith and God's noncoercive way of creating faith in "the spiritual government."

The Constitutional Provisions on Religion

Scholars debate endlessly the original meaning of the First Amendment: "Congress shall make no law respecting an establishment of religion or prohibiting the free exercise thereof. . . ." The interpretation that I find most plausible is that these provisions are jurisdictional and do not express substantial principles or a philosophy of religious freedom.[66] These provisions state what the national government cannot do: it cannot establish a national church or restrict religious freedom, and it cannot interfere in state establishments.[67]

Two facts support this interpretation. One is that in the ratification process, in Congress and in the states, the amendment was not controversial. Given that the states had different Christian traditions and different understandings and practices concerning establishment and religious freedom, one would expect that an amendment dealing with religion and the federal government would be very controversial and even divisive. That, however, was not what happened. The religious provisions were drafted to avoid controversy and to voice agreement, which would not have been possible if they were expressing disputable principles.

The second fact is that nothing changed with their adoption. The religious provisions reaffirmed "the jurisdictional status quo."[68] They confirmed "what virtually everyone did agree on — namely, that religion was within the jurisdiction of the states, and that the institution of a new national gov-

---

66. Smith, *Rise and Decline*, pp. 48-57.

67. During the ratification process for the Constitution, Madison argued: "The Government has no jurisdiction over it [religion]." Quoted in Michel I. Meyerson, *Endowed by Our Creator: The Birth of Religious Freedom in America* (New Haven: Yale University Press, 2012), p. 158. Madison did not think that an amendment was necessary since the Constitution did not mention religion. When some voiced fear that the federal government might create a national church as existed in Europe, Madison in order to gain support for ratification agreed to support adding an amendment. See Smith, *Rise and Decline*, p. 58.

68. Smith, *Rise and Decline*, p. 55.

ernment was not calculated to change that situation."[69] When states did disestablish, it was "the result of the democratization of American society and of the dynamics of American religion, specifically . . . the Second Great Awakening."[70] The Supreme Court's early decisions on religion were based on federal common law, not on the First Amendment.[71] The first free exercise decision did not come until a century later, in 1879.[72]

Smith maintains that through a decades-long "meandering amendment of constitutional meaning,"[73] provisions originally designed "to confirm the jurisdiction status quo came to express major and more affirmative constitutional commitments." One such commitment is to the "separation of church and state," which "is something like the classical commitment to freedom of the church."[74] Court decisions have shown "a commitment to keeping churches independent of governmental control or regulation." The other commitment is to "the free exercise of religion" (interchangeable with "freedom of conscience") that "came to be understood in more unqualifiedly substantive or affirmative terms."[75] Both have roots in the Christian tradition.

When seen as a whole, the Constitution does not acknowledge (or deny) God, rejects a religious test for office, and does not incorporate religion into the structures of government. It does not follow, however, that the absence of a reference to God means that the government created by the Constitution was to be "Godless" or "religionless."[76] The people who wrote and ratified the Constitution appointed chaplains, proclaimed national days of prayer, and "used religious language routinely in their official acts and statements."[77]

69. Smith, *Rise and Decline,* p. 56.

70. Hutson, *Church and State in America,* p. 163.

71. John Witte Jr. and Joel A. Nichols, *Religion and the American Constitutional Experiment,* 3rd ed. (Philadelphia: Westview, 2011), p. 244.

72. Smith, *Rise and Decline,* pp. 140-43. *Reynolds v. United States,* 98 U.S. 145 (1879) was the first decision that used Jefferson's "wall metaphor." Donald L. Drakeman argues that the Court's later overreliance on two Virginians is due to Chief Justice Waite's decision in the *Reynolds* case. Donald L. Drakeman, *Church, State, and Original Intent* (New York: Cambridge University Press, 2010), p. 3.

73. Smith, *Rise and Decline,* pp. 66-71.

74. Smith, *Rise and Decline,* p. 69.

75. Smith, *Rise and Decline,* pp. 71-72.

76. Religion "was banished from the Constitution for political considerations not because of any generalized enmity to it. It is, accordingly, more appropriate to speak of a politique Constitution than a 'Godless' one." Hutson, *Church and State in America,* p. 144.

77. See Smith, *Rise and Decline,* pp. 63-64, for Laura Underkuffler's documentation. Witte and Nichols list the variety of ways state governments "patronized religion" in the eighteenth century. *Religion,* p. 61. Meyerson writes: "Moreover, the willingness to employ

Yet the Constitution does not take a position on the God question; it is "prudently agnostic: it studiously declines to affirm either secularism or religion, atheism or theism."[78] It does not establish a Christian government, nor does it establish a secular, nonreligious one. Martin Marty writes, "Although the founders included the Latin root (*saeculum,* of this age) of the word secular in their motto, it would not have occurred to them to use such a term to show that they were forming a 'secular' state in modern senses of such a term."[79]

A Secular Worldview

While in the early republic religion played a primary role in social life and strongly influenced government, today government plays a primary role and strongly influences the role played by religion in social life.[80] Whereas in the eighteenth century Christianity and democracy were moving together, by mid-twentieth century "the two strands in the double helix had been winding away from each other for some time," leading to a growing reciprocal alienation between the two. A distinctive public doctrine was undermining Christianity's cultural authority, one "veering toward un-Christian commitments to worldly progress, autonomous self-realization, and idolatrous patriotism."[81]

---

explicitly religious references shows that the framers were not afraid of official discussions of religion and did not intend to eliminate religious language from public discourse." Meyerson, *Endowed by Our Creator,* p. 5.

78. Smith, *Rise and Decline,* p. 104. "[T]he agnostic Constitution . . . steadfastly declines to align itself with any party, or with either the providentialist or secularist visions of the country." Proponents of the "godless" Constitution work to subvert this agnosticism "and to elevate one of the longstanding interpretations — namely, the secularist interpretation — to the status of constitutional orthodoxy. They thereby subvert a valuable strategy for maintaining unity amid diversity." Smith, *Rise and Decline,* pp. 104-5.

79. Martin Marty, "Getting Beyond 'The Myth of Christian America,'" in *No Establishment of Religion: America's Original Contribution to Religious Liberty,* ed. Jeremy T. Gunn and John Witte (Oxford: Oxford University Press, 2012), p. 370.

80. Harold J. Berman, "Religious Freedom and the Challenge of the Modern State," in Hunter and Guinness, eds., *Articles of Faith,* pp. 42-43.

81. Heclo, *Christianity and American Democracy,* pp. 80, 214. Heclo describes the reigning public doctrine in terms of autonomy, inclusiveness, and a tolerance in which all views are equally valid. Truth and values amount to personal opinion, and religion is a personal and private matter. Heclo argues that commitment to the democratic faith and to the culture of choice provides a unifying secular identity that transcends other identities, including religion. Heclo, *Christianity and American Democracy,* pp. 95-96.

The growing role of government is evident in the Supreme Court's increased activity in matters of religious freedom. For the first 150 years of the republic, the Court's role was limited to the federal level. With the incorporation of both religious provisions in the 1940s, the door opened for the Court to make hundreds of decisions during the next seventy-five years that now apply to all levels of government.[82] As many scholars argue, the Court's religious freedom decisions and discourse do not form a coherent body of law. Nevertheless, citizens today enjoy a high degree of religious freedom,[83] a reality due more to society's pluralism and citizens' beliefs and practice of tolerance than to what the Court says. Yet, in having the final word on the legal meaning of the Constitution's provisions on religion, the Court's influence has been and will continue to be very significant.

The dominant discourse on religious freedom in the courts and legal scholarship expresses a worldview built around key concepts such as "autonomy," "separation," "private" (religion), "neutrality," "equality," and "secular."[84] I will focus on the understanding of "secular" and its counterpart "religion."

82. See the listing and brief description of cases up to 2010 in Witte and Nichols, *Religion,* pp. 306-38.

83. Smith speaks of "a paradox": "On the one hand, no society in history has afforded greater scope and protection for a diverse range of religious belief and conduct. . . . On the other hand, there is something approaching unanimity on the proposition that the prevailing *discourse* of religious freedom — or the official framework and language within which issues of religious freedom are argued about and judicially resolved — is deeply incoherent. . . . As our practice has improved, it seems, our understanding and discursive facility have deteriorated." Steven D. Smith, *Getting Over Equality: A Critical Diagnosis of Religious Freedom in America* (New York: New York University, 2001), p. 10.

84. On "autonomy" see Sandel, "Freedom of Conscience"; according to Sandel, a new "version of liberalism" informs "the reigning interpretation of religious liberty," an interpretation that views the human being as "a choosing self, independent of its desires and ends." This "unencumbered self" is "sovereign . . . the author of the only obligations that constrain." Sandel, "Freedom of Conscience," p. 75. In *Cantwell v. Connecticut,* 310 U.S. 296 (1940), p. 303, for example, the Supreme Court stated: "Freedom of conscience and freedom to adhere to such religious organization or form of worship *as the individual may choose* cannot be restricted by law." Quoted in Sandel, "Freedom of Conscience," p. 85.

On "separation" see Philip Hamburger, *Separation of Church and State* (Cambridge, MA: Harvard University Press, 2002), pp. 2-3. The idea that church and state are separate in structure is an indispensable element for the church to be free from political domination or interference as well as to keep the church from wielding the sword. Hamburger acknowledges this positive understanding of separation when he writes that the term also "alludes to a differentiation or distinction between church and state." Hamburger, *Separation,* p. 3. But he also shows that "separation" understood as "a distance, segregation, or absence of

Historically, "secular" is a biblical and Christian term, essential for theology. It is an intrinsic part of the doctrine of two ages. Its meaning depends on eschatology: "secular" names "this age," this passing age, before God's final age. The term that corresponds with "secular" is not "religious" but "eternal."[85] Secular authorities are God's agents to deal with matters of this age. For Christian faith, the "secular" is "religious," that is, it too "pertains to God." The secular is "a specialized area of God's domain."[86] There is no "godless" sphere of life.

In the worldview of much First Amendment jurisprudence, "religion" and "secular" take on very different meanings. "Secular" comes to mean "nonreligious," that is, the opposite of "religious." Whatever "religion" is thought to be, it is understood to be a section of life separate from the secular world, partitioned off from law, politics, culture, and economics. All reality and language is either "secular" or "religious"; something cannot be both at the same time. The Supreme Court and constitutional scholars function with one kind of language and ban the other. It is the sovereign state — through its laws, regulations, or court decisions — that determines what is and is not "religious" for its purposes.[87]

---

contact" between the two has a detrimental effect on religious freedom. Hamburger, *Separation*, p. 2. For more on the various meanings of "separation," see Witte and Nichols, *Religion*, pp. 51-57. See also John Witte Jr., "The Serpentine Wall of Separation Between Church and State," in *God's Joust, God's Justice: Law and Religion in the Western Tradition* (Grand Rapids: Eerdmans, 2006), pp. 207-42.

On "private" (religion) see Marsden, *The Twilight of the American Enlightenment*, p. 158.

On "neutrality" see Smith, *Rise and Decline*, pp. 128-38; Steven D. Smith, *Foreordained Failure: The Quest for a Constitutional Principle of Religious Freedom* (New York: Oxford University Press, 1995), pp. 78-97. "Perhaps the most common modern version of neutrality holds that government can remain neutral in matters of religion by confining itself to the realm of the secular." Smith, *Foreordained*, p. 81.

On "equality" see Smith, *Rise and Decline*, pp. 147-58; Smith, *Getting Over Equality*, pp. 10-26.

On "secular" see Smith, *Disenchantment*, especially pp. 107-50.

85. O'Donovan, *Desire of the Nations*, p. 211.

86. Nomo Stolzenberg, quoted in Smith, *Disenchantment*, p. 114.

87. For example, the Department of Health and Human Services (HHS) defined "religious employer" in this manner in its regulations for the Affordable Care Act: "The amended interim final regulations specified that, for purposes of this exemption, a religious employer is one that: (1) Has the inculcation of religious values as its purpose; (2) primarily employs persons who share its religious tenets; (3) primarily serves persons who share its religious tenets; and (4) is a non-profit organization. . . ." "Group Health Plans and Health Insurance Issuers Relating to Coverage of Preventive Services Under the Patient Protection and Af-

In this modern sense, "secular" still refers to "this age" but without an eschatological horizon. There is only one age, or perhaps, only one age that counts in legal discourse. Whatever might be said about the age-to-come must be reinterpreted to fit the accepted ideology of this one age. A secular jurisprudence may not be, or may not consider itself to be irreligious, yet in practice and often in theory, it considers "secular" to be a domain independent of God, if there is a God.[88] This worldview became prominent in the twentieth century. According to Noah Feldman, "until the 1870s, the word 'secular' did not even figure in American discussions of church and state."[89] A Webster's dictionary of 1913 defines "secular" as "pertaining to this age."[90] In contrast, the first definition of an online dictionary from 2006 illustrates a common understanding of secular in our time: "of or relating to the doctrine that rejects religion and religious considerations."[91]

One who interprets the First Amendment through the lens of a secular worldview with religion as private belief might say something like this: "We were a religious (or largely Christian people), *but* we established a secular government." In other words, these Christians, for some reason, didn't want their religion to influence government, so they created a secular, that is, a nonreligious government. It sounds counterintuitive, and, as I have noted, it does not correspond to the history of the early republic. Change one word in the sentence and place it within Christian two-age, dual-jurisdiction theology, and it says: "We were a religious (or largely Christian) people, *so* we established a secular government." Because they were Christians, they insisted

---

fordable Care Act," *Federal Register* 77, no. 31 (February 15, 2012): 8725. http://www.gpo .gov/fdsys/pkg/FR-2012-02-15/pdf/2012-3547.pdf. For my criticism of these regulations, see my article, "When Government Defines 'Religious' (Church): An Historical Example," *Journal of Lutheran Ethics* (March 2012), http://www.elca.org/Faith/Journal-of-Lutheran -Ethics.

88. Brian Leiter is one constitutional scholar who denies that *religious* freedom is special on the basis of "philosophical naturalism" since "it is no longer rational to believe in gods or other super-natural beings." Because religion may have psychological value for the individual, it should be tolerated on an equal basis with other claims of conscience. Leiter's atheism shows how questions concerning the rationale for *religious* freedom are often theological. Brian Leiter, preface to his paperback edition of *Why Tolerate Religion?* p. 3 (forthcoming), http://papers.ssrn.com/sol3/papers.cfm?abstract_id=2396866.

89. Quoted in Smith, *Rise and Decline,* p. 91.

90. *Webster's Revised Unabridged Dictionary* (1913), http://machaut.uchicago.edu/ ?resource=Webster%27s&word=secular&use1913=on. The first definition is "coming or observed once in an age or in a century."

91. "Secular-WordNet (r) 3.0 (2006)," *Online Dictionary,* http://onlinedictionary .datasegment.com/word/secular.

that their government be secular, that is, one that deals with the matters of this passing age and not those of the new age-to-come, which are outside its jurisdiction. The matters of this age, they would add, are also God's concern, and Christians are to deal with them on the basis of the convictions and attitudes of their faith. Here they "have no lasting city" (Heb. 13:14, RSV), yet they are "to seek the welfare of the city" in which they find themselves (Jer. 29:7, RSV), as God does.

However, a secular worldview with its nontheological categories of "religious" and "secular" has no room for the theological belief that "God has ordained two governments."

> The confinement of discourse to the secular rules out . . . the fundamental and essentially jurisdictional premise that gave rise to the whole debate and tradition in the first place — the belief that God has divided life into spiritual and temporal domains and has assigned different authorities to each domain. For this reason among others, debates about religious freedom no longer have the *jurisdictional* character they once had. Instead, we now have a problem of *justice,* broadly conceived, or of "fairness."[92]

No Longer a Special Freedom?

Smith wants us to imagine "a community in which most people believe in and only care for the temporal." In such a community, Smith asks, "would there be room, or any reason, to give special honor or legal status to religious freedom?"[93] Any theory about this situation would not be one of *religious* freedom, since it would not offer protection to *religion* as religion, that is, because of its *religious* character. "Rather the theory protects religion as a temporal human activity and because that activity is thought to affect temporal interests."[94] Government would not interfere with religious choices because it would violate a person's autonomy, for example.[95]

In contrast, Michael Stokes Paulsen has a clear answer to what is special about religious freedom:

92. Steven D. Smith, "Discourse in the Dusk: The Twilight of Religious Freedom?" *Harvard Law Review* 122, no. 7 (2009): 1882.
93. Smith, *Getting Over Equality,* p. 50.
94. Smith, *Getting Over Equality,* p. 51.
95. Smith, *Getting Over Equality,* pp. 46-50.

Religious freedom only makes entire sense as a social and constitutional arrangement on the supposition that God exists (or very likely exists); that God makes claims on the loyalty and conduct of human beings; and that such claims, rightly perceived and understood, are prior to, and superior to, the claims of any human authority.[96]

Paulsen, in echoing Madison, is saying what many Christians and other religious people would say if asked why religious freedom is a special freedom. It seems commonsensical that an indispensable reason that we have religious freedom is because a living God communicates with people, or so many believe. If there were no God, and people believed there was no God, why *religious* freedom?

George P. Fletcher defends the special character of religious freedom with the concept of loyalty. He finds inadequate the common justifications of religious freedom based in the idea that religious beliefs are simply important, personal psychological beliefs. "The imperative of loyalty to a higher power provides the most compelling account of our deferring to religious obligations. The religious life, as we know it in the West, is based on the individual's having loyalties to a transcendental authority. These loyalties preclude giving wholehearted allegiance to a secular authority."[97] Religious beliefs arise in communities of believers and "represent a submission to an external authority that commands obedience." For Fletcher, religious claims, because of their nature, "generate exemptions from statutes that apply neutrally to everyone."[98]

As compelling as these justifications are to many, they have a fatal flaw: they are theological, or they are tied to a theistic understanding of religion. In the secular worldview of constitutional discourse, they are excluded from addressing the question, "Why *religious* freedom?" They are constitutional "heresy." Justifications, if there are any, must be secular or nonreligious.

Douglas Laycock, a prominent leader in defending religious liberty, is confident that he can offer a secular account for why religion should receive special treatment, one that does not entail "commitments to any proposi-

96. Michael Stokes Paulsen, "The Priority of God: A Theory of Religious Liberty," *Pepperdine Law Review* 39, no. 5 (2013): 1160, http://digitalcommons.pepperdine.edu/plr/vol39/iss5/8.

97. George P. Fletcher, *Basic Concepts of Legal Thought* (New York: Oxford University Press, 1996), pp. 181-83.

98. Fletcher, *Basic Concepts of Legal Thought,* pp. 181-83.

tion about religious belief."[99] For him, it should be sufficient reason to say "because the Constitution says so," but apparently for many, it is not. He recognizes that theological beliefs played an important, perhaps indispensable, role in constitutional guarantees of religious liberty. "But," he writes, "these religious beliefs cannot be imputed to the Constitution without abandoning government neutrality on religious questions."[100] Theological rationales violate the Constitution's no-establishment clause. Laycock bases his "religion-neutral case for religious liberty" on three "secular propositions": Since government suppression of religious views has caused great suffering, religious freedom is needed to minimize conflict and create a peaceful society; religion has "extraordinary importance" for the individual; and "beliefs at the heart of religion . . . are of little importance to the civil government."[101]

For the sake of religious freedom, one hopes Laycock's rationale is convincing, yet I doubt if it provides a secure basis for why religion should receive special treatment. Accounts of what counts as religion, as Smith says, "are typically over- and underinclusive. They cover more than 'religion' and less than everything we think of as 'religion.' "[102] For example, yes, religion may be extraordinarily important to an individual but so are other kinds of beliefs for others. Moreover, to claim that "beliefs at the heart of religion . . . are of little importance to the civil government" is hardly convincing, since it would, for example, discount the historical significance for government of the dual-jurisdiction doctrine.

Laycock defines "religion" broadly, so that it becomes an expansive and elastic term. For him, "religion" is "any set of answers to religious questions, including the negative and skeptical answers of atheists, agnostics, and secularists."[103] Other inclusive definitions understand religion in broad functional, subjective terms: an individual's ultimate concern, the deeply

---

99. Douglas Laycock, "Religious Liberty as Liberty," in *Religious Liberty*, vol. 1, *Overviews and History* (Grand Rapids: Eerdmans, 2010), p. 67.

100. Laycock, "Religious Liberty as Liberty," p. 67.

101. Laycock, "Religious Liberty as Liberty," pp. 58-61.

102. Smith, *Rise and Decline*, p. 147.

103. Laycock, "Religious Liberty as Liberty," p. 69. I wonder if this definition is the operative one in his three propositions. As far as I can see, Laycock does not define or clarify what is and is not a "religious question," which pushes the definitional question down the line. Many apparently secular questions easily become religious ones, such as: Is it true that America is "the last, best hope" for human society? Many philosophy courses would be "religious." The focus on "religious question" may lead to an intellectualistic and individualistic view of religion.

held moral convictions of an autonomous self, or a person's profound beliefs.[104] When "religion" becomes so general and vague, it becomes difficult to know what makes "religion" special, which consequently leads to denying its specialness. Some may adopt a broad functional definition of religion for the Free Exercise Clause and a narrow, substantivist one for the Establishment Clause; such an attempt, however, betrays an arbitrary "double standard."[105]

But perhaps the most telling criticism of a secular rationale is that many who like Laycock function within a secular worldview no longer believe religion is special, and they no longer seek a rationale for religious freedom. A recent op-ed piece states the case:

> Most Western societies have, for historical reasons, come to think of "religious freedom" as a special kind of liberty. . . . From today's perspective, it is easier to see that religious freedom is not a special kind of liberty, but one expression of a broader set of freedoms of conscience, belief, assembly and action.[106]

This notion is widespread:

> We [Witte and Nichols] are . . . troubled by a growing tendency among some scholars to deny that religion is special and deserving of special constitutional protection. Various writers now say that such a constitu-

104. The Supreme Court stated that the test of religious belief is whether it is a "sincere and meaningful belief which occupies in the life of its possessor a place parallel to that filled by the God of those admittedly qualifying for the exemption." *United States v. Seeger,* 380 U.S. 163 (1965), p. 176. http://supreme.justia.com/cases/federal/us/380/163/case.html. The statement illustrates a nonjurisdictional understanding of religion.

105. See James Davison Hunter, "Religious Freedom and the Challenge of Modern Pluralism," in Hunter and Guinness, eds., *Articles of Faith,* p. 72.

106. Kenan Malik, "Religious Freedom, Secular Forum," *International New York Times* (Jan. 12, 2014), http://nyti.ms/1eAyUad. "Today," he writes, "we live in a different world. Religion is no longer the crucible in which political and intellectual disputes take place. Questions of freedom and tolerance are not about how the dominant religious establishment should respond to dissenting theological views, but about the degree to which society should tolerate, and the law permit, speech and activity that might be offensive or hateful, that might challenge the state or undermine national security." Malik illustrates his view: "There is nothing wrong with the American government's requiring Catholic-run hospitals to give employees health insurance that includes free contraception." Once "religion" no longer involves jurisdictional questions, religious freedom claims are easily dismissed.

tional vision of religion, if it even existed in the eighteenth century, has become obsolete in this postmodern and postreligious age. Religion is too dangerous, divisive, and diverse in its demands, the argument goes, to be accorded special protection. Religion is better viewed as just another category of liberty and expression and given no more preference than its secular counterparts. Indeed, to accord religion special treatment is an unconstitutional establishment of religion, and discriminates against the nonreligious.[107]

Smith writes that ordinary citizens might consider it "radical" to think "there is no longer any warrant for singling out *religious* freedom as a special constitutional commitment." "Far from being audacious," in an academic environment "the argument might more accurately be characterized as ho-hum."[108] He quotes Laycock: "Scholars from all points on the spectrum now question whether there is any modern justification for religious liberty." Laycock adds: "For the first time in nearly 300 years, important forces in American society are questioning the free exercise of religion in principle — suggesting that free exercise of religion may be a bad idea, or at least, a right to be minimized."[109] If the proposal to do away with religious freedom as a special freedom comes to be accepted, Smith envisions that "the outcome would be in one sense the last chapter in the story of American religious freedom."[110]

107. Witte and Nichols, *Religion,* p. xv.
108. Quoted in Smith, *Rise and Decline,* p. 139.
109. Quoted in Smith, *Rise and Decline,* p. 140.
110. Smith, *Rise and Decline,* p. 141. According to Smith, Kent Greenawalt's massive *Religion and the Constitution,* vol. 2, is another example of the unstable character of secular rationales for religious freedom. Smith writes that the author finds himself in an "awkward position": he is trying to respect a legal and cultural commitment to the special legal treatment of religion, yet he refuses to rely on religious rationales to do so. Greenawalt "acknowledges this 'paradox,' as he calls it. His hope is that the special commitment to religious freedom can be grounded in the *fact* that people still believe in special treatment for religion, even if that belief cannot (or can no longer) be supported with any very satisfying *justifications.*" Smith concludes "that the constraints of modern secular discourse effectively preclude Greenawalt from offering any justification for his prescriptions beyond unconvincing appeals to supposedly shared axioms or commitments." Smith, "Discourse in the Dusk: The Twilight of Religious Freedom," *Harvard Law Review* 122 (2009): 1904-5.

Conclusion: What Then?

With these historical and theological reflections, I have sought to show that there are two fields of discourse concerning the basis of religious freedom. Secular or nonreligious discourse has marginalized or banned theological discourse. If my claim has validity, then the message is: "If you want to defend the principle of religious freedom, don't talk about God." But a secular discourse is having trouble justifying religious freedom as a special freedom. This inability threatens *religious* freedom in the long-term.

Fortunately, Lutherans might think, we have a theoretical solution to the divide I have described; it's called "the two kingdoms." We divide the world into spheres. We recognize the secular world as autonomous with its own language and rules, and we value reason as the way this world operates. Our faith is our motivation to do the best possible in the secular world according to its own requirements. We are free to accept the secular discourse and restrictions of constitutional jurisprudence and to leave the truth claims of our faith behind us. Perhaps we will have opportunity to translate our faith commitments into the ongoing language of the legal community without loss. Our challenge is to learn to smuggle these commitments into secular discourse without anyone noticing.

This sounds like a caricature of the two kingdoms, or does it? I fear it may represent a tendency in some Lutheran circles to capitulate to a worldview that puts brackets around the church's faith in the public arena. How can Lutherans rest content with an account of religious freedom that denies God's dual jurisdictions? How can we acquiesce or even baptize an understanding of law that presupposes that the secular is the only reality? How can we pretend that God's Word has nothing do to with matters of this age?

Should we not rather begin by recognizing this worldview for what it is? Long ago Paul Tillich labeled it "self-sufficient autonomy."[111] Hütter sharpens Tillich's critique. He calls this worldview *"sovereign secularism,"* which is "comprehensive, immanentist self-sufficiency." Secularism, he writes, entails "an arrogation to itself of the divine attribute of sovereignty."[112] Should not Lutherans approach this secular worldview with such a critical spirit?

If there is an alternative to the present hegemonic worldview, it would give space to the religious vitality in the American experience in all its plu-

---

111. Paul Tillich, *The Protestant Era* (Chicago: University of Chicago Press, 1948).
112. Hütter, *Dust,* p. 103.

ralism. Perhaps the alternative would be something like Smith's "American settlement." Smith discerns "two contending views, or families of views" throughout American history, which he calls "providentialist" and "secularist." Since America has affirmed the "principle of openness," or the "principle of contention," both interpretations of the American experience "were, and would continue to be, legitimate contenders." Neither "position would be permitted to establish itself as *the* constitutional principle or, conversely, to banish the other as a legitimate interpretation of the American constitutional order."[113] Instead of adopting either providentialism or secularism, the American settlement has embraced, and could in the future embrace, the principle "of constitutional agnosticism and constitutional contestation among the various interpretations."[114] Under this principle, defenses of religious freedom from the perspective of dual jurisdictions would be a welcomed perspective in contention with other views. Smith's worthy plea is for democratic debate and negotiation on many of the questions that are now closed in a secular worldview. It is a call for "a genuine pluralism" that includes a variety of religious and secular viewpoints.[115]

What then do Lutherans do? Let us support personal and corporate religious freedom for all, knowing that all are created in the image of God. May we exercise our own religious freedom with respect for the proper role of government and by adhering to legitimate civil law. Let us deepen and teach the theology of dual jurisdictions in our churches and advocate its importance in the public square. Let us encourage society to welcome this Christian novelty as a "legitimate contender" in the democratic debate about the meaning of the First Amendment, which requires that the ban on theology be lifted so that it is no longer considered to be "constitutional heresy." And ought not we Lutherans renew our commitment to the "freedom of the church"?

Vatican II in its "Declaration on Religious Freedom" stated: "The freedom of the Church is the fundamental principle in what concerns the relations between the Church and governments and the whole social order."[116] In addressing political rulers, Pope Paul VI asked: "And what does the Church ask of you today? . . . She asks of you nothing but freedom — the freedom to

113. Smith, *Rise and Decline*, p. 103.
114. Smith, *Rise and Decline*, p. 109.
115. Marsden, *The Twilight of the American Enlightenment*, p. 167.
116. "Declaration on Religious Freedom *(Dignitatis humanae),*" in *The Documents of Vatican II,* ed. Walter M. Abbott, S.J., and Very Rev. Msgr. Joseph Gallagher (New York: Guild Press, 1966), p. 693.

believe and to preach the faith, the freedom to love God and to serve Him, the freedom to live and to bring to men her message of life."[117]

A Lutheran social statement sets forth a similar principle: "Our concern is that the church be free to be the church, the state to be the state, each true to its own God-ordained functions."[118] "The Nature of the Church and Its Relationship with Government" gave voice to the church's freedom.[119] In our time when government reach continually expands, Lutherans need to develop our understanding of "the freedom of the church," which is so vital a part of the theology of dual jurisdictions.

What about the future? Heclo concludes his essay on Christianity and democracy by predicting and asking: "The tension between religious commitment and political allegiance [between Christian discipleship and American citizenship] will grow and vary depending on whether the person defines his or her life as a Christian American or an American Christian. What is the 'fundamental' term, and which the mere modifier? Each person's answer will make all the difference in the world and, some believe, beyond it."[120]

Toward the end of his recent book, Smith predicts that "the fate of religious freedom will likely depend to a large extent on the fortunes of 'the church.'" "[I]f the church continues to be a vigorous and vital institution in society, religious freedom will probably be okay. Conversely, if the church declines, religious freedom (and, perhaps, much else) is likely to go down with it."[121]

These are predictions worth thinking about.

117. "Declaration on Religious Freedom," n. 53, p. 693.

118. The American Lutheran Church, "Church-State Relations in the USA" (1966), p. 3.

119. See note 48. Consistent with the freedom of the church, the Supreme Court recently gave special protection for religious institutions in a unanimous decision upholding "ministerial exceptions." *Hosanna-Tabor Evangelical Lutheran Church and School v. Equal Employment Opportunity Commission,* 132 S. Ct. 694 (2012).

120. Heclo, *Christianity and American Democracy,* p. 144.

121. Smith, *Rise and Decline,* pp. 163-64.

CHAPTER 3

African Americans and Secular Law:
A Paradoxical Relationship

Richard J. Perry Jr.

*The rules may be color-blind, but people are not. The question re-
mains, therefore, whether the law can truly exist apart from the color-
conscious society in which it exists, as a skeleton devoid of flesh; or
whether law is the embodiment of society, the reflection of a particular
citizenry's arranged complexity of relations.*

Patricia J. Williams[1]

Setting the Context

One of the frightening and instructive experiences I have had involved an
encounter with the Detroit Police Department. I use the adjectives "frightening" and "instructive" because as a naïve middle-class African American
male, I was unaware of how white police officers treated African American people. I knew an African American police officer who lived in our
neighborhood and attended the same church our family attended. It was
not until the Detroit Rebellion of 1967 that I became aware of how white
police officers treated African American people in some parts of Detroit,
especially in the poor areas, when they ran afoul of the law; and I learned
the extent to which police would go to restore order.[2] However, it was not
until my personal experience with white police officers that I was instructed

---

1. Patricia J. Williams, *The Alchemy of Race and Rights* (Cambridge, MA: Harvard University Press, 1991), p. 120.
2. "Detroit Race Riot (1967)" at http://www.blackpast.org/aah/detroit-race-riot-1967.
Accessed December 31, 2014.

on the relationship between members of the African American community and the police force.

During the late 1960s, I was a student at Michigan Lutheran College in Detroit. After classes, members of the bowling team from church and I went bowling one evening. Afterwards, I went to the church (located on the east side of Detroit) where I was working as a youth director. Around 10:00 p.m., I gathered my briefcase (with all my books and papers in it) and my bowling bag (which only contained my bowling ball and shoes), and locked up the church. Since I had a blown engine in my car during those days, I either took the bus or walked home from church. This particular evening the bus was late, so I started walking at a brisk pace.

I noticed that a police car with two white policemen had driven by after I started walking. I did not think much about it because police presence in this part of town was normal. Normal in the sense that drug dealing was on the rise in the neighborhood and break-ins were occurring on a regular basis. After I had walked several blocks, however, the same police car pulled up alongside me and the police officer on the passenger side asked, "What do you have in there?" I innocently responded, "My books and my bowling ball and shoes." The officers got out of the car, told me to put my hands on the trunk and to "spread them." One officer kicked my ankles to the distance he wanted my legs. I was nervous, and my arms began to shake because this was my first encounter with the Detroit police force. The officer wanted to know why my arms were shaking so much. I told him "I'm nervous. Did I do anything wrong? I was wondering, why are you doing this? I work at the church down the street."

Meanwhile, the other officer was rummaging through my briefcase and bowling bag. The officer who patted me down said I was clean. His partner replied that everything was all right with the briefcase and bowling bag. Still shaking and with a heart pumping furiously, I gathered up my belongings. After the officers got back into their car, the officer who patted me down said, "That bowling ball can be considered a weapon. I suggest you not carry it with you at this time of night." "All right, officer," I said as I begin to walk home. About seven or eight blocks later, the police officers drove by again. This time they kept going.

I learned this kind of interrogation was a normal practice in the church's neighborhood. White police officers would drive up and tell a group of African American males to "spread them." One of the members of the church's basketball team who learned of my encounter said, "Welcome to the 'hood, Rev. Welcome to the 'hood." I also learned that police officers had performed a "search and seizure routine," sometimes called "stop and frisk," on me. And it was all legal: if the officers had a "reasonable suspicion" that a person was armed, they could stop and frisk that person.[3] Ever since that incident, my heart pumps fast and I shake whenever I am stopped by the police.

After years of confronting explicit white racism, I learned that what I experienced was the result of "unconscious racism."[4] The "stop and frisk" law is one example of the unconscious way that white police officers exercise their hidden racial prejudices and power over African American people and their bodies.

I remembered this incident as our nation recently confronted two events involving the killing of young black men. The first was the trial of George Zimmerman for killing an unarmed African American male, Trayvon Martin. I was an unabashed spectator of the televised trial because I was curious with how the court system would handle the case, especially since the victim's side of the incident could not be told. The second event was the shooting of Michael Brown, an unarmed African American male, in Ferguson, Missouri. Once again, I was curious about how the grand jury would respond to the actions of a white police officer. Both of these events confirmed suspicions I had: the white men would not be held responsible by the law for these deaths.

The Enduring Problem

These two events raise what I consider to be an enduring problem in the U.S.: the troubled relationship between people of color and police officers, mediated and justified by the law.[5] This enduring problem has been exposed

3. *Terry v. Ohio*, 392 U.S. 1, 88 S. Ct. 1868, 20 L. Ed. 2nd 889 (1968).

4. Charles R. Lawrence III, "The Id, the Ego, and Equal Protection: Reckoning with Unconscious Racism," *Stanford Law Review* 39 (January 1987): 317-88.

5. I am following the designation of people of color as defined in the Evangelical Lutheran Church in America's Social Statement, *Freed in Christ: Race, Ethnicity and Culture* (Chicago: Department of Studies, Division for Church and Society, 1993). Since the adoption of this Social Statement, "African Americans" has been changed to "African Descent" and "African Nationals" and "Caribbean" has been added. In addition, Arab and Middle Eastern have been added and Hispanic has been changed to "Latino/as." These classifications follow closely the categories employed by the U.S. Office of Management and Budget (OMB) Directive 15. Those categories related to race are: American Indian or Alaska Native, Asian or Pacific Islander, Black, and White with two categories related to ethnicity: "Hispanic or Latino" and "Not of Hispanic origin." Directive 15 was changed to include the following

in racial profiling practices that expose the disproportionately high number of African American and Latino people, especially males, being stopped by police, and the rising number of unarmed African American and Latino males who are shot to death. What does "equal justice under the law" mean if one is a person of color living in the United States? As Prof. Williams's epigraph at the beginning of this essay asks, is it possible for there to be colorless law in a color-conscious society like the United States? Does the African American religious and ethical tradition offer any guidance about the meaning of just and unjust secular law?

A Proposal of Paradox

This chapter represents my struggle as an African American male, a Lutheran pastor, and an ethicist to answer those questions. My proposal is that African Americans have a paradoxical relationship with secular law. A paradox is the apparent lack of resolution of opposing statements, yet both are true. In Lutheran social ethics, this is captured by Martin Luther's understanding of the Christian moral life. Writing in "The Freedom of a Christian," Luther says, "A Christian is perfectly free lord of all, subject to none. A Christian is a perfectly dutiful servant of all, subject to all."[6] Said differently, Christians are free of any service or responsibilities to or for the other, yet Christians are bound to service and responsibilities to and for the other.

By secular law, which I am challenging here, I mean social and moral laws (including the legal system proper) that are created by human beings to govern personal conduct and social relations in society. For example, "stop and frisk" laws are adopted through a supposedly democratic process to govern personal conduct and social relations. They have racial and racist overtones because of the population those laws are applied to on a daily basis.[7] Paradoxically, despite racial and racist overtones of some secular

---

categories: race — American Indian or Alaskan Native, Asian or Pacific Islander, Black or African American, White, and ethnicity — Hispanic origin and Not of Hispanic origin. See "Revisions to the Standards for the Classification of Federal Data on Race and Ethnicity." Available at: http://www.whitehouse.gov/omb/fedreg_directive_15. Accessed May 25, 2014.

6. Martin Luther, "Freedom of the Christian," *Luther's Works*, vol. 31, *Career of the Reformer I*, ed. Harold J. Grimm, trans. W. A. Lambert and Harold J. Grimm (Philadelphia: Fortress Press, 1957), p. 344.

7. *Report: NYPD Stop-And-Frisk Activity in 2012 (2013)*, available at http://www.nyclu.org/publications/report-nypd-stop-and-frisk-activity-2012-2013.

laws, African Americans fundamentally believe in the authority and power of the secular law and those legal human rights documents that order human existence in the world. For example, the original language of the United States Constitution essentially defined most African Americans as property, nonhumans. As such, that document has racial and racist overtones. Yet, African Americans exhibit a strong sense of loyalty to the Constitution and an interpretation that promotes equal citizenship and justice.[8] They also bring a strong critique and protest against secular law and documents when they are unjust, unjustly applied, or have unjust implications, sometimes in the name of the Constitution. Loyalty and protest, in a preliminary way, express our paradoxical relationship to secular law.

Second, I make the claim that the paradoxical relationship with secular law is shaped by the permanent nature of white racism in America.[9] Admittedly, this is a deeply pessimistic view about the capacity of white America to transform its practice of white racism. The insidious nature of America's "original sin," in both its conscious and unconscious expression, originates, I believe, in a faulty understanding of what it means to be a human being.[10] While a "stop and frisk" law may be adopted under the guise of trying to cut down crime and remove guns from the streets, it is an unconscious expression of racism. Carrying out the law, especially when it is done by white police officers, disproportionately affects African American and Latino/Latina youth and their bodies. They are subjects to be controlled rather than human beings with feelings, thoughts, and ambitions.

Third, I claim that the Rev. Dr. Martin Luther King Jr.'s understanding of just and unjust laws is an adequate understanding of the Lutheran interpretation of secular law. More specifically, I claim that King's theology, although he was a member of an African American Baptist denomination, embodies what Lutherans identify as the "two kingdoms doctrine."[11] King's interpre-

8. Dorothy E. Roberts, "The Meaning of Blacks' Fidelity to the Constitution," *Fordham Law Review* 65 (1997): 1761.

9. I have been deeply influenced by Derrick Bell's understanding of the permanent nature of racism. See his book *Faces at the Bottom of the Well: The Permanence of Racism* (New York: Basic Books, 1992).

10. Jim Wallis, "Racism: America's Original Sin," *Sojourners,* available at http://sojo .net/print/blogs/2013/7/29/racism-americas-original-sin. Accessed March 17, 2014.

11. This doctrine has been variously identified as "Two Realms" and "Two Governances" within the Lutheran theological and ethical tradition. See Martin Luther, "Temporal Authority: To What Extent It Should Be Obeyed" (1523), in *Luther's Works,* vol. 45, *The Christian in Society II,* ed. Walther I. Brandt, trans. J. J. Schindel (Philadelphia: Fortress Press, 1962), pp. 75-129.

tation, when set side by side with traditional Lutheran interpretations, is an authentic *Christian* (i.e., biblical) understanding of the Christian's relationship to government and the laws it enacts to govern personal, institutional, and social relationships. Before delving into this theology, however, I want to focus on the claim that white racism is permanent and how this reality is confronted by some African American religious and legal scholars in combating structural white racism.

White Racism and Its Permanent Nature

White racism exists as a permanent dimension of American social and institutional life. The disparity in perceptions and experience between African Americans and white Americans, especially in regard to the legal system, lies in the institutionalization of the inferiority of people of color. Although white racism can be expressed individually and institutionally, my focus here is on the systemic expression of white racism. Systemic white racism is "a phenomenon that employs race as a proscriptive principle for denying rights and opportunities, that is, a principle of societal exclusion."[12] The most telling example of this principle emerged in the formulation of the Constitution of the United States. Seeking to exact a compromise with southern states that saw abolishing slavery as a threat to their economic survival, the framers embedded racial difference into the institutional life of society. Systemic white racism determined, in part, who African American people were, are, and what they will be from the perspective of free white propertied males. The challenge for African Americans was and is today how we will resist institutionalized white racism.

"Don't Confuse Me with Facts. You Are What I See!"

The reader may be wondering why we should focus on the issue of race and white racism in an article on law. He or she may claim, "Isn't the law neutral? Don't we live in a colorblind society? Are not the most prominent actors within the legal and criminal justice system (i.e., the lawyers, prosecutors, juries, and judges) called upon to suspend their experiences, racial biases,

12. Peter Paris, *The Social Teaching of the Black Churches* (Philadelphia: Fortress Press, 1985), p. 3.

and thoughts and just apply the law?" Since the civil rights movement purportedly has attained all of its goals, some citizens might believe the election and reelection of an African American president is emblematic of the success of the American citizenry in overcoming issues of race and white racism.

Such a belief, however, exhibits great naïveté about issues related to race and white racism. Moreover, race and white racism have been enormously difficult conversation topics for Americans. Some of the difficulty resides in our ability, and sometimes the inability, to listen to various understandings of what race means. Some people may believe that any discussion of race is useless because the existential situation of people of color will now be transformed by post–civil rights era successes in political, economic, and social life. Other people may believe that any discussion of race is "impolite"; and consequently, persons wanting to discuss race become known as "bad people." I agree with theologian James H. Cone that we have to break the silence on the issue of white racism. While that process must begin with dialogue, quite honestly, this is where my pessimism begins. How can anyone engage in honest dialogue with people of color when they do not know or want to know about the *historical* and *contemporary* experience of people of color on the planet Earth? Genuine dialogue is only possible through honest attempts to make sense of what race and white racism mean from the perspective of Americans of color.[13] All of us must ask, what do some African American religious, scientific, or even legal scholars have to say about what race and racism mean? Which standpoint is "normative"? Who decides which standpoint is normative? The multidisciplinary nature of the meaning of race is complex and difficult terrain to navigate. However, it is important to be aware of the ongoing academic discussions on this matter to begin a meaningful conversation, so I will briefly review major themes below.

A Theological Perspective on Race

I want to begin with what it means to be a human being in a race-conscious society.[14] Central to my contention is the view that the community of white

13. James H. Cone, "The Challenge of Race: A Theological Reflection," in *Ethics Matters: African, Caribbean, and African American Sources,* ed. Marcia Y. Riggs and James Samuel Logan (Minneapolis: Fortress Press, 2011), pp. 78-86.

14. Discussion of what it means to be a human being is normally understood to be theological anthropology. Accordingly, "*Theology* is critical reflection about the God-human relationship, and *anthropology* is rational inquiry into and understanding of human beings

Americans, despite all of that community's diversity, perpetuate a faulty understanding of what it means to be human. People who practice white racism both consciously and unconsciously are contesting the work of God, who created all people in God's image (Gen. 1:26-28). Racism becomes a religion that supplants faith in God.[15] This is the sin that the Old Testament calls idolatry, a violation of the first commandment. Those who practice white racism institutionally, by making policies and laws and supporting destructive institutions, make their racial heritage and culture the normative standard for what it means to be human.

African American womanist theologian M. Shawn Copeland offers a more contemporary understanding of what it means to be a human being. At the center of her thinking about what it means to be a human being is the experience of poor, exploited African American women and how others treat their bodies.[16] Copeland traces, through the gaze of white European male philosophers, attitudes and ideas that have supported popular assumptions about race that have dehumanized people on the basis of skin color.[17] Borrowing the category of horizon from Bernard Lonergan, Copeland writes that a horizon shaped by the race of the other "hides the 'other' from my own, and renders the 'other' invisible." That is, no matter what the facts are, you are what another sees that you are, a body whose skin (whose race) leads to behaviors that control and separate one human being from the other.[18] A crucial example of how the bodies of poor exploited African American women are objectified and controlled is the life of Saartjie Baartman, who became known as "the Hottentot Venus." Baartman was the victim of a form of science that viewed the bodies of African American women as objects of pleasure to be put on display.[19] This objectification of African American women continued throughout slavery because the master's economic well-being was dependent upon the production and reproduction of African American women. Racism, therefore, results in the complete terrorization of African American bodies, especially African American women's bodies,

---

and culture." Linda E. Thomas, *Living Stones in the Household of God: The Legacy and Future of Black Theology* (Minneapolis: Fortress Press, 2004), p. vii.

15. See the classic work of George D. Kelsey, *Racism and the Christian Understanding of Man* (New York: Charles Scribner's Sons, 1965).

16. M. Shawn Copeland, *Enfleshing Freedom: Body, Race, and Being* (Minneapolis: Fortress Press, 2010), pp. 14-15.

17. Copeland, *Enfleshing Freedom,* pp. 9-11.

18. Copeland, *Enfleshing Freedom,* pp. 12-15.

19. Copeland, *Enfleshing Freedom,* pp. 11-12.

from an institutional standpoint. Racism, as Copeland opines, "goes beyond prejudice or even bigotry by binding negative or vicious feelings or attitudes to the exercise of putatively legitimate power."[20] Simply stated, at bottom, race is a social construct.

Scientific Perspectives on Race

A growing contribution to the conversation on the meaning of race and white racism emerges from the dialogue between science and religion. The growth of genetic technology has created a window of opportunity for religion and science to make a contribution toward a uniform understanding of race. As Copeland's argument subtly suggests, human beings engage in myth-making around the concept of race. Joseph L. Graves Jr., an evolutionary biologist, calls this "the race myth," which means letting what one sees (race) carry more importance than what the Other shows himself or herself to be. As racial categories are developed, humankind is ranked according to phenotypical differences such as skin color, hair, body type, and facial features. Of course, this is biological determinism and a pernicious and contradictory (?) ideology.[21] On one hand, when African Americans engage in conversation with white Americans, they sometimes hear, "When I see you, I don't see race."[22] This is denial of the obvious — skin color. On the other hand, African Americans constantly experience white Americans "seeing" race when white security guards follow them in stores, racially profile them, and falsely identify them as perpetrators of a crime. Through the lens of racism, human beings are socialized by institutions (family, religion, education, politics, law, and economy) to ignore the reality that is before them. Graves's conclusion is that race "is a social construct, a myth in the service of social dominance: which can be defeated."[23]

Barbara Holmes, a lawyer and religious ethicist, approaches an understanding of race from the direction of cosmology and quantum physics. Her book, *Race and the Cosmos: An Invitation to View the World Differently,*

20. Copeland, *Enfleshing Freedom,* p. 109.
21. Joseph L. Graves Jr., *The Race Myth: Why We Pretend Race Exists in America,* with a New Preface by the Author (New York: Plume, 2004), chapter 1.
22. Derrick Clifton, "11 Things White People Should Stop Saying to Black People Immediately," at http://mic.com/articles/96144/11-things-white-people-should-stop-saying-to-black-people-immediately_br (accessed January 1, 2015).
23. Graves, *The Race Myth,* p. 207.

serves as a threat to the black religious and theological establishment: the principal reason is that Holmes invites the black religious and theological establishment to take account of science.[24] Her thesis is that "the quest for justice is a social, theological, and scientific construct, and by that I mean that liberation must take the entire life space (including science) into account."[25]

Holmes's understanding of race, I think, augments what Copeland and Graves have to say about race. Holmes argues that "race signifies the way in which we orient ourselves toward one another based on perceived categorical differences of color, culture, or ethnicity."[26] In Holmes's view, there is a connection between what we think about ourselves and what we think of the world. There is an ethical dualism that supports reality as it is (i.e., reinforcing the importance of race for determining social relations and policies) rather than reality as it should be (i.e., making race irrelevant to social and political relations). Holmes's solution is to adopt the language of cosmology to stimulate human imagination. That language engenders an invitation to see that "darkness" matters in a positive sense.[27] Embracing darkness is valuable for two reasons, says Holmes: "In the place of discourses of inferiority and marginalization, dark matter is a symbol of power and relevance. It also offers dark people an opportunity to begin to see themselves as metaphorically connected to a darkness that is predominant in the universe."[28] Viewing one's self positively through darkness rather than through light, often portrayed as the normative gaze, is certainly a novel contribution to the debate about the permanence of race and racism in America. Holmes, however, is more concerned about inviting people to view the world differently. And science can help in that process of liberating all people.

A Legal Perspective on Race

The conversation around race becomes more complex when the contributions of diverse legal perspectives on the meaning of race are considered. First, there is complexity because of the number of players involved in

24. Barbara Holmes, *Race and the Cosmos: An Invitation to View the World Differently* (Harrisburg, PA: Trinity Press International, 2002).
25. Holmes, *Race and the Cosmos*, p. 55.
26. Holmes, *Race and the Cosmos*, p. xvi.
27. Holmes, *Race and the Cosmos*, pp. 106-10.
28. Holmes, *Race and the Cosmos*, p. 106.

determining the meaning of race. Legislators, lawyers, judges, and American citizens are all stakeholders in arriving at the meaning of race for legal purposes. If it is the case that judges are trained to leave their emotions and life experiences aside when rendering decisions, what does that mean for an African American client who senses that the judge really does not care about his or her case? What is the role of the African American lawyer who challenges a white judge who shows racial bias? What does it mean when an African American judge, who has been active in civil rights activity in his or her community, renders a decision that white defendants fail to accept? Is it the responsibility of an African American judge to recuse himself or herself from the case? Second, what is a legal definition of race? Who determines the definition of race when people of color are excluded from social power on the basis of race? What purpose(s) does a legal definition of race serve? These questions are crucial for exploring what African American legal minds can contribute to the conversation about race and secular law.

The debate about the legal construction of race in America begins with the principal document that governs life in the United States. The United States Constitution, although amended by the Thirteenth, Fourteenth, and Fifteenth Amendments, clearly signals in the first instance who are citizens of the United States. Article 1, section 2, clause 3 of the United States Constitution reads as follows,

> Representatives and direct Taxes shall be apportioned among the several states which may be included within this Union, according to their respective Numbers, which shall be determined by adding to the whole Number of free persons, including those bound to Service for a term of years, and excluding Indians not taxed, three fifths of all other persons.[29]

Some African American legal scholars have not let go unnoticed the fact that African American people have been identified as nonhuman or inferior since before the Constitution was even drafted. Leon Higginbotham Jr., a prominent African American jurist and scholar, writes that African people were deemed inferior before 1787. Inferiority, Higginbotham writes, reflects "a state of mind and logic of the heart. It poses as an *article of faith* that African Americans were not quite altogether human. What's more, 'inferiority'

---

29. The U.S. Constitution. Available at http://constitutionus.com/. Accessed March 22, 2014.

did not owe its existence to the legal process. Although the law came to enforce the precept, it did not create it."[30]

Building on Higginbotham's work, we can note several important things about racial inferiority. First, he establishes that inferiority became a faith that was already prominent in the psyche of white Americans. Certainly the analysis offered by Shawn Copeland on how the Enlightenment period contributed to the subjugation of African American people, especially poor African American women, makes common cause with Higginbotham's thinking. Second, although I hesitate to argue against Higginbotham's claim that the legal process did not create the status of inferiority experienced by modern African Americans, I must do so. The legal process *did* create the status of *legal, as well as social,* inferiority as evidenced by the number of legal cases brought in the United States over what constituted the race of a person. Ian Haney Lopez's book *White by Law: The Legal Construction of Race* documents how the law created racial categories as a method of maintaining legal differences between racial groups. White European Americans became defined by what they were not; that is, to be a white European American meant one was defined from a negative — dark race — as society understood and practiced that definition.[31] Despite this gloomy reality, I will argue that we may find in Martin Luther King's conceptualization of just and unjust law a resonant and hopeful African American Lutheran understanding of the nature and possibilities of secular law.

An African American Interpretation of Secular Law

Martin Luther King was the twentieth century's greatest drum major for human rights and social justice, as evidenced by the voluminous number of books, articles, and essays written on various dimensions of King's public work. However, there is more to King than the nonviolent direct action he taught so famously. King drastically reformed society's perception of African Americans from being viewed as mere objects to being treated with rancor and viciousness to being seen as African Americans, having ideals worthy of sharing and being heard in the public sphere.

---

30. A. Leon Higginbotham Jr., *Shades of Freedom: Racial Politics and Presumptions of the American Legal Process* (New York: Oxford University Press, 1996), pp. 3 and 9.

31. Ian Haney Lopez, *White by Law: The Legal Construction of Race,* Revised and Updated 10th Anniversary Edition (New York: New York University Press, 2006).

A little-known dimension of King's theological work was King's understanding of the Christian's relationship to the state and the courts. King fundamentally saw good in both the state and the courts. He reflected the best of the African American religious tradition, a paradoxical embrace reflecting both loyalty and critique. On the one hand, King saw, the state or government was needed to restrain humankind from itself. In a paper on Reinhold Niebuhr, King expressed the notion that "government is very necessary, for men (sic) inevitably corrupt their potentialities of love through a lust for self-security which outruns natural needs."[32] Government's legitimate (?) role, he opined, was to regulate the behavior of human beings. On the other hand, government itself was corrupted by human sin; and the role of the Christian and the Christian church was to critique it when it evidenced such corruption.

Over time, the courts became an ally of King. If state policies, laws, and documents failed to respond to the needs of society's downtrodden and racially oppressed people, the courts were viewed as one system that would protect individual citizens and their rights. When social institutions failed in their responsibility to provide equally for all of the citizens of the United States, King gave high praise to the courts. One speech, "Give Us the Ballot — We Will Transform the South," typifies King's thinking since his days in Montgomery. He says,

> So far only the judicial branch of the government has evinced this quality of leadership. If the executive and legislative branches of the government were as concerned about the protection of our citizenship rights as the federal courts have been, then the transition from a segregated to an integrated society would be infinitely smoother.[33]

King, however, was ever a realist. He sensed that the courts would not be the cure-all for the freedom of poor, oppressed people. It would also take nonviolent direct action, especially when unjust laws were instituted to control the lives of American citizens.

The foundation of King's thinking on law finds its expression in his belief

---

32. Martin Luther King Jr., "Reinhold Niebuhr's Ethical Dualism," in *The Papers of Martin Luther King, Jr.,* vol. 2, ed. Clayborne Carson et al. (Berkeley: University of California Press, 1994), p. 147.

33. Martin Luther King Jr., "Give Us the Ballot," in *A Testament of Hope: The Essential Writings of Martin Luther King, Jr.,* ed. James M. Washington (New York: HarperOne, 2003), p. 198.

about God and the ethical principle of human dignity. King believed deeply in a personal God. In a sermon titled "A Knock at Midnight," King writes,

> I am convinced of the reality of a personal God; . . . it is a living reality that has been validated in the experience of everyday life. . . . So in the truest sense of the word, God is a living God. In [God] there is feeling and will, responsive to the deepest yearnings of the human heart; this God both evokes and answers prayer.[34]

This living and personal God was the foundation of all existence. And, this personal God was intimately involved in the environment that, using law as its weapon, was negating the dignity and worth of African Americans and all poor people.

The King literary corpus reveals that he employed a number of resources to reinforce his thinking on just laws and unjust laws.[35] However, the "Letter from Birmingham Jail" is probably the most closely reasoned and systematic in its thinking and argumentation. As many are aware, the "Letter" was written in response to a group of clergy who published a statement in the local Birmingham, Alabama, paper challenging the Southern Christian Leadership Conference (SCLC) and King about their activity in Birmingham and asking them to be patient about law reform.[36] King wrote the "Letter" while he was in jail for disobeying a court injunction which, in King's view, was an abuse of legal power because it reinforced segregation laws. Those segregation laws and subsequent injunctions also hindered free expression guaranteed by the First Amendment of the U.S. Constitution.

In the "Letter," King builds his case for why he is in Birmingham (to combat racial injustice) and his perspective on just and unjust laws. After reviewing the components of nonviolent direct action, its philosophy, and the purpose of nonviolent direct action, King describes the experience of racial segregation and the impact it has on African American people, both parents and children. African American people, he suggests, can no longer wait for their rights, as the clergy statement suggested.

The "Letter" combines both natural law and personalism. While King

34. Martin Luther King Jr., "A Knock at Midnight," in *Strength to Love* (Philadelphia: Fortress Press, 1963, 1981), p. 62.

35. See for example King's *Stride Toward Freedom* (New York: Harper & Row, 1958), pp. 33-34 and chapter 4.

36. Martin Luther King Jr., "Letter from Birmingham Jail," in *Why We Can't Wait* (New York: New American Library, 1963, 1964), pp. 76-95.

may not have been a traditional natural law proponent, he would argue that there is a connection between law and morality. Thus, he thought, decisions that any person would make are shaped by his or her moral beliefs and lived experience. Positive law, on the other hand, reflects a more distant involvement with human life, and supporters of positivist approaches to law argue that one's moral beliefs have no place in administering the law: the law is the law.[37] In the positivist view, one has to accept the decisions made by the courts, and judges must make legal decisions disregarding their personal feelings or sense of morality. (Ironically, this is not unlike African American contemporary experience.) Some might argue that recent decisions to not indict or find guilty police officers who shot and killed unarmed African American people are beyond belief.

King's religious understanding of natural law emphasizes that there is a "higher law" influencing moral decisions. This "higher law" is a lens through which one must understand how secular law must be shaped. Higher law can be known by human beings through their capacity to reason. However, this capacity is not useful or sufficiently well informed unless American citizens feel the depth of racial oppression that has been experienced by African American people.

After setting forth this framework, King is prepared to state his belief about just and unjust laws. His bottom line is paradoxical. That is, on the one hand, King would obey secular laws, recognizing one has "a moral responsibility" to do so. But the other side of the paradox is that if a law is unjust, one has a moral responsibility to disobey. A just law is one that is consistent with the law of God. An unjust law is a law that is "out of harmony with the moral law."[38] King calls upon St. Augustine and St. Thomas Aquinas as his authorities. With Augustine, King agrees that an unjust law is no law at all. With Aquinas, King agrees an unjust law is not grounded "in eternal law or natural law." The ethical dimension of his analysis is that laws which support racial segregation are unjust because of what they do to those who are segregated and what they do to the persons who practice segregation. Unjust laws are grounded in human reason. Consequently, King argues that racial segregation is "morally wrong and sinful." The appropriate moral action is to disobey an unjust law through nonviolent protest, bringing critique to the governmental body enforcing racial segregation laws.

37. Richard Wollheim, "Natural Law," in *The Encyclopedia of Philosophy*, vol. 5, ed. Paul Edwards (New York: Macmillan and The Free Press, 1967), pp. 450-54.

38. King, "Letter from Birmingham Jail," p. 82.

King embodies, I think, a paradoxical perspective in his discussion of "higher law" that reflects a truer (?) biblical understanding about higher law. That is, his faith in a living God who is intimately involved in the human condition is reflected when King says, "Any law that uplifts human personality is just. Any law that degrades human personality is unjust."[39] Although King was trained as a systematic theologian, his preaching skill surfaces in the discussion of when individuals should disobey unjust law. For example, King interprets a critical story for him, the story of Shadrach, Meshach, and Abednego (Daniel 3), to mean that the three people in the fiery furnace chose to disobey the "laws of Nebuchadnezzar, on the ground that a higher moral law was at stake."[40] Accordingly, one's experience with a corrupt governmental agency, an unjust secular law, or abusive representatives of a governmental agency warrants disobedience because obedience would require worship of a human being and his or her unjust policies. A crucial concept that King continually injects into the public sphere is that God endows all human beings with dignity and worth. Human beings are created in the "image of God." Therefore, human beings are to be respected not because of their race, skin tone, or whether they obey perpetrators of unjust laws. Human beings are to be respected because of their love of their creator. In many ways, therefore, King converges with Lutheranism and its embrace of Acts 5:29 — namely that one must disobey humankind on the basis of loyalty and commitment to a "higher law." King, as with Lutherans, would argue that *agape* (love) is the higher law. Love becomes the regulating motif for enacting the ethical principle of justice in society. King did not focus on the human capacity for reason as the basis for human beings knowing the "higher law." Rather, King's focus was on the love of God that pervades one's heart, a love that manifests itself for victims of white racism and even for those who practice institutional white racism.

Conclusion

I have attempted in this essay to argue that African Americans have a paradoxical relationship with secular law. This relationship has been demonstrated in diverse disciplines and their contributions to understanding the nature of race. They have achieved some consensus that systemic white rac-

39. King, "Letter from Birmingham Jail," p. 82.
40. King, "Letter from Birmingham Jail," p. 84.

ism creates a false perception of African Americans' reality, and that consequently, the existence of African Americans is principally constituted by systemic white racism reinforced by the implementation of secular law. In response, I have offered Martin Luther King's interpretation of secular law, where he distinguishes between just and unjust law, which is similar to a Lutheran interpretation of secular law. In both interpretations, when a law is just and the state is just, we have a moral responsibility to obey. When a law is unjust, and the state unjustly applies unjust laws, we have a moral responsibility to protest and to disobey. In the words of King, "It may be true that morality cannot be legislated, but behavior can be regulated. The law may not change the heart, but it can restrain the heartless."[41] Our task as both religious people and stakeholders within the system of secular law must be to continue to dialogue with institutional oppressors in order to free victims and perpetrators from the evil of systemic white racism.

41. Martin Luther King Jr., "An Address Before the National Press Club," in *Testament of Hope,* p. 100.

PART II

Reflections on Property and Larger Creation: Property Law and the Environment

CHAPTER 4

U.S. Property Law Reconsidered in Light of the Lutheran *Finitum Capax Infiniti*

Mary Gaebler

It is generally understood that one cannot jump out a window ten stories up and expect to fly; for with the greatest possible probability, the law of gravity will teach a person what she has apparently failed to observe, even as she bumps up hard against the ground below. If our choices and actions fail to take account of what is real, there will be painful consequences. Sincere belief is not the same thing as knowledge, and as Icarus discovered, human beings are not designed to fly.[1] In his explanation of the first commandment, Luther begins with the warning from chapter 20 of the Book of Exodus — "I am the Lord your God, mighty and jealous, visiting the iniquity of the fathers upon the children to the third and fourth generation of those who hate me, and showing mercy to many thousands of those who love me and keep my commandments" (Exod. 20:4, RSV).

While we may think it appallingly unfair of God to visit the consequences of our actions upon our children, this is not commensurate with Luther's belief in a world where divine presence is hidden behind an observable continuity and interpenetration of all that exists. That this appears to us as unjust reflects our mistaken belief that each human being is a separate entity, autonomous from every other, and therefore responsible only for his or her individual actions. Civil law rests upon this presupposition, as does the related belief in the separation of each part from the others that underscores U.S. property law in particular. The devastating effects of this

---

1. Icarus, failing to respect the real circumstances of his situation, paid the consequences with his death. Having been given a pair of artificial wings held together with wax, Icarus ignored the fact that wax melts when heated, soared toward the sun, and, as the wings fell to pieces, fell into the sea and was drowned. From the myth of Daedalus and Icarus.

presupposition on the environment today will most certainly pose acute challenges for those who deal with them tomorrow. Thus, whatever the ultimate causation, there is no denying that in the face of environmental degradation, our children's children, even to the third and fourth generation, are bound to suffer from our inability or unwillingness to act in accordance with what is true.

This chapter begins by focusing on a uniquely Lutheran view of a God-infused world that is commensurate with the world science is discovering — a unified world of mutually interdependent parts, where the actions of each entity radiate outward in ever-widening concentric circles, with consequences even to the third and fourth generation. Informed by the analysis of Joseph Sax, I argue that it is precisely this interdependency that U.S. property law fails to take into account, thereby ushering in dangers that will resonate for decades to come.[2] Stanley Hauerwas has pointed out that we cannot act rightly until we can see what is true.[3] Is it possible that we, for the most part, do not in fact really apprehend the environmental consequences of our collective action (and inaction)? What is it that we are failing to grasp and why are we so resistant to responding rationally to the facts? This problem, I suggest, exceeds the "prisoner's dilemma."[4] It is not so much a logical failure based on the absence of critical information as the failure of logic under the influence of anxiety and greed.

As Luther often observed, reason is only too happy to blind itself by clinging to false gods. Thus the second portion of this chapter focuses on the problematic distortion of reason that is one of the consequences of sin.

2. Joseph L. Sax was a prominent legal scholar who helped shape environmental law in the United States. In what the *New York Times* calls a "signal achievement," Sax retrieved ancient Roman law to formulate a legal doctrine recognizing natural resources as a public trust that must be protected from private encroachment. From his obituary by Douglas Martin, "Joseph Sax, Who Pioneered Environmental Law, Dies at 78," *New York Times*, March 10, 2014, available at http://www.nytimes.com/2014/03/11/us/joseph-l-sax-who-pioneered-legal-protections-for-natural-resources-dies-at-78.html?_r=0. Accessed August 23, 2014. It appeared on the same date in print on p. B16 of the New York edition.

3. Stanley Hauerwas and William H. Willimon, *Resident Aliens: Life in the Christian Colony* (Nashville: Abingdon, 1989), p. 88.

4. "The prisoner's dilemma" is a tool of game theory to explain how self-interested reason, logically applied, results in self-defeating consequences. The assumptions of game theorists about what rationally constitutes "self-interest" fail to take account of the deep interdependency upon which individual flourishing depends. These assumptions, I will suggest, are themselves a manifestation of the blind self-delusion associated with sinfully distorted reason.

If Sax is particularly instructive in demonstrating the failure of U.S. property law to acknowledge what is real, Lutheran theology may be able to help us understand what it is that we are refusing to see and why we are refusing to see it. Yet, Lutheran theology always moves beyond warning to promise, and this chapter will do the same. Preceding the warning from Exodus 20 that visits the sins of the parents upon their offspring, we find these words, "I am the Lord your God, who brought you out of the land of Egypt, out of the house of bondage" (Exod. 20:2, RSV). If God's presence is a warning, it is also a promise that there is more at work than meets the eye, suggesting that our blindness might be overcome. Narratively speaking, it is akin to the promise that Harry Potter hears when, on his eleventh birthday, Hagrid arrives to declare to him that he is not "just Harry" but a wizard. In a similar moment of self-discovery, Luther found himself in the lead role of a very important theodrama, and with new purpose exhibited the clarity and courage necessary to forge a Reformation. If the law shows us what we are not, then the promise teaches us what we are when we relinquish a false autonomy for a "theonomous" understanding of ourselves and the world in which we live — recognizing that we are also "wizards" and potential reformers — by way of God's in-forming and empowering presence.[5]

A God-Infused World: Moving beyond Dualisms

Martin Luther's panentheistic understanding of God's presence in, with, and under the created order is unusual, if not unique, within Western Christianity.[6] Beginning with a Christological emphasis on the inseparable relation between the two distinct natures of the God-Man Jesus, who is described in the Chalcedonian Creed as totally human and totally divine, Luther finds God ubiquitously and infinitely present throughout the finite world.[7] "[T]he power of God cannot be . . . determined and measured," he

---

5. Tillich coined the term "theonomous" and the distinction it represents. Paul Tillich, *A History of Christian Thought from Its Judaic and Hellenistic Origins to Existentialism,* ed. Carl E. Braaten (New York: Simon & Schuster, 1967), p. 185.

6. "Panentheism" is distinguished from "pantheism" by the idea that God is both more than nature (pan-EN-theism) and simultaneously identified with nature (PAN-en-THEISM). Many argue that there are important similarities between Luther's view and that of Eastern Orthodoxy.

7. This creed was formulated at the Council of Chalcedon in 451. The text of the Chalcedonian Creed appears in Philip Schaff, *The Creeds of Christendom, with a History and*

writes, "for it is uncircumscribed and immeasurable, beyond and above all that is or may be."[8] "On the other hand," Luther continues,

> [the power of God] must be essentially present at all places, even in the tiniest tree leaf. The reason is this; it is God who creates, effects, and preserves all things through his almighty power and right hand, as our Creed confesses. For he dispatches no officials or angels when he creates or preserves something, but all this is the work of his divine power itself. If he is to create or preserve it, however, he must be present and must make and preserve his creation both in its innermost and outermost aspects. Therefore, indeed, he himself must be present in every single creature in its innermost and outermost being, on all sides, through and through, below and above, before and behind, so that nothing can be more truly present and within all creatures than God himself with his power.[9]

This description of a God-infused world has been captured by the later Lutheran tradition in the phrase *"finitum capax infiniti"* or "the finite can bear the infinite." The phrase is intended to distinguish the Lutheran position on this matter from the Reformed, who teach, conversely, that "the finite cannot bear the infinite."

The theological debate regarding the relation between the finite and infinite took form around the Eucharistic practice and teaching of the Reformation. The Bible speaks of the risen Jesus, seated at "the right hand of God" (Col. 3:1, RSV). Thus, it is unreasonable, Calvin concluded, to hold that Christ could be *bodily* present anywhere other than there. Rather than offering the real body and blood of Christ in the bread and wine of the communion meal, as the Roman Catholic tradition teaches, Calvin insisted that those predestined for salvation are spiritually transported to commune with Christ "at the right hand of God." Luther argues instead "that the right hand of God is not a specific place in which a body must or may be, such as on a golden throne, but is the almighty power of God, which at one and the same time can be nowhere and yet must be everywhere."[10] Thus, while the Reformed tradition views God in Christ as far away, the Lutheran tradition

---

Critical Notes, 6th ed. rev. and enlarged, vol. 1 (New York: Harper & Brothers, 1877, c. 1919 by Philip Schaff), pp. 29-33.

8. Martin Luther, "This Is My Body" (1527), in *Luther's Works,* vol. 37, *Word and Sacrament III,* ed. and trans. Robert H. Fischer (Philadelphia: Fortress Press, 1961), pp. 57-58.

9. Luther, "This Is My Body," pp. 57-58.

10. Luther, "This Is My Body," pp. 57-58.

holds that the incarnation brings God "down" and into the created order to stand wholly with, yet simultaneously distinct from, this "fallen" world. For Luther and for Lutherans, then, there simply is no "spiritual body of Christ" apart from the humanity of Jesus, which reveals the infinite God present in, with, and under the finite world, even as Christ's body and blood are truly present in, with, and under the real bread and wine at the communion table.

Yet, the Reformed and Catholic traditions share an important presupposition that the Lutheran tradition rejects. Klaas Zwanepol suggests that both Catholics and Reformed share an underlying premise that the finite and the infinite are incompatible, reflecting "the absolute disproportionality between Creator and creature."[11] Catholic Eucharistic practice teaches that the bread and wine are ontologically changed — *transubstantiated* — into Christ's body and blood by way of priestly intervention, even as the faithful are themselves elevated and ontologically changed in the spiritual journey from earth to heaven.

Luther's relational approach to ontology begins instead, not with Aristotelian substances, but with Christ's words. "Since [Jesus] says 'here . . . this is my body,' he certainly can and does make it so," Luther writes.[12] Thus, for Luther the bread and wine offered in the communion meal are real bread and wine to be sure, but simultaneously they are *revealed* in and through the spoken words of Jesus *to be* wholly the true body and blood of Christ. Instead of an "either/or" relation, Luther's theology begins with a "both/and." For Luther the question of *how* Aristotelian substances can be two things simultaneously is of little interest. Divine promise overrides materialist presuppositions in matters of faith so that Luther describes (rather than explains) this paradoxical relationship between the finite and the infinite as Christ's bodily presence "in, with, and under" the bread and the wine.[13] While Jesus' words authorize Luther's theological conviction on this point, the incarnation itself reveals the finite and the infinite in their immediate relation, providing the nondualistic lens through which everything else is to be understood. "The Lutheran tradition," Zwanepol writes,

> concludes from God's incarnation in Christ that by this very fact finite reality became apparently capable of bearing the infinite. That the Word

11. Klaas Zwanepol, "Lutheran and Reformed on the Finite and the Infinite," *Lutheran Quarterly* 25, no. 4 (2011): 414.

12. Luther, "This Is My Body," p. 47.

13. The language of "consubstantiation" (replacing "transubstantiation") reflects the Aristotelian interests of later Lutheranism.

has become flesh is the basis of the Lutherans' *capax* claim. Lutherans have tended to imbue incarnation with a structural meaning which puts the relationship between finite and infinite into a completely new light — with far-reaching consequences. The incarnation brings about a new impression of God as well as of humans and the world.[14]

Of particular importance for this chapter, then, is Zwanepol's suggestion that, for Lutherans, the relationship between God and the world is changed in God's decision to identify fully with the created order. It is "the concept that God descended once and for all into our finite reality and that here is where God has become our companion" which brings about the "far-reaching consequences" summarized by Zwanepol as "a new impression of God as well as of humans and the world."[15]

Part of what it means to act ethically is to act in accordance with what is true. For Luther, what is true is a world where the presence of the living God calls everything and everyone into a vast interdependent web of life. Called to be what they are, persons, in response to God's address, become this ontological "community" manifest in love, through the divine presence uniting all that exists.[16] Thus the distinctively Lutheran understanding of a God-infused creation has important ethical implications for the way human beings are to enact relations with one another and all that makes up the "natural world." Given the Lutheran panentheistic perspective, nature can never be apprehended as a collection of separate objects subject to human ends. Rather, the created order provides the context in and through which God is constantly speaking creation into being and calling human persons into right relation with God and neighbor.

Right relation, understood structurally on the basis of incarnation, implies that the paradoxical distinction between Christ's humanity and divinity is replicated in a similarly paradoxical distinction between self and neighbor, even as it is replicated in that faith relationship binding persons to God in Christ. The Lutheran paradoxical structure begins, like Luther's Eucharistic theology, with a "both/and" way of thinking rather than a dualistic "either/or." Thus individual distinction *never* implies separation in Luther's thought;

14. Zwanepol, "Finite and Infinite," p. 416.
15. Zwanepol, "Finite and Infinite," pp. 428, 416.
16. It must be noted that Luther's understanding of God's presence in the world is made manifest in the "living word," which "in, with, and under" the created order constantly speaks creation into being. This is a dynamic model and therefore different from those views of creation that posit a fixed and static divinity intermingled with the material universe.

far from it — human beings are most fully themselves when they recognize God's presence in, with, and under their own being and doing, even as they retain self-identity. Thus freed from false individualistic alienation, persons become "masks" of God — extensions of God's relational, enlivening grasp. Understanding oneself as theonomous rather than autonomous allows a false competition between individuals to be replaced with an ability to see what is true — that one's personal good resides in that which also benefits the neighbor. Common good and individual good are brought together in and through God's presence — a reality revealed via an empirically verifiable natural interdependency. "Christians are called not only to consider their personal interests and needs, but also to address the needs and interests of their neighbors — indeed the whole community — in the context of the common good," writes Ronald Duty. In his chapter, "Law, Grace, Climate Change, and Water Rights in the American Southwest" (included in this collection), Duty provides a Lutheran understanding of the "benevolence" such a calling entails by way of five criteria — sufficiency, sustainability, participation, solidarity, and equity, applying these to our shared dependency on water (water being itself a mask for God's ubiquitous life-giving and sustaining presence).

False Presuppositions and U.S. Property Law: Dividing What Nature Has Not

Property law in the United States offers quite a different picture of the relationship of human beings to one another, to nature, and to God. Not only does it divide natural systems into independent entities, but it makes nature particularly vulnerable to human greed and mistakenly sets individual benefit against the common good. Though modern scholarship has made our biological and social interdependency clear in recent years, U.S. property law fails to acknowledge this. Joseph L. Sax, in his 2008 article examining "Environmental Law Forty Years Later," notes that "in the Anglo-American legal system we have a highly individualistic conception of property."[17] "It consists," he suggests,

---

17. Joseph L. Sax, "Environmental Law Forty Years Later: Looking Back and Looking Ahead," in *Biodiversity, Conservation, Law and Livelihoods: Bridging the North-South Divide,* IUCN Academy of Environmental Law Research Studies, ed. Michael I. Jeffery, Jeremy Firestone, and Karen Bubna-Litic (New York: Cambridge University Press, 2008), pp. 9, 12.

of the view that almost anything can be owned, and that ownership embraces the full range of uses that can be made, so long as one does not invade the like rights of others — what might be called the trespassory or nuisance limit on ownership. In this system, there is almost no notion of use entitlements that are withheld because of some interest of the public; nor is there any affirmative obligation to use one's property in a way that is beneficial to the public. The system rests on a fundamental market-driven assumption that ultimately what is good for the owner is good for the public.[18]

Given the Lutheran understanding of the Creator's relationship to the creation, such notions of property appear deeply askew; and though Sax is not prepared to speak of divine presence, he does insist that whatever ownership means, it must allow for both a recognition of environmental insights and the common ownership of certain public goods essential to the flourishing of the whole. Yet, Sax suggests, U.S. property law works in the opposite direction, affirming *jus abutendi,* or a "right of destruction," which is "essentially the notion that one can do as he wishes with his own property, even wasting or destroying it, however much of a loss that might be to the society at large."[19] According to this view, the functional importance a parcel of real property plays in a larger environmental context is of no importance. In Sax's view, then, the U.S. emphasis on individual property rights dangerously supersedes the broader rights of the community. "[T]he nature and magnitude of environmental problems still confronting us," writes Sax, "global warming and biodiversity impoverishment, to name only the most familiar — is daunting; [and] the United States, which once offered forward-looking leadership in both the legal and administrative spheres, does not [any longer] under its current governance . . . play that role."[20]

In a review of the Supreme Court decision in *Lucas v. South Carolina Coastal Council,* 112 S. Ct. 2886 (1992), Sax explores property rights in light of environmental concerns, by juxtaposing two "economies."[21] The present (and problematic) emphasis on absolute individual property rights Sax identifies with a *"transformative economy."* The transformative economy, writes Sax, "builds on the image of property as a discrete entity that can be

18. Sax, "Environmental Law," p. 12.

19. Sax, "Environmental Law," p. 13.

20. Sax, "Environmental Law," p. 9.

21. Joseph L. Sax, "Property Rights and the Economy of Nature: Understanding *Lucas v. South Carolina Coastal Council,*" *Stanford Law Review* 45 (1992): 1443, available at: http://scholarship.law.berkeley.edu/facpubs/1017.

made one's own by working it and transforming it into a human artifact."[22] It treats the land as a passive object awaiting human domestication.[23] Thus, "the world is submitted to an inventory that analyzes it into an array of stocks and resources that can be moved from place to place, broken down through fire and force, and assembled through human decisions into a new object-world, the result of work."[24] The *economy of nature,* on the other hand, views the world not as a collection of passive independent entities but "as consisting of systems defined by their function." Here, land "is already at work, performing important services in its unaltered state"; thus, writes Sax, "[a] forest would be [characterized as] a habitat for birds and wildlife, rather than simply [as] a discrete tract of land containing the commodity timber."[25]

Sax's description of the two economies trades on a central distinction in relation to the natural world: a false view of nature on the one hand, understood as a collection of independent entities passively awaiting the creative work of human beings to become something of value, and a view of nature described as a network of natural systems on the other, characterized by the work (or "service") they already provide for the whole ecosystem. In particular Sax wants to demonstrate how property law legally (and dangerously) pulls apart what is inseparable according to nature. "Conventional pollution laws," for example,

> do not demand that adjacent land be treated as part of a river's riparian zone nor that it be left to perform natural functions supportive of the river as a marine ecosystem. On the contrary, such laws assume that a river and its adjacent tracts of land are separate entities and that the essential purpose of property law is to maintain their separateness. . . . Benefits that adjacent lands and waters confer upon each other can, with rare exceptions, be terminated at the will of the landowner, because the ecological contributions of adjacent properties are generally disregarded in defining legal rights.[26]

With his discussion of *Lucas,* Sax drives his point home. At stake in the *Lucas* case was the development of shoreline property containing dunes

22. Sax, "Understanding *Lucas,*" p. 1442.
23. Sax, "Understanding *Lucas,*" p. 1442.
24. Sax, "Understanding *Lucas,*" pp. 1442-43. Sax is quoting from Philip Fisher, *Making and Effacing Art: Modern American Art in a Culture of Museums* (New York: Oxford University Press, 1991), p. 223.
25. Sax, "Understanding *Lucas,*" pp. 1442, 1445.
26. Sax, "Understanding *Lucas,*" p. 1444.

that provided an important protective barrier for the region. When South Carolina, intending to protect this barrier, adopted a regulation preventing development in the area (including, significantly, the land owned by Lucas), Lucas complained that if he couldn't develop his land, then it was, in effect, worthless. In a decision that Sax sees as demonstrative of a much deeper problem, the Court agreed with Lucas, demanding that he be compensated. Quoting from Coke's Institutes, the Court noted, "for what is land but the profits thereof?"[27] "The possibility that some property may not be suitable for developmental use because of the natural services it provides to the public," notes Sax, "never seems to have been contemplated as a possibility by the Justice [i.e., Antonin Scalia] who wrote the Court's opinion."[28] Significantly, the decision of the Court to compensate Lucas, Sax warns, sends the "operative message . . . that the public must buy back the right to maintain the remaining elements of its biodiversity from owners who have a property right to destroy it."[29] The irrationality of such a view seems to Sax obvious.

Likewise, in his discussion of *Lujan v. Defenders of Wildlife,*[30] Sax reveals just how deeply this conception of property rights has skewed the Court's ability to see clearly and to act effectively. When the plaintiffs sought to trigger consultation requirements of the Endangered Species Act in a situation where a U.S.-funded project jeopardized the continued existence of a listed endangered species, the Supreme Court focused on whether the alleged injury was sufficient to try the case. The only legal interest identified by the Court emphasized nature's entertainment value to human beings, thus rejecting the plaintiffs' interest in protecting biodiversity. "What is genuinely significant about the *Defenders* case, and deeply distressing," writes Sax, "is that it shows how the Justices perceive the significance of the [Endangered Species Act], what it means to be 'injured' by violations of the Act, and who is thereby injured."[31] "The court," he warns, "cannot conceive of anyone having a legal entitlement in the safeguarding of biodiversity."

---

27. This refers to a collection of laws published by Sir Edward Coke under the title *Institutes of the Laws of England*. Published in the early to mid-seventeenth century, these have come to be recognized as the foundation of common law. Reference to Coke's Institutes by the Supreme Court is not unique to the *Lucas* case.

28. Sax, "Environmental Law," p. 14.

29. Sax, "Environmental Law," p. 14.

30. *Lujan v. Defenders of Wildlife,* 504 U.S. 555 (1992).

31. Sax, "Environmental Law," p. 19.

Yet it hardly seems an exaggeration to say that the protection of biodiversity is at the very core of the environmental enterprise. Indeed, the essential things that the Court rejects as being legally cognizable are the very essence of environmental perils: [these include] the fact that the most significant hazards are pervasive; that they threaten essentially everyone across the globe; that they are generally impending rather than actualized, and thus not injurious in the conventional legal sense; and that they most often present hazards — such as loss of sustainability and impoverishment of future generations — that are not within the conventional legal category of "concrete injury."[32]

Reinforcing the juxtaposition of the two "economies," Sax argues that the Supreme Court's decision in *Lucas* was, in fact, intended to answer and negate a pro-environmental position taken by the Wisconsin Supreme Court in *Just v. Marinette County.*[33] That opinion includes the key point Sax is eager to protect:

An owner of land has no absolute and unlimited right to change the essential natural character of his land so as to use it for a purpose for which it was unsuited in its natural state and which injures the rights of others. . . . [W]e think it is not an unreasonable exercise of [the police] power to prevent harm to public rights by limiting the use of private property to its natural uses.[34]

Justice Scalia's opinion, on the other hand, declares that "leaving land in its natural condition is in fundamental tension with the traditional goals of private property law," according to Sax.[35] In his analysis of the *Lucas* decision Sax notes a number of oddities — in particular a novel nuisance test, designed to block an application of any "nuisance" law that might suggest private property could have inherent public attributes that could trump landowner rights.[36] Scalia, Sax suggests, is concerned about a possible "shift from a conception of property rights that defines what owners cannot do . . . to what they can do," thereby reinforcing a notion of ownership as "some irreducible right to use by the private landowner."[37] "[T]he oddities of the

32. Sax, "Environmental Law," p. 21.
33. *Just v. Marinette County*, 201 N.W.2d 761 (Wis. 1972).
34. *Just v. Marinette County*, 768, quoted in Sax, "Understanding *Lucas*," p. 1439.
35. Sax, "Understanding *Lucas*," p. 1441.
36. Sax, "Understanding *Lucas*," p. 1441.
37. Sax, "Understanding *Lucas*," p. 1441. Sax recognizes that "[t]here is certainly a

[*Lucas*] opinion," writes Sax, "can best be viewed as doctrinal devices which separate the demands of the transformational economy from those of the economy of nature."[38] Both Sax and Scalia, then, view these two accounts (transformational economy and the economy of nature) as fundamentally opposed. With *Lucas,* Sax suggests, "the issue [of conflict] . . . has finally come to the surface. As the demands of the economy of nature mounted, exposure of the *fundamental tension between* the economy of nature and the transformational economy was inevitable. *Lucas,*" Sax concludes, "is just the vehicle for its emergence."[39]

False Presuppositions: Individual Greed and the Common Good

Sax's concern for the common good as it is related to nature's systemic interdependence finds a parallel in Luther's concern for the common good as it is made manifest in social and political interdependency. In both cases, human greed appears to be the motivating factor that puts the wider community at risk.

Luther discovered to his dismay that the more he preached about God's free gift of salvation, the worse people behaved; and the worse people behaved, the more communities suffered. "It is true," Luther writes,

> you have the true gospel and the pure Word of God, but no one as yet has given his goods to the poor. . . . nobody extends a helping hand to another, nobody seriously considers the other person, but everyone looks out for himself and his own gain, insists on his own way, and lets everything else go hang.[40]

---

risk that a majority of neighbors will be able to oppose undesired urban development by exaggerating the importance of ecological services performed by undeveloped land in their neighborhood." Sax, "Understanding *Lucas,*" p. 1454. However, Sax continues, "As the services of the economy of nature are increasingly recognized . . . a consensus can be expected to develop as to which functions are important enough to demand maintenance." "Understanding *Lucas,*" p. 1446.

38. Sax, "Understanding *Lucas,*" p. 1446. The "oddities" Sax identifies are "the distinction between land and personal property, the total loss requirement, the novel nuisance test, the elimination of the harm/benefit distinction, the focus on historical use, and the requirement that restrictions be in the 'title to begin with.'"

39. Sax, "Understanding *Lucas,*" p. 1452.

40. Martin Luther, "The Seventh Sermon at Wittenberg, 1522," in *Luther's Works,* vol. 51, *Sermons I,* ed. John Doberstein (Philadelphia: Fortress Press, 1959), p. 96.

Whereas previously, towns of four or five hundred had been able to gather as much as seven hundred gulden for the mendicant monks, now, Luther complains, "when they are asked to contribute one or two hundred gulden toward good schools and pulpits, they cry, 'you would reduce us to rags and make beggars of us!'"[41] Thus, as Luther points out, the people will jeopardize their collective future. Poor teachers will undermine the schools from which future civic leaders ought to emerge, while the absence of pastors will deprive sinners of a saving faith, which can only be ignited by the word of God, rightly preached. Ignorance now and hell later is the collective future for a community of individuals unwilling or unable to recognize the interdependent aspect of their situation.

The relation of neighbor-love to community well-being is highlighted again by Luther when, during the plague of 1527, he cautions that by failing to use the common sense God gave them, people are "tempting God" and threatening the common good. "[I]t is . . . shameful," Luther warns, "for a person to pay no heed to his own body and to fail to protect it against the plague the best he is able, and then to infect and poison others who might have remained alive if he had taken care of his body as he could have."[42] Such people "are much too rash and reckless," he exclaims. "They disdain the use of medicines; they do not avoid places and persons infected by the plague, but lightheartedly make sport of it and wish to prove how independent they are." Yet, no one, Luther warns, is independent in such a way. During this crisis, Luther calls upon the people to shoulder their God-given responsibilities with regard to the estates of government, church, and family. Pastors should remain behind to serve the laity in this time of crucial need; governing officials are called upon to keep order; masters and servants, too, are to care for one another, as are parents, children, and neighbors. Those who can find adequate replacements for themselves are free to depart in good conscience. Indeed, Luther suggests, there might be some who not only could, but perhaps should, leave town to protect themselves. Despite this apparent opening for the meek, the fearful, and the prudent, Luther, by the time he has reached the end of his list of relational obligations, seems to have cut off all escape. Given the fact that an extra pair of hands would

41. Martin Luther, "Exposition of Psalm 127, for the Christians at Riga in Livonia, 1524," in *Luther's Works*, vol. 45, *The Christian in Society II*, ed. and trans. Walther I. Brandt (Philadelphia: Fortress Press, 1962), p. 319.

42. Martin Luther, "Whether One May Flee from a Deadly Plague, 1527," in *Luther's Works*, vol. 43, *Devotional Writings II*, ed. Gustav K. Wiencke, trans. Carl J. Schindler (Philadelphia: Fortress Press, 1968), p. 131.

presumably always be helpful in such a crisis, everyone seems to be included when he says, "Yes, no one should dare leave his neighbor unless there are others who will take care of the sick in their stead and nurse them."[43]

For Luther, individual good is deeply interwoven with the good of the whole community; and in this he reveals communal presuppositions that are not much different than Sax's environmental concerns. Sax rejects the idea that what is good for the individual owner is good for the whole community, suggesting that the common good is *not* well served when we begin and end with individual rights. Luther likewise criticizes any assumption that individuals operate independently from a responsible relation towards their neighbors. Though largely in agreement, their positions are, nevertheless, not identical. While both maintain that individual "right" must give way to the common good when individual claims or actions jeopardize the well-being of the whole, they differ on the status of individual "rights."

This is most visible in Luther's attack on greed. In 1520 Luther published a sermon on trade and usury. Four years later he wrote a longer piece on the same subject.[44] His concern was the growing acceptance of greed as a socially acceptable motive for what he viewed as the unholy robbery of the poor. "Among themselves," he writes, "the merchants have a common rule which is their chief maxim and the basis of all their sharp practices where they say, 'I may sell my goods as dear as I can.'"

> *They think this is their right.* Thus occasion is given for avarice, and every window and door to hell is opened. What else does it mean but this: I care nothing about my neighbor; so long as I have my profit and satisfy my greed, of what concern is it to me if it injures my neighbor in ten ways at once? There you see how shamelessly this maxim flies squarely in the face not only of Christian love but also of *natural law. . . .* On such a basis trade can be nothing but robbing and stealing the property of others.[45]

We note the maxim that Luther rejects; it is the rule that teaches me I need "care nothing about my neighbor so long as I have my profit and satisfy my greed." Why should I care if it "injures my neighbor in ten ways at once?" The "why should I care about my neighbor?" question is reflected in

---

43. Luther, "Plague," p. 122.

44. Martin Luther, "Trade and Usury" (1524), in *Luther's Works*, vol. 45, *The Christian in Society II*, ed. Walther I. Brandt, trans. Charles M. Jacobs and Walther I. Brandt (Philadelphia: Fortress Press, 1962).

45. Luther, *Trade and Usury*, p. 247; emphasis added.

Sax's concerns about the Court's failure to see beyond the narrowest possible interpretation of individual property rights in the *Lucas* case, thereby placing the good of the whole community in jeopardy. "The most significant hazards are pervasive," Sax writes, and "they threaten essentially everyone across the globe."[46] Though both Luther and Sax seek to protect the public good, and while both appear to position individual interests as structurally in conflict with the interests of the whole, Luther's rejection of greed as a genuine benefit deemed worthy of protection reveals a view of human good that differs from Sax's. Luther's God-infused world is one where individual benefit is understood as harmonious with the good of the whole — a fact that he thinks should be apparent to reason. That the merchants see it otherwise is a reflection of their blind misapprehension of what is true. Greed damages both the victim and the thief, reflecting and reinforcing wrong relations with God and neighbor. Like the plague itself, greed that fails to take account of the neighbor's good threatens to infect the whole community. Luther's both/and approach begins with the presupposition that greed is irrationally self-defeating, because it fails to acknowledge natural interdependency. While Sax shares Luther's understanding that individual life is dependent upon a balanced and flourishing ecosystem, he resists extending this to judgments on the authenticity of "benefits" claimed by individuals.

The Power and Limits of Reason

Properly employed, reason allows human beings to understand the laws of nature. Luther clearly believed that regard for one's neighbor is not a command particular to the Christian tradition. The maxim that teaches us to rob and steal the property of others, he writes, "flies squarely in the face . . . of . . . *natural law*." Though Luther rejects the application of Aristotelian reason to matters of the Spirit, he affirms reason when it is applied to the world as "the most important and the highest in rank among all things and, in comparison with other things of this life, the best and something divine."[47]

46. See note 37 above.

47. Martin Luther, "Disputation Concerning Man" (1536), in *Luther's Works,* vol. 34, *Career of the Reformer IV,* ed. and trans. Lewis W. Spitz (Philadelphia: Fortress Press, 1969), p. 137. Brian Gerrish suggests that "if we are to do justice to the complexity of Luther's thought, we must carefully distinguish: (1) natural reason, ruling within its proper domain (the earthly kingdom); (2) arrogant reason, trespassing upon the domain of faith (the heavenly kingdom); (3) regenerate reason, serving humbly in the household of faith, but always

Sax's observation that the Court's failure to take account of "significant" and "pervasive" environmental hazards that "threaten essentially everyone across the globe," together with his argument that these hazards must be considered for the good of the whole, demonstrate that Luther's confidence in reason is not misplaced. Sax sees the need clearly and responds rationally. Reasoned analysis of our everyday experience allows us to discover what leads to flourishing and what thwarts it. Scientists systematically analyze their observations of the world to discover fixed patterns, revealing, for example, the natural environment as an interconnected set of relationships among all those things within it. The Ten Commandments reflect, in Luther's view, *naturally intelligible relations,* both social and biological, among human beings, and are thus authorized, not by the Bible, but *by the creation itself.* "Moses," Luther claims, "agrees exactly with nature";[48] and the basic content of the Ten Commandments was "spread over the whole world, not only before Moses but even before Abraham and all the patriarchs."[49] The Lutheran Confessions reiterate Luther's confidence in reason, insofar as it is applied to this world, noting that "to some extent human reason naturally understands the law since it has the same judgment naturally written in the mind."[50] Thus, all persons of reason should be able to grasp the "external" works that are commanded with little difficulty. It is these natural laws, which reveal our deep interdependence and the critical role played by biodiversity, that, in Sax's view, the Court is failing to acknowledge, to the peril of all. Because God's will is made visible to reason through natural law, the Lutheran tradition affirms explicitly that

> God requires the righteousness of reason. Because of God's command, honorable works commanded in the Decalogue should be performed. . . . For God wants this civil discipline to restrain the unspiritual, and to preserve it

subject to the Word of God. Within the first context, reason is an excellent gift of God; within the second, it is Frau Hulda, the Devil's whore; within the third, it is the handmaiden of faith." Brian A. Gerrish, *Grace and Reason: A Study in the Theology of Luther* (Oxford: Clarendon, 1962), p. 26.

48. Martin Luther, "How Christians Should Regard Moses" (1525), in *Luther's Works,* vol. 35, *Word and Sacrament I,* ed. and trans. Theodore Bachmann (Philadelphia: Fortress Press 1960), p. 168.

49. Martin Luther, "Against the Sabbatarians: Letter to a Good Friend," in *Luther's Works,* vol. 47, *The Christian in Society IV,* ed. Franklin Sherman, trans. Martin Bertram (Philadelphia: Fortress Press, 1971), p. 89.

50. "Apology of the Augsburg Confession," 7, *Book of Concord,* ed. and trans. Theodore G. Tappert (Philadelphia: Fortress Press, 1959), p. 108.

he has given laws, learning, teaching, governments, and penalties. [And] to some extent, reason can produce this righteousness by its own strength.[51]

Yet, with all the intrinsic incentives that nature provides, it is hard to understand why we fail, as often as we do, to recognize and respect these laws of nature. Why is it that "reason can produce . . . righteousness by its own strength" only "to some extent"? Our drive for survival combined with the human ability to recognize and adapt our behavior to contextual demands, suggests there should be a considerably higher degree of success than we see in the socially destructive greed of the merchants, and the environmentally dangerous decisions of the Court. Luther's explanation for this failure is sin; and Lutheranism takes seriously the ravages of sin as idolatry distorts the capacity of reason to do the work it should.

Idolatry and the Distortion of Reason

We opened this chapter with the declaration of God's creating and sustaining presence ("I am the Lord your God") and the first "commandment," requiring that human beings worship God alone. That the latter does not necessarily follow from the former is, for Lutheranism, a foregone conclusion; for in Luther's view false gods are everywhere. "There has never been a people," he writes, "that did not establish and maintain some sort of worship. Everyone has set up a god of his own, to which he looks for blessings, help, and comfort. . . . Everyone made into a god that to which his heart was inclined."[52] Whatever "your heart clings to," Luther explains, "whatever it entrusts itself [to]" — that, he warns, "is really your God."

> Many a person thinks he has God and everything he needs when he has money and property; in them he trusts and of them he boasts so stubbornly and securely that he cares for no one. Surely such a [person] also has a god — mammon by name, that is, money and possessions — on

51. "Apology of the Augsburg Confession," p. 110. The "Augsburg Confession" is arguably the single most important document defining what it means to be Lutheran. "The Apology to the Augsburg Confession" is a further elucidation of key points. For historical background to the composition and eventual publication of the "Apology," see the "Editors' Introduction to the Apology of the Augsburg Confession," *Book of Concord*, p. 110.

52. Martin Luther, *The Large Catechism*, "Ten Commandments," in *Book of Concord*, ed. and trans. Theodore G. Tappert (Philadelphia: Fortress Press, 1959), p. 367.

which he fixes his whole heart. It is the most common idol on earth. He who has money and property feels secure, happy, fearless, as if he were sitting in the midst of paradise.[53]

"This desire for wealth clings and cleaves to our nature all the way to the grave," Luther insists. "So . . . if anyone boasts of great learning, wisdom, power, prestige, family, and honor, and trusts in them, he also has a god, but not the one, true God."[54] No one is outside the reach of this first commandment, for just as reason seeks survival, so too does it require that we make our survival meaningful; thus reason presses us to fix on something that gives our lives purpose. In today's world (as in other ages) the list of false gods includes not only the money, wisdom, power, prestige, and family mentioned by Luther, but ideological gods as well. Absolute obedience to this kind of god often requires rigid political positioning. For Luther, whose central battle cry was "justification by faith alone," such self-righteous rigidity, so often viewed by the pious as "good works," reveals the most seductive and pernicious false god of all.[55] We worship this god when we "seek comfort in [our] own works and presume to wrest heaven from God," writes Luther.[56] In this situation, he continues, a person keeps an accounting of good deeds, and "on such things [she] relies and of them . . . boasts, unwilling to receive anything as a gift from God, but desiring . . . to earn or merit everything. What is this," he asks rhetorically, "but setting up *ourselves* as God?"[57]

False gods are particularly dangerous, Luther suggests, because the worship of idols distorts our ability to see things clearly. Thus, there is, in his view, a direct and causal connection between our adherence to the first commandment and our ability to fulfill the other nine.[58] While Scalia may be wrong in missing "the very essence of [those] environmental perils [which] . . . threaten essentially everyone across the globe," he is hardly insincere. An inability to see what is true leads us in turn to rationalize and defend choices that damage the common good — a phenomenon well documented by Lang-

53. Luther, *The Large Catechism*, p. 365, paragraphs 5-7.
54. Luther, *The Large Catechism*, p. 366, paragraphs 9-10.
55. Or "God alone" or "Christ alone" — the point being that the accomplishment of what seemed to Luther a mighty task was entirely God's work.
56. Luther, *The Large Catechism*, First Commandment, p. 367, paragraph 22.
57. Luther, *The Large Catechism*, p. 367, paragraph 23.
58. Luther, *The Large Catechism*, p. 369, paragraph 31.

don Gilkey in his book *Shantung Compound.*[59] As a young teacher, fresh out
of Harvard, and caught in China when America entered the Second World
War, Gilkey found himself locked away in a Japanese internment camp. He
describes a "strange dilemma" that nearly drove their little community to
self-destruct — a situation that might well have put all their lives in danger.[60]
In their fear, and apparently blinded by the false god of security, the people
failed to observe that their attempts to protect themselves (by stealing food
and space from their neighbors) only hastened the very thing they feared
the most. Gilkey observes,

> When . . . a man [*sic*] gives his ultimate devotion to his own welfare . . . he
> is no longer free to be completely moral or rational when he finds himself
> under pressure. Whenever the security of the object of this commitment is
> threatened, he is driven by an intense anxiety to reinforce that security.[61]

Though the moral and rational powers did not disappear in those who "acted
immorally and unjustly," these powers were distorted as they were pressed
into service by that acute anxiety eager to justify selfish (though ultimately
self-defeating) choices.[62] "In this situation," Gilkey argues,

> no amount of intelligence or of ideals and good intentions will change [a
> person's] behavior or free him from his selfishness so that he can be good.
> The more acute mind of the intelligent man may well fashion more plau-
> sible rationalizations than can the slower mind of his neighbor. In each
> of our crucial moral issues this pattern repeated itself: over and over the
> more educated and respectable people defended their self-concern with
> more elegant briefs.[63]

Summing up the situation, Gilkey notes that "[i]njustice to other men . . . is
the social consequence of an inward idolatry, the worship of one's own self or
group."[64] Such self-delusion nearly always results in a race to claim the moral
high ground, and a corresponding inability to hear or respond to alternative

59. Langdon Gilkey, *Shantung Compound: The Story of Men and Women Under Pressure*
(New York: Harper & Row, 1966 [paper 1975]).
60. Gilkey, *Shantung Compound,* p. 162.
61. Gilkey, *Shantung Compound,* p. 231.
62. Gilkey, *Shantung Compound,* p. 231.
63. Gilkey, *Shantung Compound,* p. 232.
64. Gilkey, *Shantung Compound,* p. 232.

points of view.[65] Hence, appeals to reconsider a given choice in light of the possible consequences were, in Gilkey's experience, unsuccessful.

Luther would agree that human beings cling to their denial of what is actually the case out of a deep, if hidden, anxiety about human finitude. In such a state of anxiety, reason responds to whatever appears as a threat, attempting to overcome it — including that vulnerability which comes from being an interdependent part of a community. The greed displayed by individuals in Shantung Compound who were prepared to steal food from the community, like the greed of property owners unwilling or unable to take environmental costs into account in their eager desire for profit, and like the merchants who took it as their right to squeeze every last gulden out of their neighbors — all suggest an inability to recognize and respect those bonds upon which survival depends. The profundity of Gilkey's argument rests on his observation that reason, on its own, cannot overcome the deep anxiety associated with finitude and false gods. Rather, reason is put to work, under the power of anxiety, to creatively rationalize decisions that appear good to us when we are afraid. St. Augustine likewise observed that our "prideful" desire to resist God through self-assertion leads to a reversal whereby the intellect is no longer master, but becomes instead the servant of a fearful and anxious will. The only thing that can master this, in the view of Augustine, Luther, and Gilkey (not to mention the apostle Paul), is a faith that finds its ground, not in false idols, but in God.

Sax's Proposal: Problems and Promise

We have already noted Sax's juxtaposition of two economies. On the one side, reflecting the transformative economy, is the Court's rigid insistence on a view of property law that presupposes a world of independent entities — autonomous persons with absolute power over particular parcels of the natural world. It is this presupposed ontological independence and power of human beings that property law, in Scalia's view, rightly endorses. In "fundamental tension" with this view is the economy of nature, which presupposes a world made up of interdependent communities where every discrete entity also participates fully in the whole. This is the world that environmentalists like Sax observe, analyze, and describe. Given Sax's focus on the failure of our legal system to take these observations into account, he apparently views

---

65. Gilkey, *Shantung Compound*, p. 232; for example, see pp. 85-87.

the economy of nature as essentially true, and the transformative economy as a theory based on presuppositions that are false. Yet, having laid out this tension very clearly, Sax's surprising solution is to "balance" the interests reflected in the two competing views of nature. "[E]nhanced judicial willingness to protect against arbitrary governmental regulation" is needed, he suggests, "to assure proportionality . . . [and] to achieve an acceptable balance between the demands of the transformational economy and those of the economy of nature."[66] Sax rebukes the Court, in reference to *Lucas,* which "should have asked whether notions of property law can be reformulated to accommodate ecological needs *without impairing the necessary functions of the transformational economy*" (emphasis added).[67]

Given the similarity between Sax's understanding of persons according to the transformative economy and Luther's view of persons caught up in idolatrous self-aggrandizement who think and act as if "they are a law unto themselves," such a "balance" between these two opposing perspectives appears, from a Lutheran perspective, to be a deal with the devil. Sax introduces the "usufructuary model," which begins with presuppositions about human beings in relation to the larger created order — presuppositions that do not "balance" the two opposing views Sax describes, but offer, rather, a third position commensurate with Luther's. "Blackstone," notes Sax, "speaks of the *usus fructus* as a temporary right of using a thing, without having the *ultimate* property, or *full dominion* of the substance" (emphasis added).[68] In this third model the rights of the individual are contingent upon something larger. They exist within and as part of a domain that is ultimate — a domain that has "full dominion of the substance." While Sax may identify this larger domain jurisprudentially with the public interest or common good, it can also be understood theologically as that divine presence which permeates the entire created order, "speaking it into existence without pause."

Notably, for Luther, as, perhaps, for Blackstone, "temporary" power and penultimate dominion do not imply passivity in the face of that which is ultimate. Nor, for Luther, would this relationship be understood as producing an agency that is one part God's work and one part human work. Rather, in Luther's thinking the duality is overcome in the *theonomous self.*[69] God is

---

66. Sax, "Understanding *Lucas,*" p. 1454.

67. Sax, "Understanding *Lucas,*" p. 1446.

68. Sax, "Understanding *Lucas,*" p. 1452, n. 90.

69. For a more complete discussion of Luther's understanding of the theonomous self and of its importance in his mature theology, see my *The Courage of Faith: Martin Luther and the Theonomous Self* (Minneapolis: Fortress Press, 2013).

wholly present in, with, and under the choices that human beings make as responsible agents, in a way that is reminiscent of that paradox which holds the divine aspect of Christ in unity with the human — "one person in two natures." Human agents who are grasped by and subjectively engaged with the divine ground — persons, that is, whose actions reflect their faith in God — are those whose reason is free from the effects of idol-worship so that they can see clearly, and respond flexibly and creatively to an ever-changing historical context.

Sax identifies a similar kind of flexibility and creative response with the adaptive development he expects to see in the judicial decisions of the Court, as judges reinterpret property law in the context of changing public goals. The new wisdom of the courts that Sax predicts will be forthcoming, in his view, promises novel approaches to the adjudication of interests, representing the development of natural resources on one side (transformational economy) and the care that must be taken to preserve the health of ecological systems on the other (economy of nature). Thus, the response Sax describes reflects not a balance of competing interests but a cooperative act, whereby each may be benefited in the exchange.

Courage in the Face of Environmental Challenges

When, on his eleventh birthday, Harry Potter finds that he is not merely the unwelcome nephew of the Dursleys, but a real wizard with an important destiny, he is drawn into a battle between good and evil that unleashes a courage and determination he did not know he possessed. Indeed, these virtues would presumably not have been his had he failed to embrace the destiny that was thrust upon him. Finding that he is part of a much larger story, Harry is himself enlarged and en-couraged.

It is in the theonomous merging of the divine will with the freely made human decision to embrace a destiny already bestowed upon us that the way for such courageous empowerment is opened. Something like that happened to Luther, too, when he unexpectedly found himself in the midst of a conflict that he had neither invited nor expected. Nevertheless, as the conflict rapidly took on epic proportions, Luther came to believe that God had called him into the fray; and as he observed himself being pulled into the midst of what he took to be a cosmic battle between God and the Devil, Luther could only say over and over that it was God's Word which was driving him forward. Though fully expecting to die a heretic's death, Luther neither succumbed to fear nor hid from the responsibility he believed was his alone. Luther and Harry Potter both, once clear that they had been marked and called into the cosmic drama, found that they could accept whatever penultimate outcomes came to pass because they had placed their ultimate security in an ultimate ground. While Harry's story is a work of fiction, Luther's is not; and it was his real experience of self-discovery that was later fashioned into the Lutheran theology of vocation — a theology which, against all odds, had the effect of allowing millions of people to view their lives in a new light, thereby empowering a bold new enthusiasm for the task at hand. Rather like Harry, these people discovered that they were not merely "muggles." As Luther's contemporaries came to believe that they too were known, named, and marked with particular roles to play in a great, cosmic theodrama, a vast new energy erupted across northern Europe, powerful enough to spawn a Reformation.[70]

Our world is again being drawn into crisis as we face an environmental catastrophe of epic proportions. From a Lutheran perspective, the question is whether we will recognize and embrace the larger story in which we are all players with specific callings and purpose. Neighbor-love, in a world described paradoxically as something both natural and divine, calls upon each to recognize and honor the other. The Lutheran claim that the "finite bears the infinite" implies that human beings can recognize and receive, embrace and engage the very near presence of God, with potentially "transformative" effects — yet without eclipsing the nature of this material world which functions as God's "mask." The collective being in which each life shares suggests that individuals can never be understood as an absolute law unto themselves, or as absolute masters of a world that is ultimately the "property" of God. Rather, as Sax's usufructuary model suggests, persons are rationally equipped to enjoy a temporary "right" of use commensurate with the contingency of human existence (to which Luther would quickly add, "rationally equipped" insofar as reason is freed by faith from idolatrous anxiety). But thus empowered, Luther promises, the future beckons, as persons and the communities in which they participate are enabled to flourish in rational conformity with God's sustaining presence and purpose.

---

70. The Lutheran practice of adding "for you" as the Eucharistic bread and wine are delivered to individual Christians reflects Luther's vocational theology, whereby persons are called, not in general, but personally, according to the unique relational context in which they stand.

CHAPTER 5

Law, Grace, Climate Change, and Water Rights in the American Southwest

Ronald W. Duty

Public redress through a judge is not forbidden but expressly commanded, and it is a work of God.

Apology to the Augsburg Confession, Art. XVI, 7

As a practical matter, striking changes are being required of those who hold, and aspire to hold, water rights. We are in a time of basic change in relation to our resources. . . . There is time for a fairly gradual shift, and the sooner the need for change is recognized, the sooner planning for change can begin, and the less painful the ultimate changes will be.

Joseph L. Sax, "The Constitution, Property Rights, and the Future of Water Law"

In 1952, the State of Arizona sued the State of California in the federal courts, claiming a larger share of water from the Colorado River was due to it than Congress had authorized in the Boulder Canyon Project Act of 1928. The case of *Arizona v. California* was at that time the latest skirmish in a ninety-year-old history of political, legal, cultural, and economic conflicts

---

I thank John Fox for his assistance with legal research about some of the cases discussed in this chapter, and Mark Carlson for his help locating state legislation amending the California Water Code. I also thank Marie Failinger and Mary Gaebler for their critical comments and suggestions on an earlier draft of the chapter.

over water, water rights, and economic development in the arid American Southwest.[1]

These struggles over water have continued down to the present. They swirl around two fundamentally different beliefs and understandings about how the West should be settled and developed, both different versions of what Joseph Sax calls a "transformational economy."[2] In such an economy, people believe that human labor is required to transform their natural environment for more productive and desirable uses in order to produce things for human consumption, and that the natural world is "in a passive state, waiting to be put to use."[3] Apart from human activity and purposes, the natural environment in this view has no value of its own and performs no significant functions. One variant of this economy is the vision of John Wesley Powell who strongly believed that the aridness of the territory west of the 100th Meridian places significant environmental limits on how the West could be feasibly and sustainably settled.[4] Powell bluntly wrote: "but at 20 inches [or less of annual rainfall] agriculture will not be uniformly successful from season to season. Many droughts will occur; many seasons in a long series will be fruitless; and it may be doubted whether, on the whole, agriculture will prove remunerative."[5] Others employing the transformational view take a more aggressive approach and in their "hydrological optimism" have mistakenly assumed that water is as abundant in the West as in the East; it just needs to be moved to where it is needed.[6] They simply have not believed Powell's

1. The case became known as *Arizona v. California*, 373 U.S. 546 (1963).

2. For discussions of the concept of a transformational economy, see Joseph L. Sax, "Property Rights and the Economy of Nature: Understanding *Lucas v. South Carolina Coastal Council*," *Stanford Law Review* 45 (1992): 1447-49; and "Ownership, Property, and Sustainability," *Utah Environmental Law Review* 31 (2011): 5.

3. Sax, "Property Rights and the Economy of Nature," p. 1442.

4. John Wesley Powell, "The Irrigable Lands of the Arid Region," *Century Magazine* (March 1890): 766-76, reprinted in Powell, *Seeing Things Whole: The Essential John Wesley Powell*, ed. William deBuys (Washington, DC: Island Press, 2001), p. 278. The 100th Meridian runs along the eastern edge of the Texas panhandle up into Canada. For more on John Wesley Powell's life and work, see, for example, Wallace Stegner, *Beyond the Hundredth Meridian: John Wesley Powell and the Second Opening of the West* (Boston: Houghton Mifflin, 1953, 1954); Philip L. Fradkin, *Wallace Stegner and the American West* (New York: Alfred A. Knopf, 2008); and Jackson J. Benson, *Wallace Stegner: His Life and Work* (Lincoln: University of Nebraska Press, 1996).

5. John Wesley Powell, "Report on the Lands of the Arid Region" (1878), in *Seeing Things Whole*, p. 157.

6. The expression "hydrological optimism" to describe this aggressive perspective on

argument about the limits and fragility of arid western land, and have thought that water "should be used to promote public policies such as population growth and economic prosperity."[7] They refuse to accept the constraints on transformational development and water use that Powell's argument entails.

The key elements of Powell's strategy for a western institutional, legal, and infrastructural framework were two assumptions: first, that irrigation was absolutely needed for both farming and ranching, and, second, that irrigation of such lands required a different kind of water law than that which prevails in the East.

The more aggressive advocates of the transformational western economy, and most western states, have incorporated the doctrine of appropriation into their own vision, and their view of western development ultimately prevailed over Powell's. But their victory had legal and ecological consequences, some of which Powell foresaw. One was a lot of litigation over water. Powell bluntly told the International Irrigation Congress in 1893, "you are piling up a heritage of conflict and litigation over water rights for there is not sufficient water to supply the land."[8] All this litigation occurs against the backdrop of what Philip Fradkin sees as the fundamental contradiction and issues of the West: which "were — and remain to this day — the aridity that breeds sparseness and the denial of that condition, which leads to overdevelopment."[9] Many western policy-makers and citizens are in denial about what western aridity and sparseness mean both for their common life and their individual lives, and have intensively used rivers of the Southwest, resulting in the over-allocation of their water.[10]

Human transformational attitudes, individual and corporate behavior, and public water policies and water laws about the natural environment have put at serious risk the lives, water rights, and livelihoods of Southwestern residents, their communities, and states.[11] The transformational economy

water is taken from Cristiana Z. Peppard, *Just Water: Theology, Ethics, and the Global Water Crisis* (Maryknoll, NY: Orbis, 2014), p. 25.

7. Joseph L. Sax, "Reserved Public Rights in Water," *Vermont Law Review* 36 (2012): 535-36.

8. Quoted in Stegner, *Beyond the Hundredth Meridian*, p. 343.

9. Fradkin, *Wallace Stegner and the American West*, p. 167.

10. William deBuys, *A Great Aridness: Climate Change and the Future of the American Southwest* (New York: Oxford University Press, 2011), pp. 9, 36, 154-55, 162-63.

11. For the purposes of this chapter, the region of the American Southwest includes the states of Arizona, California, Colorado, Nevada, New Mexico, Texas, Utah, and Wyoming.

in which they operate has also caused serious disruption to the hydrological functioning of the Southwestern environment. This risk of serious harm is intensified because of climate change and the prospect of a significant reduction in water supply in the Southwest. The current regimes of water rights will, in all likelihood, need both to be transformed and adapted to new climatic conditions and to reflect the value of the natural environment.[12]

This chapter will review this risk and harm by reviewing three federal cases after describing Luther's understanding of the operation of natural law as a consequence of human behavior for the creation, and the correlative effects of that law as creation rebounds upon human beings and societies. Employing Luther's understanding of water as an example of daily bread and his explication of the Seventh Commandment on theft of property and possessions, we will consider how the principles of precaution, sufficiency, sustainability, participation, solidarity, and equity help both to evaluate water use, policy, and water rights in the Southwest and to guide possible future changes in these things. Through these principles of practical moral reasoning, Christians and others can exercise their responsible moral agency as God works through them to bring their uses of water and public policies for water into greater conformity with God's intention for creation.

Texas is included here because a significant part of the state lies west of the 100th Meridian and it has historically considered itself part of the Southwest. It also figures in two of the cases discussed below. Wyoming is included because the watershed of the Green River in the southwestern part of the state is part of the Colorado River Basin and the state is a member of the Colorado River Compact.

12. See Sax, "The Limits of Private Rights in Public Waters," *Environmental Law* 19 (1988): 474-75; "The Constitution, Property Rights, and the Future of Water Law," *University of Colorado Law Review* 61 (1990): 269, 277, and 281-82; "Property Rights and the Economy of Nature," pp. 1442-55; "Reflections on Western Water Law," *Ecology Law Quarterly* 299 (2007); "An Environmental Agenda for Our Time," Blue Planet Prize Commemorative Lecture sponsored by the Asahi Glass Foundation, Tokyo, June 2008, pp. 35-37, accessed June 28, 2014, available from: http://www.af-info.or.jp/blueplanet/doc/essay/2007essay-sax .pdf; "The Unfinished Agenda of Environmental Law," public lecture delivered at the Blue Planet Prize Commemorative Lecture sponsored by the Asahi Glass Foundation, Tokyo, June 2008, pp. 41-43, and 45-46, accessed June 30, 2014, available from: http://www.af-info .or.jp/blueplanet/doc/essay/2007essay-sax.pdf; "Environmental Law Forty Years Later: Looking Back and Looking Ahead," in *Biodiversity, Conservation, Law and Livelihoods: Bridging the North-South Divide,* ed. Michael I. Jeffery, QC, Jeremy Firestone, and Karen Bubna-Litic (Cambridge: Cambridge University Press, c. 2008 by the IUCN Academy of Environmental Law), pp. 10-12; and "Ownership, Property, and Sustainability," *Utah Environmental Law Review* 31, no. 1 (2011): 9, 16-17.

RONALD W. DUTY

Daily Bread, Natural Grace, and Water Rights

Water figures significantly in Luther's understanding of "daily bread." The Seventh Commandment against theft is linked both to Luther's understanding of "daily bread" and to the relation between his theology of creation and his understanding of natural law. In his explanation of the First Article of the Apostles' Creed, Luther says that God not only gives creatures life but also "constantly sustains" them with both the physical means that make it possible for life to continue daily, and with the political and legal means — "good government, peace, and security" — that makes those physical means secure.[13] God's creating and preserving action is ongoing and the creation itself is not static but dynamic.[14] Water is one of those physical means of sustenance and support. Luther affirms God's mastery over water, both to sustain faithful people and to punish the unfaithful.[15]

Human alienation and estrangement from God affects the whole creation.[16] There is a profound interdependence between the natural order, human action, and cultural processes, Michael Welker argues.[17] The Hebrew scriptures tell of human sin's "devastating effects on other creatures," says biblical theologian Terence Fretheim, and even describe its "adverse cosmic effects."[18] This is concisely expressed by the prophet Hosea:

13. Martin Luther, *The Large Catechism,* 13-15, in *The Book of Concord: The Confessions of the Evangelical Lutheran Church,* trans. Charles Arand et al., ed. Robert Kolb and Timothy J. Wengert (Minneapolis: Fortress Press, 2000), p. 412. The First Article of the Apostles' Creed is: "I believe in God the Father Almighty, Creator of Heaven and Earth."

14. Martin Luther, *Lectures on Genesis, Chapters 1–5,* in *Luther's Works,* vol. 1, ed. J. Pelikan (St. Louis: Concordia, 1958), pp. 16, 41, 47, 50-51, and 75-76, where Luther writes: "God created all things through the Word: 'Let the sea bring forth fish; the earth, herbs, beasts,' etc.; likewise: 'Grow, fill the earth and the sea.' These words are in force until today, and for this reason we see increase without end. . . .

"... God, through His Word, extends His activity from the beginning of the world to its end. For with God there is nothing that is earlier or later, swifter or slower; but in His eyes all things are present things. For He is simply outside the scope of time."

15. Luther uses the example of the Exodus of Israel from Egypt to make this point. *Lectures on Isaiah, Chapters 40–66,* ed. Hilton C. Oswald, trans. Herbert J. A. Bouman, in *Luther's Works,* vol. 17, ed. J. J. Pelikan, H. C. Oswald, and H. T. Lehmann (St. Louis: Concordia, 1972), pp. 96-97.

16. Terence E. Fretheim, "Is Genesis 3 a Fall Story?" *Word & World* 14, no. 2 (Spring 1994): 152-53.

17. Michael Welker, *Creation and Reality* (Minneapolis: Fortress Press, 1999), p. 17; see also p. 16.

18. Terence E. Fretheim, *God and the World in the Old Testament: A Relational Theology*

Hear the word of the LORD,
  O people of Israel;
For the LORD has an indictment
  against the inhabitants of the land.
There is no faithfulness or loyalty,
  and no knowledge of God in the land.
Swearing, lying, and murder
  and stealing and adultery break out;
  bloodshed follows bloodshed.
Therefore the land mourns,
  and all who live in it languish;
together with the wild animals
  and the birds of the air,
  even the fish of the sea are perishing. (Hos. 4:1-3, NRSV)

Hosea uses the form of the lawsuit discourse to draw connections between the mourning of the land and the languishing and perishing of wildlife, on the one hand, and human sin and faithlessness toward God, on the other.[19] The morality or immorality of human acts, the justice or injustice of social arrangements, and the behavior of the powerful have tragic cosmic effects. "I have no doubt," writes Luther, "that before sin the air was purer and more healthful, and the water more prolific; yes, even the sun's light was more beautiful and clearer. Now the entire creation in all its parts reminds us of the curse that was inflicted because of sin."[20] These connections go both ways and express, for Luther, the operation of natural law in which the consequences of human wrongdoing rebound upon the actor: "Because everyone robs and steals from everyone else," Luther wrote, "God has mastered the art of punishing one thief by means of another."[21]

For Dietrich Bonhoeffer, "the Natural" arose when "creation" became "nature" through human sin.[22] In the Natural, God places life "at the service

---

of Creation (Nashville: Abingdon, 2005), 19. Fretheim cites the examples of Deuteronomy 11:13-17, Jeremiah 4:22-26, Hosea 4:1-3.

19. Walter Brueggemann, "The Uninflected *Therefore*," in *Reading from This Place*, vol. 1, *Social Location and Biblical Interpretation in the United States*, ed. Fernando F. Segovia and Mary Ann Tolbert (Minneapolis: Fortress Press, 1995), pp. 239-40.

20. Luther, *Lectures on Genesis*, vol. 1, p. 204.

21. Luther, *The Large Catechism*, p. 419.

22. Dietrich Bonhoeffer, *Ethics*, ed. Clifford J. Green, trans. R. Krauss, C. C. West, and

of other lives and of the world," and duties and tasks flow from God's gift of life.[23] Even in its sinful state, this nature is the object of God's "created grace," which "is exactly the grace that inheres in the world by virtue of a gracious God."[24] The interdependent realms of the human and the "web of nature" become both the occasion and the place of created grace.[25] God still continues the creating activity and shares it with, and works through, both humans and nonhuman elements in nature, which become for Luther the "masks" of God's creating.[26] Thus, for example, water is an actor in creating as well as something in, with, and through which God works, and must be respected as such and as a part of the creation. Moreover, through created grace, argues Fretheim, "the chaotic elements . . . finally . . . have divinely constrained limits in their ability to destroy" or disrupt.[27]

Luther has this kind of natural grace in mind when he explains what "daily bread" means in the Lord's Prayer. Daily bread includes

> everything that belongs to our entire life in this world; only for its sake do we need daily bread. Now, our life requires not only food and clothing and other necessities for our body, but also peace and concord in our daily business and in associations of every description with the people among whom we live and move — in short, everything that pertains to the regulation of our domestic and our civil or political affairs. For where these two relations are interfered with and prevented from functioning

---

D. W. Scott, *Dietrich Bonhoeffer Works* (English Edition), vol. 6 (Minneapolis: Fortress Press, 2005) pp. 173-74.

23. Bonhoeffer, *Ethics,* pp. 178, 180.

24. Joseph Sittler, "Ecological Commitment as Theological Responsibility," in Sittler, *Evocations of Grace: Writings on Ecology, Theology, and Ethics,* ed. Steven Bouma-Prediger and Peter Bakken (Grand Rapids: Eerdmans, 2000), p. 83.

25. Joseph Sittler, *Essays in Nature and Grace* (Philadelphia: Fortress Press, 1972), pp. 2, 87, and 94.

26. Martin Luther, *Lectures on Genesis, Chapters 38–44,* in *Luther's Works,* vol. 7, ed. Jaroslav Pelikan and Walter A. Hansen, trans. Paul D. Pahl (St. Louis: Concordia, 1965), p. 184; and Martin Luther, "Psalm 101," trans. Alfred von Rohr Sauer, *Luther's Works,* vol. 13, *Selected Psalms II,* ed. Jaroslav Pelikan (St. Louis: Concordia, 1956), p. 197. God creating *through* humans and other creatures is an example of the finite bearing the infinite in Luther's theology as particular finite human beings, for example, at certain times and places manifest in distinct ways God's creating activity in particular instances. See the discussion by Mary Gaebler in part 1 of her essay "U.S. Property Law Reconsidered in Light of the Lutheran *Finitum Capax Infiniti*" elsewhere in this volume.

27. Fretheim, *God and the World in the Old Testament,* pp. 279-82. The quote is from p. 282.

properly, there the necessities of life are also interfered with, and life itself cannot be maintained for any length of time.[28]

Within "everything," Luther includes all that is "required to satisfy our bodily needs, such as food and clothing, house and home, fields and flocks, money and property; . . . seasonable weather . . . and the like."[29] Luther regarded such listings as illustrative rather than complete and definitive. Therefore, it is fitting for us to include both water and water rights (a form of property protected by law) in the metaphor of daily bread.[30]

Luther's theology and ethic are relational.[31] Although our primary relation is to God through faith, we also stand in relation to our earthly neighbors. We are responsible to God, argues Gustav Wingren, both for fearing, loving, and trusting God above all things and for fulfilling our responsibility to and for our neighbor through our Christian vocations.[32] Responsible moral agency marks Luther's mature anthropology and ethic.[33] A Christian acts to address the needs or further the interests of neighbors in what Mary Gaebler calls "a cooperative alliance with the indwelling Spirit" such that "God's active and cooperating presence is at work in, with, and under her own agency."[34] In doing so, we again become God's mask for our neighbor. For God, Luther says, "wants us to act in accordance with [God's] ordered power."[35]

As responsible moral agents, Christians have considerable freedom to respond to their neighbors. Luther emphasizes their freedom in discern-

28. Luther, *The Large Catechism,* p. 430. I have explored the contemporary significance of Luther's understanding of daily bread for economic rights in "The Right to Property and Daily Bread: Thinking with Luther about Human Economic Rights," *Journal of Lutheran Ethics* 9, no. 2 (February 2009), accessed February 3, 2009, found at http://www.elca.org/ JLE/Articles/408.

29. Luther, *The Small Catechism,* p. 437.

30. For a recent discussion of the dimensions of the metaphor of daily bread in the Lord's Prayer, connecting the rights to water needed to grow the cereals and grains used to bake the literal bread people eat, see Rebecca P. Judge and Charles C. Taliaferro, "Companionable Bread," *Word & World* 23, no. 4 (Fall 2013): 267-372.

31. Gustaf Wingren, *Luther on Vocation,* trans. Carl C. Rasmussen (Philadelphia: Muhlenberg Press, 1957), pp. 5, 50.

32. Wingren, *Luther on Vocation,* p. 120.

33. Wingren, *Luther on Vocation,* p. 120.

34. Mary Gaebler, *The Courage of Faith: Martin Luther and the Theonomous Self* (Minneapolis: Fortress Press, 2013), p. 175.

35. Martin Luther, *Lectures on Genesis, Chapters 15-20,* in *Luther's Works,* vol. 3, ed. Jaroslav Pelikan, trans. George V. Schick (St. Louis: Concordia, 1961), p. 274.

ing how they fulfill obligations to others that the commandments impose. Luther's characteristic formula explaining the commandments begins, "We are to fear and love God" and then continues, "so that we do not" harm our neighbor in various ways, but respond to their needs or interests and uphold their reputations. Luther also connects his understanding of the human to Christian freedom: "A Christian is a perfectly free lord of all, subject to none. A Christian is a perfectly dutiful servant of all, subject to all."[36] Christians are allowed — even expected — to exercise discernment and reason, and to use different modes of action.[37] Luther presumes that people can understand, from common human experience and reason, the various ways in which they might scheme to get their neighbors' possessions dishonestly or unethically, and therefore can also refrain from doing so. Similarly, in exhorting Christians to help their neighbor improve and protect their property and income, Luther does not tell them how to do that. They are free to discern, exercise reason and judgment about, think through, and decide these things, and to act for themselves.[38]

Luther regards reason very highly and praises the important results achieved when people put it to good use. For, "Right reason is the principal part of man."[39] Yet, because a person's reason is often focused on his or her concern for the self, God gives the Law as a guide for reason, "to illumine and help man and to show him what he should do and what he should avoid,"

36. Martin Luther, "The Freedom of a Christian," in *Luther's Works*, vol. 31, *Career of the Reformer I*, ed. Harold J. Grimm, trans. W. A. Lambert and Harold J. Grimm (Philadelphia: Fortress Press, 1957), p. 344.

37. Luther includes "my reason and understanding" among the things God gives humans when they are created (*The Large Catechism*, p. 432). And the reason or intellect that humans were given was "sound" (*Lectures on Genesis*, vol. 1, p. 141). In his "Disputation Concerning Man" (1536), Luther writes: "[Reason] is the inventor and mentor of all the arts, medicines, laws, and of whatever wisdom, power, virtue, and glory men possess in this life. . . . That is, that it is a sun and a kind of god appointed to administer these things in this life. Nor did God after the fall of Adam take away this majesty of reason, but rather confirmed it." *Luther's Works*, vol. 34, *Career of the Reformer IV*, trans. and ed. Lewis W. Spitz (Philadelphia: Fortress Press, 1960), p. 137. See also Gary M. Simpson, " 'Written on Their Hearts': Thinking with Luther about Scripture, Natural Law, and the Moral Life," *Word & World* 30, no. 4 (Fall 2010): 419-28, for a helpful discussion of Luther's understanding of human moral and practical reason.

38. Gaebler recognizes the role of discernment in the Christian's exercise of her or his theonomous agency. Gaebler, *The Courage of Faith*, p. 178. Likewise, Wingren also recognizes the importance of discernment and freedom in Luther's doctrine of vocation as the Christian acts in "elastic constancy toward others." Wingren, *Luther on Vocation*, pp. 208-9.

39. Martin Luther, "The Disputation Concerning Man," pp. 137 and 144.

and how rightly to help the neighbor, or to legislate, administer, or adjudi-cate the civil laws.[40] Once illumined by faith in God, "the work is incarnated and incorporated into it." Luther calls this "another reason," "the reason of faith," which becomes integral to discernment and responsible agency for Christians.[41]

In explaining the negative and positive duties that the Seventh Com-mandment prescribes, Luther applies the common natural law injunctions of nonmalevolence ("so that we do not take our neighbors' money or prop-erty, or acquire them by using shoddy merchandise or crooked deals") and beneficence ("but instead help them to improve and protect their property and income") to the lives of Christians.[42] As the precautionary principle, nonmalevolence is often expressed as the imperative to "do no harm." Re-garding water rights, nonmalevolence means eliminating or reducing harm and risk to access to water and the water rights of individuals or organiza-tions whenever possible. The commandment's exhortations correspond to the principle of benevolence, or the moral imperative to do good to others, here by helping them to protect and improve their access to water and water rights.[43]

While Luther's primary pastoral concerns in his *Large* and *Small* cat-echisms were the conduct of individual Christians toward their immediate neighbors, he also considered these principles to be applicable to questions of social justice and the vocation of princes and other public officials in his commentary on Psalm 82.[44] Elsewhere, Luther wrote, "[I]t is the duty of the

40. Martin Luther, *Lectures on Galatians, Chapters 1–4* (1535), *Luther's Works*, vol. 26, ed. Jaroslav Pelikan and Walter A. Hansen, trans. Jaroslav Pelikan (St. Louis: Concordia, 1963), p. 183.

41. Luther, *Lectures on Galatians, Chapters 1–4,* pp. 267 and 362.

42. Brian Tierney traces the antecedents of these two principles to the medieval De-cretist Rufinus's distinction of commands, prohibitions, and demonstrations in natural law in the twelfth century. See Tierney's *The Idea of Natural Rights* (Grand Rapids: Eerdmans, 2001), p. 62. See also Jean Porter, *Natural and Divine Law: Reclaiming the Tradition for Christian Ethics* (Grand Rapids: Eerdmans, 1999), pp. 254-55. On Luther as a natural law thinker, see Simpson, " 'Written on Their Hearts,' " pp. 419-28; and Simpson, "Putting on the Neighbor: The Ciceronian Impulse in Luther's Christian Approach to Practical Reason," in *The Devil's Whore: Reason and Philosophy in the Lutheran Tradition,* ed. Jennifer Hockenbery Dragseth (Minneapolis: Fortress Press, 2011), pp. 31-39.

43. In Luther's day, these principles were standard aspects in the discussion of natural law. Luther was quite familiar with them and used them in his explanations of the com-mandments. See Gary M. Simpson, " 'Written on Their Hearts,' " pp. 421-42 and p. 422, n. 5.

44. Martin Luther, "Psalm 82," in *Luther's Works*, vol. 13, *Selected Psalms II*, ed. J. Pe-likan, trans. C. M. Jacobs (St. Louis: Concordia, 1956), pp. 39-72.

authorities to consider and to do what is necessary for the best government of the common people who are committed to their care."[45] As citizens and participants in economic life, or as public officials, Christians are called not only to consider their personal interests and needs, but also to address the needs and interests of their neighbors — indeed the whole community — in the context of the common good. The principles of nonmalevolence and benevolence thus are applicable to action by — and toward — individuals, social groups, and whole societies concerning their access to water and their water rights.

Water Rights as Property

While Luther dealt with property and possessions as a moral matter in his catechisms, he certainly understood property also as a matter of secular law that gave people certain legal rights and responsibilities and imposed certain penalties for violating the law. Property is a legal and moral relation among natural or artificial persons, such as corporations, with respect to things.[46] These relations are necessarily, as political theorist John Meyer says, "embedded in a web of social and ecological relationships."[47] In modern societies, property is a creature of civil law.[48] The law creates formal legal

45. Martin Luther, "Trade and Usury" (1524), in *Luther's Works*, vol. 45, *The Christian in Society II*, ed. Walther I. Brandt, trans. Charles M. Jacobs and Walther I. Brandt (Philadelphia: Fortress Press, 1962), p. 287.

46. Morris R. Cohen, "Property and Sovereignty," in Cohen, *Law and the Social Order: Essays in Legal Philosophy* (New Brunswick, NJ: Transaction Books, 1933, 1982), p. 45. Our possessions and property are also things that we individually value and that may help to inform our personal identities. Cultures also have various social ways of interpreting both possessions and property. See *Having: Property and Possession in Religious and Social Life*, ed. William Schweiker and Charles Mathewes (Grand Rapids: Eerdmans, 2004). The quotation is taken from the editors' "Introduction," p. 6.

47. John M. Meyer, "The Concept of Private Property and the Limits of the Environmental Imagination," *Political Theory* 37, no. 1 (February 2009): 99-127; Sax, "Ownership, Property, and Sustainability," pp. 12-13; See also Joseph L. Sax, "Review of the Laws Establishing the SWRCB's Permitting Authority over Appropriations of Groundwater Classified as Subterranean Streams and the SWRCB's Implementation of Those Laws," Final Report No: 0-076-300-0 to the California State Water Resources Control Board, January 19, 2002, pp. 7-11 and 281 (unpublished), accessed July 2, 2014, available from: http://scholarship.law.berkeley.edu/cgi/viewcontent.cgi?article=3235&context=facpubs.

48. Jeremy Bentham, *The Limits of Jurisprudence Defined*, ed. Charles Warren Everett (New York: Columbia University Press, 1945), pp. 61, 79-81.

title for someone to objects or assets, giving them certain legal powers or claims in relation to others. A property *right* is a "bundle" of legal claims any of which the owner of the property is entitled to make on certain others.[49] Property owners seldom, if ever, possess all these powers all at once. This bundle of (mostly) rights usually is distributed among different parties in various ways that also create relationships among those who hold any of those rights-claims as well as among those who are under the corresponding duties that those rights-claims impose.

Today, water rights are a species of property all their own.[50] Who, then, "owns" the water in a river? In one respect, this is a trick question. In U.S. law, "water is publicly owned but amenable to private rights of use."[51] The Supreme Court reaffirmed this principle in 1913 in *The United States v. Chandler-Dunbar Co.*: "Ownership of a private stream wholly upon the lands of an individual is conceivable, but that the running water in a great navigable stream is capable of private ownership is inconceivable."[52] While the public seldom, if ever, holds the whole bundle of powers over water today, it does hold the powers of possessing the water and the ultimate right

---

49. Jeremy Waldron, *The Rule of Law and the Measure of Property*, The Hamlyn Lectures (Cambridge: Cambridge University Press, 2012), p. 66. Honoré describes this bundle of powers and claims with respect to real property as follows: "[O]wnership comprises the right to possess, the right to use, the right to manage, the right to the income of the thing, the right to the capital, the right to security [of ownership for the foreseeable future], the rights or incidents of transmissibility [i.e., her ability to transfer ownership to others through, for example, her will or by selling to others] and absence of [a time limit on her possession and use of the farm], the prohibition of harmful use, liability to [to be seized by creditors if, for example, she fails to make her loan payments], and the incident of [a residual right to the farm if, for example, a leaseholder on the land is unable to continue terms of the lease]: this makes eleven leading incidents." A. M. Honoré, "Ownership," in *Oxford Essays in Jurisprudence* (First Series), ed. A. G. Guest (Oxford: Clarendon, 1961), p. 113.

50. Douglas S. Kenney, "Prior Appropriation and Water Rights Reform in the Western United States," in *Water Rights Reform: Lessons for Institutional Design*, ed. Bryan Randolph Bruns, Claudia Ringler, and Ruth Meinzen-Dick (Washington, DC: International Food Policy Research Institute), p. 172. "Hardly anyone outside of the arid West knows much about water law," Sax says, "but it embraces one of the most extraordinary conceptions of property rights in the whole of our jurisprudence." Sax, "Reserved Public Rights in Water," p. 535.

51. Sax, "Reserved Public Rights in Water," p. 535. Elsewhere in the same paper (p. 538), Sax observes, "The distinctive message of the law is that water ultimately belongs to the community; and while individuals should of course benefit from it, it must always be used in ways that also benefit the community." See also "Environmental Law Forty Years Later," p. 22.

52. *The United Sates v. Chandler-Dunbar Water Power Co.*, 229 U.S. 53 (1913), p. 69.

to manage it as a public trust through state and federal governments.[53] But, in another sense, parties can acquire rights to *use* water from the public — usually through state governments — by showing that those rights would be in the public interest because they would put the water to productive use. Those use-rights are their property, subject to various conditions and public claims.[54] Their permits typically specify the amount of water they are entitled to draw for immediate use or storage and the dates they may do so. "Public rights must sometimes trump private rights," notes Sax, "but don't [necessarily] abolish them."[55]

Laws about water rights may be structured differently. Most western states adopted the "doctrine of appropriation," in which surface water rights are awarded to the first party who can put water to beneficial use, actually diverts the water from its source to where it is used, and uses the water in a timely manner.[56] Such rights are recognized by the date the right was awarded; earlier rights have seniority over rights awarded later. Those rights are tied to the land they irrigate rather than the source of the water because the land is often some distance from its immediate source.[57] By contrast, the doctrine of riparian rights prevalent in states on or east of the Mississippi River gives the water right to the owner of the land adjacent to the water

53. Joseph L. Sax traces the understanding of the diversion of water from a river for off-stream uses as a matter of public trust to the California case known as *Nat'l Audubon Society v. Superior Court,* 658 P.2d 709 (1983), *cert. denied,* 464 U.S. 977 (1983) in "Reflections on Western Water Law," *Ecology Law Quarterly* 34 (2007): 300. On natural resources, including water, as a public trust, see Joseph L. Sax, "The Public Trust Doctrine in Natural Resource Law: Effective Judicial Intervention," *Michigan Law Review* 68 (1970); Sax, "Environmental Law Forty Years Later," pp. 24-25; Joseph L. Sax, "Our Precious Water Resources: Learning from the Past, Securing the Future," paper given to a meeting of the Resource Management Law Association, New Zealand (2009), pp. 6-7, accessed June 27, 2014, available from: http://www.rmla.org.nz/upload/files/rmla08_josephlsax_ourpreciouswaterresources.pdf; Sax, "Reserved Public Rights in Water," p. 3; and Sax, "The Limits of Private Rights in Public Waters," pp. 474-82.

54. Sax, "Property Rights and the Economy of Nature," p. 1452; and Sax, "The Limits of Private Rights in Public Waters," p. 476.

55. Sax, "Our Precious Water Resources," p. 7.

56. Craig Bell and Jeff Taylor, *Water Laws and Policies for a Sustainable Future: A Western States' Perspective* (Murray, UT: Western States Water Council, 2008), p. 67, quoting *Simmons v. Inyo Cerro Gordo Mining & Power Co.,* 192 P. 144, 150 (Cal. App. 1920). Found at: http://www.westgov.org/wswc/laws%20&%20policies%20report%20(final%20with%20cover).pdf, accessed June 11, 2014; and Kenney, "Prior Appropriation and Water Rights Reform," p. 170.

57. Powell, "Report," pp. 204-6.

source, with those who have been awarded rights earlier gaining priority over later-requesting owners.

Rights to water and real property both may be dealt with differently by the law depending upon what philosophical assumptions legislators or judges make about the nature and function of property.[58] The *transformational economy,* as described by Sax and the one that informs most legal cases, is not the only way to think about how water rights will be understood and interpreted. In transformational economies, property and water rights are regarded as discrete and separate entities unconnected to the property of others and are controlled by owners pursuing their self-interest. All uses of land and water transforming them for beneficial purposes are considered equal and are at the complete discretion of rights-holders.[59] (This understanding is consistent with the principle of nonmalevolence as it works to protect the property interests of owners, but it ignores Luther's understanding of the principle of benevolence by disconnecting individual owners from others.[60]) In such economies, all water in streams is fully allocated and none is left for in-stream ecological functions, which are not regarded as of immediate human use. The administration of water rights is inflexible, assumed to be automatic and routine, and without need for active management once water rights are assigned. Voluntary and involuntary reallocation of surface water is "extremely burdensome, complex, and expensive." The burden of any water shortages is borne entirely by the most junior rights-holders.[61] Finally, the moral and legal claims of persons who are not directly harmed by an owner's use of land or water can be ignored because they have no legal interest in the effects of that use.[62]

By contrast, in a *natural economy,* as described by Sax, water and land are viewed as a continuous habitat that is characterized both by their natural ecological functions and the results of this functioning, rather than as

58. Sax, "Property Rights and the Economy of Nature," pp. 1437-46, where Sax critically analyzes the majority U.S. Supreme Court decision by Justice Antonin Scalia in the case named in the title of the article.

59. Sax, "Property Rights and the Economy of Nature," pp. 1445-46. In transformational economies, the moral and legal claims of persons who are not directly harmed by an owner's use of land or water can be ignored because they have no legal interest in the effects of that use.

60. See Mary Gaebler's essay "U.S. Property Law Reconsidered in Light of the Lutheran *Finitum Capax Infiniti*" in this volume.

61. Sax, "Our Precious Water Resources," pp. 2-3.

62. Joseph L. Sax, "Understanding Transfers, Community Rights and the Privatization of Water," *West-Northwest* 14 (2008): 33-39.

discrete and separate units whose boundaries are determined by human beings for primarily human transformational uses.[63] In natural economies, rights to use land and water are shaped according to the physical nature of the resource and its role in the larger ecology of the area. Maintaining the ecological functions of the property is seen as the owner's responsibility for the common good, making the distinction between private and public rights not as sharp as in transformational economies. Owners therefore have a custodial role with a dual function that is both economically productive and ecological. The public has a stake in how owners maintain those functions.

Sax believes that natural systems can support a human developmental economy that produces the goods and services required for a prosperous human community.[64] Natural economies require legal systems that are flexible and adapted to protecting the functions of water and land habitats, treating them as a common heritage and a public trust, and using both restrictions and incentives to shape human behavior to be conducive to such protection while also providing humans the ability to earn a viable livelihood.[65] The value here of Sax's contrast of these two types is that the understanding of law in the ideal type of natural economies could help to address some significant issues of water rights and administration today that are more difficult in the law of actual transformational economies. Taking the environment's needs for water during climate change into account in water policy and land management as a natural economy would require,

63. Sax, develops his notion of a natural economy over a number of works, including "Property Rights and an Economy of Nature," pp. 1442-46; "An Environmental Agenda for Our Time," pp. 35, 41, and 46; "Ownership, Property, and Sustainability," pp. 5, 9, and 12-13; "The Unfinished Agenda of Environmental Law," p. 41; and "The Constitution, Property, and the Future of Water Law," p. 276. The functions of this natural economy are, Sax argues, to produce and maintain abundant biodiversity in relatively balanced ecological relationships, efficiently use and reuse water, produce oxygen and recycle carbon dioxide, and recycle waste, among others.

64. Sax, "Property Rights and an Economy of Nature," pp. 1445-46, 1451, and 1453; Sax, "An Environmental Agenda for Our Time," pp. 35-37.

65. Sax, "Ownership, Property, and Sustainability," pp. 36-37 and 44; "An Environmental Agenda for Our Time," pp. 35 and 42-43; "Ownership, Property, and Sustainability," pp. 10 and 25; "Our Precious Water Resources," p. 7. Sax contends that in those legal systems oriented to a natural economy, the public as a whole would have both a public entitlement and a stake in how particular owners of water rights or land use their property. Diverse collections of actors could legally hold particular owners responsible for the degradation or destruction of parts of the natural system, even though those actors might not have the direct material interest in those water systems or parcels of land that is now required to demonstrate harm to themselves and to qualify for compensation.

however, will be difficult both because Southwestern environments will be in flux in the short term, and the long-term needs of those environments are also difficult to predict because the new normals for those environments are very difficult to foresee.

Analyzing Legal Disputes over Water Rights

In recent years, landowners, Native American tribes and pueblos, irrigation districts, states, those who administer interstate compacts, and the federal government all have claimed interests or rights-claims to the water of various Southwestern rivers or aquifers. The issues in these cases arise because most people and authorities in the Southwest — except some Native American tribes — act from the mindset of the transformational economy.

Interstate River Compacts

Interstate river compacts are legal agreements between states that share the same river system to apportion water among them. Typically, river compacts are first negotiated among the relevant states, and then are made federal law by Congress under the Commerce Clause of Article II, Section 8 of the U.S. Constitution, which gives Congress the authority to regulate commerce "among the several States, and with the Indian Tribes." Rivers that border or pass through more than one state and are at least potentially navigable — and hence capable of interstate commerce — are covered under this clause.

Interstate river compacts and commissions are only one among the parties sharing an interest in the same sources of surface water in an interstate river system. The first dispute involves the Colorado River Compact, which was created by Congress in 1922. In *Arizona v. California*, at stake was how much water each state would receive to support both its present population and its agricultural sectors as well as to support its future growth — in effect, how many people could actually live and work in those states. Also at issue were the powers and responsibilities of the federal government to, among other things, support Native American tribes, including how much water they would have for the foreseeable future.

In its decision, the Supreme Court ruled that water allocations made by Congress in authorizing interstate river compacts are legally binding and cannot be changed by the courts, even though the Supreme Court had previously reapportioned water among states using a legal doctrine called "equitable apportionment" to make its own apportionment.[66] Consequently, Arizona's claim to a larger share of the 7.5 million acre feet (MAF) apportioned under the Compact to the states in the Lower Colorado Basin at California's expense was invalid. Similarly, the Court rejected California's claim to portions of the water of the tributaries of the Colorado which, if granted, would have redistributed 1 MAF of Lower Basin water annually to California from other basin states. Federal and state courts are generally deferential to legislative actions provided they pass constitutional and other legal tests, and the Court saw no reason to apply that doctrine in this case.[67]

Citing two precedent cases, the Court also ruled that the United States was entitled to reserve an amount of water necessary for the needs of certain Native American tribes on five reservations and various federal lands such as national forests, recreation areas, and wildlife areas.[68] In creating reservations, the federal government also in effect reserved enough water to irrigate their arable land, and the Court acknowledged that since these reservations were created prior to the Compact, reservation water rights should have priority over the rights allocated by the Compact. Thus, the Court rejected Arizona's contention that it ought to reserve enough water to meet the future needs of the people who would live there, arguing that it could only guess at what those needs may be.[69]

In a second case currently before the Supreme Court, *State of Texas v. State of New Mexico and State of Colorado,* Texas filed suit in 2013 against these two members of the Rio Grande Compact, created in 1930, alleging that they had violated its terms with respect to Compact water allocations among the states, Compact governance, the relationship between surface water in the river and groundwater pumping in nearby aquifers, and an operating agreement between irrigation districts in Texas and New Mexico and

66. *Arizona v. California,* at 565-67. For discussions of the doctrine of equitable apportionment, see Chad D. Orr, "'Unless and Until It Proves to Be Necessary': Applying Water Interest to Prevent Unjust Enrichment in Interstate Water Disputes," *California Law Review* 101 (2013); George William Sherk, "Equitable Apportionment After *Vermejo:* The Demise of a Doctrine," *Natural Resources Journal* 29 (Spring 1989): 565-83; and Richard A. Simms, "Equitable Apportionment — Priorities and New Uses," *Natural Resources Journal* 29 (Spring 1989): 549-63.

67. Sax, "The Public Trust Doctrine in Natural Resource Law," pp. 542-43.

68. The two precedent cases cited were *Winters v. United States,* 207 U.S. 564 (1908) and *United States v. Powers,* 305 U.S. 527 (1939).

69. *Arizona v. California,* pp. 596 and 600-601.

the U.S. Bureau of Reclamation about the supply of the Rio Grande Project which would go to the two irrigation districts.[70]

Texas contends, supported by the U.S. Solicitor General, that New Mexico "allowed and authorized Rio Grande Project water intended for use in Texas to be intercepted and used in New Mexico . . . causing grave and irreparable injury to Texas."[71] New Mexico's responding brief argues that Texas cannot show that New Mexico violated either any of the Compact's terms or any obligations for water delivery to Texas under the Compact.[72] The Supreme Court appointed a Special Master in the case in November 2014 "to direct subsequent proceedings, to summon witnesses, to issue subpoenas, . . . to take . . . evidence," and to submit reports to the Court as he deems necessary. Other parties were given until January 29, 2015, to intervene in the case.[73]

Texas's lawsuit emerged from a related case, *New Mexico v. United States,* filed in 2011 in Federal District Court in New Mexico, in which the State of New Mexico sued the U.S. Bureau of Reclamation seeking to invalidate a 2008 Operating Agreement between the Bureau and irrigation districts in New Mexico and Texas which benefit from the Rio Grande Project and to permanently prevent the Agreement's use.[74] New Mexico alleged that the Agreement reallocated significant amounts of water from New Mexico to Texas resulting in a reduction of the New Mexico irrigation district's share of Project water from 57 percent to 38 percent. New Mexico also accused the Bureau of an illegal transfer of 33,000 acre feet of water from the Compact to the Project.

Texas v. New Mexico and Colorado and its preceding dispute, *New Mexico v. United States,* illustrate both the underlying complexity of some water

---

70. The Project originated with an act of Congress in 1905. The Compact was authorized by Congress in 1930. The Compact was intended to supply water to users in the Upper Reach of the Rio Grande from its origins in Colorado to Ft. Quitman, Texas. The Project was intended to supply Rio Grande water specifically to irrigation districts near El Paso, Texas, and near Elephant Butte, New Mexico.

71. State of Texas, *Complaint, State of Texas v. State of New Mexico and State of Colorado,* accessed October 13, 2013, available from: http://sblog.s3.amazonaws.com/wp -content/uploads/2013/04/1-7-13-Texas-v-NM-booklet.pdf.

72. State of New Mexico, *New Mexico's Brief in Opposition to Texas' Motion for Leave to File Complaint,* available at: http://sblog.s3.amazonaws.com/wp-content/ uploads/2014/01/12-27-13-NM-Supp-Brf-in-Opp2.pdf, accessed May 4, 2013.

73. Order of the Supreme Court, November 3, 2014, Docket Number 220141 ORG, available at: http://www.supremecourt.gov/search.aspx?filename=/docketfiles/220141 .htm, accessed December 10, 2014. Four responses to briefs were filed on January 29, 2015, and the Elephant Butte Irrigation District was given additional time to reply to each of them,

74. *New Mexico v. United States et al.,* D.N.M. 11-CV-691 (2011).

disputes and the fact, noted above, that the powers of water and other property rights are usually distributed among a network of different parties. The latter dispute shows the complexity of relations among holders of various water rights that underlies the former dispute. The federal government holds the ultimate control of the Rio Grande according to Article I, Section 8 of the U.S. Constitution, but has granted the Compact authority to allocate its water among its member states. They, in turn, grant rights to use water to parties in the state, such as municipalities, farmers and ranchers, corporations, irrigation districts, etc. Other parties also hold rights granted prior to creation of the Compact in 1938. For example, Congress also created the Rio Grande Project in 1905 authorizing the federal Bureau of Reclamation to erect and operate reservoirs on the Rio Grande to help supply specific shares of water to the Elephant Butte Irrigation District in New Mexico and El Paso Irrigation District No. 1 in Texas, both of which serve agricultural producers in each district. Although the water rights of the two districts and their members were granted prior to the Compact, both New Mexico and Texas claim that through the Compact they have some powers over the Project and how the Bureau of Reclamation administers Project water. Under a 1905 treaty with the United States, Mexico has a claim to a portion of Rio Grande water for use by Ciudad Juarez and in its surrounding agricultural areas.

Interstate Water Transfers

As states, cities, or other jurisdictions grow in population or economic activity, they commonly try to increase their available water supply. They can do this by drilling wells or purchasing water or water rights from other sources. Again, control of the water affects both current populations, farms, and ranches as well as potential for future growth for a state or city.

Interstate market mechanisms for water transfers are not well developed.[75] However, direct voluntary dealings between water holders and parties seeking to acquire water do occur.[76] The U.S. Supreme Court has ruled

75. Bryan Randolph Bruns, Claudia Ringler, and Ruth Meinzen-Dick, "Reforming Water Rights: Governance, Tenure, and Transfers," in Bruns, Ringler, and Meinzen-Dick, eds., *Water Rights Reform*, p. 288. For a discussion of some of the challenges of creating and regulating water markets, see Bryan Randolph Bruns and Ruth Meinzen-Dick, "Frameworks for Water Rights: An Overview," in Bruns, Ringler, and Meinzen-Dick, eds., *Water Rights Reform*, pp. 9-10.

76. See, for example, *Water Transfers in the West: Projects, Trends, and Leading Practices*

in *Sporhase v. Nebraska* that while states have a legitimate interest in the conservation and preservation of their groundwater, interstate transfers of water are constitutional under the Commerce Clause, and states may not discriminate against out-of-state parties in such transfers.[77]

In 1984, the City of El Paso sued the State Engineer of New Mexico over legal barriers it alleged New Mexico had erected against the export of water outside the state.[78] In *City of El Paso v. Reynolds,* the federal district court ruled that New Mexico had imposed an embargo against out-of-state use of its groundwater in a state statute in violation of the Commerce Clause and enjoined New Mexico from enforcing the embargo or denying El Paso's permit applications to drill wells in three New Mexican aquifers with a capacity to pump 300,000 acre feet annually for export to the city.[79]

Despite New Mexico's attempt to meet the court's objections by revising the state water code to permit interstate transfers subject to state regulation, under *Sporhase* the federal court invalidated the legislation for violation of the Commerce Clause because it required the State Engineer to consider the criteria of conservation of water and public welfare for out-of-state applicants *but not for in-state applicants.*[80] The Court also found that the State Engineer's administration of drilling applications under a two-year moratorium "on new appropriations of ground water hydrologically connected to the Rio Grande below Elephant Butte," "disclose[d] an impermissible, discriminatory purpose" and "only substantiates the conclusion that the true purpose of the statute is to prevent El Paso from obtaining any ground water from New Mexico."[81]

---

in Voluntary Water Trading (Denver: The Western Governors' Association, 2012), which has extensive discussion of issues in water transfers, accessed March 15, 2014, available from http://www.westgov.org/reports?start=8.

77. *Sporhase v. Nebraska ex rel. Douglas* 458 U.S. 941 (1982).

78. *City of El Paso v. Reynolds* 597 F. Supp. 694 (D.N.M. 1984). During droughts, groundwater pumping tended to increase. Groundwater basins, however, were not recharging to their traditional levels. In 1980, the City of El Paso applied to New Mexico's State Engineer for authorization to develop wells in the Mesilla Bolson groundwater basin. The City also requested permits to drill 326 wells in two other basins and draw 296,000 acre feet annually for export to El Paso ("Water Litigation," pp. 24-26).

79. *El Paso v. Reynolds,* pp. 696-97, summarizing *City of El Paso v. Reynolds,* 563 F. Supp. 379 (D.N.M. 1983). See also "Water Litigation," p. 24; and *City of El Paso v. Reynolds,* 597 F. Supp. 694 (D.N.M 1984), p. 696.

80. *El Paso v. Reynolds,* pp. 705-6.

81. *El Paso v. Reynolds,* pp. 697, 707. The relation between groundwater and surface water has been a murky issue in water administration and water law until recently, when

Because they are committed to a transformational economy, these authorities desired to project population and economic growth, and adopt policies and plans that would enhance such an economy. Their implementation has created both an actual and a perceived water scarcity that led to the perpetual search for greater water supplies. The City of El Paso has judged that its current sources of water could not support its aspirations and projected growth, and sought to drill for and transfer water from New Mexico. Texas, New Mexico, Arizona, and California jealously guard their own compact apportionments at the same time that they jockey for advantage and more water to support their own aspirations for growth. Their common vulnerability with respect to water has created perpetual legal and legislative conflict among these public authorities rather than cooperation over water supplies governed by the compacts.[82] Instead of acting to help each other protect and improve their economies through use of existing or projected water supplies, as Luther suggests they should, they squabble and legally scheme seemingly over every drop of surface and groundwater in what they see as a zero-sum game in order to deprive the other of water they themselves are eager to use for further transformational economic growth. If lawsuits can't accomplish their purposes, states will use the legislative process to do so, as with New Mexico's efforts to prevent export of groundwater.[83] This is not to dismiss

---

laws in various states began to reflect hydrological science's findings that surface and underground waters constitute an interconnected system. Groundwater administration was the substantive issue behind the suit in *El Paso v. Reynolds*. Similarly, groundwater figured in the facts of *New Mexico v. United States* because a key issue of the 2008 operating agreement of the Rio Grande Project was the factoring of groundwater pumping into the water allocation formula of the agreement to which New Mexico took exception. The New Mexico State Engineer was attempting to adopt integrated management of surface and groundwater in the state. His office had already been concerned about groundwater supplies in the state for some time. Between 1961 and 1982, the New Mexico State Engineer identified and declared groundwater basins below the lower Rio Grande stream system and assumed administrative authority over the groundwater of the Lower Rio Grande basin in the state by creating the Lower Rio Grande Water Master District in 2004 and also began metering most wells in the district ("Water Litigation," p. 24). Moreover, there is hydrological evidence of interaction between the Rio Grande and nearby groundwater because the river occasionally disappears from its bed only to emerge from underground again further downstream. Neil W. Ackerly, "Evolution of the Rio Grande," *Water Challenges on the Lower Rio Grande: Forty-third Annual New Mexico Water Conference Proceedings*, WRRI Report No. 310 (March 1999, New Mexico Water Resources Research Institute), p. 28. Accessed December 24, 2013, available from: http://wrri.nmsu.edu/publish/watcon/proc43/contents.html.

82. DeBuys, *A Great Aridness*, p. 37.
83. The Central Arizona Project carries 1.5 MAF of Colorado River water annually from

the positive use, importance, or "good fruit" of lawsuits, which the *Apology* to the *Augsburg Confession* praised in an epigraph at the beginning of this paper and with which Luther concurred, but only to indicate how public bodies, like individuals, can be curved in upon themselves rather than being primarily directed toward the common good of all.

The Principles of Nonmalevolence and Benevolence and Southwestern Water Rights

I have argued that the principles of nonmalevolence and benevolence are applicable to action by — and toward — individuals, social groups, and whole societies concerning their water rights. The principle of benevolence has various dimensions that are highly significant for water rights: precaution, sufficiency, sustainability, participation, solidarity, and equity. Together, they help to parse out on the matter of water rights the sort of thing Luther had in mind when he explained what the principle of benevolence means in the case of property. We will use these dimensions of the principle of benevolence to evaluate these legal cases as well as other aspects of water rights in the Southwest.

Precaution

To help people have effective water rights, water should not be polluted, over-allocated, or wasted by human users, and water-related habitats should not be deprived of water necessary to maintain environmental habitats in a healthy condition for the foreseeable future because the well-being of people and their communities and the health of their environment are interconnected. The principle of precaution operates this way. The states of the Southwest are now confronting the fundamental dilemma of the region we saw earlier that Fradkin identified: "the aridity that breeds sparseness and the denial of that condition, which leads to overdevelopment."[84] Southwestern

---

Lake Havasu near Parker on the Colorado River southeast to the San Xavier Indian Reservation southwest of Tucson. It supplies water to the metropolitan areas of Phoenix, Mesa, Tucson, and communities in between. Forty-seven percent of its water is designated for Indian water rights settlements under the Arizona Water Settlements Act of 2004 (http://www.cap-az.com/, and http://www.cap-az.com/index.php/tribal-water, accessed July 28, 2014).

    84. See note 9 above.

rivers are "over-allocated" and the historical limits of water that these rivers can supply are being approached if not already surpassed.[85] Southwestern aquifers also are becoming increasingly depleted. In contrast with Luther's use of the principle of nonmalevolence with respect to people's property, this incautious overdevelopment exposes present and future water rights holders and water users as well as the natural environment to considerable risk.[86] The principle of *precaution* casts a critical gaze on the assumptions, practices, and legal interpretation of transformational economies by the courts.

"This imbalance [between water supply and demand] will grow in the future if the potential effects of climate change are realized and demands continue to increase," according to the Bureau of Reclamation.[87] The climate of the future, which is unlikely to be the "normal temperate climate" generally prevailing since the last ice age, will invalidate conventional assumptions about the availability and uses of water. According to Richard Seager, "The cycle of natural dry periods and wet periods will continue [in the Southwest], but they continue around a mean that gets drier [over time]."[88] The *Third National Climate Assessment* projects for the Southwest that as mean temperatures rise, swings in weather patterns will be greater, winters will be warmer, the lower-altitude snowpack will melt earlier, and annual rainfall amounts will decline. Although the magnitudes of decline projected by these studies differ, they agree in projecting a trend of significant declines over the century.[89] These declines may severely restrict how much water users

85. Connie A. Woodhouse, David M. Meko, Glen M. MacDonald, Dave W. Stahle, and Edward R. Cook, "A 1,200-year Perspective of 21st Century Drought in Southwestern North America," *PNAS* 107, no. 50 (December 14, 2010): 21283. An annual deficit in water supply of 3.2 MAF is projected by 2060 in the Colorado Basin alone. U.S. Department of the Interior, Bureau of Reclamation, *Colorado River Basin Water Supply and Demand Study: Final Study Report* (Washington, DC: Bureau of Reclamation, 2012), pp. SR-34–SR-35. Found at: http://www.usbr.gov/lc/region/programs/crbstudy/finalreport/Study%20Report/CRBS_Study_Report_FINAL.pdf, accessed April 29, 2014.

86. Current levels of delivery of Colorado River water, for example, likely will not be sustainable as climate change intensifies. Daniel R. Cayan et al., "Future Dryness in the Southwest U.S. and the Hydrology of the Early 21st Century Drought," *PNAS* 107, no. 50 (December 14, 2010): 21275.

87. Bureau of Reclamation, *Colorado River Basin Water,* p. SR-6. See also deBuys, *A Great Aridness,* pp. 8-9.

88. Quoted in deBuys, *A Great Aridness,* p. 26.

89. A recent climate study projects the average flow of the Colorado River to decline about 10 to 40 percent over roughly the next fifty years. Bell and Taylor, *Water Laws and Policies for a Sustainable Future: A Western States' Perspective,* p. 161; and Colorado River Governance Initiative, "Rethinking the Future of the Colorado River: Interim Report" (Boul-

can draw from tributaries of Southwestern river systems.[90] More extreme weather events are expected, which will cause greater flooding and erosion, silting of rivers, generally lower water quality, and less percolation of water into aquifers. Hotter summers will raise evaporation rates. When they occur, droughts will be longer and more severe. These trends are likely to be even greater in the southern half of the region where the Rio Grande flows.[91] As with Luther's understanding of natural law, the consequences of people's best intentions and well-meaning actions to develop the West for a transformational economy, together with climate change, are rebounding upon them and threatening themselves, their communities, and their futures.

Larry Rasmussen observes, "Our destiny is uncertain because the new planet doesn't work the same way the old one did," requiring a multidimensional transition entailing perspectival, economic, demographic, polity, policy, and religious and moral transitions from current ways of thinking and acting to new ones.[92] William deBuys makes three pertinent observations

---

der: University of Colorado Law School Western Water Policy Program, December, 2010), p. 71, accessed April 29, 2014, available from: http://www.circleofblue.org/waternews/wp-content/uploads/2011/01/CRGI-Interim-Report.pdf. Another study suggests that annual average water runoff from the Colorado River Basin will decline by about 2.8 to 17.6 percent between 2041 and 2099. G. Garfin et al., *Southwest Climate Change Impacts in the United States: The Third National Climate Change Assessment,* ed. J. M. Melillo, Terese Richmond, and G. W. Yohe, U.S. Global Change Research Program. Doi:10.7930/JO8GIHMN, pp. 462-86. Found at: http://nca2014.globalchange.gov/report/regions/southwest, accessed May 7, 2014. Modeling studies of future temperature and flow of the river basin suggest that "for each 1° C increase in temperature, runoff will decrease from 2-8% in the Colorado River Basin" (Woodhouse et al., "A 1,200 Year Perspective of 21st Century Drought in Southwestern North America," p. 21287). See also Cayan et al., "Future Dryness in the Southwest and the Hydrology of the Early 21st Century Drought," p. 21275.

90. Amy C. Lewis, Karen MacClune, Kari Tyler, et al., "Climate Change and the Santa Fe Basin: A Preliminary Assessment of Vulnerabilities and Adaptation Alternatives," report prepared for the U.S. Bureau of Reclamation, the City of Santa Fe, and Santa Fe County (Boulder: Institute for Social and Environmental Transition, February 2013), pp. 23-24.

91. G. Garfin et al., *Southwest Climate Change Impacts in the United States,* pp. 462-86. Numerous other effects are also forecast. For other discussions of projections of Southwestern warming and its effects, see Cayan et al., "Future Dryness in the Southwest"; Richard Seager and Gabriel A. Vecchi, "Greenhouse Warming and the 21st Century Hydroclimate of Southwestern North America," *PNAS* 107, no. 50 (December 14, 2010): 21277-282; Glen M. MacDonald, "Water, Climate Change, and Sustainability in the Southwest," *PNAS,* 107, no. 50 (December 14, 2010): 21256-262; and Woodhouse et al., "A 1,200 Year Perspective of 21st Century Drought."

92. Larry L. Rasmussen, *Earth-honoring Faith: Religious Ethics in a New Key* (Oxford: Oxford University Press, 2013), p. 70.

about this transition: First, *"the human contribution to change in the natural world more often catalyzes than dictates the outcome."* Second, *"the forces latent in nature have the potential to move ecological systems toward multiple future states; human activities help select the direction of the move."* Third, human beings and societies adjust to change because of *"the enormity of the human capacity for adaptation."*[93] Thus, there is plenty of room and opportunity for responsible human agency at both the individual and social levels.

Water law may initially be an obstacle to dealing with climate change and addressing the principle of precaution.[94] Nevertheless, Sax concluded "that the way is constitutionally clear for changes that will bring water law into phase with contemporary needs."[95] He advocates moving toward reinterpreting these areas of law more flexibly according to the assumptions of the "natural economy."[96] This might help authorities and users address the principle of precaution more effectively.

Policy changes consonant with the principle of precaution could include realistic water projections by interstate river compact commissions, which would anticipate their effects on state water allocations. Revised estimates will help states and other users reduce expectations about the available water supply to more realistic levels.[97] This will encourage public authorities and others to plan for more realistic population levels, economic growth, water policies and procedures, and other steps that will help to reduce or eliminate water deficits.

Although legislative action on water issues will be both urgent and politically difficult, the principle of precaution suggests that harm to rights and access to water in the Southwest will only increase the longer confronting both these issues and the risk to various parties' water rights is delayed. State and federal courts are incapable of deliberating and deciding the fundamental public policy issues of water under climate change, however much they may be able to adjudicate individual cases over water rights.[98] If courts inter-

---

93. DeBuys, *A Great Aridness,* pp. 13 and 16, italics in the original.

94. Sax observes that "our [current] legal system . . . is quite ill-suited to meet the goals of an economy of nature" (Sax, "The Unfinished Agenda of Environmental Law," p. 42). He argues that although currently we can use the law to protect parts of nature, the law does not "engraft the values of the economy of nature onto traditional notions" of property rights (Sax, "Property Rights and the Economy of Nature," p. 1446). See also Sax, "Environmental Law Forty Years Later," pp. 11-13.

95. Sax, "The Constitution, Property Rights, and the Future of Water Law," p. 281.

96. Sax, "Property Rights and the Economy of Nature."

97. Sax, "The Constitution, Property Rights, and the Future of Water Law," p. 269.

98. Sax, "Environmental Law Forty Years Later," p. 18.

pret current laws consistent with the assumptions of the natural economy, as Sax urges, it may help some in the Southwest adapt to climate change. But those basic policy issues for the region will have to be addressed by state legislatures, Congress, and administrative actions.[99]

Sufficiency

The principle of sufficiency holds that my individual neighbor should not only have a right to sufficient water for his or her needs, but also that there be water sufficient to satisfy the needs of the whole community whose members share the water.[100] The Christian tradition recognizes the importance of a sufficient supply of water for all people, especially those most vulnerable, who are apt to be among the first to be deprived of good-quality water when it is scarce.[101] Luther's interpretation of the Seventh Commandment by extension requires people to help all to have, improve, and protect their rights to water. Yet, the creation of a transformational economy from a vast wilderness, and its effect on water demands, has come at the expense of Native American and Alaskan Native tribes, and people of Spanish and Mexican descent.

Seager believes that "[t]he fundamental structure of the Southwest's water budget [under climate change] points toward sustained and severe shortage."[102] The Southwest's population is projected to grow by 68 percent to 94 million people by 2050 alone.[103] If even just a sizeable fraction of that growth occurs, it will exacerbate the expected water shortage even more. Geographer Glen MacDonald argues that "even restricting population growth by 50% would not allow current per capita water usage to be sustained under many water-supply scenarios."[104] Sax argues therefore that future population

99. On this general point, see Waldron, *The Rule of Law and the Measure of Property,* pp. 103-7.

100. This particular formulation of the sufficiency principle is based on Per Anderson, "Agriculture, Food, and Responsible Biotechnology," in *Lutheran Ethics at the Intersections of God's One World,* ed. Karen L. Bloomquist (Geneva: The Lutheran World Federation, 2005), p. 183.

101. Christine E. Gudorf, "Water Privatization in Christianity and Islam," *Journal of the Society of Christian Ethics* 30, no. 2 (2010): 29.

102. Quoted in deBuys, *A Great Aridness,* p. 31.

103. Garfin et al., *Southwest Climate Change Impacts in the United States,* p. 463.

104. MacDonald, "Water, Climate Change, and Sustainability in the Southwest," p. 21261.

and economic growth likely will have to be accommodated either by current or declining amounts of water.[105] How might this be possible?

The combination of traditional growth policies and limited water availability will put considerable stress upon all Southwestern interstate water compacts and exacerbate existing over-allocations of water. The current provisions of these compacts may become obsolete under those conditions. For, "no compact features a commission expressly empowered to modify apportionments or administration based on climate change considerations. . . . Additionally, climate change is likely to force attention on many other topics currently omitted from compacts."[106] Changing these allocations would require difficult political negotiations as well as an act of Congress.[107] This may make litigation over water apportionments even more likely.[108]

Without policy changes, water rights holders with permits relatively low in seniority will be unable to draw some — *or any* — of the water to which they are entitled, substantially reducing or eliminating the usefulness and value of their water rights, and making their current livelihoods economically infeasible.[109] This likely will result in diminished opportunities for many. As one water policy expert recently said, "We're moving increasingly into a water economy. Those that have water are better positioned to grow and prosper. Those that need it see their options closing, or they have to go find it."[110]

Authorities need not wait for legal reallocation to factor reduced water deliveries into their planning. All parties in the Southwest can begin now to

105. Sax, "Our Precious Water Resources," p. 11.

106. Douglas S. Kenney et al., "Impact of Earlier Spring Snowmelt on Water Rights and Administration: A Preliminary Overview of Issues and Circumstances in the Western States," Final Project Report (review draft) (Boulder: Western Water Policy Program, Natural Resource Law Center, University of Colorado, September 3, 2008), p. 8, found at: http://wwa.colorado.edu/publications/reports/, accessed December 24, 2013.

107. Sax underscores the difficulty of securing legal change, "The Limits of Private Rights in Public Waters," pp. 482-83.

108. Kenney et al., "Impact of Earlier Spring Snowmelt," p. 12.

109. David Gutzler, "Climate Change and Water Resources in New Mexico," *New Mexico Earth Matters,* Summer 2007, Part 3, pp. 1-4, available at https://geoinfo.nmt.edu/publications/periodicals/earthmatters/7/n2/em_v7_n2.pdf.

110. Mark Davis, director of the Institute for Water Law and Policy, Tulane University, quoted in Brett Walton, "Texas Water District Finds Few Friends in Quest for Water in Oklahoma," accessed October 11, 2013, available from: http://www.circleofblue.org/waternews/2013/world/texas-water-district-finds-few-friends-in-quest-for-water-in-oklahoma/.

plan policies, procedures, business plans, and other steps to work toward conservation, efficient use, storage, and distribution of water in line with more realistic projections of water supplies.[111] These measures also need to take the water requirements of the environment into account from the start. A variety of measures might be considered, including economically effective and realistic pricing for water to encourage conservation and recycling.[112]

Voluntary transfers of water are legally permissible where explicit congressional authorization is not required. A recent report by the Western Governors' Association suggests that the importance of water transfers may increase as a way of managing water supplies.[113] Both the number and size of water transfers within states have risen significantly in recent years, and likely will continue to do so.[114]

Despite some changing administration of water rights because of climate change, existing laws are relatively inflexible. Mounting confusion over

111. See deBuys's discussion of the Central Arizona Project, which brings Colorado River water to Arizona communities, for an example of why the regulation of housing development and zoning are critical to Arizona's future where water is concerned.

112. These might include more efficient distribution and plumbing for agricultural, urban, and industrial uses, different water pricing practices encouraging water conservation, mandating the use of more arid-tolerant landscaping as some southwestern cities are already beginning to do, and more. Conservation, efficiency, and water pricing are recognized in the *Colorado River Basin Water Supply and Demand Study*, at least in connection with agricultural conservation (p. SR-44) although pricing policies are not discussed with respect to municipal and industrial conservation or in any other context. This is a significant lacuna in the study. In her discussion of Muslim and Christian approaches to water privatization, the connection of efficient use and water pricing is also recognized by Gudorf, "Water Privatization in Christianity and Islam," p. 30. Developing other sources of supply by itself is an inadequate approach to water sustainability. As mentioned, Southwestern aquifers are being depleted faster than they are replenished, and so drilling more wells is not sustainable. Desalinization of water and importing water from other watersheds for the Colorado Basin are either expensive and inefficient or of doubtful political feasibility.

113. Western Governors' Association, *Water Transfers in the West*, p. 7. Elsewhere (p. 18), this report calls water transfers "a critical tool for water allocation in the future."

114. Western Governors' Association, *Water Transfers in the West*, p. 9. Transfers within the western states have risen from slightly above 50 per year in 1988 to about 325 in 2008. The annual flows of such transfer have risen from about 550,000 acre feet in 1988 to over 2.5 MAF in 1991, 1994, 2000, and 2005 before declining to about 120,000 acre feet in 2008. Fluctuations appear partially related to drought conditions. In the Southwestern states, the number of water transfers between 1988 and 2009 are as follows: Texas — 336; New Mexico — 138; Colorado — 1,977; Wyoming — 65; Utah — 79; Nevada — 604; and California — 638. This totals 3,837 intra-state water transfers in the Southwest of 27.95 MAF of water between 1988 and 2009. Almost half of the water was transferred inside California (p. 14).

these changes may increase litigation.[115] Rather than stretching limited administrative flexibility to the breaking point, Sax argues that the water law needs to be significantly more flexible and responsive to extended drought through reductions to water users' permit amounts on a percentage basis, which would be less disruptive to users and spread burdens of reduced water availability more equitably. His other recommendations include incentives for efficient use, flexible water permits allowing for reductions in emergencies or water use on an "interruptible basis," employing voluntary abandonment or involuntary forfeitures of water rights, markets for water sales and exchanges, and water banking, to deal with environmental emergencies.[116]

State prioritization of uses and users may also be called for. Reallocation of water uses is increasing already, favoring urban and commercial users over less efficient agricultural users.[117] But the access of the most marginal members of society to water is vulnerable to compromise, and must be considered and protected.[118] An example one hopes will be adopted by other states is the 2012 California law declaring "that every human being has the right to safe, clean, affordable, and accessible water adequate for human consumption, cooking, and sanitary purposes." It requires that "all relevant state agencies shall consider this state policy when revising, adopting, or establishing policies, regulations, and grant criteria when those policies, regulations, and criteria are pertinent to the uses of water."[119]

115. Kenney et al., "Impact of Earlier Spring Snowmelt," p. 12.

116. Sax, "Our Precious Water Resources," pp. 1-13.

117. Sax, "The Limits of Private Rights in Public Waters," p. 483.

118. Gudorf, "Water Privatization in Christianity and Islam," pp. 33-34. For example, in approving a comprehensive settlement of Native American and other water claims to the Gila River System, the Arizona Supreme Court held that all tribes in Arizona have a right to water under Arizona law that is not tied to irrigable acres, as stipulated in *Arizona v. California* for the federal government. (This is the assessment of a report to the Navajo Nation regarding a proposed settlement of Northeastern Arizona Indian water rights claims.) "Proposed Navajo Nation Council Resolution: An Action Relating to Resources and Intergovernmental Relations; Approving the Proposed Northeastern Arizona Indian Water Rights Settlement . . ." (2010), p. 2. Found at: http://eagle51.fatcow.com/docs/20100716settlement agreement.pdf, accessed October 11, 2013. The report was interpreting the Arizona Supreme Court's ruling, *In re: The General Adjudication of All Rights to Use Water in the Gila River System and Source*, 35 P.3d 68, 76 (Ariz. 2001), accessed August 7, 2014, found at: http://www.narf.org/nill/bulletins/state/documents/wateradjudication.pdf. Appropriations of water based on the number of irrigable acres may be insufficient. Authorities ought not to assume that the economies and water allocations of Native American reservations should be based on agricultural acreage alone.

119. State of California, "An Act to Add Section 106.3 to the Water Code, Relating to

Sustainability

To help people protect their property, further their interests, and serve their neighbors,[120] the use of water should be sustainable for the foreseeable future; this is the principle of sustainability. From a Christian perspective, ethicist Christine Gudorf argues, "decisions [about water] must neither sacrifice just access for sustainability nor sacrifice sustainability for just access," particularly for poor and marginalized people.[121]

Sustained and severe water shortage from climate change will put considerable stress upon interstate river compacts and their intermediaries, which will be unable to deliver contracted amounts of water to their end users.[122] Changing current practices will likely prove less disruptive than failing to adopt more sustainable policies and practices for water storage and distribution that reduce seepage and evaporation, thus conserving water supplies. Water users can also be given incentives to adopt sustainable water practices or install more efficient equipment.

Flexibility of water laws and their administration by interstate river compacts can enhance the sustainability of water supplies and their use. The current inflexible provisions of existing compacts may, however, create a major procedural and political problem. Litigation over water apportionments may increase if compact policies, regulations, and practices do not change to address the challenges of climate change.[123] How might compact policies, regulations, and practices be changed to meet the challenge? The Colorado River Governance Initiative rejects renegotiating the Colorado River Compact as politically unfeasible. It suggests three possible "pathways" forward for the Compact: clarify and enforce existing governance rules, consider new interstate arrangements, and augment river flow from additional sources. The Initiative also suggests both establishing a series of substantive objectives for addressing future challenges for managing the river's water supply and considering which pathway may be most likely to

---

Water," accessed July 19, 2014, available from http://www.leginfo.ca.gov/pub/11-12/bill/asm/ab_0651-0700/ab_685_bill_20120925_chaptered.pdf.

120. Martin Luther, "The Ten Commandments" (explanation of the Seventh Commandment), *The Large Catechism*, p. 417.

121. Gudorf, "Water Privatization in Christianity and Islam," p. 35.

122. For example, deliveries of water from the Colorado River at current levels likely will not be sustainable as climate change intensifies. Cayan et al., "Future Dryness in the Southwest U.S.," p. 21275.

123. Kenney et al., "Impact of Earlier Spring Snowmelt," p. 12.

achieve them.[124] The first two pathways are consistent with Sax's favoring of flexible water laws and administration and the examples of flexibility he suggests.[125]

The 68 percent population growth projected for the region by 2050, however, is a wild card that threatens to undermine all efforts to achieve sustainability in water use in the Southwest. Public policies to increase the efficiency and sustainability of water use will be important tools to cope with the two challenges of climate change and population growth. Zoning policies, building codes, and landscaping regulations will be particularly important, as higher-density development is a more efficient and sustainable way to deliver and use water than lower-density development that tends to be favored by residential real estate developers.[126] Policies to reuse as much water as possible can also enhance sustainability of water use.

Authorities could adopt policies to encourage patterns and practices of water use that can be sustained over significant periods of time, that ensure and protect people's access to water — especially for those most vulnerable — and that provide for sufficient and sustainable amounts of water needed for the coming drier natural environment. Among the key elements of a sustainable water policy are "conservation of existing supplies, reallocation through marketing, and protection of instream flows to protect natural systems."[127]

The principle of sustainability requires that the effects on the natural environment and communities from which water is transferred by sale need to be addressed. Sax argues that there is currently no legal doctrine to deal with such issues. But he thinks ways could be developed to mitigate the effects of permissible transfers on those communities, especially poorer communities

124. Colorado River Governance Initiative, "Rethinking the Future of the Colorado River: Interim Report," pp. 2, 11, and 26.

125. Sax, "Our Precious Water Resources," pp. 2-6.

126. See deBuys, *A Great Aridness*, pp. 174-203, for a discussion of these issues in Arizona.

127. Sax, "The Constitution, Property Rights, and the Future of Water Law," p. 281. Some of these steps could conceivably be taken to partially set in motion the implementation plans of the 2012 Colorado River Basin Water Demand and Supply Study. See Bureau of Reclamation, *Colorado River Basin Water*, SR-41–SR-49, SR-52–SR-56, SR-74, and SR-77–SR-82; U.S. Department of the Interior, Bureau of Reclamation, "Moving Forward to Address the Challenges Identified in the Colorado River Basin Water Supply and Demand Study" (Washington, DC: Bureau of Reclamation, June, 2013), found at: http://www.usbr.gov/lc/region/programs/crbstudy/MovingForward/FactSheet_MovingForward.pdf, accessed April 29, 2014.

least able to adapt.[128] Rasmussen and Peppard both object to the mere com-modification of water regardless of other considerations in the current trans-formational economy.[129] Sax contends, however, that if water is first used for needs of the natural environment as a transition toward a natural economy requires, he sees "no reason to inhibit, and every reason to allow, ordinary economic activity among water users, such as sales and exchanges of use rights."[130] A healthy environment can, among other things, contribute to sustainability by retaining more water on the land. There may also be reallo-cation of water among various uses in the future through achieving various efficiencies and transfers.[131] Protection of natural systems in combination with certain transfers and reallocation of uses, therefore, can contribute to increased sustainability of water use.

Participation

"Participation," for theologian Per Anderson, "means that all living things exist within communal relations created by God and that the interests of the living should be heard and taken into consideration when decisions are made." To assure that there is water sufficient both for the present and the foreseeable future, all people, including the vulnerable and marginalized, should have a voice in deliberations about policies and practices on how water is obtained, stored, priced, delivered, and disposed of, who has ac-cess to it, and to what uses it is put. This is the principle of participation. Participation is concerned to encourage "free inclusive discourse" and seeks to empower all and to remove barriers to active involvement in decision-making about things in which people are vitally interested.[132] From Luther's perspective, one way I can help my neighbors to have sufficient, sustainable access to water is to ensure their participation in the community's policy-making and decisions about its water supply.

Decision-making about water has been largely nonparticipatory in most of the situations out of which the legal cases discussed above have

128. Sax, "Understanding Transfers: Community Rights and the Privatization of Water," pp. 33 and 36-38.

129. Rasmussen, *Earth-honoring Faith*, pp. 263-73, and Peppard, *Just Water*, pp. 36-51.

130. Sax, "Our Precious Water Resources," p. 13.

131. Sax, "Our Precious Water Resources," p. 11.

132. Anderson, "Agriculture, Food and Responsible Biotechnology," pp. 177-78.

arisen. Average water users were not invited to take part.[133] The Bureau of Reclamation claims to have adopted a more participatory approach to the Colorado River Basin Water Supply and Demand Study and its follow-up implementation efforts. Study participation, however, was disappointingly limited to the addition of county, water district, and municipal officials and professionals, and the public is invited to respond to implementation plans only on its website after implementation proposals are made.

Instead, public authorities and citizen groups at both federal and state levels can work together to assure widespread public participation so that the perspectives, opinions, and desires of the public — including the marginalized and most vulnerable — inform policies and plans. Public participation will also ensure public support for the hard decisions Southwestern states face about current and future water policy. But much depends upon when and where the participation of such groups is allowed in the planning and administrative processes.[134] In some states, more participatory processes in water planning have been used, including in Colorado's Statewide Water Resources Initiative.[135] If more participation from all groups and classes in

133. Perhaps the closest that any of the organizations involved in these cases comes to wide participation is in the decision-making of the Elephant Butte and El Paso No. 1 irrigation districts. One indication of how restricted water policy discussions in New Mexico are to policy or technical experts and public officials, for example, without much participation from the general public, is the annual water conference of the New Mexico Water Resources Research Institute. A perspective of women on water has been heard only once, and its middle-class white perspective was not representative of Latinas, Native American women, or even poor white women. Fern Lyon, "Women's Interest in Water Problems," *Water for New Mexico to the Year 2000 and 2060: Thirteenth Annual New Mexico Water Conference Proceedings* (Las Cruces: Western Water Resources Research Institute, New Mexico State University, 1968), pp. 82-89. Only three times in those fifty-five years were Native Americans or their representatives invited to make a presentation.

134. See Bureau of Reclamation, *Colorado River Basin Water Supply and Demand Study*, pp. SR-10–SR-12; Appendix 4: Study Participants found at: http://www.usbr.gov/lc/region /programs/crbstudy/finalreport/Study%20Report/StudyReport_Appendix4_FINAL.pdf, accessed May 16, 2014; Appendix 5: Public Involvement Plan, found at: http://www.usbr .gov/lc/region/programs/crbstudy/finalreport/Study%20Report/StudyReport_Appendix5 _FINAL.pdf, accessed May 16, 2014; and Bureau of Reclamation, "Moving Forward to Address the Challenges," pp. 1-4.

135. Kathleen A. Miller, "Climate Change and Water in the West: Complexities, Uncertainties and Strategies for Adaptation," *Journal of Land, Resources, and Environmental Law* 27, no. 1 (2007): 95. For the Colorado example, see Statewide Water Supply Initiative, 2010, *Colorado's Water Supply Future*, Appendix A: "Roundtable Members" (Denver: Colorado Water Conservation Board, Department of Natural Resources, January 2010). Avail-

society is achieved in a carefully structured and led process, there is a better chance that the public can deliberate and decide about access and rights to water in a way that enhances human solidarity where access to sufficient water on a sustainable basis is concerned.[136]

Solidarity

People who depend upon and use the same water sources should see and treat themselves as interdependent members of the same community, so that none are excluded from key decisions about water policies and practices. This is the principle of solidarity.[137] Luther assumes the moral requirement of solidarity in explaining the commandment about theft. Helping our neighbors "improve and protect their property and means of making a living" presumes relationships of mutuality and solidarity that entail concern and action on behalf of the neighbor. The use of the term "neighbor" itself implies some level of communal solidarity, although the parable of the Good Samaritan (Luke 10:29-37) strongly suggests that such solidarity also transcends the bonds of local communities, common ethnicity, or nationality.

The principle of solidarity suggests that our access to water can hold or bring us together in mutuality and community, especially where sharing the resource or making decisions about its use is concerned. Solidarity is more than the cooperation of people with different interests to achieve a measure of personal or social advantage or utility, exemplified by interstate compacts. Treating water legally as a public entitlement that is available to all of the public — including the poor, Hispanics, African Americans, Native Americans, and new immigrants, whom water rights can help — is also important.[138] Their access to clean water, however, can easily be ignored or forcefully suppressed when it is politically expedient to do so, as the California water wars of the 1920s demonstrate.[139] The wrenching changes in

_____

able at http://cwcb.state.co.us/water-management/water-supply-planning/Documents/SWSI2010/Appendix%20A_Basin%20Roundtable%20Members.pdf.

136. On the importance of well-structured and -led participatory processes, see Baogang He, "Deliberative Culture and Politics: The Persistence of Authoritarian Deliberation in China," *Political Theory* 42, no. 1 (2014): 63 and 74.

137. Anderson, "Agriculture, Food and Responsible Technology," p. 181.

138. Sax, "Takings, Property & Public Rights," *Yale Law Journal* 81 (1971): 155-59, 160-64.

139. The City of Los Angeles ignored the residents of the Owens Valley in the 1920s

access to water that are likely to come may not secure that access for the marginalized unless there is a public recognition of solidarity between them and people in more privileged positions.

Equity

Parts of the previous analysis strain toward equity in access and rights to water.[140] Luther's explanation of the commandment about theft and possessions calling on Christians to refrain taking what is our neighbors' and to help neighbors protect and improve what is theirs is a call for equity without using the term. In Psalm 82, God admonishes the rulers of earth to "[g]ive justice to the weak and the orphan; maintain the right of the lowly and the destitute" (82:3, NRSV). Simpson notes that "Luther tethered power tightly to distributive justice for the common good and especially for the well-being of the most vulnerable among us and for all of us in our vulnerability."[141] This applies as much to water as to anything else that is necessary to our well-being. Yet, discerning equity in access to water is not simple. We may view the issue of equity in water as having two interrelated aspects: equity in access to water among the people of the Southwest, on the one hand, and equity between different broad categories of the use of water, on the other. The relation between these two aspects of water equity lies in the fact that it is human beings who use water in these different ways. Although technology can help increase the equitability of rights to water, it cannot bear the full weight of assuring equity, which is a matter of justice and human judgment.

Transformational economies in the Southwest have disproportionately

---

during a severe drought when Los Angeles refused to divert some Owens River water, to which the city had purchased rights, in order to relieve the plight of local residents who otherwise lacked access to sufficient water. Los Angeles' callousness provoked a militant and violent response from valley residents known as the California Water Wars. See William Kahrl, *Water and Power: The Conflict of Los Angeles Water Supply in the Owens Valley* (Berkeley and Los Angeles: University of California Press, 1982).

140. The need to consider equity in the context of climate change was forcefully argued by Cynthia D. Moe-Lobeda in her paper, "Climate Change as Climate Debt: Forging a Just Future," presented to the 56th Annual Meeting of the Society of Christian Ethics, January 9, 2015, Chicago, Illinois.

141. Gary M. Simpson, "Retrieving Martin Luther's Critical Public Theology of Political Authority for Global Civil Society Today," in *Theological Practices That Matter,* ed. Karen L. Bloomquist, Theology in the Life of the Church, vol. 5 (Minneapolis: Lutheran University Press under the auspices of the Lutheran World Federation, 2009), p. 166.

disadvantaged some people, such as Native Americans, Latinos, and the poor, and favored others such as middle-class European Americans. The effect of climate change on the availability of water will put considerable pressure on equity in sufficient, sustainable access to water in the future. Those low on seniority lists of water rights are likely to have their access to water curtailed significantly or completely, regardless of their needs for it to support their lives and livelihoods, unless some other criteria or priorities are used. California's recognition of the right to water sufficient for personal and household needs for all its citizens points the way to one dimension of equity in rights to water. Other measures to assure or enhance equity in the rights to water, however, may also be needed, such as regulations about water use or pricing water to encourage its efficient use or conservation, or as a measure of its value in economic production.

Currently, agriculture uses 70 percent of fresh water worldwide, industry uses 22 percent, and domestic uses take up 8 percent.[142] State prioritization of uses and users may sometimes be called for. During the recent drought, the State of California diverted some water intended for agricultural use to urban users. How much water *should* go to various economic uses or those who engage in those activities? Particularly intensive agricultural or industrial uses of water could perhaps be discouraged through water pricing or taxation. Incentives to switch from one product or process to others might also help achieve some conception of equity among users of water rights.

Finally, if equity includes the sharing of water between human beings and their communities, on the one hand, and the rest of the environment, on the other hand, considerable thought will need to be given to what constitutes equity in the shares of water given to humanity and other aspects of the Southwestern environment. As noted above, requirements of the environment as the climate changes are continually changing and difficult to ascertain. But the need for such assessment and appropriate allocation for environmental requirements for water remains.

Conclusion

The institution of interstate river compacts and the system of water rights based on seniority are relatively inflexible and ill-suited to adapt to climate

---

142. Peppard, *Just Water,* p. 23.

change. But, as Rasmussen says, "Change cannot be dialed back."[143] The environment of the Southwest, its communities, and its people have all been put at risk by the normal workings of the transformational economy, even as its future supply of water is in doubt and the water rights of its people are of uncertain effectiveness and value in the future. There may not be as much water as our unrealistically extravagant desires wish for. Southwesterners may have a real challenge fashioning both their individual and corporate lives together in ways that are viable, sustainable, and equitable. Not everyone who has a water right today will necessarily have the same water right in the future. Sustainable access to sufficient water for all will likely come to mean something much different to us than it means now, and our expectations may change significantly.

What does this mean for what Sittler called God's created grace? The harm, change, and risk climate change brings does not mean that God's ordinary or created grace ends. Luther emphasizes that "God, through His Word, extends His activity from the beginning of the world to its end." "He works not only by preserving His creation but also by changing and renewing His creation."[144] Reflecting upon God's care for the physical needs of the people of Israel in the desert for food and water after the exodus from Egypt, Luther preached, "there must be a way where there is no way; and water, where there is no water; stones must become water."[145] A more flexible system of water rights and water administration grounded in a working understanding of the ecological nature of the Southwest's water and land resources might better help the region adapt to climate change and secure sufficient water on a sustainable basis for the future needs of the region. Should that happen, Christians might see it as the gift of God's creating work and created grace. God may act both through the mask of human beings and in other ways to sustain and renew the region. God is up to something, endeavoring to renew creation, partly through some of us and perhaps also apart from us. If we trust in God's created grace, there may be sufficient water to sustain humanity and the creation through long, hot, and arid times.

143. Larry Rasmussen, "Climate Change as a Perfect Moral Storm," *Journal of Lutheran Ethics* 14, no. 2 (February 2014): paragraph [28]. Available from: http://www.elca.org/JLE/Articles/41, accessed February 3, 2014.

144. Luther, *Lectures on Genesis, Chapters 1–5*, pp. 76, 77.

145. Martin Luther, "Sermon for the First Sunday in Lent" (1522), *Sermons of Martin Luther*, vol. 2, *Sermons on Gospel Texts for Epiphany, Lent, and Easter*, ed. and trans. Nicholas Lenker (Grand Rapids: Baker, 1983), p. 131. The text for this sermon was Matthew 4:1-11.

PART III

Lutheran Reflections on the Law of Human Dignity and Human Need

CHAPTER 6

A Lutheran Feminist Critique of American Child Protection Laws: Sins of Sexual Nature

Kirsi Stjerna

One particularly insidious form of exploitation of human beings is trafficking of minors. Out of four million persons trafficked each year, about two million are children aged five to fifteen. Commercial sexual exploitation or sex trafficking, best characterized as a form of slavery,[1] constitutes a growing part of the trafficking of minors on the global scene.

Sex trafficking is a crime from which no neighborhood is safe: it victimizes children globally, as well as locally. Tens of thousands of children are transported by force in and out of the United States; and hundreds of thousands of children are subjected to sex servitude that involves various forms of abuse, torture, molestation, oppression, and terror.[2] Millions of children die a slow death in their daily hells, created by their abusers and exploiters to meet the increasing international market for "sex for sale."[3] International travel and the Internet have only expanded opportunities for criminal sexual

1. The *Victims of Trafficking and Violence Protection Act of 2000* defines commercial sexual exploitation as "the recruitment, harboring, transportation, provision or obtaining of a person for the purposes of a commercial sex act," which is "any sex act on account of which anything of value is given to or received by any person." Children are victims of a particularly severe form of trafficking, "in which a commercial sex act is induced by force, fraud or coercion, or in which the person induced to perform such an act has not attained 18 years of age." 22 U.S.C. §7102 (3) (8), (9) (2000). National Center for Missing and Exploited Children Fact Sheet, http://www.missingkids.com/en_US/documents/CCSE_Fact_Sheet .pdf (visited June 25, 2014).

2. See "Domestic Violence & Sex Trafficking," Sanctuary for Families website, http:// www.sanctuaryforfamilies.org/index.php?option=com_content&task=view&id=56& Itemid+85 (visited March 14, 2014).

3. "Domestic Violence & Sex Trafficking," Sanctuary for Families website.

engagement with children, and they facilitate manifold ways of making profit at the expense of children.

Much of the general public is either ignorant of these facts or simply does not care; but it is also true that most state and national laws are inadequate to prevent trafficking. In fact, in many ways they actually enable the ongoing sexual exploitation of children. Even as late as 2010, the state of Ohio, which is no stranger to violent crime against minors, did not consider trafficking a person a crime. Protected Innocence Initiative research has demonstrated that at least in 2011, five states — Maine, Massachusetts, Virginia, West Virginia, Wyoming — had no criminal laws prohibiting human trafficking, not to mention special provisions regarding child victims.

Initiatives against sex trafficking are in motion in many states and local governments, while the federal government is currently developing laws that more efficiently target domestic trafficking of minors. The first state law that directly prohibits human trafficking was passed in Washington State in 2003. In 2007, New York made sex trafficking a crime and particularly targeted the methods most commonly used by the exploiters to enslave, conceal, and use children for gain.[4] Sex trafficking is now a Class B Felony with a potential sentence of five to twenty-five years' imprisonment in New York.

However, significant inconsistencies in state trafficking laws — including continued misidentification of sex trafficking victims as prostitution criminals in the justice system, insufficient penalties, and ambiguity in reporting mechanisms — stand in the way of proper protection of children.[5] These statutes carry over the same weaknesses as modern rape and sexual assault laws — e.g., regarding the age through which someone should be considered a "minor" in criminal prosecutions for so-called "statutory" rape, presumed to be consensual; the criteria for sufficient "use of force" and "nonconsent"

---

4. The National Center for Missing and Exploited Children notes that patterns for trapping children are well established: "Pimps and traffickers target vulnerable children and lure them into prostitution and other forms of sexual exploitation using psychological manipulation, drugs, and/or violence. . . . Often traffickers/pimps will create a seemingly loving and caring relationship with their victim in order to establish trust and allegiance. This manipulative relationship tries to ensure the youth will remain loyal to the exploiter even in the face of severe victimization. These relationships may begin online before progressing to a real-life encounter." National Center for Missing and Exploited Children, "Commercial Sexual Exploitation of Children: A Fact Sheet," p. 1, found at: http://www.missingkids.com/en_US/documents/CCSE_Fact_Sheet.pdf.

5. For a review and comparison of state laws on human trafficking, see the Polaris Project's "2014 State Ratings on Human Trafficking Laws," at: http://www.polarisproject.org/what-we-do/policy-advocacy/national-policy/state-ratings-on-human-trafficking-laws.

necessary to prosecute a rape charge; and the lack of appropriate severity and forms of punishment in proportion to these sex crimes. Behind these disagreements on what constitutes a crime and what should be the proper punishment for it stand fundamental social disagreements and confusion about the nature of sex/gender, sexuality, women's rights, and childhood and children's rights, on the one hand, and the effectiveness of different legal and rehabilitative responses and use of force, on the other. Last but not least, money and profit are factors at all levels.

In this chapter, I will discuss Luther's vision of children as a gift from God and his theological claim that society shares "parental" responsibility with mothers and fathers to take care of all children, for the benefit of the children themselves and society at large. I will focus on Luther's treatment of the fifth commandment as a basis for Lutheran approaches to address sex crimes against children. This theology permits naming sex trafficking in children as a sin, theologically speaking, and as a human rights violation and a grave legal transgression against another person that calls for diligent adjustments in current laws at local, state, and federal levels.

As a Lutheran theologian and a feminist, and on the basis of Lutheran understanding of Christian freedom and equality, and the concept of Christian vocation *coram hominibus* (i.e., before humanity), I will argue that some current initiatives for legislative reforms promise better protection of children than others. These include the Safe Harbor Laws of 2008 passed in New York and San Francisco, and the Trafficking Victims Protection and Justice Act being proposed in New York. The nonprofit Polaris Project that was founded to end human trafficking has also played a key role in legislative reform.

Kissing Children with Holy Respect, according to Luther

Quoting St. Cyprian, the sixteenth-century reformer Martin Luther wrote: "One should kiss the newborn infant, even before it is baptized, in honor of the hands of God here engaged in a brand new deed." With his comment that "God makes children," Luther reminds his readers that children are a gift from God,[6] not given to us for our pleasure and enjoyment, but, rather

6. Martin Luther, "The Estate of Marriage," *Luther's Works*, vol. 45, *The Christian in Society II*, ed. and trans. Walther I. Brandt (Philadelphia: Fortress Press, 1962), pp. 13-15, 17-49; WA 10/2:275-304. "God makes children," *Luther's Works*, vol. 45, p. 48; see the treatise

meant for our "salvation" and for the glory of God.[7] This is the starting point, for Luther, for how to treat, relate to, and consider children: with a significant amount of the holy fear of God.

Martin Luther, a monk turned reformer and a married man with children, knew children as a gift both instinctively and from his reading of scripture and observations on life, before he ever held his own newborns in his arms, or before he witnessed his wife Katharina nursing an infant. With all his erudition and experience, Luther confidently argued, preached, and taught that parenthood was a holy calling par excellence.[8] Caring for children, he considered, was worth serious investment at home, at church, and in society.

Luther began his public reflections on children when he was addressing the benefits and the calling of marriage in the context of arguing for the right and "need" for priests to marry, though the Catholic Church forbade them from doing so.[9] To have and to raise children was a primary reason to marry in his opinion; speaking as a medieval man for those who married, he promised: "They can do no better work and do nothing more valuable either for God, for Christendom, for all the world, for themselves, and for their children than to bring up their children well."[10] His words from that 1519 sermon — written while he was still an unmarried, childless man — indicate the complexity of his views about the heavenly responsibility of parenthood, a responsibility placed on all Christians which must be carried out for the well-being of the whole of Christendom. Far from a marginal issue, children were at the center of his attention. He wrote, "If we want to help

---

in WA 10/2:275-304. WA references from *D. Martin Luthers Werke: Kritische Gesamtausgabe* (Weimar: Bohlau, 1883-).

7. Luther, "The Estate of Marriage," p. 46; see the treatise in WA 10/2:275-304.

8. Luther said about paternal and maternal duties, "A wife too should regard her duties in the same light, as she suckles the child, rocks and bathes it, and cares for it in other ways; and as she busies herself with other duties and renders help and obedience to her husband. These are truly golden and noble works." Likewise, when a father washes diapers, he may be ridiculed by some as an effeminate fool, but "God, with all his angels and creatures, is smiling — not because the father is washing diapers, but because he is doing so in Christian faith." Luther, "The Estate of Marriage," p. 40; see the treatise in WA 10/2:275-304; see also Martin Luther, "A Sermon on the Estate of Marriage" (1519), in *Luther's Works,* vol. 44, *The Christian in Society I,* ed. and trans. James Atkinson (Philadelphia: Fortress Press, 1966), p. 12; treatise in WA 2:166-71.

9. A recent treatment on this, in light of contemporary debates on gay and lesbian persons' right to marry, is Kirsi Stjerna, "On Marriage, with Luther, for Gay and Straight," *Seminary Ridge Review* 16, no. 2 (April 2014): 64-85.

10. Luther, "A Sermon on the Estate of Marriage," pp. 7-14; 12.

Christendom, we most certainly have to start with the children."[11] Children are "nothing else but an eternal treasure from God."[12]

Luther reminded his listeners and readers that all children's health — in body and soul — was entrusted to the parents. But by parents, he meant not only fathers and mothers in charge at home but also all citizens, and particularly those in positions of authority in the society such as the lawmakers and those who enforce the law. In this wider sense of parenting, God's two kingdoms described by Luther intertwine in particular ways: the orders of society are responsible to ensure that children are protected, and to restore children to God "from whom [parents] received them to take care of them" in the first place.[13]

When he discussed caring for children, Luther meant concrete responsibilities, such as supplying basic needs like food and shelter and education. Thus, for example, the early reformers were active in creating and funding Common Chests to help orphans and others in need. In taking pioneering steps to establish community schools for boys and girls, Luther demonstrated what the gospel requires and what it prompts Christians to do *coram hominibus* for the sake of children. With his vision of the vital importance of all children's education in preparing them for their duties in society, he used all of the available media to get his message across, to educate, and — importantly — to implement law and order that would ensure that this vision would be realized.[14]

How Luther understood Protestant educational reforms is noteworthy in terms of contemporary discourse, including on the question of sex trafficking: first, he stressed the importance of education of all people, particularly the role of education in promoting values and reconsideration of "right and wrong." He believed that such education would instill moral accountability and awaken people's conscience. Second, Luther was not only a vital participant, but also a leader, in legislative initiatives and social resource allocation as ways to enforce positive change. Luther understood the important role of money in this endeavor: in the task of caring for children, he wrote,

11. For our modern Lutheran theological discussions addressing secular law for the greater protection of children, we need to replace the word "Christendom" in Luther's quotation with "the world" since we are addressing this problem in a religiously and culturally pluralistic situation.

12. Luther, "A Sermon on the Estate of Marriage," p. 13.

13. Luther, "A Sermon on the Estate of Marriage," p. 13.

14. See, for example, Martin Luther, "To the Councilmen in All Cities in Germany That They Establish and Maintain Christian Schools," in *Luther's Works*, vol. 45, pp. 347-78.

we should not spare ourselves, our money or expense, nor our trouble or effort, because the children are the altar, the vigil, the mass, the true benefit.[15]

On Basic Laws and Responsibility with Luther: Interpreting the Fifth Commandment as Applied to Trafficking of Children

In one of his most significant and still widely used texts, the *Large Catechism* of 1529, Luther lays out the ground rules for how we should live in this world as Christians, how we must express, fortify, and apply our faith in this life, and how we can channel that faith through all aspects of life. In this powerful pedagogical and spiritual treatise, Luther's explanation of the Ten Commandments is a foundational text for reflection on Lutheran responses to legislation and law reform.

In the case of sins against children, such as sex trafficking, Luther's explanation of the fifth commandment resonates as particularly poignant for the contemporary discussion. In his explanation of the ancient and universally understood law "you shall not kill," Luther not only expanded the meaning of the word "kill" but also broadened the scope of human accountability to include not only those who actively take a life but also those who observe, witness, enable, benefit, stand passively by or look away from such violence, or who do not seek to prevent such a crime in all its manifestations.

First, we can imagine what Luther would say if he knew of the prevalence of crimes against children who are neglected, abused, stolen, used, raped, and killed. Luther's words about the fifth commandment resonate with the trafficking "cesspools" in our society: "But inasmuch as there is such a shameless mess and cesspool of all sorts of immorality and indecency among us, this commandment is also directed against every form of unchastity, no matter what it is called . . . every kind of cause, provocation, and means, so that your heart, your lips, and your entire body may be chaste and afford no occasion, aid, or encouragement to unchastity."[16] He also remarked, "Let all people know, then, that it is their duty, on pain of God's displeasure, not to harm their neighbors, to take advantage of them, or to defraud them by any faithless or underhanded business transaction."[17] It is

---

15. Luther, "Sermon on the Estate of Marriage," p. 14.

16. Martin Luther, *The Large Catechism,* in *The Book of Concord: The Confessions of the Evangelical Lutheran Church,* ed. Robert Kolb and Timothy J. Wengert, trans. Charles Arand and others (Minneapolis: Fortress Press, 2000), 414:202-3.

17. Luther, *Large Catechism,* 417:233.

safe to assume that he would use the power of the word to urge his fellow citizens to "guard against harming our neighbor in any way."[18]

Applied to crimes in child trafficking, with Luther we expand the verdict of "guilty" to those not acting to prevent or protect against such crimes (e.g., by way of reporting), and those benefiting financially from trafficking of persons, and those paying for sexual favors from persons held prisoner by traffickers, as well as all who have any knowledge of such crimes and fail to act. "For although you have not actually committed all these crimes, as far as you are concerned, you have nevertheless permitted your neighbors to languish and perish in their misfortune. It is just as if I saw someone who was struggling in deep water or someone who had fallen into a fire and I could stretch out my hand to pull him out and save him, and yet I did not do so. How would I appear before all the world except as a murderer and a scoundrel?"[19] He also wrote "God's commandment is violated not only when we do evil, but also when we have the opportunity to do good to our neighbors and to prevent, protect, and save them from suffering bodily harm or injury, but fail to do so."[20]

Luther's words resonate strongly in light of both current scandals and initiatives for law reforms as well. For example, as a society, we have had to revisit the issue of whose responsibility it is to report crimes against children and who is culpable by witnessing and not reporting or responding to suspected child abuse in the aftermath of the Penn State child abuse scandal that broke in 2011.[21] After longtime Penn State football coach Jerry Sandusky was charged with abuse of at least eight boys without any witnesses or university authorities reporting his crimes to the police, states have recognized the urgency of revising their legislation on reporting suspected or known child abuse crimes to better comport with the requirements of the federal Clery Act (20 USC §1092[f]) (promulgated in 1990), which requires that schools gather and report information on suspected crimes on campus.[22]

18. Luther, *Large Catechism,* 413:200.

19. Luther, *Large Catechism,* 412:192.

20. Luther, *Large Catechism,* 412:189; *Die Bekenntnisschriften der evangelisch-lutherischen Kirche,* 6. Hrsg (Göttingen: Vandenhoeck & Ruprecht, 1967), pp. 541-733. On the Fifth Commandment, see pp. 605-10.

21. See Tom Watkins, "Child-protection Laws under Scrutiny in Wake of Scandals," CNN.com. http://www.cnn.com/2011/11/17/Pennsylvania-sandusky-case/ (visited February 28, 2014) (noting the inconsistency of the legal system and the call of the group Stop It Now! for fundamental change).

22. Watkins, "Child-protection Laws under Scrutiny in Wake of Scandals," p. 1 (quot-

Luther's explanation of the fifth commandment also resonates with on-going efforts to redirect funds to provide support for child victims and pro-vide resources and mechanisms to stop the cycle of victimization. Luther's words have an amplified meaning in light of what we know the problems are and where reforms are needed: "Therefore, God rightly calls all persons murderers who do not offer counsel or assistance to those in need and peril of body and life."[23] Even in the sixteenth century, Luther was aware of the need for a systemic response in the face of suffering, and he lobbied actively for those in positions of authority to take action when he reminded his fellow citizens that they were called to defend, protect, and rescue their neighbors whether they themselves were in danger or need or not.[24] "Therefore parents and governmental authorities have the duty of supervising the youth that they will be brought up with decency and respectability."[25]

Thus, with Luther, we can target every single person's failure to proac-tively take action to prevent crimes from happening; every single person's failure to report crimes he or she may witness or suspect are occurring; and our willingness to accept or approve of inadequate legislation that fails to protect little ones and to prosecute and punish with sufficiently tough measures those who are guilty in any stage of these trafficking crimes. In the spirit of Luther, we could say that all persons, communities, churches, societies, and legal systems that fail to prevent crimes against children share in the guilt of the sins that hurt children, or even that every member in the society is as guilty as the rapist, murderer, abuser, or kidnapper of a child. That is the unpleasant news.

The good news is that we have many options to instigate reforms Lu-theran theology calls for. Luther writes with confidence, "Therefore it is God's real intention that we should allow no one to suffer harm but show every kindness and love."[26] In contemporary terms, Luther's vision instills accountability and responsibility to all parties, all structures, all offices, and all citizens, in public and in private. His vision draws children and children's issues to the center, offering seeds for critique of systems not considering children's issues as a priority in every sense of the word, including not allo-

---

ing Lisa Fones, author of *Child Abuse and Culture — Working with Diverse Families,* recom-mending changes in reporting requirements).

23. Luther, *Large Catechism,* 412:191.
24. Luther, *Large Catechism,* 414:203.
25. Luther, *Large Catechism,* 415:218.
26. Luther, *Large Catechism,* 412:193. "Whenever you fail to do this," however, "you are just as guilty as the culprit who commits the act." *Large Catechism,* 414:204-5.

cating funds and resources appropriately. Luther had a psychologically and socially astute theological conviction to share: What we do with and for our children is what will come to bless us, or haunt us, in the hour of our death. The fate and well-being of children is, then, for Luther not a marginal issue but a central issue embedded in the Ten Commandments, and a theological concern with ramifications of our failures in this life and beyond.[27]

Knowing what we know of Luther's concern for the children, it would seem that Lutherans have a solid theological and historical foundation from which to act and engage in decision-making on child sex trafficking, and, importantly, offer theological-anthropological principles that can shape decision-making. Lutheran identity requires staying engaged and taking leadership in the matters of reform including, characteristically to Lutheran tradition, educating citizens broadly on matters at stake, and finding ways for both church and society to build mechanisms that support the smallest of citizens, and thus build for the future. Calling sexual crimes against children "sins" is a way to name them as something that is not part of God's creation *coram Deo* (i.e., before God), and crimes that are unacceptable also *coram hominibus*.

Trafficking Sins against Children

Sexual exploitation and sex trafficking of children is an abominable human rights violation in legal and moral terms, and a sin in theological terms. It is not an "inevitable sin" as Lutheran theology describes original sin, which predisposes all human beings to falter and transgress against God and one another. Quite to the contrary: in the Lutheran understanding of the two kingdoms and *coram hominibus* doctrines, human laws are of instrumental importance exactly because of the reality of sin. They are not a matter of or means to salvation but a means for establishing good order in God's kingdom on earth. Socially speaking, child sex trafficking is also a grave legal transgression that calls for diligent adjustments in current laws from local to state and federal levels, as well as fundamental changes in the general population's attitudes toward children and the gender inculturation of girls and boys. Statistics shed light on the gravity of the problem, as does naming the crimes of exploitation as sins.[28]

---

27. Luther, "The Estate of Marriage," p. 46; see the treatise in WA 10/2:275-304.

28. According to the Polaris Project, "The commercial sexual exploitation of children refers generally to exploitation committed by any person, whether the pimp, the

The world is not a safe place for children — not safe in the suburbs, jungles, slums, or metropoli where children are abducted, shot, raped, drugged, pimped, molested, abused and neglected, and trafficked for sex. According to Sanctuary for Families:[29]

> Each year 4 million people are trafficked; 2 million girls between age 5 and 15 are brought into the sex industry (UN). Tens of thousands of these victims are smuggled into the U.S., and many exist under the radar — enslaved, and unseen by law enforcement or victim service agencies. The vast majority of trafficking victims, as many as 80%, are women and girls. Of these, the majority are trafficked for purposes of sexual exploitation. Women and girls trafficked for labor exploitation frequently encounter and endure sexual violence.[30]

In other words, as the Polaris Project puts it:

> Human trafficking is a form of modern-day slavery where people profit from the control and exploitation of others. Every year, human traffickers generate billions of dollars in profits by victimizing millions of people around the world, and here in the United States. Human trafficking is considered to be one of the fastest growing criminal industries in the world.[31]

The Polaris Project describes the way in which traffickers gain control over their victims:

> The dynamics of human trafficking mirror the dynamics of power and control that characterize domestic violence. . . . Amnesty International

purchaser of sex acts or some other knowing beneficiary of a child's commercial sex acts. Under federal law and some state laws, sex trafficking of a minor is defined as the recruiting, enticing, harboring, transporting, providing or obtaining of a minor knowing that the minor will be caused to engage in a commercial sex act." http://www.polarisproject.org/storage/documents/policy_documents/model%20laws/model%20safe%20harbor%20law%20overview%20final-1.pdf.

29. See "Who We Are," Sanctuary for Families Website, http://www.sanctuaryforfamilies.org/index.php?option=com_content&task=view&id=13&Itemid=42 (accessed February 2, 2014) (describing Sanctuary for Families' mission to advocate for victims of domestic and gender violence and sex trafficking).

30. "Who We Are," Sanctuary for Families Website (accessed February 2, 2014).

31. See "Human Trafficking," Polaris Project, http://www.polarisproject.org/human-trafficking/overview (accessed February 28, 2014).

defines these tactics as psychological torture. They include isolation of the victim; induced debility, producing exhaustion, weakness, or fatigue (e.g. sleep or food deprivation); threats of harm to the victim or her family and friends and other forms of threat; degradation, including humiliation, name-calling and insults, and denial of privacy or personal hygiene.

In addition, traffickers may use "forced drug or alcohol use" and restriction of movements. As a result of this "[p]sychological coercion, deception, and brainwashing," victims may see themselves as criminals, and may not seek help since they distrust outsiders because of their experiences "at the hands of their captors."[32]

A case in point is the infamous North American Super Bowl of 2014, which was preceded by a high-profile bust of a prostitution ring that rescued sixteen teenagers trafficked for prostitution and arrested forty-five pimps. In the Miami 2010 Super Bowl, the National Center for Missing and Exploited Children estimated that 10,000 women and children were trafficked; and in the Tampa Super Bowl of 2009, at least twenty-four children were trafficked into the city for sex, while Internet ads for child prostitution rose sharply before the game.[33]

> To understand the dynamics of human trafficking is to understand that events such as the Super Bowl could never not be breeding grounds for sexual exploitation. On the most basic level, any location that sees an exponential increase in large numbers of men travelling for entertainment will receive a proportional increase in those who purchase sex — studies conservatively indicate the number of men who purchase sex to be around 16% of the American population.[34]

Despite front-page stories that brought the ugly reality of trafficking home with the 2014 Super Bowl, almost immediately counter-reports began to belittle the significance of the bust, and the general public moved on to other news and commentary on the quarterbacks and running backs playing in the Super Bowl.[35] There were no nationwide protests, no banners

32. "Domestic Violence & Sex Trafficking," Sanctuary for Families website.
33. See Judy Harris Kluger, "The Super Bowl Could Never *Not* Be Breeding Grounds for Sexual Exploitation," http://www.huffingtonpost.com/hon-judy-harris-kluger/sex-trafficking-super-bowl_b_4713627.html (accessed February 28, 2014).
34. Kluger, "The Super Bowl," p. 1.
35. Kluger, "The Super Bowl," p. 1.

urging "No More Super Bowl" until "No More Slavery." Even if the press attention to this problem fluctuates, the statistics remind us of the ugly reality that demands legal action, on international, domestic, federal, and state levels.[36]

Reflections on Trends in State Legislation

Some states have taken proactive but widely varying approaches to the problem of sex trafficking, which I evaluate in this section. Leslie Klaassen has categorized the most common of these approaches as the "model structure," the "individualist approach," and the "structuralist approach." In the "model structure," which borrows from Department of Justice model legislation, trafficking is subsumed under a single definition, which makes charging crimes easier but does not recognize sex trafficking as a particularly egregious harm for sentencing purposes.[37] This approach also emphasizes prosecution over rehabilitation of victims.[38] Other states take the "individualist approach," which stresses autonomy and the individual's right to become part of the sex trade. This approach decriminalizes prostitution and related crimes, but may provide more services to those who are coerced into sex crimes.[39] Finally, some states take the "structuralist" approach influenced by feminist ideology, defining the sex trade as pervasively coercive because of women's social and economic inequality, and adopting blanket protections for both adult and juvenile victims of trafficking.[40]

From a Lutheran feminist perspective, laws that follow the structuralist approach best reflect the fundamental feminist critique of unjust power systems and hierarchy in the eyes of the law. This approach sheds light on the direct and indirect uses of force against women and children and the legal system's failures to punish these crimes appropriately. It also sheds light on

36. "Violent Crimes Against Children," About Us, FBI Website, http://www.fbi.gov/about-us/investigate/vc_majorthefts/cac/innocencelost (accessed February 28, 2014), noting the more than 1.9 million reports of suspected child abuse (1998-October 2013) and rescue of 34,000 children, conviction with lengthy sentences and property seizures of nearly 1,500 pimps, madams, and their associates who exploit children through prostitution.
37. Leslie Klaassen, "Breaking the Victimization Cycle: Domestic Minor Trafficking in Kansas," *Washburn Law Journal* 52 (2013): 595.
38. Klaassen, "Breaking the Victimization Cycle," p. 595.
39. Klaassen, "Breaking the Victimization Cycle," p. 596.
40. Klaassen, "Breaking the Victimization Cycle," p. 596.

the manifold ways that society and the law objectify and victimize women and children systematically, culturally, and religiously. It most clearly exposes the business of coercive sexual practices for profit.

One of the important legislative models embodying structuralist reforms comes from New York's and San Francisco's Safe Harbor Laws. The Polaris Project notes:

> The signing into law of the New York State Safe Harbor for Exploited Children Act in September 2008 was a watershed moment in the fight against the commercial sexual exploitation of children (CSEC) in the United States. The law is the result of years of advocacy work in New York and around the country advancing the simple proposition that children in prostitution are not criminals or delinquents but victims of a brutal form of child sexual abuse who need special services. A related law was signed in California, also in September 2008, creating a similar pilot program for Alameda County in the San Francisco Bay Area.[41]

Another powerful initiative supported by the Sanctuary has also originated in New York: the Trafficking Victims Protection and Justice Act of New York (TVPJA) promotes changes in legislation that would specifically target the "continued criminalization of trafficking victims and the impunity of those who prey on them — the pimps, traffickers, and buyers." While the bill was passed by the New York State Senate, its key provisions are still at risk in both the New York State Assembly and Senate Codes Committees. The Sanctuary Legal Center Director Dorchen Leidholdt urges: "Assembly and Senate leaders need to exert their political will to break the partisan log jams. We must amend New York State Law to end the re-victimization of trafficked children in our justice system and hold those who exploit them accountable."[42]

In a nutshell, the TVPJA revisions would recognize that selling children for sex is inherently coercive, ensure that these victims are not convicted of prostitution and that they receive services and shelter, and grade sex trafficking as a violent felony.[43]

41. Polaris Project website.
42. http://sanctuary.nonprofitsoapbox.com//index.php?option=com_content&task=view&id=573&Itemid=135.
43. "The Trafficking Victims Protection & Justice Act Is at Risk," Sanctuary for Families website, http://www.sanctuaryforfamilies.org/index.php?option=content&task=view&id=573 (accessed June 10, 2014).

The TVPJA's identification of the inherent coercion in selling children for sex, and its labeling of sex trafficking as a violent felony with higher penalties, emphasizes the ways in which the existing legal system provides both insufficient retribution and insufficient rehabilitation for victims.[44] For example, in California, a conviction in trafficking is punishable by four to eight years in prison; and in North Carolina, minor sex trafficking can lead to fifty-eight to seventy-three months in prison.[45] From a Lutheran feminist point of view, such laws do not adequately address the long-term harm toward and vulnerability of women and minors in systems that allow coercion, and they harbor inequality and gender bias within the law by responding to crimes against minors and sexual crimes with relatively minor punishments.

By contrast, by increasing the penalty to more years in prison, redefining minor sex trafficking crimes as minimally a Class B Felony like New York does, and taking other steps such as including violations of sex trafficking laws under "sex offenses" for the purposes of sex offender registry, states can increase the value society places on children's lives. Other issues on the legislative table include recognizing that sex trafficking constitutes a violation of human rights of children, redefining the age of minority for trafficking crimes from eighteen to twenty-one, and adjusting necessary evidentiary requirements for establishing *mens rea* (intent) and liability.

Recognizing trafficking as a crime of coercion and violence and a human rights issue are necessary steps for securing punishments appropriate to the severity of the crime. From a Lutheran feminist perspective, ensuring services and shelter for trafficked victims and "clarifying that sex trafficking victims should not be convicted of prostitution crimes" are important reforms.[46] They proceed from more sound principles of gender equality, and recognize the many ways of victimizing women and children that will continue without proper legal attention or control mechanisms. In the cases of prostitution and exposing trafficking operations, it is of utmost importance to adjust notions of who is a victim and who is guilty and to guard against all processes that threaten to revictimize the victim found "guilty" by participation — voluntary or forced — in the trafficking and prostitution business. The suggested reforms redirect punitive measures to penalize the "johns" and the "madams and pimps," and positive resources to rehabilitate the victim, the one exploited in prostitution and sex trafficking. These steps

44. Sanctuary for Families website.
45. Sanctuary for Families website.
46. Sanctuary for Families website.

offer hope to encourage victims who otherwise would not dare to call for help out of fear of being imprisoned and labeled, with no resources or income or support systems to build a new life. Without such strong legalized support, their attempts to call for help and break free from a prostitution ring would be a dead end.

These suggested changes reflect basic feminist critique of (1) any use of force against or abuse of women and children, (2) culturally condoned false images of women and children shaped by sexist ideas about sex and gender, and (3) power structures and relations that maintain inequality and feed injustice and abuse of power. They embody the best feminist advocacy for the use of public funds for women's and children's needs; build support systems for the female victims of sex crimes and trafficking, and secure resources for restoring victims' positive self-image, which is necessary to empower the female victim to move on to a new life that she controls with her newfound sense of empowerment.

State "Safe Harbor" Laws

As stated, from a Lutheran feminist point of view, the commercial sexual exploitation of children is an urgent crime and sin that deserves attention on local and state levels. Exemplary steps are already taken with such initiatives as the "Safe Harbor Laws" in New York.[47] Perhaps the most important change in New York's Safe Harbor Act is that an underage person charged with prostitution is presumed to be trafficked and a "person in need of supervision" under the 2000 TVPA legislation.[48]

One objective of these changes is to

[r]emove minor victims of commercial sexual exploitation from the jurisdiction of the criminal justice and juvenile delinquency systems. This step can be achieved through modifying the criminal prostitution statutes to decriminalize children in prostitution while ensuring that other legal mechanisms are in place for the state to take temporary protective custody of these children. The goal is to remove the victim from the control of

47. These objectives are described by the Polaris Project, http://www.polarisproject .org/ (accessed February 28, 2014).

48. Polaris Project, "Sex Trafficking of Minors and 'Safe Harbor,'" http://www.polaris project.org/what-we-do/policy-advocacy/assisting-victims/safe-harbor.

the pimp and help to break any unhealthy emotional attachment that has formed. A legislative alternative to technical decriminalization of these children may involve diversion of arrested children from juvenile delinquency proceedings to child protection proceedings.[49]

This goal to reform laws to empower the child victims of trafficking and secure their safety — their physical safety and also safety in the eyes of the law — resonates with Luther's vision that the community is responsible for the protection of its children in the broader sense of "parenting." The state can thereby assume the role of parenting for the sake of protection of the children who by themselves are powerless.

A second objective of the Safe Harbor Act is to

[p]rotect these children and provide them with specialized services, in recognition of their status as victims of crime and of the unique trauma that child victims of sex trafficking endure. Child victims of sex trafficking have very specialized needs that may include: safe houses, longer-term residential options, mental health care, access to GED or other remedial education programs, and life skills learning.[50]

This objective resonates with Luther's vision of procuring resources and properly allocating the use of shared resources for the benefit of the children in jeopardy. The contemporary medical community's wisdom on the effects of abuse and trauma on children's development — and of the particular trauma inflicted on the victims of sexual abuse — can constructively contribute in redesigning the procedures, protocols, and programs, as well as shaping popular perceptions and awareness.

---

49. Polaris Project, "Overview of State Legislative Policy to Address the Commercial Sexual Exploitation of Children — State 'Safe Harbor' Laws," p. 1, available at: www.polaris project.org/.../model%20safe%20harbor%20law%20overview%20final-1.pdf.

50. "Overview of State Legislative Policy to Address the Commercial Sexual Exploitation of Children — State 'Safe Harbor' Laws," p. 1. The Polaris Project notes that "experienced practitioners have learned that mainstream programs of the child abuse and neglect system routinely fail these children" and that the most successful programs place these children away from others without trafficking experience, provide mentors who are survivors or other caring professionals who understand the trauma of commercial sexual abuse, and ensure immediate placement without "undue questioning from untrained law enforcement officers." Available at http://www.polarisproject.org/storage/documents/policy _documents/Issue_Briefs/issue_brief_safe_harbor_february_2013.pdf.

A third objective of the Safe Harbor Act, which I have already emphasized, is to

> [a]mend state statutes prohibiting sex trafficking of children or pimping
> and pandering of children, to ensure that stiff penalties apply and that
> force or coercion is not a required element of the crime. Similarly to
> statutory rape laws, our criminal law should recognize the basic fact
> that children do not have the legal, psychological or emotional capac-
> ity to consent to engage in commercial sex acts. Therefore, we should
> severely penalize child predators without requiring evidence that they
> used force or coercion to induce the child victim to engage in commer-
> cial sex acts.[51]

This objective is important to the broader feminist project of redefining the
nature of coercion based on women's and children's particular experiences
of abuse and coercion. It furthers the feminist critique of sex/gender ste-
reotypes and prejudices embedded in legislation and in culture, and legal
assumptions regarding alleged "choices" and "consent" involved in sexual
exploitation. Feminist perspectives embodied in this objective shed light
on the issues of force and pain in sexual behavior and expose their harmful
impact on the experience of women and children. One change that promises to provide a more realistic definition of "coercion" would be to raise
the age for protection of "minors" from eighteen to twenty-one to reflect
the fact that girls aged eighteen to twenty-one are still subject to emotional
and psychological coercion. Along with tightening penalties and broadening
the spectrum of those implicated in the crime, this step is fundamental to
making changes with a ripple effect on social attitudes on gender. Another
fundamentally important step would be to categorically reject the argument
or assumption that any child ever would be capable of offering, or willing to
offer, her/his consent in sexual exploitation.

A final important objective of the Safe Harbor Acts is to

> [p]revent commercial sexual exploitation of children through training of
> law enforcement officers and other state officials and educating the gen-
> eral public about its dangers. . . . Law enforcement officers, judges, social
> workers, school officials, and the broader community need to learn about

---

51. Polaris Project, "Overview of State Legislative Policy to Address the Commercial
Sexual Exploitation of Children — State 'Safe Harbor' Laws," p. 2.

the problem of commercial sexual exploitation of children, in order to identify victims, recognize children at risk, and prevent sex trafficking.[52]

Training and heightened awareness of the realities of trafficking echo Luther's insistence on communities sharing the responsibility for children, being vigilant, and considering the accountability of all in paying attention, saying and doing the "right" thing, for the protection of the most vulnerable and precious: the children.

Conclusion

Recent initiatives against child sex trafficking are, from a Lutheran perspective, promising in terms of meeting the expectations that Luther laid down for parents and communities with respect to safeguarding children. The federal government is developing protective laws with child victims of trafficking in mind. However, the resources that would comprehensively address sex trafficking crimes in light of the inconsistency in state trafficking laws are inadequate to ensure protection of children from these crimes. Until then, there are several systems in place to further federal anti-trafficking efforts, including deliberate efforts to educate and empower the public.[53] In addition to initiatives to reform laws, other actions can be taken to better provide for protection and care of children. A robust resource is in Sanctuary for Families, easily accessed through their helpful website.[54]

As we think about these current issues and initiatives, Luther's reminder motivates us: children are a gift from God and parenting is a holy responsibility for all communities to make their priority. This is the foundation for Lutheran positions on contemporary legislation designed to protect children. Many of the contemporary societies that fail children by allowing devious public sins, such as sex trafficking in children, embody systems and ideologies infused by and supporting sexism and — the root of many evils — false images of women as sexual beings. Advocacy for changes in current legislation must begin, through feminist critique, by revising notions of sex/ gender, sexuality, and the dynamics pertaining to the use of power in sex/

52. Polaris Project, "Overview of State Legislative Policy to Address the Commercial Sexual Exploitation of Children — State 'Safe Harbor' Laws," p. 2.

53. See "Trafficking," http://www.polarisproject.org/human-trafficking/overview/ anti-trafficking-efforts.

54. Sanctuary for Families website, http://www.sanctuaryforfamilies.org/index.php.

gender relations. Revising these notions is the starting point for calling attention to the internationally and locally mushrooming organized sex trafficking of children. Lutheran theology's priority for the well-being of children, and the complex feminist critique of sexist ideologies and systems that "allow" or feed trafficking crimes, can be employed to support important changes in laws that matter for the future of our children.

The bottom line issue is this: working with law and order *coram hominibus* is one thing, and an important justice concern, but beyond that lies the enormously difficult challenge of altering cultural perceptions of what it means to be a woman and a man, and what healthy sexuality entails.

CHAPTER 7

Hiding in Plain Sight:
Lutheran Reflections on Human Trafficking

Wanda Deifelt

Human trafficking has become a major concern for governments and agencies in the past decade, often being compared to a modern form of slavery. While slavery was abolished in the United States in 1865, modern-day slavery exists through the trafficking of human beings.[1] Trafficking involves a continued relationship of forced labor or other form of exploitation that benefits the trafficker. The characteristics and attributes of human trafficking are described in detail by the Palermo Protocol:

> "Trafficking in persons" shall mean the recruitment, transportation, transfer, harboring or receipt of persons, by means of the threat or use of force or other forms of coercion, of abduction, of fraud, of deception, of the abuse of power or of a position of vulnerability or of the giving or receiving of payments or benefits to achieve the consent of a person having control over another person, for the purpose of exploitation. Exploitation shall include, at a minimum, the exploitation of the prostitution of others or other forms of sexual exploitation, forced labor or services, slavery or practices similar to slavery, servitude or the removal of organs. . . . The consent of a victim of trafficking in persons to the intended exploitation set forth [above] shall be irrelevant where any of the means set forth [above] have been used.[2]

---

1. Slavery was banned in 1865 with the ratification of the Thirteenth Amendment to the United States Constitution.

2. *The Protocol to Prevent, Suppress and Punish Trafficking in Persons, especially Women and Children* (also referred to as the Trafficking Protocol or UN TIP Protocol) was adopted by the United Nations in Palermo, Italy, in 2000.

Trafficking is coercive, deceptive, and abusive, but concrete information (data) on the magnitude of the problem is difficult to assess due to its very nature.[3] It is hard to determine the actual number of people involved in trafficking, with worldwide numbers ranging between 700,000 and 4 million new victims per year.[4] It is commonly agreed, however, that trafficking in human beings is an extremely lucrative business.[5] Its annual profits are estimated in the billions every year, with a seemingly endless supply of persons to traffic, especially due to economic instability, social dislocation, and gender inequality. Trafficked persons, typically women and children, are treated as merchandise that can be sold and resold. Promised a better and brighter future, they incur debt and are often forced to pay back the costs incurred in their transport and purchase.

A Violation of Human Rights

Along with drugs and weapons, human trafficking is among the most profitable and fastest-growing industries in the world. Given its global impact, there is great demand that political leaders and nations present results, but few traffickers have been prosecuted and comparatively few women have received assistance in order to escape trafficking. Many are revictimized by being deported from the countries in which they are found and ostracized by their families and communities of origin. In this context, women are often treated as victims or data figures, with little attention to the com-

---

3. At the launch of the United Nations "A Global Report on Trafficking in Persons," the Executive Director of UN Office on Drugs and Crime, Antonio Maria Costa, acknowledged: "We have a big picture, but it is impressionistic and lacks depth. We fear the problem is getting worse, but we can not prove it for lack of data, and many governments are obstructing." http://www.unodc.org/unodc/en/human-trafficking/global-report-on-trafficking-in -persons.html (accessed January 5, 2015).

4. Dina Francesca Haynes, "Used, Abused, Arrested and Deported: Extending Immigration Benefits to Protect the Victims of Trafficking and to Secure the Prosecution of Traffickers," *Human Rights Quarterly* 26, no. 2 (2004): 223.

5. A recent International Labour Office report states, "Globally, two-thirds of the profits from forced labour were generated by commercial sexual exploitation . . . amounting to an estimated $99 billion [U.S. dollars] per year." "Profits and Poverty: The Economics of Forced Labour," *International Labour Office* (2014), p. 15, quoted in Belinda Luscombe, "Inside the Scarily Lucrative Business Model of Human Trafficking," *Time,* May 20, 2014, http://time.com/105360/inside-the-scarily-lucrative-business-model-of-human -trafficking/ (accessed May 25, 2014).

plexity of their own choices and decisions.⁶ Some authors have concluded that intergovernmental and governmental responses to sex trafficking have largely developed with secondary consideration to the actual women and their situation.

Women and girls are often lured by traffickers into leaving their hometowns, believing that they will work as dancers, hostesses, or nannies. Instead, they find themselves forced to have sex for the profit of the men and women who purchased them. This might happen within a particular country, but it often involves trafficking from one country to another. Women are forced to sell themselves in brothels, frequently receiving several clients per day, in situations that are unsafe and violent. They rarely see any wages for their work. In order to secure their silence and compliance, traffickers threaten, beat, rape, drug, and deprive their victims of legitimate immigration or work documents. In such situations, their passports or personal identifications are taken. Because they might not speak the local language, they are afraid to ask for help. Most women and girls are kept in indentured servitude and told that they owe their traffickers or the brothel owners for their own purchase price and for the price of procuring working papers and travel documents.

> The rings of traffickers are often vast, extremely well connected to police and government officials, well hidden, and reach across borders and continents. Traffickers in human beings are also known to traffic in weapons and drugs, and to use trafficking in human beings to bring in initial cash flow to support the riskier traffic in drugs and arms. Human beings, being reusable commodities that can be sold and resold, are both more lucrative and less risky to traffic than drugs and arms, in that traffickers of human beings are rarely prosecuted for this particular offense.⁷

Although it is a monumental problem (attested by the research and changes of policy in the past decade), human trafficking remains a hidden problem. Because of its invisibility, trafficking has a high return-to-risk ratio, making it an attractive enterprise. Forced labor includes agriculture, do-

6. This essay addresses the persons caught in trafficking both as victims and as agents of transformation. They are victims because their human rights have been violated, and they are entitled to call upon the state for support and protection. The challenge, then, is how they can become subjects. Extending legal rights to victims empowers them, rendering them less vulnerable to further economic and social exploitation.

7. Haynes, "Used, Abused, Arrested and Deported," p. 226.

mestic servitude, maid service, sweatshops, begging, marriage, and sexual exploitation (commercial sex industry or prostitution). Jo Goodey states that trafficked women, particularly those involved in the sex industry, are not perceived as victims by criminal justice agencies because they are often labeled as morally deviant and are frequently charged as prostitutes:

> In turn, the cultural meaning of women's sexuality is central to any interpretation of how criminal justice authorities, and societies in general, respond to the problem of sex trafficking. While prostitutes have always been labelled as "criminal" and as "socially deviant," the men who visit prostitutes are generally regarded in a less negative light. In responding to cases of sex trafficking, criminal justice agents, from the police through to the judiciary, are no more immune from this negative labelling than the society in which they are culturally situated.[8]

When compared with other victim categories, such as children and survivors of sexual and physical abuse, trafficked women are often seen as complicit in their own exploitation. This is true both in their country of origin and their host country. There seems to be a categorization between more "innocent" and "deserving" victims among the women trafficked into the sex industry. Because they agreed to work abroad, or, in some cases, agreed to work as prostitutes, they are considered less than blameless. Hiding behind moralizing arguments, it would be easy to explain that the women who endure suffering because of trafficking have brought this upon themselves. It would also exempt civil society from taking a closer look at the inhuman conditions of trafficking. This false reasoning, however, falls into the pitfall of blaming the victims, instead of paying closer attention to the hidden stories that they actually represent.

A Violation of Human Autonomy

Human trafficking has only recently been addressed as a human rights issue. The Palermo Protocol states that trafficking involves deprivation of choice at some stage, either through fraud, coercion, deception, force, or threats.

8. Jo Goodey, "Sex Trafficking in Women from Central and East European Countries: Promoting a 'Victim-Centred' and 'Woman-Centred' Approach to Criminal Justice Intervention," *Feminist Review* 76 (2004): 33.

In the case of women trafficked into the sex industry, the question of agency is relevant. Of course, prostitution and trafficking are not one and the same, even if some treat them as such. Although there may be a gray area involving different degrees of choice, consent, and free will, it is commonly accepted that prostitution involves persons willingly engaging in sex work. In other words, there is a degree of agency and self-determination. Naturally, a valid argument could be made that gender imbalances as well as economic and social factors drive women to consent to such labor as their chosen profession, thus challenging the degree of agency in any woman's self-determination. Trafficking in humans, however, goes beyond this discussion because in trafficking, there is no gray area. Whether a trafficked woman was initially willing or unwilling when she entered into sex work should make no legal difference when the outcome is enslavement or forced servitude. "While some trafficked persons may be willing to work in the sex industry, they do not anticipate being forced to pay off large forcibly imposed debts, being kept against their will, having their travel documents taken from them, or being raped, beaten, and sold like chattel."[9] Trafficking implies enslavement and forced labor, making it inadmissible.

David A. Feingold points out that trafficking is often migration gone terribly wrong. Although it is organized in some parts of the world, it is also "disorganized crime" in the sense that individuals or small groups are linked on an ad-hoc basis. Traffickers range from truck drivers to village "aunties" to labor brokers and police officers. Traffickers are as varied as the circumstances of their victims. It is true that some trafficking victims are kidnapped, but most leave their homes voluntarily — under the promise of employment and better life conditions — and become trafficked on their journey. Besides the push of poverty or political and social instability, trafficking is also motivated by the draw of bright lights, big cities, and the expectation of a different lifestyle than that of their local communities.[10]

The lure of better living conditions helps to account for why, in parts of Africa, girls from medium-sized towns are more vulnerable to trafficking than those in rural villages. It might seem puzzling, but often relatives are instrumental in introducing young women and children into the sex trade. The motivations are complex, ranging from resorting to prostitution as a means of survival to attempts to support a drug or alcohol addiction. To fill the demand for ever-cheaper labor, "many victims are trafficked within the

9. Haynes, "Used, Abused, Arrested and Deported," p. 231.
10. David A. Feingold, "Human Trafficking," *Foreign Policy* 150 (2005): 26-32.

same economic class or even within a single country. In Brazil, for example, girls may be trafficked for sex work from rural to urban areas, whereas males may be sold to work in the gold mines of the Amazon jungle."[11]

The question, ultimately, is whether there is agency, whether the women themselves have a say in their own life stories. In addition, the conditions that lead to trafficking need to be better addressed. Women already disenfranchised within their own communities are more likely to fall prey to traffickers. Ostracized minorities, women without employment or future economic prospects, and girls without family members to look out for them or who have fallen outside of the educational system in their home countries are more prone to be lured with false job opportunities promised by traffickers, through a network of acquaintances or even advertised in the media.

The methods employed by traffickers are diverse. They can be complex transnational crime rings or small-scale, family-style channels or individuals. There is always a network that includes recruiters, document forgers, transporters, and purchasers. People may accept jobs they know might be risky, but they do not expect to work in slavery conditions when promised employment. According to the United Nations *Global Report on Trafficking in Persons,* the most common form of human trafficking (79 percent) is sexual exploitation, and the victims of sexual exploitation are predominantly women and girls.[12]

Multiple aspects need to be taken into consideration when addressing human trafficking. Feminization of poverty, gender inequality, and lack of access to educational and professional opportunities make women and young adults particularly vulnerable to trafficking. Not only females, but also males are victims of trafficking. It is believed that boys are widely overlooked as victims because the attitudes of law enforcement officials are still weighed down by gender biases, pinning females as victims and males as perpetrators.[13] The sex industry has thrived and grown into worldwide pro-

---

11. Feingold, "Human Trafficking," p. 32.

12. See "Global Report on Trafficking in Persons," United Nations Office on Drugs and Crime (2009), http://www.unodc.org/unodc/en/human-trafficking/global-report-on -trafficking-in-persons.html (accessed January 5, 2015).

13. Young males remain a largely invisible population in the reports on sex trafficking, yet may represent half of children trafficked in the United States. Male victims in custody often fall through the cracks of services that could be offered to help them because they are not properly assessed for sexual exploitation. See Yu Sun Chin, "Trafficked Boys Overlooked," *The Chicago Bureau,* http://jjie.org/trafficked-boys-overlooked-underrepresented/ (accessed April 23, 2014).

portions, making the commodification of bodies accessible regionally and transnationally, trafficking women and young adults from place to place to supply a global sex market. Authors and researchers talk about "push" and "pull" factors in terms of the supply and demand of the market place. This has produced a climate where human beings are prostituted under slave-like conditions, with little or no attention to their well-being and agency in this process.

A Lutheran Theological Framework for Engaging Trafficking

Martin Luther's theological corpus connects both theological and political ideas in a way that reflects the medieval worldview but also pushes it further. Obviously, Luther is not a modern thinker familiar with a state separate from the church. Rather, he discusses the nature of government and politics in light of humanity's relationship with God. Luther's best-known political views — as described in his "two kingdoms theory" — place both the secular and the religious under God's domain. Luther claimed it was the responsibility of the political authorities to achieve economic, political, and social reforms that would also affect the church. Conversely, it was the task of the church to confront the political authorities with God's will. Both kingdoms have a common foundation (God is the Lord) and a common goal (human well-being).

In Luther's two kingdoms theory, the earthly and heavenly realms are the manifestations of two divine gifts. While the state oversees social and public order, ruling over bodies, the church exercises spiritual power and looks after the well-being of the soul. Guided by the gospel, the church makes use of the power of the Word. Guided by the law, the state makes use of the power of the sword. In the secular realm, the law has the purposes of exercising justice, coercing humans, and bringing them punishment when needed. In the spiritual realm, the law is still needed because it reveals human shortcomings and reminds Christians of the need to repent. Wrongdoings in the earthly kingdom are met with punishment, whereas in the heavenly kingdom, they are met with forgiveness. These two realms complement each other as two different ways in which God cares for creation.

Although it might seem dichotomous at first, Luther's theory about the two realms in fact reflects a consistent paradoxical approach. So, whereas the secular kingdom gives witness to God's efficacy in providing governance and overseeing the earthly realm by assuring social order, the heavenly kingdom gives witness to God's power by means of spiritual and ecclesiastical order, making sure that matters of the soul and salvation are attended. This paradoxical view is best described in Martin Luther's own words, whereby he praised secular government for its divinely ordained purpose to bring order into the world. Justice is how God's love is experienced in the secular realm, in the public and political arena.

Luther's theology has often been misinterpreted, leading either to acquiescence to authoritarian regimes or passivity toward arbitrary governmental rule. However, Luther's system offers an imperative for a Christian's ethical and political participation in matters that pertain to the common good. It is evident that, for Luther, issues of public and private nature are not as distinctively separate as they are for modern human beings. Nevertheless, Luther seems quite "modern" in the sense that citizenship is a matter of participation in the *res publica,* in the common affairs, for Christians are called to be involved in public matters.

In his two kingdoms theory, Luther does not refer to two distinct physical realms with different governments. What governs both realms, ultimately, is God. Because both kingdoms are rooted in divine authority (both are created by God), they cannot be opposed to each other. In the heavenly kingdom, the law of the gospel finds its meaning through Christ (justification by faith through grace). The secular kingdom is ruled by civil law and worldly rulers to maintain society (functioning as God's instruments in the world). The two kingdoms reflect two different modes of moral thinking — each pertaining to the life of a Christian.

Luther's theology, particularly his focus on the role of believers in society, shows that Christians have an important role to play not only in the church but also in the secular realm. This is clear from his paradoxical statement, "A Christian is a perfectly free lord of all, subject to none. A Christian is a perfectly dutiful servant of all, subject to all."[14] Justification by faith, one of the tenets of Lutheran doctrine, is never the end of the story. It frees us to love the neighbor and serve the world in need. We love others because we are loved by God — and this creates a nurturing environment that affirms the vocation of Christians in the world. The love of neighbor is not simply the promotion of well-being for other church members, or Christians, or fellow citizens. Rather, it is the search to secure well-being for all creatures.

True Christians would have no need for law, since they already do more

---

14. Martin Luther, "The Freedom of a Christian," in *Martin Luther: Selections from His Writings,* ed. John Dillenberger (New York: Random House, 1962), p. 53.

than the law requires. Because Christians do not live and labor on earth for themselves, but for the well-being of the neighbor, they will ensure that laws are created and enforced to constrain evil, keep the peace, and do what is good. Without laws to coerce and punish the wicked, human beings would treat each other as savage beasts. The sword is a great benefit and necessity, and Christians will submit to it not because they require it for themselves, but to ensure justice. These are works of love: "Because the sword is a very great benefit and necessary to the whole world, to preserve peace, to punish sin and to prevent evil, [the Christian] submits most willingly to the rule of the sword. . . . Although he needs none of these things for himself and it is not necessary for him to do them, yet he considers what is for the good and profit of others."[15]

Luther's two kingdoms theory demonstrates the creative tension in which Christians live, affirming that both church and state are under the rule of God, and both function as places for Christian engagement. They are two different modes of moral thinking, each applying to the Christian life in different circumstances. To acknowledge this is to give Christians a social responsibility, a call to live a Christian life in the world. As Gustaf Wingren explains Luther's two kingdoms theory, it is only before God (in heaven) that the individual stands alone. In the earthly realm, a human being stands in relationship, each one always bound to another.[16] By centering Christian vocation on care for the other, Luther emphasizes human interdependence and responsibility. This service is a labor of love.

> Our duties as children, parents, spouses, employers, employees, friends, and citizens are particular expressions of God's command to love God and neighbor. . . . In their purest form, God's callings are not "summons" of a divine "Commander," whom the obedient soldier strenuously and reluctantly obeys. Rather they are impulses of the indwelling Spirit, calling us forth to discover our lives anew in loving service to God and neighbor.[17]

Luther's theological perspective offers important insights for the ethical implications of what it means to be a Christian in this world. We are citizens

15. Martin Luther, "Secular Authority: To What Extent It Should Be Obeyed," in *Martin Luther: Selections from His Writings*, p. 373.
16. Gustaf Wingren, *Luther on Vocation*, trans. Carl C. Rasmussen (Eugene, OR: Wipf & Stock, 1957), p. 5.
17. Douglas J. Schuurman, *Vocation: Discerning Our Callings in Life* (Grand Rapids: Eerdmans, 2004), p. 63.

of heaven, in the eschatological perspective, through our salvation in Christ; we are also citizens of this world, responsible for earthly affairs, to answer for the questions of this age. The framework for this earthly engagement is to seek not one's own well-being, but that of others — primarily those who are poor, outcast, and whose dignity is jeopardized. It implies using one's station in life to advocate for others.

This ethical concern is particularly important in the context of citizenship. Commonly understood, citizenship refers to the rights and obligations one has by being born of a particular nationality. One benefits from the privileges of citizenship — ranging from the right to vote to personal security — but citizenship also entails demands, such as the duty to pay taxes. Luther's understanding of citizenship includes a third dimension: the responsibility we have toward each other to care for the well-being of the neighbor, to use our stations in life (vocation) to serve God by meeting the needs of those around us, by holding offices not to secure our own interests but to ensure the flourishing of others. In short, the role of the Christian in the public square is to advocate for those in need, who are disenfranchised, who might not benefit from the privileges granted by one's nationality or the citizenship rights that holding a particular passport might entail.

A Christian is concerned, therefore, that existing laws grant protection and make provision not only for those who are entitled to the protection of the law, but also for those who fall through the cracks. A Christian engages in works of justice seeking the well-being of the neighbor, not his or her own interests. To seek the security and welfare of another instead of pursuing one's own benefits goes against the grain of society, where one's own life, liberty, and pursuit of happiness are exercised in detriment or at the expense of other human beings. Faith is active through love when we aid those in need, when the strong member serves the weaker, when we care and work for the other, carry each other's burdens, and so fulfill the law of Christ.[18] The command to love one's neighbor shifts the moral focus away from the self toward others.

For Luther, the law that trumps all others is that of Christ: "The first is . . . 'Love the Lord your God with all your heart and with all your soul and with all your mind and with all your strength.' The second is this, 'Love your neighbor as yourself.' There is no commandment greater than these."[19] Vocation focused on service to the neighbor solidifies God's presence in our lives.

18. Luther, "The Freedom of a Christian," p. 74.
19. Mark 12:30-31.

It places advocacy at the center of our attention: "In what concerns you and yours, you govern yourself by the Gospel and suffer injustice toward yourself and as a true Christian; in what concerns the person or property of others, you govern yourself according to love and tolerate no injustice toward your neighbor."[20] In other words, Luther's understanding of the law is not one that is premised on self-interests and rights, but one that functions as a way to secure the well-being of those around us.[21]

> If the State and its sword are a divine service, as was proved above, that which the State needs in order to wield the sword must also be a divine service. There must be those who arrest, accuse, slay and destroy the wicked, and protect, acquit, defend and save the good. Therefore, when such duties are performed, not with the intention of seeking one's own ends, but only of helping to maintain the laws and the State, so that the wicked may be restrained. . . . For, as was said, love of neighbor seeks not its own, considers not how great or how small, but how profitable and how needful for neighbor or community the works are [1 Cor. 13:5].[22]

Reforming Existing Secular Legal Approaches to Human Trafficking

Frank Laczko and Marco A. Gramegna, from the International Organization for Migration, point out that human trafficking is currently one of the most interdisciplinary topics of our day, involving human rights, gender, health, law enforcement, and social services.[23] Given the magnitude of the problem and the fact that so many international agencies and governments have given high priority and devoted extensive resources to combating human trafficking, it is puzzling that the actual number of people identified as victims of trafficking and assisted to break free from it is very small, and that the number of traffickers prosecuted is even smaller. In her research on trafficking in the United Kingdom, Julia O'Connell Davidson concludes

20. Luther, "Secular Authority," p. 375.

21. One could press the argument further and state that, regarding oneself and one's property, a Christian must follow Jesus' command to love the enemy and turn the other cheek. When dealing with others and their property, however, the Christian can and sometimes must make use of the sword.

22. Luther, "Secular Authority," p. 381.

23. Frank Laczko and Marco A. Gramegna, "Developing Better Indicators of Human Trafficking," *Brown Journal of World Affairs* 10, no. 1 (2003): 179-94.

that, far from representing a step forward in terms of "securing rights and protections for those who are subject to exploitative employment relations and poor working conditions in the sex trade, the current policy emphasis on sex slaves and [victims of trafficking] limits the state's obligations towards them."[24] In other words, the regulations in place seem to exempt national governments from assisting trafficked persons.

A similar conclusion is reached by Dina Francesca Haynes in her research titled "Used, Abused, Arrested and Deported":

> the best of the "jail the offender" and "protect the victim" models should be combined. The new model should incorporate advice from grassroots organizations that work directly with trafficked persons, in order to craft anti-trafficking programs that promote protection of victims. This new model should include immigration protection, should hit traffickers where it hurts, and should prioritize full implementation.[25]

International agreements, such as the 2000 UN Convention Against Transnational Organized Crime, together with its Trafficking Protocol, require an integrated, cross-national, and multi-agency approach to trafficking. If we consider that a complex problem requires a complex solution, governmental regulations and policies alone will not be able to fully address all elements of prevention, prosecution, and protection that human trafficking entails. Prevention of trafficking and victimization, prosecution of offenders, and protection of and assistance to victims of trafficking establish a comprehensive approach to human trafficking and allow us to make visible what is otherwise made invisible.

In order to accomplish these goals, it is first necessary to look at the power imbalance that women and children face:

> gender inequality is a major factor contributing to the problem of trafficking of women for sexual exploitation. In addition, strong social and cultural constraints mean that addressing unequal gender relations and the social construction of women's roles is difficult. These barriers and constraints severely limit the contributions that NGOs can make to addressing both supply and demand factors of trafficking. Prevention measures aimed at

24. Julia O'Connell Davidson, "Will the Real Sex Slave Please Stand Up?" *Feminist Review* 83 (2006): 20.
25. Haynes, "Used, Abused, Arrested and Deported," p. 225.

raising awareness of trafficking, risk recognition, vulnerability avoidance, and support networks are essential components of any anti-trafficking strategy.[26]

If we see trafficking not only as an individual problem of victims brought into forced work, but as a migratory response to current globalizing socio-economic trends, it can affect not only the way we describe human trafficking but also how we address it. Poverty needs to be addressed as well. So, for instance, initiatives to counter trafficking must target the underlying conditions that impel people to accept dangerous labor migration assignments in the first place. Experts in the field agree that the international legal response to the problem falls short in terms of offering long-term solutions. Janie Chuang, for instance, goes as far as saying that "by failing to assess the long-term implications of existing counter-trafficking strategies, these responses risk being not only ineffective, but counterproductive."[27] I agree with her assessment and propose that, besides the policies already in place, we need more focused inquiry into prevention strategies and a more complex way of examining human trafficking that also considers the economic, social, and cultural aspects that sustain human trafficking.

This is a global challenge that involves not only the analysis of a social problem or an immediate solution for it. It is an opportunity to reflect on the human component and the theological dimension of human dignity. The challenge is to offer visibility and agency to those who are otherwise perceived as victims and creating solutions that involve many partners.

There is a consensus among human rights activists that mainstream anti-trafficking models, namely, those that pursue the prosecution of the trafficker over the protection of the victim, do not adequately address immigration options that could serve to protect the victim and provide the necessary means for her to have a decent livelihood.[28] It is also necessary to address the trafficked women directly, developing educational materials for migrant women in destination countries and providing training and technical and financial assistance to their partners from the countries of origin.

26. Marina Tzvetkova, "NGO Responses to Trafficking in Women," *Gender and Development* 10, no. 1 (2002): 67.

27. Janie Chuang, "Beyond a Snapshot: Preventing Human Trafficking in the Global Economy," *Indiana Journal of Global Legal Studies* 13, no. 1 (2006): 139.

28. Haynes presents data specific to Central and Southeastern Europe, but the overall analysis applies as well to the continental reality. Haynes, "Used, Abused, Arrested and Deported," pp. 221-72.

Janie Chuang offers an insightful analysis of human trafficking and the shortcomings of governmental initiatives in addressing the three-pronged framework of prosecuting traffickers, protecting trafficked persons, and preventing trafficking.[29] Governments, in general, have adopted a "law and order" approach that is less concerned with the broader socioeconomic reality that drives human trafficking. Although there is a strong international foundation for cooperation — drawn primarily on initiatives and support of international agencies and protocols such as the Palermo Protocol — the level of interconnection might lack the advocacy approach that Christian ethics can supply.

The American Scenario: Legal Responses[30]

American law has been inadequate in addressing trafficking both within U.S. borders and outside, though some efforts have been made in the last two decades. Addressing the legal status of trafficked persons in America who are not U.S. citizens, Kathleen Kim and Kusia Hreshchyshyn identify a tension between immigration law and civil rights legislation.[31] Both the more restrictive immigration and the more expansive civil rights laws help identify the "full members" of the U.S. political community, assessing who has stronger rights and whose claims are weaker or nonexistent due to their citizenship status. While immigration laws are enforced by public bodies to determine who has the right to be in the country or not (based on citizenship), civil rights laws are enforced by private actors and expand rights by combating discrimination based on citizenship and national origin.

These two lines of American law meet in federal trafficking legislation that responds to both in-country and international trafficking. In the United

29. Chuang, "Beyond a Snapshot."

30. This portion of the essay relies on the legal work presented by Polaris, a nonprofit organization that works to combat and prevent modern-day slavery and human trafficking. "About Us," *Polaris,* http://www.polarisproject.org/about-us/overview (accessed January 7, 2015). Polaris offers a comprehensive overview of current federal laws related to human trafficking. "Current Federal Laws," *Polaris,* http://www.polarisproject.org/what-we-do/policy-advocacy/national-policy/current-federal-laws. For the purpose of this essay, only the summaries of the legislation pertaining specifically to the trafficking of persons (the Trafficking Victims Protection Acts — TVPAs) will be analyzed.

31. Kathleen Kim and Kusia Hreshchyshyn, "Human Trafficking Private Right of Action: Civil Rights for Trafficked Persons in the United States," *Hastings Women's Law Journal* 16, no. 1 (2004): 1-36.

States, the Trafficking Victims Protection Act (TVPA) of 2000 establishes several methods of prosecuting traffickers, preventing trafficking, and protecting victims and survivors of trafficking.[32] The act establishes human trafficking as a federal crime and mandates that restitution be paid to victims. The act also establishes the Interagency Task Force to Monitor and Combat Trafficking (which assists in the implementation of the TVPA) and the Office to Monitor and Combat Trafficking in Persons. This office publishes a *Trafficking In Persons* (TIP) report each year, describing and ranking the efforts of countries to combat human trafficking.

In its annual TIP report, the U.S. Department of State grades the scale and severity of people-trafficking and other forms of modern slavery in 188 countries and territories. Since 2001, the report has played an important role as a tool to engage foreign governments on the issue of trafficking and slavery within their borders. As such, it has served both as a means of assessment and as a resource for advocacy and campaigning for anti-trafficking in the United States and abroad. It reports people-trafficking and slavery within each country and, using a three-tier system, ranks how countries comply with the Trafficking Victims Protection Act.[33] As a result of the report, countries that repeatedly failed to improve their counter-trafficking efforts, such as Russia and China, were downgraded to Tier 3, the lowest possible ranking, which leads to damage to their national reputation, possible non-trade sanctions, restrictions on U.S. foreign assistance, and restricted access to global financial institutions such as the World Bank.[34]

The TVPA protects victims and survivors of human trafficking by establishing the "T visa," which allows victims of human trafficking and their families to become temporary U.S. residents and eligible to become permanent residents after three years. However, with the T visa regulations, the burden of proving eligibility is placed upon the applicant, who needs to take the initiative to seek out protection. Traffickers often achieve compliance from their victims by threatening to harm the trafficked persons and their families or to turn them over to law enforcement or immigration authorities, by confiscating their documents, and by employing psychological torture

32. *Victims of Trafficking and Violence Protection Act of 2000,* Public Law 106-386, *U.S. Statutes at Large* 114 (2000): 1464-1548.

33. See "U.S. Laws on Trafficking in Persons," U.S. Department of State, http://www.state.gov/j/tip/laws/, for a list of legislation dealing with trafficking in persons.

34. Annie Kelly, "How NGOs Are Using the Trafficking in Persons Report," accessed March 24, 2014, http://www.theguardian.com/global-development-professionals-network/2013/jun/21/ngos-using-trafficking-persons-report.

(such as confinement and seclusion) and physical abuse (beatings, starvation, sexual assault, and rape).

Services and protections for trafficked victims are related to cooperation with law enforcement. However, fear of retaliation from traffickers against themselves or family members (in the country of arrival or back home), distrust of law enforcement due to an absence of rule of law or government corruption in the country of origin, and the severe physical and psychological hardship the trafficked person has undergone make it difficult to seek legal help. Even if victims report their case and are willing to cooperate, it is not guaranteed that a prosecutor will pursue an investigation since prosecution is within the prosecutor's discretion. If there is no supporting evidence from law enforcement, a candidate may face complications in receiving a T visa. Only 5,000 T visas may be granted per fiscal year, when by all estimates the contingent of trafficked persons is well above this number.[35]

The Trafficking Victims Protection Reauthorization Act of 2003 (TVPRA of 2003)[36] has established a federal, civil right of action for trafficking victims to sue their traffickers. It also added human trafficking to the list of crimes that can be charged under the Racketeering Influenced Corrupt Organizations (RICO) statute. Additional provisions for protection of victims and their families from deportation were included in this Act, such as extending to nonimmigrant alien family members the same benefits and services available to a trafficking victim. The Act also required that the Attorney General report to Congress annually on the activities of the U.S. government in the fight against trafficking.

Using civil litigation as a strategy for compensating victims of trafficking is an additional tool to curb modern-day slavery. In contrast to the prosecutorial approach, a civil action can provide compensation to victims, allowing them to control and direct the legal process. Kathleen Kim and Kusia Hreshchyshyn argue that such civil litigation "empowers trafficked persons individually to pursue greater damage awards in the form of compensatory, punitive, and/or pecuniary damages."[37] Defendant traffickers

35. Kim and Hreshchyshyn, "Human Trafficking Private Right of Action," p. 4.

36. *Trafficking Victims Protection Reauthorization Act of 2003,* Public Law 108-93, *U.S. Statutes at Large* 117 (2003): 2875-87. http://thomas.loc.gov/cgi-bin/bdquery/z?d108:h.r.02620.

37. Kim and Hreshchyshyn, "Human Trafficking Private Right of Action," p. 16. The authors explain: "In a criminal prosecution, the TVPA provides for mandatory restitution and criminal forfeiture of assets. However, a restitution award depends largely on the aggres-

are not just held for crimes against the state but are directly accountable to their victims.

Nevertheless, the challenges of civil litigations are similar to criminal prosecution: trafficked persons may be prevented from seeking legal aid due to limited resources, lack of information, or intimidation. Threats of retaliation and violence may prevent trafficked persons from coming forward as criminal witnesses or as civil plaintiffs. Given the secrecy of the trafficking enterprise, defendants and their assets might not be easy to locate.

The Trafficking Victims Protection Reauthorization Act of 2005 (TVPRA of 2005) has also expanded measures to combat trafficking internationally, including provisions to fight sex tourism, and the development of a pilot program for treatment of trafficking victims abroad.[38] It has strengthened regulation of government contracts to ensure they are not made with individuals or organizations involved in human trafficking. Under it, the federal government has carried out a pilot program for sheltering minors who are survivors of human trafficking, and enabled grant programs to assist state and local law enforcement agencies to combat trafficking.[39]

These targeted efforts to combat trafficking have led not only to locating trafficked persons but also to increasing their willingness to share their accounts with a wider public. For instance, in 2013, a four-part report on human trafficking, titled "Saving Bobbi: A Teen's Sex Trafficking Ordeal," appeared in the *Twin Cities Star Tribune*. Teenager Bobbi Larson was lured by drugs, used by pimps, and became a victim of human trafficking.[40] She and her family went public with the ordeal to help other girls avoid the trauma she endured.[41] The condition in which she was found was deplorable:

---

siveness of the prosecutor and the court to inform the criminal defendant that restitution may be an element of the sentence. Since prosecutors are most focused on incarceration, restitution is easily forgotten to the detriment of the victim."

38. See *Trafficking Victims Protection Reauthorization Act of 2003,* Public Law 109-64, *U.S. Statutes at Large* 119 (2003): 3558-73.

39. Worldwide, almost 20 percent of all trafficked people are children. In some parts of Africa they are the majority. "UNODC Report on Human Trafficking Exposes Modern Form of Slavery," United Nations Office on Drugs and Crime, http://www.unodc.org/unodc/en/human-trafficking/global-report-on-trafficking-in-persons.html (accessed January 5, 2015).

40. Pam Louwagie, "Saving Bobbi: A Teen's Sex Trafficking Ordeal," *Star Tribune* (Minneapolis), Sunday, November 17, 2013, A1, A8-A9.

41. The entire series "Saving Bobbi" is available as an e-book by startribune.com/ebooks. Proceeds go to the MN Girls Are Not for Sale, an initiative of the Women's Foun-

The girl was huddled with a friend on a grimy mattress on the floor, lolling in a methamphetamine haze. Instruments of modern day bondage lay scattered about: A drug pipe keeping her in a meth-induced stupor, willing to do almost anything for the next high. A prepaid credit card. Three cellphones, tethering the girls to pimps and johns 24/7. . . . Pimps liked to target the particularly vulnerable ones — kids with abuse in their past, autism, fetal alcohol syndrome. When those challenges combined with teenage rebellion, and kids bolted from home to the streets, they were easy prey.[42]

In addition to increasing the likelihood of public awareness of these crimes, the Trafficking Victims Protection Reauthorization Act of 2008 (TVPRA of 2008) has included several new prevention strategies, including requirements that the government provide information about workers' rights to all people applying for work and education-based visas.[43] It has required that unaccompanied alien children be screened as potential victims of human trafficking. It has enhanced criminal sanctions against traffickers, and expanded definitions of various types of trafficking to make prosecution easier. It has also put in place new systems to gather and report human trafficking data. In addition to the prevention strategies, the 2008 reauthorization has expanded the protections available with the T visa. It has extended the time period for granting a T visa and waived the disqualification for lack of good moral character for T visa holders applying for adjustment to permanent resident status if the disqualification was caused by or incident to the trafficking.

The move to decriminalize the acts of victims and help children and teenagers in situations of prostitution has been accompanied with a change of language and concept: the term "sex trafficking" has replaced the term "prostitution" even if the victims were not transported across state or national borders. In the past, juveniles who were lured into the sex trade were arrested and prosecuted as prostitutes. In recent years, however, federal and some state laws have changed to define them as victims rather than criminals. State laws criminalize adults that have sex with children under statutory rape laws. However, these laws were not applied in cases where the adult

dation of Minnesota to end child sex trafficking. See "MN Girls Are Not for Sale," Women's Foundation of Minnesota, www.wfmn.org/mn-girls-are-not-for-sale.

42. Louwagie, "Saving Bobbi," p. A1.

43. *William Wilberforce Trafficking Victims Protection Reauthorization Act of 2008,* Public Law 110-457, *U.S. Statutes at Large* 122 (2008): 5044-91.

purchased sex. The result was that children, recognized under both state and federal law as victims of a crime, were arrested and convicted of prostitution. This has changed under the safe harbor laws, which provide both legal protection and provision of services.[44] According to the U.S. Department of Justice, child sex trafficking is now defined as recruitment, harboring, transportation, provision, or obtaining of a person for a commercial sex act, if the person is under eighteen years of age, regardless of whether any form of coercion is involved.[45]

The Trafficking Victims Protection Reauthorization Act of 2013 (TVPRA 2013) was passed as an amendment to the Violence Against Women Act.[46] Among other things, it prevents child marriage and strengthens programs to ensure that U.S. citizens do not purchase products made by victims of human trafficking. It also establishes emergency response provisions within the State Department to respond quickly to disaster areas and crises where people are particularly susceptible to being trafficked. The reauthorization also strengthens collaboration with state and local law enforcement to ease charging and prosecuting traffickers.

Law enforcement authorities are also working together with businesses (especially hotels and airlines) to identify people who are being moved around against their will. For instance, the pattern of booking a series of hotel rooms on a credit card, then paying in cash, should raise suspicion. Large sporting events are also on the radar of trafficking activists: "Because sex trafficking spikes around the Super Bowl, hotel employees are being asked to be particularly vigilant during that time. And the NFL has been asked to only host the Super Bowl in states that have robust anti-trafficking laws."[47] Education and awareness are essential tools in curbing human trafficking.

Nevertheless, there are still flaws in federal and state trafficking legislation. For instance, the state of Iowa, according to its criminal law, regards human trafficking as less serious than drug cases. Whereas drug charges

---

44. "Sex Trafficking of Minors and 'Safe Harbor,'" *Polaris,* http://www.polarisproject.org/what-we-do/policy-advocacy/assisting-victims/safe-harbor (accessed January 7, 2015).

45. "Trafficking in Persons: A Guide for Non-Governmental Organizations," United States Department of Labor, http://www.dol.gov/wb/media/reports/trafficking.htm (accessed March 26, 2014).

46. *Trafficking Victims Protection Reauthorization Act of 2013,* Public Law 113-14, *U.S. Statutes at Large* 127 (2013): 54-139.

47. Luscombe, "How to Spot a Trafficking Victim at an Airport," http://time.com/3445807/how-to-spot-a-trafficking-victim-at-an-airport/ (accessed December 5, 2014).

are Class B felonies, punishable up to twenty-five years imprisonment, trafficking charges are Class D felonies and carry a five-year maximum, with a possible increase to ten years if the victim is a minor.[48] It is deeply troubling that the consequences of possessing drugs are harsher than the act of selling human beings.

A Lutheran Commitment to Human Well-Being and Human Dignity

While the policies in place articulate the legal aspects of trafficking, it is important to understand the ethical impetus behind such laws if we are going to ensure that they are reformed and enforced to protect victims. Christian ethics reminds us that at stake is the well-being of actual human beings. A Christian ethics is concerned that justice needs to be reestablished to rectify wrongdoings, that there be the reaffirmation of human dignity after so much pain and abuse for victims, and that healing needs to take place after so much hurt. Such care draws from the Lutheran faith commitment toward the well-being of human bodies and the development of a spirituality that affirms the interconnection of the whole of creation. In the Lutheran tradition, the service carried out for the well-being of human beings who are most broken and vulnerable is part of Christian vocation, so that "each one should become as it were a Christ to the other."[49]

In the three-pronged approach of prosecuting traffickers, protecting trafficked persons, and preventing trafficking, scholars agree that more emphasis goes into prosecution than into protection and prevention. If we change the focus to protection and assistance to trafficking victims, we can put a range of social and criminal justice responses into place to support those who have been trafficked. Working with criminal justice responses that present a more comprehensive legal approach, churches, NGOs, and other advocacy groups can be involved by offering protection and assistance to victims. Jo Goodey offers a concrete list:

Under the terms of social responses, these can include: short-term residence permits; housing; welfare payments; education; employment; and

48. Anne Easker, "Iowa's Penalty for Sex with Enslaved Prostitute Has Been Pale When Compared to Drug Charges," IowaWatch.org, http://iowawatch.org/2014/04/15/iowas-penalty-for-sex-with-enslaved-prostitute-pale-when-compared-to-drug-charges/ (accessed December 30, 2014).
49. Luther, "Freedom of a Christian," p. 76.

health-care. Criminal justice responses can incorporate: provision of information to victims on the substance and progress of their case; specialist victim support and counselling services; restitution and compensation from State and/or offender; protection of witness's privacy; and a comprehensive witness protection "package" incorporating any or all of the following: police protection for the duration of the case; right to testify away from open court and anonymously; change of identity; relocation of victim and/or family, either within a State or to another State.[50]

Sending victims home may simply place them back in the same conditions that endangered them in the first place. In situations of armed conflict or political unrest, if criminal gangs are involved in the trafficking, they will likely threaten the safety of victims and their families.[51] Trafficked persons only get to enjoy the full range of social benefits, such as a temporary residence permit and access to education, if they agree to cooperate with the authorities by providing the police with information and/or testify against traffickers.

However, victim cooperation does not always provide the necessary conditions for the women themselves due to the danger that cooperation entails. After all, because human trafficking is such a lucrative business, a single witness could not hamper the entire enterprise. It is a complex network that infiltrates not only local and familial connections but also includes law enforcers and people in high-power positions. When victims are asked to collaborate in identifying and bringing their captors or handlers to justice, there often is tension. The criminal justice authorities want criminal intelligence and, ultimately, testimonies against traffickers. Yet, what trafficked persons are able and willing to give is not always full cooperation in light of the dangers posed to them if they agree to help in a criminal investigation.

The support for trafficked women in destination countries often takes the form of outreach work with sex workers, practical assistance to women who have managed to escape trafficking, and training initiatives for women who have been granted permits to remain. Shelter in countries of destination is provided to women who have escaped from trafficking situations or who have been rescued by the police and granted temporary residence permits

50. Goodey, "Sex Trafficking in Women from Central and East European Countries," p. 31. Although Goodey refers to the European experience, her comprehensive list offers concrete suggestions for other global initiatives.
51. Feingold, "Human Trafficking," p. 30.

while they decide whether to testify against their trafficker. There is a need for a safe place under police protection where women survivors of trafficking can be accommodated. However, women who hold the status of illegal immigrant, or who have been involved in illegal prostitution, will be fearful of coming to a police shelter since they risk detention. Those who wish to escape from prostitution, but do not want to return to their country of origin, cannot benefit from accommodation provisions if they hold the status of illegal immigrants. Trafficked women who have decided to continue to work as prostitutes independent of pimps and brothel owners will be unable to access shelter services.[52]

The safety of the survivors is vital. Although some trafficked persons are willing to return to their families, in many cases this is a dangerous solution. There is also limited funding to ensure that they have the means to maintain themselves emotionally and financially. There are even fewer resources to safeguard that they have received the necessary support to become self-sufficient and self-reliable. At the end of the day, everyone wants something from these women: the clients want sex, the pimp his money, the prosecutor reliable testimony, and governments just want to send them to their home countries. True advocacy for trafficked persons should ensure that funding and programs necessary to assist victims in recovering from being trafficked are in place.

Values such as advocacy, solidarity, and empowerment take new meaning in the context of human trafficking. The care given to others is not simply carried out on behalf of others or for them. But, in mutuality, it challenges us into accountability. To assure the well-being of people being trafficked, and to advocate on their behalf, is an act of justice. It is to see that victims of human trafficking are treated as victims, rather than criminals. A clean record will give them the confidence to move ahead and seek opportunities without having to worry about a criminal conviction. Respect, dignity, and justice become the means by which Christians love their neighbors and witness Christ to one another.

52. Tzvetkova, "NGO Responses to Trafficking in Women," p. 63.

CHAPTER 8

Bearing So Much Similar Fruit: Lutheran Theology and Comprehensive Immigration Reform

Leopoldo A. Sánchez M.

Current scholarship on U.S. immigration policy written by authors inspired in the Lutheran tradition offers different visions of immigration reform. Two relatively recent approaches prove the point. On the one hand, Peter Meilaender argues for the right of nation-states to craft immigration policies that give priority to the needs of their citizens and their visions of what constitutes community.[1] Stephen Bouman and Ralston Deffenbaugh, on the other hand, focus on the church's evangelical hospitality toward the stranger as the driving biblical principle leading to strong advocacy for the needs and rights of immigrants.[2]

These seemingly competing visions of immigration reform raise the issue of Lutheran identity in determining approaches to secular law. What exactly constitutes a Lutheran approach to immigration reform? This essay argues that a Lutheran theological matrix composed of four different points of departure or themes — namely, love of neighbor (including the stranger), obedience to the law (including civil law), God's work in the two kingdoms (spiritual and temporal realms), and vocation — helps to make sense of the disparity and tension between contrasting Lutheran positions on immigration. The same matrix is then used as an interpretative lens to explore how these themes of Lutheran theology might be used to engage or approach comprehensive immigration reform. In the end, I argue that, in spite of the seemingly opposite points of departure in Lutheran proposals for immigration reform today, a common commitment to basic theological

---

1. Peter C. Meilaender, *Toward a Theory of Immigration* (New York: Palgrave, 2001).
2. Stephen Bouman and Ralston Deffenbaugh, *They Are Us: Lutherans and Immigration* (Minneapolis: Fortress Press, 2009).

themes and frameworks still leads Lutherans with different viewpoints to bear much similar fruit in terms of offering a moral compass for assessing U.S. immigration law.

Should Not All Lutherans Agree?
A Lutheran Spectrum on Immigration

At Concordia Seminary, St. Louis, we offer a course titled *Theology of Compassion and Human Care.* The course description reads as follows: "A consideration of the theological rationale for the church's efforts in the world toward bringing justice, caring for the poor, relieving human suffering, preserving and protecting creation." For a number of years, I have been invited to speak to the class for the sessions on poverty and immigration. One of the pedagogical strategies I use in approaching the often-polarizing issue of immigration lies in showing students how Lutherans actually embrace a spectrum of positions on immigration law and reform. This strategy initially comes as a shock to some students. Should not all Lutherans agree on such an important issue?

Somewhat predictably, the two basic lines of argument in the classroom reflect those in the national debate. On one hand, students who are strong advocates for respecting the divinely ordained temporal authority of the state's "rule of law," and thus the rights of its citizens and legal residents, often tend to favor tighter enforcement policies and may not immediately see why there is even an immigration debate at all: "What part of 'illegal' do you not understand?" They focus on the need to uphold the laws of the land, whatever they might be, and thus tend to frame their concerns alongside the political spectrum of legality and illegality.

On the other hand, students who are strong advocates of immigrants and their families, whether documented or not, as well as the church's work of gospel proclamation and mercy among the strangers, tend to highlight the divinely ordained church's "Great Commandment" and "Great Commission" without legal conditions attached: "What part of 'love your neighbor as yourself' and 'go and make disciples of all nations' do you not understand?" They focus on the immigrants themselves, their needs and contributions to the church, family, and society, and therefore tend to look at matters more along a social spectrum of hospitality and hostility toward neighbors. At least initially, neither side considers that perhaps Lutheran theology can make some sense out of this disparity and tension, allowing for a deeper and more complex conversation about immigration and immigrants to take place, one that ultimately makes room for a diversity of more nuanced positions enriched by such dialogue.

To highlight the spectrum of Lutheran ideas on immigration, I have my students read two contrasting examples of reflections on the issue by Lutherans today. On one end of the spectrum, we have Bouman and Deffenbaugh, who, reminding Lutherans of their own immigrant roots and historic efforts in resettling Lutheran refugees, focus on the church's evangelical hospitality toward the stranger as the main biblical/theological basis and guiding principle for advocating on behalf of immigrants, their needs and rights. While these authors are not against the need for immigration law, they nevertheless stress the need to move beyond immigration policies focused solely on enforcement. The authors do not advocate a policy of "open borders," but rather call for sensible reform that accounts fairly for the contributions of immigrants and their families to our way of life. While Bouman and Deffenbaugh hold to the importance of the rule of law, they also believe that the immigration system itself is broken or unworkable, and therefore ends up setting itself up for failure in enforcing the very rule of law it seeks to uphold.[3] Finally, as a theological reflection on immigration written by Christians who see themselves as representatives of a historically immigrant Lutheran church, the overall thrust of their presentation is, understandably so, informed by the principle of hospitality toward aliens or foreigners with whom we share a common humanity and immigrant identity — thus the title of their book, *They Are Us*.[4]

On the other end of the spectrum, political theorist Peter Meilaender, focusing on a people's right for self-definition in their view of political community and national identity, argues for the rights of modern nation-states such as the U.S. to regulate and enforce immigration. Are they really us? Not so fast, Meilaender might say, asking instead the provocative question: "May (or perhaps must) we prefer 'our own' — our families, friends, neighbors, and compatriots, the shared way of life we develop together, even the

<hr/>

3. Bouman and Deffenbaugh, *They Are Us,* pp. 54-69.

4. Martin Marty sums up well the authors' intention: "Everyone recognizes that not all doors of all nations can be wide open all the time and in all circumstances. But policy questions have to come in after, not before, we consider the meaning of immigration, the needs and rights of immigrants, and — though this is often forgotten — the gifts they bring to the republic. The first word for Christians has to be Christian. . . . [F]ollowers of the gospel of Jesus Christ *get* to welcome the stranger in his name, to practice hospitality, and to share in the gifts that come in the exchange with the stranger." Martin E. Marty, foreword to Bouman and Deffenbaugh, *They Are Us,* pp. xii-xiii.

familiar vistas of our native land — to other people, in different places, with different ways of life?"[5] Meilaender is particularly critical of what he sees as "one-sided" statements by church officials that focus "almost entirely on the needs of immigrants, both legal and illegal, while giving virtually no attention to the issue of securing the border or the social costs of unenforced immigration laws."[6] Meilaender does, however, pose the possibility that immigrants over time can become "*de facto,* if not *de jure . . .* one of us" due to their proximity to our families, friends, and community, so that "[o]ur obligations to them gradually begin to mirror those we owe fellow citizens, of which the refusal to expel them from the country is basic."[7]

Making Sense of Lutheran Differences: A Theological Framework for Assessing Lutheran Approaches to Immigration

A Lutheran theological matrix can make some sense out of the disparity between contrasting Lutheran positions on immigration reform. In a relatively recent report of the Commission on Theology and Church Relations (CTCR) of the Lutheran Church–Missouri Synod (LCMS), titled *Immigrants Among Us* — a document I had the privilege to be involved with as its main drafter — the Commission draws attention to four theological themes Lutherans can utilize in framing their conversations about immigrants and proposals on immigration reform.[8] Moving from more general frameworks that Lutherans share with other Christians to those that are more specifically Lutheran in focus, these thematic points of departure are the following:

General Frameworks:
1. God's command to his people to "love the neighbor as yourself," including the alien or stranger (cf. Lev. 19:18, 33-34).
2. God's command to obey the authorities and honor the law for the sake of peace and order in society (cf. Rom. 13:1-7; 1 Pet. 2:13-17).

5. Meilaender, *Theory of Immigration,* p. 3.

6. Mark Amstutz and Peter Meilaender, "Public Policy and the Church: Spiritual Priorities," *The City* 4 (Spring 2011): 5.

7. Peter Meilaender, "Immigration: Citizens and Strangers," *First Things* 173 (May 2007): 12, http://www.firstthings.com/article/2007/05/immigration-citizens-strangers.

8. Commission on Theology and Church Relations (CTCR), *Immigrants Among Us: A Lutheran Framework for Addressing Immigration Issues* (St. Louis: LCMS, 2013). This document is available online in English and Spanish from http://www.lcms.org/ctcr.

Specifically Lutheran Frameworks:

3. Two Kingdoms Theology: God works in the world through the spiritual realm for the sake of justification before God (right-hand kingdom, spiritual government) and through the temporal realm for the sake of justice before humans (left-hand kingdom, temporal government).

4. Vocation: God's manifold work on behalf of many neighbors through the callings of his people in various estates, offices, or orders established by God (e.g., marriage, government, church, education, economy, etc.).

Each lens or point of departure contributes something different to the discussion and does not claim to solve all the issues involved.

Our fourfold theological matrix helps explain in part why authors from the same theological background and confession such as Bouman/ Deffenbaugh and Meilaender can have contrasting views on immigration reform. In short, these authors start from different points of departure and thus read the situation with certain priorities in mind. With the immigrant neighbor as their central concern, Bouman and Deffenbaugh focus on God's command to his people to love the strangers in their midst as their guiding biblical value:[9]

> "When a stranger sojourns with you in your land, you shall not do him wrong. You shall treat the stranger who sojourns with you as the native among you, and you shall love him as yourself, for you were strangers in the land of Egypt: I am the Lord your God." (Lev. 19:33-34, ESV)

The focus on immigrant neighbors works well to highlight not only their basic dignity as God's creatures, but also their marginality or vulnerability, making them special objects of compassion. Moreover, this approach serves to warn against the use of harsh rhetoric, fueled by racist or discriminatory language, against immigrants. The call for self-identification with immigrants today because of our national or our church's spiritual fathers' and mothers' immigrant past also fits well under this entry point into the conversation on immigrants.[10] In this approach, the concern for locating immigration issues in the context of the polarity of legality or illegality is not a primary concern, since God's love and compassion for the aliens or strangers in our

9. Bouman and Deffenbaugh, *They Are Us*, pp. 8-24.
10. Bouman and Deffenbaugh, *They Are Us*, pp. 25-53.

midst — and vulnerable neighbors in general — is not conditional upon the fulfillment of any legal requirements.[11]

Meilaender, on the other hand, focuses on the second framework, which includes the rights of modern nation-states to create, enact, and enforce immigration laws that give priority to the well-being of their citizens and residents before attending to the needs of others.[12] When the relationship between immigration law and national identity becomes the main focus of the conversation, Meilaender argues that more attention can be given to policy considerations such as "the purposes of politics, relationships between insiders and outsiders, and the foundations of international order."[13] In this legal framework, more attention is given to what constitutes just, fair, or adequate law in a political context that assumes "special relationships" among its citizens. The priority of love, as it were, is therefore extended to citizens who are closest to us *first* and then to strangers — not the other way around. While Meilaender agrees that "we owe something to each person simply by virtue of his or her humanity," he adds that "we also stand in particular relationships to certain persons for whom we bear special responsibilities," including "fellow citizens."[14]

Undoubtedly, using the law as a lens for approaching immigration will yield different views on policy matters. Lutherans will find themselves holding various positions along a spectrum that gives more or less weight to different aspects of the immigration debate such as border enforcement and national security, human rights of immigrants and humane enforcement of immigration laws, family unification for those torn apart (or in danger of being separated) by deportation, and/or economic factors such as the need for worker visas to deal with labor demand. We will unpack some of these issues in the third section of this chapter.

The very possibility of respectful and fruitful dialogue on these matters concerning both citizen and immigrant neighbors among Lutherans can actually "reflect an earnest desire to respect the rule of law and to test

---

11. The CTCR report notes that "the divine command to love the alien as our neighbor remains valid and is not fundamentally tied to the fulfillment of any specific obligations on the part of the alien. This suggests that legal or illegal status cannot be a prerequisite for the church's concern about the basic dignity of aliens and their families . . . their fair and just treatment in society, and their need to hear the Gospel and receive the sacraments." *Immigrants Among Us*, p. 18.

12. Meilaender, *Theory of Immigration*, pp. 81-171.

13. Amstutz and Meilaender, "Public Policy and the Church," p. 13.

14. Meilaender, "Citizens and Strangers," p. 11.

the validity of a specific law and so to provide a larger measure of justice."[15] Indeed, using civil law as a point of departure in the immigration debate will yield a number of positions among Lutherans on how to deal with reform.[16] Some may believe that current law, though imperfect, is good enough as it stands. Some will engage in peaceful protests to dramatize perceived injustices against citizens and/or immigrants. Others will push for reform, through the power of the vote or the exercise of civil disobedience, in certain areas of the current law deemed inadequate or perhaps unjust. Such an area might be the law's inability to provide an adequate number of worker visas to keep up with U.S. labor demand, which in turn encourages unfair labor practices such as hiring people without permission to work or exploiting workers without the protection of the law. Another area might be the law's inability to reunite families in a reasonable amount of time due to the huge backlog in processing visa applications, which in turn encourages families to cross the border or overstay visas to be together with their loved ones.

Others will opt for peaceful coexistence with those immigrant neighbors (e.g., undocumented children) who are not a dangerous threat to society until some legal remedy is made available to deal with their ambiguous legal circumstances. A recent example of such a temporary remedy lies in the option available since 2012 for undocumented children, who were brought to the U.S. by their parents illegally before they reached the age of sixteen, to request "Consideration of Deferred Action for Childhood Arrivals (DACA)." Described by the U.S. Citizenship and Immigration Services (USCIS) as "a use of prosecutorial discretion," DACA may also make the applicant "eligible for work authorization," but "does not provide lawful status."[17] The rationale provided for the temporary remedy lies in the Administration's desire "to focus its enforcement resources on the removal of individuals who pose a danger to national security or a risk to public safety."[18]

While Lutherans share with other Christians the same biblical concerns for hospitality toward strangers and obedience to government authorities, two more specifically Lutheran theological lenses contribute further to re-

---

15. CTCR, *Civil Obedience and Disobedience* (St. Louis: LCMS, 1966), p. 6.

16. CTCR, *Immigrants Among Us*, p. 32.

17. USCIS, "Consideration of Deferred Action for Childhood Arrivals (DACA)," http://www.uscis.gov/humanitarian/consideration-deferred-action-childhood-arrivals -daca (accessed August 4, 2014).

18. USCIS, "Frequently Asked Questions," http://www.uscis.gov/humanitarian/ consideration-deferred-action-childhood-arrivals-process/frequently-asked-questions (accessed August 4, 2014).

flection on immigration law and reform, namely, the distinction between the two kingdoms/realms and the teaching on vocation.[19] Bouman/Deffenbaugh and Meilaender assume these categories in their respective views of immigration. Bouman and Deffenbaugh, for instance, highlight the church's "ministry" of hospitality among immigrants in the right-hand realm as a catalyst for immigration reform in the left-hand realm.[20] God's people are given the command to care for the stranger without distinction as a fundamental value that must shape one's thinking in the left-hand realm, even though Christians may disagree on particular immigration policy.[21]

In making the move toward a biblically grounded " 'preferential option' for the stranger, the alien, the poor, and defenseless," the authors assume the Lutheran teaching concerning the church's call to do its work in the right-hand or spiritual realm regardless of the current state of the law in the left-hand or temporal realm.[22] The authors surely call for comprehensive reform in immigration law, but they also see the church's work of ministry in the spiritual realm as a non-negotiable factor that should precede policy considerations per se.

Meilaender's proposal highlights the notion of "special relations" to neighbors who are closest to us as a basis for nation-states to give priority to their citizens in crafting of immigration law over against the needs of foreigners. He argues that "[i]mmigration regulations are a way of embodying in policy a preferential love for our fellow citizens and the way of life that we share."[23] By making the move toward "special relations" in his approach to immigration, the author implicitly appropriates the Lutheran teaching on vocation, which calls Christians to first attend to those neighbors whom they have been especially given to serve in the world. While Christians may serve all neighbors as they have opportunity, vocation makes the general commandment to love the neighbor more concrete and practical by drawing attention toward those closest to us.[24] This idea of "special relations" leads

19. See Martin Luther's classic work "Temporal Authority: To What Extent It Should Be Obeyed," *Luther's Works*, vol. 45, *The Christian in Society II*, ed. Walther I. Brandt, trans. J. J. Schindel and Walther I. Brandt (Philadelphia: Muhlenberg, 1962), pp. 75-129; see also Gustaf Wingren, *Luther on Vocation*, trans. Carl C. Rasmussen (Eugene, OR: Wipf & Stock, 2004).

20. Bouman and Deffenbaugh, *They Are Us*, pp. 82-94.

21. Bouman and Deffenbaugh, *They Are Us*, p. 20.

22. Bouman and Deffenbaugh, *They Are Us*, p. 10.

23. Meilaender, "Citizens and Strangers," p. 11.

24. "The world, after all, contains countless needy people who require assistance. How are we to know whom to help? So we begin with those to whom we stand in special relationships." Meilaender, "Citizens and Strangers," p. 11.

Meilaender to suggest, for instance, that, while "enforcement-only" proposals in immigration reform are not sufficient to deal with the complexity of the problem, "enforcement-first" proposals must not necessarily be put off the table.[25] As we shall point out soon, however, Meilaender's narrow use of the principle of "special relations" to argue for the priority of citizens over foreigners has its limits, since the Lutheran teaching on vocation allows for a broader application of the principle that includes other neighbors in close proximity to us. Special relations include commitments to fellow citizens, but also to family members, church members, and even immigrant neighbors who work and live in our midst.

Using the Lutheran distinction between the two realms/kingdoms and the distinctive Lutheran teaching on vocation as frameworks for immigration has further advantages. I have argued that the Lutheran distinction between the two realms is helpful in the practice of ministry. It allows Christians to promote the proclamation of the gospel and do the works of mercy that flow from the gospel among immigrants in the spiritual realm, regardless of the particular positions Christians might hold on immigration law in the temporal realm. Positions on immigration law should not be an obstacle to the church's unity in Christ and its mission in the world.[26] There is a certain freedom for disagreement among Lutherans on left-hand realm issues dealing with the preservation of justice, order, and peace in the world (including immigration law and reform). Yet these issues do not (or at least, should not) get in the way of the basic Lutheran commitment to the work of holistic ministry among immigrants in the spiritual realm, which deals with justification before God through faith in Christ and the works of mercy that accompany and adorn this gospel of life as the church serves all. *The beauty of the Lutheran distinction between temporal and spiritual realms or governments is that it allows for disagreement on political issues without letting such positions get in the way of the church's unity and mission in the world.*

The Lutheran doctrine of vocation helps to explain further why Luther-

<hr/>

25. Referring to an ELCA resolution critical of "enforcement-only approaches" to immigration reform, Meilaender asks: "But what of 'enforcement-first' approaches? Some of the most promising compromise proposals aiming at immigration reform seek to pair improved border security — once security benchmarks have been met — with the possibility of amnesty for illegals, or increases in the number of work visas made available. I regard proposals of this sort as quite reasonable." Peter C. Meilaender, "Ethics without Political Science," *Journal of Lutheran Ethics* (April 2010), https://www.elca.org/JLE/Articles/311.htm.

26. Leopoldo Sánchez, "Misión e inmigración. Pedagogía para trabajar entre los inmigrantes," *Missio Apostolica* 16, no. 1 (2008): 70-74.

ans often have different positions in the immigration debate. When in 2010 Governor Jan Brewer signed into law Arizona's controversial S.B. 1070, the "Support Our Law Enforcement and Safe Neighborhood Act" bill, I argued that the decisions the Governor, an LCMS Lutheran, made as a public official in the left-hand realm, as well as the decisions of others to challenge the new state law's constitutionality, were all ultimately driven by the desire of different advocates to stand up for different sets of neighbors.[27] Governor Brewer advocated for the protection of "the citizens of Arizona," and therefore against criminal elements like drug dealers and smugglers who threatened their quality of life.[28] Inevitably, others, including Lutherans, advocated for neighbors who appeared to fall through the cracks in Arizona's enforcement-only approach to immigration:

> There will be others who will advocate for the hard-working immigrants whose legal status is questionable but over the years have contributed to the economic vitality of the state, whose children were born here and know no other country than this land of freedom and opportunity, whose families are a weird composite of citizens, residents, and illegal aliens all living under the same roof. These neighbors will have their advocates. Lutheran Immigration and Refugee Service (LIRS), for example, has chosen consistently to advocate for the unity of the family as they take a critical look at the rapidly changing nature of immigration laws everywhere.[29]

Ideally, Christians are advocating for the needs of particular neighbors as they argue for more worker visas, family unity, border enforcement, or a path toward legalization. *Implicitly or explicitly, immigration debates have*

27. Leopoldo Sánchez, "Arizona Neighbor on My Mind," ConcordiaTheology.org, May 3, 2010, http://concordiatheology.org/2010/05/arizona-neighbor-on-my-mind (accessed July 30, 2014).

28. Writing for the majority, U.S. Supreme Court Justice Anthony M. Kennedy acknowledged the concerns of Arizona, but ultimately sided with the United States, ruling that three out of four sections of S.B. 1070 were preempted by federal law. The syllabus of the Court sums up the aforementioned three sections as follows: "Section 3 makes failure to comply with federal alien-registration requirements a state misdemeanor; §5(C) makes it a misdemeanor for an unauthorized alien to seek or engage in work in the State; §6 authorizes state and local officers to arrest without warrant a person 'the officer has probable cause to believe . . . has committed any public offense that makes the person removable from the United States'; . . . " *Arizona et al. v. United States,* 567 US (2012).

29. Sánchez, "Arizona Neighbor on My Mind."

some neighbor in mind. Meilaender's theory of immigration advocates for the needs of citizens first. However, as Bouman and Deffenbaugh's work shows, immigrants will also have their advocates. What else could be expected from Christians whose main vocations at the time of writing *They Are Us* were, respectively, serving as director of Evangelical Outreach and Congregational Mission for the Evangelical Lutheran Church in America (ELCA), and as president of Lutheran Immigration and Refugee Service (LIRS)? Make no mistake about it. *Vocation drives decisions about who we serve, and who we serve first.* Vocational priorities help us to see in part why Lutherans who hold to the same confession end up at times on different sides of the immigration debate. They are standing up for certain neighbors.

Our closest neighbors are fellow citizens in some cases, but in other cases they are immigrants and their children. We have responsibilities toward them that arise because of their close proximity to us. It is not uncommon for citizens and legal residents to live in the same household with undocumented family members.[30] Their proximity to one another, in the context of their vocations or callings as family members, compels them to love, serve, and protect each other. Understandably, their commitment to family unity will take priority over concern for fellow citizens who are not as closely connected to them. It is also not uncommon for undocumented persons to live, work, and worship with us. Our children may be going to school together, or working in the same restaurants. Our families may be eating at the same potlucks, or at the Lord's Table. In a theology of vocation, levels of proximity or closeness to neighbors matter. These levels vary, and therefore, levels of advocacy in calls for reform will differ. As we have seen, even Meilaender makes room in his approach to advocate for those immigrants who have become our *de facto* neighbors and part of our communities, and goes as far as arguing for the possibility of providing amnesty as long as certain legal conditions are fulfilled such

---

30. Even though Christians are free to use the terms "illegal" and "undocumented" to refer to persons who are in the U.S. without a valid visa, I generally opt not to use the term "illegal" because of its failure to distinguish between the immigrant person and the concrete act he or she has committed that is against the law. Such language also tends to reduce the whole person to the spectrum of legality and illegality. In this sense, even the term "undocumented" is limited in its scope. The CTCR notes that both terms "offer neither a comprehensive picture of our immigrant neighbors nor an accurate portrait of the complexity of the immigration problem." CTCR, *Immigrants Among Us,* p. 23; see also Leopoldo Sánchez, "Immigrants Among Us: What Are Confessional Lutherans to Do?" *LOGIA* 19, no. 1 (Epiphany 2010): 57-58.

as "the payment of back taxes or proficiency in English."[31] The beauty of the Lutheran theology of vocation is that it gives Christians permission to advocate, fight for, and defend neighbors they have been called to serve — whoever they might be.

At the same time, we must be careful that, in advocating for particular neighbors, we do not become insensitive to the plight of others. The teaching of vocation can potentially be used in an absolute, exclusionary manner. Meilaender, for instance, has noted that a nation's right for self-determining its admission of immigrants into the country should not lead to an absolute policy of closed borders, especially in view of the international community's moral concern for groups such as refugees and its growing support for keeping close family members together.[32] In a similar vein, Bouman and Deffenbaugh acknowledge the need for "homeland security," but not at the expense of violating "people's rights," tearing families apart, or permanently marginalizing undocumented immigrants who contribute to the country and share our values.[33]

The doctrine of vocation teaches us that there is always a human face in the immigration debate. Lutheran legal scholar and professor Marie Failinger has argued precisely for a more "face-to-face" approach to immigration law — for instance, in processing requests by vulnerable strangers for entry into the U.S. — noting particularly how rules of due process should be tempered by the modern rubric in American jurisprudence of "guided discretion" in the hearing of specific cases.[34] In *Immigrants Among Us,* the CTCR states both the particular and the nonexclusionary character of Luther's teaching on vocation, especially in the context of a broader argument that vocational priority toward citizens should not trump in an absolute way appropriate concern for suffering strangers:

31. Meilaender, "Citizens and Strangers," p. 12. We should note that Meilaender's proposal does not seem to acknowledge data showing that undocumented workers pay taxes, contributing to Medicare and the Social Security Administration's "earning suspense file," from which they will get no benefit. See Kimber Solana, "Illegal Immigrants Give Billions to Medicare, Social Security with No Hope of Benefit," http://www.medicarenewsgroup.com/ context/understanding-medicare-blog/understanding-medicare-blog/2013/01/07/illegal -immigrants-give-billions-to-medicare-social-security-with-no-hope-of-benefit (accessed September 10, 2014).

32. Meilaender, *Theory of Immigration,* pp. 174-83.

33. Bouman and Deffenbaugh, *They Are Us,* p. 19.

34. Marie A. Failinger, "Recovering the Face-to-Face in American Immigration Law," *Southern California Review of Law and Social Justice* 16, no. 2 (2007): 319-70.

Although one cannot attempt to fulfill God's law in some abstract sense without some concrete neighbor in mind, Luther is also able to teach that the law of God is above this or that particular vocation, office, and neighbor. This insight adds another layer of complexity to the immigration debate and prevents us from arriving at some exclusivist approach to vocation and office that will conveniently leave out some important neighbors who might not fit neatly within our stations. . . . Christians still must find ways, whenever possible, to deal with the suffering neighbor even when he is outside his [*sic*] particular vocation(s).[35]

Gathering the Fruits of Lutheran Debate: Lutheran Identity and Comprehensive Immigration Reform

We are now in a position to ask: How might Lutheran theology seen through our four frameworks above help us to approach and address comprehensive immigration reform? At the risk of overgeneralization, comprehensive immigration reform is basically an approach to immigration law that does not focus *solely* on enforcement-based measures, but argues for reform more *broadly* by taking into consideration other factors such as economics and labor, family integration issues, and/or humanitarian concerns. Attention to Lutheran debate on such matters offers us a rich field of fruitful ideas to gather from — even more, a moral compass — as we assess how Lutheran identity might shape the national debate on immigration law and reform.

One of the fundamental premises for the drive toward comprehensive immigration reform lies generally in the belief that the current U.S. immigration system is broken. Bauman and Deffenbaugh point out three areas in which the present state of U.S. immigration law deals inadequately with deep values held by U.S. citizens — including Christians — such as family unity, the dignity of the worker and fair labor practices, and the humane treatment of those seeking freedom.[36]

---

35. CTCR, *Immigrants Among Us*, p. 43. The report cites Althaus's succinct summary of Luther's teaching on vocation: "Luther's ethics is an ethics of station and vocation, but not in an exclusive sense." See Paul Althaus, *The Ethics of Martin Luther* (Minneapolis: Fortress Press, 1972), p. 41. The report also states: "On the one hand, we must rejoice in our vocations and attend primarily to those neighbors we have been called to serve. On the other hand, we must have the needs of all our neighbors in mind when the opportunity to serve them arises — even those neighbors who are living among us illegally." CTCR, *Immigrants Among Us*, p. 44.

36. Bauman and Deffenbaugh, *They Are Us*, pp. 59-69.

Let us consider family unity. Due to the backlog in processing applications, a lawful permanent resident (LPR) of the U.S. who did not enter the country with his or her spouse and minor children "must wait at least three years and nine months to be reunited with his or her spouse. . . . If the LPR is from Mexico, he or she must wait seven years and five months."[37] The backlog problem leads to extended family separation, which in turn leads people with close bonds to do whatever they can to remain together — including resorting to illegal immigration through border-crossing or by overstaying their visas. The incentive to continue breaking the law is greater if, for example, one of the family members is already in the U.S. illegally even though his children were born in the U.S. (a "mixed-status family"), since in current immigration law, "a person deported will not be allowed to reenter the United States for at least ten years, if then."[38] The unity of the family suffers.

The brokenness of the system may also be seen in its inability to deal adequately with the basic economics of supply and demand. Unmet labor demands in the agricultural, service, and construction sectors of the U.S. economy not only entice migrants to cross the border to supply the need but actually require the work of unskilled migrants. Even though the increasing fencing of the border tells immigrants not to cross into the U.S., the powerful economic demand on the other side of the border tells immigrants that if they risk their lives to cross the border, there will be a job waiting for them on the other side. As Bauman and Deffenbaugh point out, "the demand for unskilled jobs that is not being filled by native-born workers is between 400,000 to 500,000 per year. Yet under current law, the annual number of immigrant visas for unskilled workers is only five-thousand."[39] Since economics is a major force for migration, the inadequacy of the law in allowing for an adequate number of visas to supply needed unskilled labor actually leads not only to illegal immigration, but also to unfair labor practices such as violation of wage and hour standards, unhealthy working conditions, and extortion of workers by employers who threaten to call Immigration on them.

Finally, the authors see yet another indication of a broken system in the way the U.S government deals with a number of vulnerable immigrants who pose no threat to society. In particular, the increasing use of

37. Bauman and Deffenbaugh, *They Are Us,* p. 60.
38. Bauman and Deffenbaugh, *They Are Us,* p. 66.
39. Bauman and Deffenbaugh, *They Are Us,* p. 63.

detention centers for the "overwhelming majority of these asylum seek-ers" — including children — is seen as "drastic," leading the authors to argue for other forms of monitoring that do not include imprisonment for such low-risk individuals.[40] For a nation that extols the value of free-dom, the authors find it problematic that such freedom is unnecessarily curtailed for those immigrants who legitimately flee persecution and seek a more dignified life.

Meilaender does not state his case for immigration reform by appealing to the moral inadequacy of the broken immigration system per se, largely because he gives a certain fundamental priority in ethical discourse to "the moral legitimacy of regimes" over "specific policy issues."[41] Otherwise stated, the more fundamental ethical question is whether a people's choice of a form of government, including one that holds to the rule of law and gives legal priority to its own citizens and their political life or national identity, is fundamentally moral or just. If it is not, then one cannot finally pledge allegiance to such government. If it is, then a subsequent discussion of poli-cies that may or not sustain the regime can take place, but always within the context of the regime's political frameworks.

While assuming this theoretical distinction between general regimes and specific policy issues, Meilaender still states two cases or nonabsolute "exceptions" in which a regime's right to define its immigration policies "may nevertheless not simply be a matter that each nation is entirely free to de-termine for itself."[42] Meilaender speaks of assistance to refugees ("the truly desperate") and the unification of close family members ("family unity") as morally compelling transnational obligations or "values that circumscribe states' freedom of action" at some level.[43] Moreover, as we have already seen, he also speaks of providing a path toward amnesty for undocumented immigrants who have become a part of our communities and contributed to our shared way of life. While it is clear that Bouman and Deffenbaugh do not approach questions on immigration reform in the same manner Meilaender does, it is remarkable to see how in spite of their unique ways to process the issues, they still hold a number of similar values such as the concern for the immediate family and vulnerable neighbors.

40. Bauman and Deffenbaugh, *They Are Us,* p. 65; for a movie that speaks to the com-plexities of the asylum system and the related use of detention centers, see *Chasing Freedom,* directed by Don McBrearty (First Look Pictures, 2005), DVD.
41. Amstutz and Meilaender, "Public Policy and the Church," p. 14.
42. Meilaender, *Theory of Immigration,* p. 173.
43. Meilaender, *Theory of Immigration,* pp. 174, 180.

For an example of a more systematic Lutheran proposal for comprehensive immigration reform, we need to look no further than the LIRS five
principles for reform.[44] They are the following:

1. Path to citizenship
2. Humane enforcement
3. Family unity
4. Protection for vulnerable migrants
5. Protection of workers

Let us look at these five principles through the lens of our fourfold Lutheran
theological matrix already discussed. We will note how these principles
assume or arise from a particular appropriation of a Lutheran lens to immigration, thus placing them within a spectrum that is legitimately tied to
Lutheran identity.

First of all, the LIRS principles clearly assume and promote the biblical
command to love the immigrant neighbor. Undocumented immigrants and
their families in particular are to be brought out of the shadows and integrated into U.S. society. This is done through a path to legalization, which
may include citizenship at some point. Humane enforcement highlights the
human dignity of the immigrant, and asks specifically for reducing the use
of detention centers and expanding community support programs for those
who do not have to be detained. The call for the protection of the family unit,
while not a uniquely immigrant need, becomes a principle of reform because
of the potential separation of immigrant families through deportation or
the lack of an adequate supply of visas to reunite separated families. The
principle of protection of immigrants highlights their vulnerability and pays
particular attention to the need for integrating refugees, asylees, survivors
of torture and trafficking, and unaccompanied minors into U.S. society. The
protection of migrant workers also assumes their vulnerability as potential
objects of abuse in the workplace.

Second, all principles assume the importance of the rule of law, even if
aspects of current immigration law are seen as needing reform. The first one
highlights the need for a regularized process of legalization that is described
as an "earned pathway to lawful permanent residency and eventual citizen-

44. LIRS, "Principles for Comprehensive Immigration Reform," http://lirs.org/wp
-content/uploads/2013/02/LIRS-Principles-for-Comprehensive-Immigration-Reform.pdf
(accessed 4 August 2014).

ship."[45] While some immigration reform proposals do not offer a path to citizenship, but only some form of legalization of status, they all presuppose the importance of some legal path out of the shadows of living in the margins of the undocumented status. The petition to reduce the use of detention centers is articulated in the framework of humane and just enforcement, presupposing the right of a nation to enforce its laws. The principle of family unity, which asks for an adequate supply of visas to bring families together, also presupposes the right of a nation to regulate the entry of foreign nationals into the country. Moreover, the proposal for the protection of migrant workers highlights the need to uphold the nation's labor laws.

While Lutherans may disagree on how the biblical command to love the immigrant neighbor or the biblical command to obey the temporal authorities should apply to contemporary questions about immigration law and reform, comprehensive immigration reform is certainly one viable application of such general theological frameworks to our situation today. There is, in a sense, nothing exclusively Lutheran about comprehensive immigration reform's incorporation of these two principles in its platform, simply because love of neighbor and obedience to civil authority are general commitments Lutherans hold in common with other Christian communions. Evangelicals and Roman Catholics in the U.S., for instance, hold to similar tenets in their versions of comprehensive immigration reform.[46] At the same time, there is

45. LIRS, "Principles for Comprehensive Immigration Reform"; Bauman and Deffenbaugh support a basic fourfold set of criteria for assessing immigration reform proposals. Such criteria are grounded in basic moral values that call for the protection of the family, the worker, and the stranger. They ask if the proposal promotes family unity, as well as human and worker rights. They also ask if the proposal enables the undocumented to come out of the shadows through a path to permanence as a full member of society. See Bauman and Deffenbaugh, *They Are Us*, p. 70.

46. The Evangelical Immigration Table (EIT) calls for immigration reform that "respects the God-given dignity of every person," "protects the unity of the immediate family," "respects the rule of law," "guarantees secure national borders," "ensures fairness to taxpayers," and "establishes a path toward legal status and/or citizenship for those who qualify and who wish to become permanent residents." See EIT, "Statement of Principles for Immigration Reform," http://evangelicalimmigrationtable.com/#principles (accessed August 1, 2014). U.S. Catholic Bishops include in their position for comprehensive immigration reform "an earned legalization program," a fair "worker program," "family-based immigration reform," "restoration of due process rights," assistance in "sustainable economic development in sending countries," and "targeted, proportional, and humane" enforcement. See USCCB, "Catholic Church's Position on Immigration Reform," http://usccb.org/issues-and-action/human-life-and-dignity/immigration/churchteachingonimmigrationreform.cfm (accessed August 1, 2014).

also nothing intrinsically un-Lutheran about LIRS's particular reform platform. It represents a legitimate Lutheran application or appropriation of God's timeless mandates to love the alien as yourself and obey the authorities.

We can now move to an analysis of comprehensive immigration reform through the lens of our two more specifically Lutheran frameworks, namely, the teachings of the two kingdoms/realms and vocation. Perhaps surprisingly, the LIRS principles for reform do not speak at length about the church's role among immigrants in the spiritual realm apart from the state of immigration law in the left-hand realm. LIRS, however, encourages churches to visit people in detention centers, and its statement in favor of community support programs that can attend to those who do not need to be detained does not exclude the role churches might play in providing such support. More explicit is how the LIRS principles highlight the role that not only individual Christians, but Christian agencies with a particular charge, can (or indeed, must) play in the left-hand realm. Theirs is a public advocacy platform for immigration reform in a number of areas. At times, the reforms are specific: path to citizenship, "reducing the use of immigration detention," and providing "an adequate supply of visas for families seeking to reunite."[47] Overall, however, reform criteria are still broadly defined in the LIRS document, so that the "five principles of reform" are more fundamental than the actual legal forms such principles might take. A guiding principle is specific enough to define the scope for legal reform, but flexible enough to encompass a variety of legislative proposals within the stated scope.

When it comes to the manner in which Lutherans propose guidelines for dealing with left-hand temporal issues, the CTCR document *Immigrants Among Us* takes a more indirect approach to immigration reform questions, providing individual Christians with Lutheran theological tools for reflection on immigration so that they can make their own conscientious decisions on the matter. While the LCMS, unlike the ELCA, does not have an official public position on immigration reform "from above" in the form of a broad churchwide resolution, it does offer an approach "from below."[48] The LCMS

---

47. LIRS, "Principles for Comprehensive Immigration Reform."

48. ELCA, "Toward Compassionate, Just, and Wise Immigration Reform." Social Policy Resolution CA09.11.71, accessed August 1, 2014, http://download.elca.org/ELCA %20Resource%20Repository/Immigration_ReformSPR09.pdf. The document acknowledges the "rule of law," but also speaks of "a broken immigration system." It calls for reform that includes the following principles: "Reunite families and integrate the marginalized," "protect the rights of people at work," "establish just and humane enforcement," "revitalize refugee protection and integration," and "address root causes of forced immigration."

position is defined in its CTCR document on immigration as follows: "This approach seeks to teach not by direct, irrefutable command but through biblical and theological guidelines and principles that the Christian is meant to reflect on and contextualize."[49] If the danger of official "from above" statements on legitimately disputed issues such as immigration law and reform is that they can quench individual Christian conscience in dealing with potentially gray areas in the realm of ethics, the danger of a perhaps less intrusive approach "from below" that leaves all things to the individual Christian is that it might not be bold enough to encourage wider support for dealing with aspects of current law that might be morally questionable.

In the spectrum between public and private approaches, one could argue that the LIRS statement of comprehensive immigration reform principles fits somewhere between both. Overall, it is more public than private in scope. At the same time, it prefers to advocate for principles rather than specific legislation. Having said that, such principles are not finally meant simply to guide individual Christian reflection. The principles are used a bit more boldly to guide ongoing assessment of legislation considered in Congress. They are truly normative principles. There is, however, a difference between a Lutheran church body's official statement and a Lutheran social agency's statement. Whereas the former claims to speak for the church's position as a whole and teaches its members to follow it for the sake of obedience to God's will, the latter speaks more clearly for those neighbors whom it has been called to serve and advocate for, while also calling to action those who will heed the call to serve these neighbors in particular.

As a Lutheran social agency, LIRS fulfills a corporate vocation that compels the organization to advocate in a more public and normative manner

49. CTCR, *Immigrants Among Us*, p. 35. In a previous document, the Commission on Theology and Church Relations noted that "sensitive questions may arise for public debate concerning which God's Word provides less specific guidance. . . . In these cases it may be helpful for the Synod, while recognizing that Lutheran Christians equally committed to following God's will as revealed in Holy Scripture may come to different conclusions, to keep its members informed and offer guidance to them as they determine their own positions." The Lutheran Church–Missouri Synod, "Tuition Tax Credits and the Lutheran Church–Missouri Synod," quoted in CTCR, *Render unto Caesar . . . and unto God: A Lutheran View of Church and State* (St. Louis: LCMS, 1994), p. 51. However, there are cases where the LCMS has spoken in resolution on behalf of the whole church. In 2007, the Missouri Synod adopted Res. 6-04A "To Encourage and Assist Congregations to Respond to the Ministry Needs of Immigrants in Their Midst," encouraging government officials to exercise "compassionate mercy" toward the immigrant. In 2010, the Synod also adopted Res. 6-07A, "To Support Efforts to End Human Trafficking/Slavery."

for immigration reform precisely because its main institutional mission and vocation is to serve refugees and immigrants. Therefore, the LIRS principles for reform may be seen as operating within the context of the Lutheran teaching on vocation. One can also argue that the LCMS's more private approach "from below" in those social matters, where arguably "there is no clear consensus among all Christians on the moral failure of certain aspects of immigration law," gives individual Lutherans generous room to "contextualize" what immigration reform should mean for them from the perspective of their own vocations.[50]

Having said that, personal vocation does not have to be seen merely in individualistic terms. It can also be approached in terms of what we might call "collective vocation," in which many Christians with a similar interest come together to advocate for particular neighbors.[51] In a collective approach to vocation, individual Christians with a passion and commitment are more than welcome to join forces with agencies such as LIRS to learn and educate others about, pray for, support financially, and volunteer in activities related to immigration reform initiatives.

An implicit appeal to the Lutheran teaching of vocation is also operative in comprehensive immigration reform, given its strong support of reforms that protect the unity of the family. While the LIRS principles focus on the immigrant neighbor, they also do so arguably in the context of a broader commitment to family vocation. The pathway to citizenship is both for undocumented immigrants "and their families," and concern for "unaccompanied minors" is in the end an argument for the protection of the family.[52] So is the appeal for the reduction of detention centers and, by extension, deportations, which often affect and divide families. There is a sense in which the principle of family unity, grounded in the most fundamental vocation to care for those who are closest to us, is broader than the other principles or the values that undergird them. By advocating for family unity, LIRS calls Lutherans to help others uphold one of the most basic God-given callings we have all been given.

The LIRS principles include both the protection of the migrant and "U.S. citizen" workers, thus showing that our vocations call us to advocate

---

50. CTCR, *Immigrants Among Us,* p. 35.

51. For the concept of "collective vocation," see Leopoldo A. Sánchez M., "The Human Face of Justice: Reclaiming the Neighbor in Law, Vocation, and Justice Talk," *Concordia Journal* 39, no. 2 (2013): 127.

52. LIRS, "Principles for Comprehensive Immigration Reform."

for various sets of neighbors — both insiders and outsiders.[53] While the document does not specifically include border security as part of comprehensive immigration reform, as some other proposals do, it uses the language of enforcement. By doing so, the document acknowledges indirectly the need for enforcement of immigration laws and thus the vocations of those who work in temporal government. Immigration officers are called to enforce the borders, albeit humanely, and they should not be demonized for doing so. At the same time, Lutheran theology allows us to honor the vocations of parents and spouses, workers and farmers, pastors and other church workers, who approach immigration law and reform from their respective callings in life. In the end, the LIRS principles for immigration reform embody the complexity of the national immigration debate and the spectrum of neighbors and vocations Lutherans move along in making sense of these issues.

Conclusion

On the basis of the general principles of love for the stranger and obedience to the temporal authorities, as well as the Lutheran distinction between the two realms and its teaching on vocation, we conclude that the LIRS principles for comprehensive reform can be seen as a viable Lutheran application of the aforementioned frameworks to immigration issues. Even writers inspired in the Lutheran tradition such as Bouman/Deffenbaugh and Meilaender, who employ different points of departure or reorder moral priorities in their approaches to immigration law and reform, still agree on basic comprehensive reform tenets such as the need for enforcement, concern for vulnerable immigrants, unification of the basic family unit, and the possibility of allowing at least some undocumented immigrant neighbors the possibility of earning legal status.

Therefore, we can posit a certain affinity between comprehensive immigration reform principles, such as the ones laid out by LIRS, and basic Lutheran theological commitments to uphold God's commands to love the neighbor and obey the authorities, God's work in the two realms or kingdoms, and God's work on behalf of many neighbors through various vocations. Finally, our research suggests that even Lutheran voices with different starting points or viewpoints on immigration law still can bear much similar fruit by offering us a moral compass to engage and discern the often exag-

---

53. LIRS, "Principles for Comprehensive Immigration Reform."

gerated, partisan, and sensational claims made in the national media and political debate on immigration law and reform — a compass grounded in Lutheran identity as expressed in the fourfold theological matrix described in this essay.

CHAPTER 9

God's Uses of the Law and the Effort to Establish a Constitutional Right to the Means to Live

Marie A. Failinger and Patrick R. Keifert

Therefore, it would be very proper to place in a coat-of-arms of every pious prince a loaf of bread instead of a lion, or a wreath of rue, or to stamp it upon the coin, to remind both them and their subjects that by their office we have protection and peace, and without them we could not eat and retain our daily bread.

The Book of Concord[1]

To the state of Maryland, Jeanette and Junius Gary were merely welfare recipients who had too many children.[2] After a number of miscarriages that led her to despair of her barrenness, Jeanette bore Junius eight children in less than seven years. Unfortunately, her health was compromised by these pregnancies, resulting in high blood pressure, arthritis, and maybe diabetes. Junius, a hard-working man with an engineering bent, who was honorably discharged from the Army after severe injuries, was employed during these years as a truck driver and chauffeur until he was in an automobile accident. He became unable to work because of dizzy spells, blackouts, and seizures, and then unexpectedly died at the age of forty-five.

Faith and family were the center of the Garys' lives. But they had to seek assistance from the state of Maryland to survive due to their disabilities. To

1. Lutheran Confessions, The Lord's Prayer, Fourth Petition, *Book of Concord: The Symbols of the Evangelical Lutheran Church,* trans. and ed. Theodore G. Tappert (St. Louis: Concordia, 1957), p. 202.

2. The facts recounted about the Gary family are taken from Julie Nice, "A Sweeping Refusal of Equal Protection: Dandridge v. Williams (1970)" in the forthcoming book *The Poverty Law Canon,* ed. Ezra Rosser and Marie A. Failinger (2016).

discourage welfare recipients from having more children, the state capped Aid to Families with Dependent Children assistance to families at $250 per month, well below the poverty line and even below the rock-bottom basic needs even the state recognized that large families had. That cap was the most any family on welfare could receive, regardless of the actual number of persons in a family, and the Garys struggled just to eat every day.

Today, many national constitutions recognize a constitutional right to the means to live. This right is even written into international law: Article 11 of the International Covenant on Economic, Social and Cultural Rights provides that "[t]he States Parties to the present Covenant recognize the right of everyone to an adequate standard of living for himself and his family, including adequate food, clothing and housing, and to the continuous improvement of living conditions. The States Parties will take appropriate steps to ensure the realization of this right, recognizing to this effect the essential importance of international co-operation based on free consent."[3] Yet, the United States has refused to ratify this Covenant, or to acknowledge any affirmative right of human beings to government assistance in meeting basic survival needs.[4] That refusal to recognize a basic right to the means to live does not distinguish between a healthy adult who has available work and others, such as children or elderly or disabled persons, their caretakers, or those who want to work but are unemployable or underemployed in changing markets.

To be sure, both federal and state governments have created numerous programs to assist low-income citizens and residents of the United States: Temporary Assistance to Needy Families (TANF) for families; Supplemental Security Income (SSI) for aged, blind, and disabled individuals; and the SNAP program (formerly Food Stamps) are among these. Some have argued that these programs are more generous than those in some countries

3. Article 11, Sec. 1, International Covenant on Economic, Social and Cultural Rights, opened for signature Dec. 16, 1966, art. 12, 993 U.N.T.S. 3, 8 (entered into force Jan. 3, 1976), available at http://www.ohchr.org/EN/ProfessionalInterest/Pages/CESCR.aspx (accessed March 14, 2014). This covenant also recognizes the right of people to self-determination, the right of the family to protection, and the rights to work, to health, education, and to cultural participation.

4. The United States signed the covenant in 1977, but Congress has refused to ratify or make accession to it since then. See United Nations Treaty Collection, Chapter 4 part 3, Covenant on Economic, Social and Cultural Rights, https://treaties.un.org/pages/view details.aspx?chapter=4&lang=en&mtdsg_no=iv-3&src=treaty (accessed March 14, 2014). As of March 2014, there were 161 parties to this treaty.

that have signed on to the International Covenant on Economic, Social and Cultural Rights, but they are not as generous as those in many industrialized nations, even those with less national wealth than the U.S.

Despite the existence of these programs, many of which date back to the Depression of the 1930s, American courts and legislatures have turned back attempts to declare that these or any programs are enforceable human rights. Perhaps most dramatically, in the Garys' lawsuit to overturn the $250 family cap on welfare benefits, which became the Supreme Court case of *Dandridge v. Williams,* Justice Potter Stewart famously responded, "the intractable economic, social, and even philosophical problems presented by public welfare assistance programs are not the business of this Court."[5] Accordingly, since the 1970s, the Supreme Court has consistently proclaimed that there is no constitutional right to the basics for survival. While the Supreme Court's refusal to recognize a right to the means to live can be explained in part by constitutional concerns such as separation of powers, federalism, and the limits of judicial competence to construct social programs, the fact is that none of the three federal branches of government has recognized such a right, nor have state governments.

While a key constitutional value in the United States is the "separation of church and state" embodied in the Establishment Clause of the First Amendment, one may wonder why the United States has refused to recognize a right to the means to live, despite the fact that most of its citizens continue to identify themselves as Christians, Jews, and Muslims, religions that all emphasize our duties to protect the most vulnerable in society. We suggest that, at least in part, this failure may be traced to theological confusion over the ways in which God uses the law, including secular law promulgated by individuals and human institutions for the sake of human community. This chapter assumes a consistent and thoroughgoing theocentric realism.[6] As we consider God's uses of the law, we will especially focus on God's uses of human law, as sin, death, and the Evil One profoundly and systemically distort it. Despite these distortions, God's primal agency in human law remains, often hidden, yet very real.[7]

Though early Western medieval literature often focused on providing for

5. *Dandridge v. Williams,* 397 U.S. 471 (1970), p. 487.

6. Michael Welker, *God the Spirit,* trans. John F. Hoffmeyer (Minneapolis: Fortress Press, 1994), pp. 46-49 (providing a more sustained description of "realistic theology").

7. For a good discussion of this theme in recent Lutheran theology, see Stephen D. Paulson, *Lutheran Theology* (New York: T. & T. Clark International, 2011), pp. 24, 42, 54-55, 67, 86, 151, 211.

the poor as a form of "works-righteousness," a way of meriting grace, early welfare law literature concerned itself primarily with the "receiving" side of welfare efforts, concentrating on the moral worthiness of recipients, describing wealth transfers as undeserved "charity" or "gift" rather than a deserved "right."[8] Individuals and families who demonstrated piety and conformed to social standards such as hard work and proper parenting were most likely to be fed and housed at public expense.[9] In some jurisdictions, the poor were consigned to "poorhouses," their children sometimes removed from their care to be apprenticed or brought up by persons who would teach them the proper moral behavior their parents had not.[10]

After the advent of the Reformation, however, social reformers had other theological paradigms to draw from, including the Lutheran views about the uses of the law. Most Lutheran scholars agree that this tradition has taught two uses of the law, the so-called civil use of the law, and the spiritual or theological use of the law.[11] The second, theological use is sometimes described as a mirror that accuses sinners, holding up their sins to them incessantly and comprehensively so they can come to see that their only salvation is through the grace of God, and not their own merit or works.[12]

8. Larry Cata Backer, "Medieval Poor Law in Twentieth Century America: Looking Back toward a General Theory of Modern American Poor Relief," *Case Western Reserve Law Review* 44, no. 3-4 (1995): 871-1061, at 871 (noting that "the benefits of status and property, however, carried with them a spiritual and quasi-legal duty of charity. In time of necessity all people were expected to share their superfluous wealth with those in need; otherwise the wealthy were under no *obligation* to donate their wealth for charitable purposes").

9. Backer, "Medieval Poor Law," p. 1029 (noting that "in the medieval period . . . [w]hile the poor were thought inferior, only the able-bodied who refused to work, and thereby violated the class and status norms of medieval society, were despised as deviants and punished as beggars, thieves, and vagabonds").

10. Joel F. Handler, "The Transformation of Aid to Families with Dependent Children: The Family Support Act in Historical Context," *New York University Review of Law & Social Change* 16 (1987-88): 457-534, at 468 (noting, "The goal of nineteenth-century welfare policy, therefore, was to distinguish the worthy poor from the pauper and to prevent the poor from passing over that line").

11. Although these uses are described somewhat differently in theological writings and confessions, we will follow the distinction between the first or civil use of the law in this earthly kingdom, and the second or spiritual use. We do not mean to avoid the continuing debate on a third use but rather to propose a theological warrant for the right to the means to live that is more irenic and can even be shared across theological traditions.

12. Edward Engelbrecht, *Friends of the Law: Luther's Use of the Law for Christian Life* (St. Louis: Concordia, 2011), p. 9. For a longer discussion of the second use, see William H. Lazareth, *Christians in Society: Luther, the Bible and Social Ethics* (Minneapolis: Fortress

Regrettably, the first, civil use of the law is often described as only preventative and punitive, established by God to deter "the wicked" from harming the earthly creation and to provide appropriate earthly retribution for them if they do. There is also a significant literature debating whether Martin Luther, or the Lutheran tradition that follows Luther, recognized a third use of the law.[13] Those modern Lutheran theologians who have advocated for a more robust third use of the law have often reverted to the traditional argument that "Gospel without Law" leads to antinomianism, i.e., the likelihood that Christians, who continue as sinners, will understand Christian freedom from the law as a license to ignore the commands of the law, deluding themselves that their freedom purchased by Christ permits everything, even those actions condemned by the Decalogue and biblical teaching. On the other side, Lutheran theologians who have resisted recognition of a third use of the law have been concerned about "Law without Gospel," i.e., about the use of the law to justify oneself through one's own holiness, the very works-righteous theology at the heart of Luther's criticism. Some modern Lutheran theologians have also argued that a third use of the law distorts the actual existence and experience of a Christian, by recasting the constant direct (which some critics describe as existential) encounter between God and the Christian into a primary relationship between the Christian and the law, separate from God.[14] The main concern of this chapter is not to settle the debate about whether Luther, or the authentic Lutheran tradition, has recognized a third use of the law. Rather, we suggest that employing the traditional first use Lutheran imagination of how God continues to use law to engage human beings in the world throughout history is a more solid basis on which Lutherans and other Christians can engage and challenge modern governments and lawmakers on issues such as the constitutional right to welfare. By contrast to more modernist, nontheological frames, this consistently theocentric frame allows for a justification for these rights that can be shared with Jews and Muslims.

Many Christians today employ an imagination about the uses of the law that bears a faint resemblance to that espoused by some of the Deist founders of the American constitutional system. In the common portrayal of the

---

Press, 2001), pp. 116-20 (noting the exposure of human sinfulness, and human discharge from the law once "the regenerate appropriate God's grace through faith").

13. See, for example, the third use description in Engelbrecht, *Friends of the Law*, pp. 79-81.

14. The work of Robert Bertram, Gerhard Forde, and Edward Schroeder, teachers and friends, has been instructive to our argument.

constitutional founders' imagination, God has given the natural law, with its foundation in the Ten Commandments, to human beings.[15] Then, while God may be continuing to create in the "natural world," God has stepped back from the human community, expecting that humans will found legal institutions and execute laws that carry out the basic contours of those commandments. This legal imagination emphasizes restraining sinners from violating the natural law and punishing those individuals who have transgressed it, thus restoring equilibrium in the secular world through retribution, among other reasons to equalize the situation of wrongdoer and victim, as death penalty proponents argue is necessary by taking a life for a life.[16] In this imagination, the law of God, in its first use, provides a minimalist order to the secular world, but does not instruct or govern most human affairs. At the same time, in this view, those who are redeemed are instructed and empowered, through the separate sanctifying action of the Holy Spirit, to live holy lives in this world, and to fill the social emptiness left by the minimalist first use of the law with more robust, charitable, and life-giving action on behalf of the neighbor. (We might note how this understanding of the Holy Spirit's action separates the persons and the work of the Trinity to reinforce the great modern divide between public and private.[17])

This dual understanding of law, roughly corresponding to what has been called the first use and the third use of the law, has its parallel in the American imagination on the role of law in meeting the needs of the neighbor, certainly at least until the Great Depression and New Deal. In that imagination, governments chiefly operate to provide some minimal order to our "public" interactions in daily life by dictating rules of restraint for governments, institutions, and individuals — rules against violence, theft, slander, etcetera punishable by fines, imprisonment, or civil judgments. These rules, while founded on key natural law expectations, are largely developed by self-regulating human beings as they encounter changing conditions and

15. Recent research has debunked the claim that "the God of the Enlightenment deists was a remote, uninvolved, watchmaker God that generated no love or warmth in people." Joseph Waligore, *Introduction to Deism,* http://www.enlightenmentdeism.com/?page_id=25 (accessed December 12, 2014).

16. See Linda E. Carter, Ellen S. Kreitzberg, and Scott W. Howe, *Understanding Capital Punishment,* 2nd ed. (Newark: Matthew Bender, 2008), pp. 11-13.

17. Many secular philosophers have raised these same questions regarding what has been called "the modern dogma," which accepts the fact-value split. See Wayne C. Booth, *Modern Dogma and the Rhetoric of Assent* (Chicago: University of Chicago Press, 1974), pp. 13-24.

new ways in which sinful persons engage in wrongdoing. Thus, criminal laws against theft of property from the person can be reimagined through human ingenuity to produce embezzlement laws and even prohibitions against insider trading and theft of intellectual property. Meanwhile, other "private" social needs are filled by the generosity of the charitable act, the voluntary largesse of individuals, social institutions such as the church, and even governments. Yet, much like the medieval conception, "givers" are expected to give out of their abundance, not to the extent that their own personal needs or desires are jeopardized. Thus, for example, modern tax schemes assume that individual taxpayers are legally and morally entitled to "keep" the income they have "earned," unless government determines that social welfare will be significantly enhanced by government collection of taxes to fund a common project that will increase community economic success, including for the "givers," e.g., the highways taxpayers use to get to work, or a football stadium that will bring employment. Even if Americans are motivated by a variety of other reasons to create social programs such as TANF and SNAP, including compassion for the needy, few of them would accede to the claim that these programs create a legal right in needy recipients to the means to live.

In constitutional terms, this imagination has been captured in the distinction between "negative rights" against government interference with personal freedom and "affirmative rights" to government assistance in order to flourish on one's freedom. The Constitution has been read by American courts and legislatures as a "negative rights" document, with some few exceptions. *Dandridge v. Williams* is a prime example of this "negative rights" understanding; the Supreme Court holds that the Gary family has no legal claim on government to perform a duty to provide for their basic subsistence needs.

We would suggest that the Lutheran tradition teaches a richer and more nuanced understanding of God's uses of the law that can better inform our human responsibilities to respond to the neighbor's need through government and secular social organizations. We will explore how five interrelated errors in the modern thinking about the relationship between God, the church, and secular law and legal institutions can be challenged by the Lutheran tradition. First, in the Lutheran understanding, God is no watchmaker who starts the world turning and then lets us fend for ourselves. Rather, God is the primal agent in our efforts; God continues to create in and with the human community, including in our creation of secular law.[18] That

---

18. Lazareth, *Christians in Society,* p. 66.

is to say, when human beings write and enforce law, God is there, moving by the power of the Holy Spirit through our work, whether we understand and acknowledge and heed or rebel against God's presence.

Second, God's uses of the secular law — God's demands on human persons and institutions — are not simply retributive, setting forth minimalist expectations to be met with punishment when we refuse to heed those demands. Rather, God works in the world of this age with us to create new human institutions, to preserve and enrich human community through our service to the neighbor, and to repair the world's brokenness. That work of repair is not only for the world's spiritual brokenness (God's second use of the law) but also its material and social brokenness, from environmental destruction and family violence to eradication of social discrimination against vulnerable groups.

Third, God moves through the law, teaching, encouraging, demanding, and punishing not just Christians but all persons. God is instructing and inspiring not only redeemed Christians to work toward "God's preferred and promised future" for us all; indeed, the law calls every human being to this task.[19] Similarly, both Christians and non-Christians fall short of God's expectations for a world that is trustworthy for all; and both Christians and non-Christians are exhorted to make the needs of the human community their own through secular law. We may anticipate failure in this task due to sin, death, and the Evil One, but that does not end God's desire, preference, command, indeed, demand on us to work for that future.

Fourth, an exclusive emphasis on the third use of the law in creating a trustworthy world risks reinstating the error of theocratic perfectionism that has characterized America's civil religion. Finally, such an emphasis can construct a wall of separation between God's work in using law to create a civil society and God's work in forming Christian community to serve that society. For the Christian, in the Lutheran view, no such wall of separation exists.

We elaborate on these points starting with the first key error that both lawyers and political activists, including Lutherans, make as they attempt to

---

19. On God's preferred and promised future, see generally Patrick R. Keifert, *We Are Here Now* (St. Paul, MN: Church Innovations Publishing, 2006). This expression is a development of the law/promise distinction building on Dietrich Bonhoeffer's reworking of that classic formulation through the language of penultimate and ultimate. This formulation follows Philip Melanchthon's in Apology of the Augsburg Confession, IV, *The Book of Concord*, pp. 32-42. One summary of Article IV for our purposes might be, "How to promote good works without losing the free promise."

shape the legal rules for the secular world on difficult issues such as abortion and same-sex marriage out of natural law understandings. That is, it is easy to proceed as if the natural law is sui generis, a static set of legal or value principles that exists "out there" rather than the ongoing will and work of God in human history. Or, to play with the title of this chapter, God's uses of the law may become "the" or "our" uses of the law, whether they are two or three or many. Even those who, if challenged, would concede that law is God's work in the world tend to reason as if this were not so. They — we — then commit a common idolatrous sin: we begin to interpret the natural law from a "thoroughly anthropomorphic" perspective, creating our own image of God and God's will for the world instead of recognizing our status as recipients of God's law, as first and foremost the creatures rather than creators of law.[20]

From this perspective, it is easy to begin to unhook philosophy of law from the ever-present intervention and command of God that emanates from and is responsive to the ever-changing nature of the creation.[21] Even humanity itself is constantly undergoing change, both biological and social. Yet, once jurisprudence and law-making are relationally unhooked from the continuously creating Trinity, and lawyers and political activists think that they can depend only on human rationality to structure secular law, their work becomes a perversion of God's will for the world. That amnesia about God's ongoing participation in our fate results in rigidified and theologically problematical assumptions about human nature that structure our views, whether conservative or liberal, on providing for our fellow human beings in need, e.g., human beings are naturally corrupt and lazy, and will never exert effort to care for themselves and their families without coercion, so families should be refused help with the means to live in order to force parents to provide for their families. Or, we might incorrectly assume, poor people like the Garys are incapable of managing their own lives, so a humane government or society must step in to provide for their basic needs, help them address their pathologies, and conform their lives in ways that let them participate effectively in mainstream societies. While each of these arguments is seemingly grounded

20. Johannes Heckel, *Lex Charitatis: A Juristic Disquisition on Law in the Theology of Martin Luther,* trans. Gottfried G. Krodel (Grand Rapids: Eerdmans, 2010), p. 27.

21. For example, in his lectures on Genesis, Luther pointed out, "God did not therefore in the seventh day cease to work in every sense, but he works still, not only in preserving his whole creation, but also in altering and new-forming the creature." John N. Lenker, *Luther on the Creation: A Critical and Devotional Commentary on Genesis 1–3* (Minneapolis: Lutherans in All Lands Co., 1904), p. 67.

in human reason and experience, they not only oversimplify the human story of vulnerable families like the Garys but do not even pretend to consider how God is working in the world to provide for the Garys' material and spiritual needs through their callings to each other and others' callings to them.

Because Lutherans recognize that human beings are co-creators of this secular world, including secular law, we are not excused from making law even though law-making necessarily relies, in part, on our own flawed and sinful experience and reasoning. Most certainly, our human understanding of secular natural law will be corrupted because, as Johannes Heckel claims that Luther argued, human understanding of the experience of true love for God and the neighbor becomes "weak, dim and crude" as a result of sin.[22] Luther, Heckel notes, emphasizes that human beings will constantly misuse the very search for the principles of secular natural law as a true search for God's will, and become arrogantly confident of their ability to "re-think God's thoughts."[23] Secular human laws will inevitably reflect the sin of human beings advocating for laws that favor themselves or their own righteousness before God, under the guise of their "discovery" of "the will" of God for creation.[24]

Therefore, Lutheran theology would counsel, pronouncements about secular natural law, and attempts to govern human communities through the positive laws that embody those understandings, must always be viewed with skepticism. They must be met with continual efforts to probe the self-justification that may be at the heart of those descriptions, and with attention to how secular positive laws that claim to reflect natural law actually operate in the real, empirical world. Visible evidence that legislation and enforcement of particular positive laws are causing damage to the environment or to intimate human relationships such as marriage is evidence that human beings may well "have it wrong" in their understanding of secular natural law, whether from human sin or simply human limitation. Thus, the "discovery" and pronouncement of what secular natural law requires must always be attended by humility, self-criticism, and the willingness to probe all claims about natural law.

People of faith, in particular, need to be asking the question, "What is God up to here? What is God's preferred and promised future for our community?" And people of faith, along with those who are not, are called to

22. Heckel, *Lex Charitatis,* p. 55, citing Luther's First Disputation against the Antinomians 1537; The Formula of Concord II, *Book of Concord,* pp. 218-19.

23. Heckel, *Lex Charitatis,* p. 56.

24. Heckel, *Lex Charitatis,* p. 56.

be continually attentive to the dynamic relationship between human beings and the wider ongoing creation of God, and to embrace the opportunity to make and remake the secular law in ways that, as best as possible, seem to contribute to the flourishing that God demands for all persons in the world.[25] This calling requires not only our best thinking from reason and experience, but also constant immersion in, and listening to, the lives and experiences of others, listening for God's Word for the world, and being certain that we will never be certain of it. Neither tradition nor idealism, which put human beings at the center of the law-making process, can serve as an ultimate good or principle if the recognition of God's ongoing work in the world is to be honored.

A second key error that Lutheran interpreters can make is to conflate Luther's teaching about the uses of God's law with the kingdoms in which God operates. In one reading, the first or "negative" use of the law is conflated with the secular, or left-hand kingdom, so that deterring or punishing evildoers becomes the secular world's only legitimate use of the law. The affirmative or positive uses of the law in structuring human community to enable it to flourish are forgotten in this discourse about the secular kingdom; they come in only as a third use of the law, a call to Christians to be holy.

Heckel, a lawyer interpreting Luther's understanding of law, described the contrast that Luther saw between divine natural law and secular natural law, two distinct though complementary ways in which God employs law in the two kingdoms, "God's kingdom under Christ" and "the kingdom of the world under the governing [secular] authority."[26]

Heckel argues that in the Lutheran tradition, divine natural law is not a set of commands about right conduct, but exclusively spiritual — the Word and the Spirit — and directed only to believing hearts. For Luther, God's commandments are radically spiritual; "God does not command anything external."[27] Divine law's only objective is to create "a God-formed will," to form a heart "seized by God's spirit." The very definition of divine natural law is uncoerced, joyful love that both binds the whole person in complete

---

25. Luther, speaking on secular authority, argued "[i]f it is God's work and creation, then it is good, so good that everyone can use it in a Christian and salutary way," and urged Christians to "serve God in government if the needs of his neighbor demands. For those who punish evil and protect the good are God's servants and workmen." "Temporal Authority: To What Extent It Should Be Obeyed" (1523), in *Martin Luther's Basic Theological Writings*, 2nd ed., ed. Timothy Lull (Minneapolis: Fortress Press, 2005), pp. 441-42.

26. Heckel, *Lex Charitatis*, p. 41.

27. Heckel, *Lex Charitatis*, p. 45.

surrender to God and also assures him or her of God's love. Divine natural law is universal because it emanates from the Creator of law; it addresses all of humankind "in the status of the incorrupt nature"; it grasps the human being in his or her totality; it lasts eternally; and it is exhaustive of, and the model for, all law valid before God.[28] Law is legislated as the divine will in the form of the Word of God that penetrates the human will as it is "resting" or "being drowned" in the will of God.[29] While the divine law demands a work from the Christian, paradoxically, that work is love for the Creator that only God can make possible, not the person.[30] The instantiation of divine natural law, the divine positive law, which God instituted after creation to order the communal life of persons in relationship to God through the institutions of marriage and the church, is not divine unless used spiritually, i.e., to transform the will into one characterized by perfect love for God and others. Notably, Heckel argues, Luther rejected the idea that the Golden Rule was an expression of the divine natural law, "first, by its content: it demands an external 'work' ('do also to them'); and second, by reference to the *I* as the standard of conduct *('you want people to do to you')*."[31] Divine natural law is not appropriate for the governance of the secular world, because love — God — provides law with its ontological basis, and "is binding only if the will of the recipient of this law affirms it as being binding," that is, only in the spiritual kingdom.[32]

Secular natural law represents the divine intervention into the affairs of human beings living their daily lives on earth, the commandment that they reject the self-involvement and self-interest that drives the world into chaos to live a life for the sake of others.[33] Secular positive law, intended to carry out the moral power of secular natural law, is that law which human beings institutionalize in government and political power (which, in Luther's view, includes the commands of the Decalogue that are borrowed into positive law).[34]

Stated another way, remembering God's agency, we might describe secular human laws as a reflection of God's mediation between the dynamics of creation and the tendencies of human agency to destroy it. Theologian Edward Schroeder reminds us that the law as Luther understood it was not

---

28. Heckel, *Lex Charitatis*, p. 48.
29. Heckel, *Lex Charitatis*, p. 49.
30. Heckel, *Lex Charitatis*, p. 50.
31. Heckel, *Lex Charitatis*, pp. 50-51.
32. Heckel, *Lex Charitatis*, p. 47.
33. Heckel, *Lex Charitatis*, pp. 56-57.
34. Heckel, *Lex Charitatis,* at pp. 57-58.

a set of rules about lawful behavior but "nomos" or *Gesetz Gottes* in German, God's "way of operating in the world," reflecting human solidarity, the membership of each in the human community, and the mutual responsibility of all to serve each other for the common good.[35] God's law is a demand for life-giving behavior from human beings. It is a description of God's preferred future for us, a description of behavior that can create a world that human beings can trust, and in that trust, can flourish and help other living beings, human and nonhuman, to flourish. *It is a demand for more than negative rights, or a minimalist state.* And it warrants itself both in the present demands of the law and the unconditional free promise of life in Jesus Christ.

Said another way, civil law, in this case welfare law, is an example of how human beings can cooperate with the ongoing creation to stem the chaos of sin that threatens the very right to life, by responding to human need and securing lives. Or, it can be an example of how human beings and institutions can use the law to create chaos, destroy human relationships, and deny some or all of us the overwhelming bounty of creation.

To give just an example of how the law can work to order or disorder creation, the Decalogue's commandment against stealing (a negative right, or a prohibition) recognizes the fact that sinners are tempted to steal, whether through a simple burglary or complex financial transactions. Each theft creates uncertainty about what human beings can expect. Working with and obeying God, we can craft legal constraints for sinful thefts that make it possible for human beings to entrust their property to each other for purposes ranging from community uses to investment.

But the law of property (an affirmative right) also gives sinful human beings the power to destroy a trustworthy world for others, when property owners "stand on their rights" as an excuse to ignore the neighbor's need for use of that property. Thus, in the United States, homeless people are constantly being arrested for camping on doorsteps or breaking into buildings that are empty, just to find a warm place to sleep. God's law for the secular world demands more than protection against interference with property rights; it demands that government cooperate with other human agents and the divine Agent in the project of creating legal rights that can guarantee a trustworthy world for these homeless people.

---

35. Email from Edward Schroeder to Marie Failinger, August 13, 2013. See also Heckel, *Lex Charitatis*, pp. 56-57 (noting Luther's view that the moral basis for the law "is the awareness of mankind's solidarity and mutual responsibility as a body whose members are called to serve one another, according to their respective talents; its goal is the common welfare").

The third and related error that can arise from conflating secular natural law and what Heckel calls divine natural law is that Christians may incorrectly believe that God's demands to order the *saeculum* (secular world) are addressed only to them. Introducing back a third use of the law directed at Christians not only risks a misunderstanding of how salvation operates in the life of a Christian. It also may imply that the heavy demands of the secular natural law — what we should be doing to others, as we would have them do to us — apply only to Christians in their status as saved persons. But if the purpose of the secular natural law is to order the secular world so that human beings and others can live in a trustworthy world in this life, then we should expect these heavy demands to be addressed to the activity of all persons, whether or not they accept the accusation of the law in its theological use, and whether or not they accept that their only recourse is salvation of God through Christ.

In this way, the narrow description of a first use as the magistrate's use of the law to punish wrongdoers in this earthly life is much too cramped, and the third use as the instruction of the Holy Spirit only to Christians to do good works potentially misleading. God's first use secular natural law as embodied in secular positive law functions to instruct, to exhort, to compel, to guide, to judge, and to punish those in this earthly life. It tells us what our duties are — e.g., to meet the daily needs of our neighbor. It encourages us that in doing so, we will be carrying out the will of God. It even expects and demands that we will do so, and that the judgment of God for our failure to do so will hang over us.

Thus, the demands of God's law on all human beings for God's ordering of our earthly world cannot be reduced to a minimalist interpretation of the Ten Commandments literally read as "negative" commands. Rather, the demands of God's law are demands upon all living persons to care for our world and to give our lives for it, as we find in Luther's Small Catechism explanations to the Ten Commandments, which are addressed to all persons as the law written on their hearts, minimalist prescriptions with maximalist demands:

The Fourth Commandment

Thou shalt honor thy father and thy mother [that it may be well with thee and thou mayest live long upon the earth].

What does this mean? We should fear and love God that we may not despise nor anger our parents and masters, but give them honor, serve, obey, and hold them in love and esteem.

The Fifth Commandment

Thou shalt not kill.

What does this mean? We should fear and love God that we may not hurt nor harm our neighbor in his body, but help and befriend him in every bodily need [in every need and danger of life and body].

The Sixth Commandment

Thou shalt not commit adultery.

What does this mean? We should fear and love God that we may lead a chaste and decent life in words and deeds, and each love and honor his spouse.[36]

To return to the Garys for a moment, a crabbed, negative first use view of the law suggests that the "secular" state of Maryland has no obligation under the secular natural law to actually meet the Garys' true needs, even the most critical of those needs, because the state's welfare programs are "supererogatory and voluntary," not obligatory responses to human need.

These issues raise a fourth error that tempts Americans, including Lutherans, in a nation whose civil religion has strong theocratic perfectionist strains: it is very easy for Lutherans who rightly seek to affirm the teaching of God's law within the church to conflate it with the belief that we have the innate ability to sanctify ourselves. In the simplest form of this error, the church suggests that Christians are morally superior to non-Christians. This error confuses the righteousness of God and of his Word with the idea that our own works make us righteous, a problem that also circles back to Luther's argument about the second use of the law.

While surely no Lutheran would admit to this error, subtler but nonetheless equally egregious moves are often made by those emphasizing the third use of the law in the care of the world. For example, this error occurs regularly when the church presumes that its holiness, grounded in the work of the Holy Spirit, grants it a morally superior stance from which to teach the rest of the world on questions of theological anthropology. Here it is very important to recognize the enduring power of sin, death, and the Devil and Lutherans' suspicion of their best moral judgments. We are *simul justus et peccator* (at once righteous and sinners) to our dying day. What holds for

---

36. *Book of Concord*, p. 160.

the individual Christian in this regard also holds for the moral teaching of the church.

In the context of the right to welfare, this error toward perfectionism leads the church to pronounce to state officials that Christians have a morally better answer to questions of proper public policy, or that some system of social welfare benefits is the morally right system to legislate. Instead, the church should be engaging policy-makers in public conversation about the moral principles at stake, and we suggest that the appropriate place to have this conversation is under the first use of the law. Here, we can learn from conversations with legal scholars like Michael Perry and Kent Greenawalt about what kinds of public arguments that take into account faith's convictions are appropriate.[37] To our mind, these would include appeals to common sense, common law, and the heritage of natural law.

Christians should also be clear about the proper use of the scriptures in this conversation with other citizens. In America, arguments from scripture are a part of the civil religion and it is hard to imagine any reasonably nonreductive public argument that would ignore them. Yet, how they will function in these diverse audiences is, after all, hardly within Christian control. We can only faithfully argue from scripture; we cannot determine how the Word of God falls upon human consciences. This is, after all, the work of the Spirit. However, unlike some uses of scripture, which consist of pronouncements about the sure will of God, Lutherans have always taken seriously the Isaiah passage, "Come now, let us reason together."[38] In this understanding, scripture functions as enthymeme, as content, and as ethos for the Christian's participation in public discourse. In some cases, we can presume a common heritage around some passages of scripture, even among citizens who are not Christian. In other cases, the scripture will function as a raw proclamation and prophetic truth-telling. In still other cases, it will reveal the character of the Christians making the witness.

In such conversations, the church cannot ignore the real possibility that Christians will be among those making policy, and this conversation may have a different effect upon their souls than for those who do not share this faith. The Holy Spirit acts upon the sinner-saint as she chooses, and in keeping with God's law and promises. In democratic public policy

---

37. See for example Michael J. Perry, *Love and Power: The Role of Religion and Morality in American Politics* (New York: Oxford University Press, 1991), pp. 83-127; Kent Greenawalt, *Private Consciences and Public Reasons* (New York: Oxford University Press, 1995), pp. 39-95.

38. Isaiah 1:18, RSV.

discourse, the coin of the realm will always be votes, as Lutherans will pay careful attention to in their arguments. For Lutherans, democracy is not a corruption of the public conversation, but an acknowledgment of the way in which community participation brings forth good fruit to the world. This is God's law at work, compelling the citizen to ask about God's preferred and promised future, and to get to the task of co-creating a trustworthy world.

A fifth error that can result from the first use/third use battle is that Christians may try to construct a wall of separation between God's work in using the law to create a civil society and God's formation of Christian community to serve that civil society. This separation or wall-building loses the focus upon our common work of forming a trustworthy community for the sake of the creation. When God cast Adam and Eve from the Garden of Eden, he did not cast them into a world where it was impossible to form community with others: in their fall, they gained the knowledge of good and evil; and although they could not truly fear, love, and trust in God above all things, they were capable of creating, with God, a world in which human need could be met. Though their toil in rock and soil would exhaust, and ultimately kill them, it also could sustain the basics of life for all. This fundamental gift of survival is the voice of God, the divine subwoofer, saying, "good, very good." As the Formula of Concord reiterates, like the rest of creation, the human person was "originally created by God pure and holy and without sin."[39] Whatever the powers of sin, death, and the Devil, they cannot end this goodness or eradicate this Word that calls every descendant of Adam and Eve to co-create a trustworthy world with God.

Conclusion

A Lutheran approach to the problem of the right to welfare, simply put, would make an appeal to God's command, "Feed the poor." All persons can understand this aspect of the Word of God as law, as written on their hearts, Christians no differently than non-Christians. Luther tells us that non-Christians, as well as Christians (who are still sinners), are likely to exercise a stubborn will, by saying, "No, I don't want to" and "I don't choose to see what you are telling me to see" or "Who, after all, really is my neighbor?"

39. Formula of Concord I, *Book of Concord,* p. 216.

Or, they will obey, but only because they reason that "something worse will happen to me if I don't."[40]

To argue that the world will be created as trustworthy primarily through the instruction of the third use of the law is to suggest that Christians forget everything they knew about this word of God as law once they have been redeemed, and they have to relearn it once again. Instead, we suggest, Christians still know the law as, in its first use, it has been written on their hearts. What is different is how they respond to the word of God as law — not stubbornly resisting but freely and happily responding, "Why not feed the poor? I can't imagine why we wouldn't. What else is God calling us to do if not to do this?" That is, grace operating with the power of the Holy Spirit in their lives should not be described as recovering a lost knowledge about the need of the neighbor and the law's demand for response to it. Rather, we should recognize that the gospel has opened Christians' eyes and hearts to the freedom they have been given in Christ's sacrifice to do otherwise than what they will do as sinners, refusing or denying the will of God, or obeying it grudgingly and fearfully.

If Christians have been freed from the bondage of their stubborn will, what is left for them to do with the secular law of human welfare? It is to think with others, Christian and non-Christian, who have all received God's good gift of reason, about *how* to feed the poor. Some of that reasoning will be in the church; Christians will exhort each other to look within the moral traditions of church and world to interpret that "how" for a modern world. Some of the church's contribution will be in forming community with the poor, creating relationships of trust, love, and respect that are not available or even realistically expected from government bureaucracies. Some of that contribution will be in partnerships with civil society, which have as their aim faithfulness to God's mission in the world.

Such community is grounded in the way that we are all created, compelling us to be in solidarity with all others, because the alternative to solidarity is the death of the world. Our calling to solidarity with those like the Garys who are also at once saints and sinners is the church's obligation to articulate and to carry out in cooperation with our fellow citizens. We might also describe the work of the law of God as this: the Spirit compels from the past

---

40. See Luther's sermon for New Year's Day on Galatians 3:23-29 (noting three attitudes toward the law — bold opposition to the law through a dissolute life, outward obedience based on a fear of death and hell, and external and inward obedience, "with the heart"). Engelbrecht, *Friends of the Law,* p. 80.

an emerging new reality and from the future breaking-in of a prophetic word that opens a space for innovation that results in solidarity. Even if we do not currently recognize a right to the basic means to live, our past and our future come to meet at a new present, a new moment for a new possibility of a right to survive. The very nature of God is this kind of creative emergence, so we should not be surprised if this perduring interest in creating a trustworthy world takes on new forms and new compelling forces and reasons, including the emerging idea of an international right to life.

CHAPTER 10

Can Luther Help Modern Lawyers
Understand Fiduciary Duty?

Susan R. Martyn

Luther put forward several uses (or functions) of "law." I will explore the modern utility of Luther's ideas by using his lens of "usefulness" to shed light on a modern body of law with ancient roots called fiduciary duty.[1] I select fiduciary law because of its ancient lineage, intuitive appeal, and relevance to Luther's thought.

Historically, fiduciary law can be traced to Roman times, and today provides a robust and expansive body of law that has proved essential to economic and social developments in democratic societies. Rudiments of fiduciary law existed in Luther's day, and there is some indication that he was aware of its potential.

Most importantly, fiduciary law affords us the opportunity to analogize to Luther's uses of the law in a modern secular context. Primarily, I will examine the ways in which fiduciary law expresses Luther's nuanced meaning of the law's functions in the civil and political realm, that is, his first use of the law.

Politically, law applies to all societies. Luther recognized the need for written law to promote justice by using external coercion.[2] Fiduciary law illustrates this secular use of the law by both preventing harm and by promoting socially useful altruism. It prevents harm by articulating fiduciary

---

1. I will use the terms "fiduciary duty" and "fiduciary law" interchangeably in this chapter. In legal parlance, "fiduciary duty" is the legal obligation of those who assume fiduciary roles. The law governing these persons is called "fiduciary law."

2. Luther referred to this use of secular law as an external means of order and coercion in the political realm by means of bodily rewards and punishments. *Only the Decalogue Is Eternal: Martin Luther's Complete Antinomian Theses and Disputations,* ed. Holger Sonntag (Minneapolis: Lutheran Press, 2008), pp. 33-36 (hereafter *Decalogue*).

duties to one who has entrusted her business to another. It promotes these socially useful relationships by enforcing fiduciary duties with a wide array of legal remedies.[3]

These obligations also promote reliance on socially useful relationships. These responsibilities are not imposed on unwilling participants. Fiduciary law promotes social order by setting a high standard, *"uberrima fides"* or "utmost good faith," to promote loyalty to the interests of another.[4] This "obligatory altruism" applies only to those who choose to enter into relationships designed to serve the interests of another.[5]

Luther also recognized that secular law prescriptions intended to prevent harm or promote human flourishing will never be comprehensive enough to foresee future situations where they might apply. He therefore advocated *epieikeia* or the practice of equity to fully understand the spirit of the law as well as its letter; that is, to realize the abundance of justice required to govern.[6]

Luther also identified a second or theological use of the law intended primarily for Christians. This accusing use of the law was meant to reflect what we truly are, humans in need of grace.[7] Here he emphasized the use of law to evaluate or accuse by mirroring our bad behavior to our conscious vision. He also recognized that secular as well as biblical law might fulfill this function.[8] Those who serve as secular fiduciaries therefore might benefit from modern fiduciary law's evaluation of other-directed service.

---

3. Luther referred to this use of the law as the "accusing law," or law as the Holy Spirit's tool to work sorrow over sin in human hearts, thus preparing us for Christ's fulfillment of the law offered in the gospel. *Decalogue,* pp. 170-72, 76, 105-7.

4. On the notion of *uberrima fides,* see, e.g., *Meinhard v. Salmon,* 164 N.E. 545, 546 (N.Y. 1928).

5. Leonard Rotman, *Fiduciary Law* (Toronto: Thomson/Carswell, 2005), p. 315.

6. Luther agreed with both Cicero and Aristotle that *epieikeia* was necessary to discern justice. Gary M. Simpson, "Luther, Martin," in *Encyclopedia of Global Justice,* ed. Deen K. Chatterjee (New York: Springer, 2011); Gary M. Simpson, " 'Putting on the Neighbor': The Ciceronian Impulse in Luther's Christian Approach to Practical Reasoning," in *The Devil's Whore: Reason and Philosophy in the Lutheran Tradition,* ed. Jennifer Hockenbery Dragseth (Minneapolis: Fortress Press, 2011), pp. 31-38.

7. James M. Kittelson, *Luther the Reformer: The Story of the Man and His Career* (Minneapolis: Augsburg, 1986), p. 93.

8. Gary M. Simpson, "Lutheran Ethics," in *Dictionary of Scripture and Ethics,* ed. Joel B. Green et al. (Grand Rapids: Baker Academic 2011), p. 499.

A Brief History of Fiduciary Obligation

Fiduciary law's intuitive appeal resonates to those of us with faith backgrounds. The source of this legal obligation is a duty undertaken for another's benefit. As Christians, we understand that we are not just about ourselves, but called on to serve others. We recognize Jesus as the perfect fiduciary, the "selfless steward who lays down his life for others."[9]

A Parable

We will begin this exploration of fiduciary obligation with a parable that illustrates it: the parable of the unjust steward.[10] You will recall that a rich man had a steward or manager who "wasted his goods."[11] Asked for an accounting and about to be fired, the steward turned to his employer's debtors, forgiving their debts to the master at a substantially discounted rate to gain the debtors' favor. When the lord discovered this, he commended rather than condemned the unjust steward, for "the children of this age are more shrewd in dealing with their own generation than are the children of light."[12] Jesus comments:

> "And I tell you, make friends for yourselves by means of dishonest wealth so that when it is gone, they may welcome you into the eternal homes. Whoever is faithful in a very little is faithful also in much; and whoever is dishonest in a very little is dishonest also in much. . . . And if you have not been faithful with what belongs to another, who will give you what is your own? No slave can serve two masters; for a slave will either hate the one and love the other, or be devoted to the one and despise the other. You cannot serve God and wealth."[13]

Jesus presumes that we realize the immorality of the manager's behavior. Modern law provides us with a vocabulary to articulate its legal shortcom-

9. Mary Szto, "Limited Liability Company Morality: Fiduciary Duties in Historical Context," *Quinnipiac Law Review* 61, no. 23 (2004): 88.

10. I borrow this idea from Austin W. Scott, "The Fiduciary Principle," *California Law Review* 37 (1949): 539. The parable itself is found in Luke 16:1-13.

11. This is the King James translation. The NRSV tells us that the manager "was squandering his property."

12. Luke 16:8.

13. Luke 16:9-13.

ings. The manager's conduct gives us a great example of a breach of a fiduciary obligation. First, the steward was a fiduciary because he was entrusted with the management of the rich man's property, just as a lawyer is a fiduciary, entrusted with a client's goals or business.[14]

Second, once undertaking a fiduciary employment, the steward also took on a legally imposed fiduciary obligation: to act solely for the master's benefit. The fiduciary requirement attached because he agreed to an entrustment position that enabled him to take advantage of the master's business for his own profit. When he assumed this role, he was obligated to act with sole loyalty for the master's benefit in the management of his lord's property.

Third, when the manager discounted the amount owed by the master's debtors, he did so for his own benefit, thereby breaching his fiduciary obligation.[15] He sought to serve his own interests, not those of his employer. In so doing, he breached his duty of loyalty to the master.

The master not only forgives the manager, but also praises him for his self-preserving efforts. In fiduciary terms, the manager finally showed zeal in his efforts to protect himself, which he should have shown in managing his employer's property. The forgiveness and praise illuminate what God would do, but what the secular law does not.

If the master in the parable sought legal redress today, such a breathtaking breach of fiduciary duty could result in a cascade of legal remedies. Like the master, courts recognize the right to dismiss faithless lawyers, employees, trustees, or guardians when they compromise the task or take advantage of that with which they have been entrusted.[16] A court also could award monetary damages to the master for the lost debt, which the employee would be responsible to pay.[17] It could further impose a constructive trust, which recognizes that all of the money paid the steward by the debtors belongs in trust for the master.[18] The employer also might be able to set aside the manager's disloyal compromises, and compel his debtors to repay the entire amount.[19]

---

14. Scott, "The Fiduciary Principle," p. 540.

15. Scott, "The Fiduciary Principle," p. 540.

16. Restatement (Third) Agency §3.10; Restatement (Third) of the Law Governing Lawyers, §32(2000) [hereinafter cited as RLGL].

17. Restatement (Third) Agency §8.01 Comment d (1); RLGL §6(1).

18. Restatement (Third) Agency §8.02 Comment e (2008).

19. Restatement (Third) Agency §8.02 Comment e (2008). For example, *Walley v. Walley*, 1 Vern. 484, 23 E.R. 609 (Ch. 1687) (faithless manager's conveyances to third parties for his own benefit set aside because all had knowledge about the manager's position of trust and his own self-interest).

If the manager has been mismanaging the master's property for his own benefit for some time, the master would be entitled to other legal relief such as a declaratory judgment establishing the rights of the master, an injunction to stop the disloyal behavior, a constructive trust on the money or property expropriated in the past, as well as a return of the manager's salary during the period he acted in breach of his fiduciary position.[20]

The Social Necessity of Fiduciary Duty

Many of the fiduciary remedies we depend on today have developed over the centuries in response to two developments. First, agency law was developed to solve the social problem of the master in the parable: how to obtain and maintain control over the conduct of a person performing a service for another.[21] Those entrusted with the property of another had obligations to treat it as they would their own, that is, to use precautions to preserve and protect it.[22]

Second, traditional courts often were not able to provide adequate remedies to enforce these obligations. Instead, courts or forums called "equity" developed new remedies, which eventually were folded into the governing law over the course of time. These procedures often were associated with some notion of the king or ruler's conscience. They were designed as a means to promote fairness in individual situations that were not available with more traditional forms of legal relief.[23]

---

20. For a case of legal relief involving a declaratory judgment establishing the rights of the master, see RLGL §6(5); *Griva v. Davison,* 637 A.2d 830, 846-48 (D.C. 1994). For an example of an injunction to stop the disloyal behavior, see *Maritrans v. Pepper, Hamilton and Scheetz,* 602 A. 2d 127 (Pa. 1992). On monetary penalties for a breach of fiduciary trust, see Restatement (Third) Agency §8.01 Comment d(2) (2008). For lawyers (who are fiduciaries), this remedy exists for "a clear and serious breach of duty to a client" (RLGL §37). The remedy is called fee forfeiture (if the fee has been billed but not collected) or fee disgorgement (if the fee has been collected).

21. Tamar Frankel, *Fiduciary Law* (New York: Oxford University Press, 2011), p. 92; Joseph Biancalana, "Thirteenth-Century Custodia," *Legal History* 22 (2001): 14-44.

22. Russ VerSteeg, "Early Mesopotamian Commercial Law," *University of Toledo Law Review* 30 (1999): 197-98.

23. See for example, Henry St. George Tucker, *Commentaries on the Laws of Virginia* (1846), pp. 28-29. ("When the world was under the dominion of princes, whose word was law, whose breath created and whose breath unmade every ordinance of their realms, the supplicant threw himself at their feet for . . . the relaxation of the rigor of the law in its oper-

Equitable doctrines can be traced to Roman times. Roman law developed the *fideicommissum*, which allowed a person to conduct a transaction through the use of a legally recognized third person faithful to the entrustor's wishes.[24] Canon law developed similar notions of third-person agency to meet the needs of church agencies that could not otherwise own property due to vows of poverty, but who wanted to sustain a spiritual life for followers.[25]

Equity courts also promoted respect for individual property holders by creating a strong law of testation combined with a fiduciary duty to carry out the testator's wishes.[26] These courts further protected property succession rights by recognizing wills and heirs who were not legally able to benefit through the creation of trusts.

These trust-like arrangements developed outside of the traditional legal systems in new, but equally official procedures. The *fideicommissum* was one of the "most versatile institutions of Roman law."[27] Roman consuls and later special prætors had the power to do equity, that is, act against tradition where formalism did not produce a desirable outcome.[28] Equity also was known in continental Europe and in England, where lawyers relied on the Roman concept of *fideicommissum*.[29]

---

ation. . . . In those days, when the papal supremacy prevailed over Europe, and the Catholic faith was universal, the king, like his subjects, had his priest and his confessor. And as the chancellor was formerly an ecclesiastic, . . . and presided over the king's chapel, he became the keeper of the king's conscience; and it was sufficiently natural, that when those who were aggrieved appealed to the foot of the throne for redress, he should refer their complaints to an officer whose learning so fitly qualifies him to judge, while his piety seems to furnish ample assurance of the purity of his decisions.")

24. Examples of the need for such fiduciary third-person agents include: soldiers could not buy goods in the provinces where they were stationed, and minors could not contract below the age of twenty-five. Ernest Vinter, *A Treatise on the History and Law of Fiduciary Relationship and Resulting Trusts*, 3rd ed. (Cambridge: W. Heffner Sons Ltd., 1955), pp. 3-4. *Fideicommissum* means "an object entrusted (commissum) to the good faith (fides) of the recipient, for the benefit of another person." David Johnson, *The Roman Law of Trusts* (Oxford: Clarendon, 1988), p. 9.

25. Frankel, *Fiduciary Law*, pp. 91-95.

26. Joshua Getzler, "Rumford Market and the Genesis of Fiduciary Obligations," in *Mapping the Law: Essays in Memory of Peter Birks*, ed. Andrew Burrows and Lord Rodger of Earlsferry (Oxford: Oxford University Press, 2006), p. 597.

27. Johnson, *The Roman Law of Trusts*, p. 1.

28. Johnson, *The Roman Law of Trusts*, p. 4.

29. Michele Graziadei, "The Development of *Fiducia* in Italian and French Law from the 14th Century to the End of the *Ancien Régime*," in *Itinera Fiduciae: Trust and Treuhand*

Commentators trace these notions of law and equity to Old Testament law. There, the strict halachic letter of the law or Levitical law, consisting of 612 commandments, requires certain acts and prohibits others. Alongside this extensive series of regulations was the equitable doctrine of *lifnim mishurat hadin,* meaning "beyond the line of the law" or "inside the line of the law."[30] This spirit of the law notion developed to explain deviations from the formal law in the interest of that which is God's desire.[31]

The need for equity has never been based on the unique characteristics of Hebrew, Greek, Roman, or other legal systems. Rather, it relates to what Plato and Aristotle recognized as the natural and conventional forms of justice.[32] The former, based on broad notions of reason, morality, and justice, can be characterized as the spirit of the law, while the latter is the letter of the law, the general legal requirements enacted by legislatures and judges.[33]

Put another way, the law must be fairly applied, and those who enact general legal requirements will never foresee all of their possible applications. Equity is necessary to maintain what the law would have done if cognizant of later specific facts and circumstances.[34] It makes static law dynamic, allowing a society to promote human flourishing.

---

in Historical Perspective, ed. Richard Helmholz and Reinhard Zimmerman (Berlin: Duncker & Humblot, 1998), p. 357.

30. Shmuel Shilo, "On One Aspect of Law and Morals in Jewish Law: *Lifnim Mishurat Hadin," Israel Law Review* 13 (1978): 359.

31. For example, in Deuteronomy 6:18 we find the admonition to "Do what is right and good in the sight of the Lord, that it may be well with you." Doing what is right is following the formal law, but we must also do what is good, that is, aspire to God's desire. Rotman, *Fiduciary Law,* pp. 163-64.

32. Roger A. Shiner, "Aristotle's Theory of Equity," *Loyola of Los Angeles Law Review* 27 (1994): 1245.

33. Cicero refers to the distinction between *æquitas* (spirit of the law) and *ius* (letter of the law). Rotman, *Fiduciary Law,* p. 173.

34. Thomas Aquinas, *Summa Theologica* (Vol. II, Part II-II, q. 120, art. 1 at 1695). ("Legislators in framing laws attend to what commonly happens: although if the law be applied to certain cases it will frustrate the equality of justice and be injurious to the common good, which the law has in view. Yet it happens sometimes to be injurious — for instance, if a madman were to put his sword in deposit, and demand its delivery while in a state of madness, or if a man were to seek the return of his deposit in order to fight against his country. On these and like cases it is bad to follow the law, and it is good to set aside the letter of the law and to follow the dictates of justice and the common good. This is the object of *epikeia* which we call equity.") (Trans. Fathers of the English Dominican Province, 2nd ed. [1920].)

Luther's Awareness of Fiduciary Duty

These principles of law and equity or letter and spirit of the law were well established in Roman and canon law when Luther studied and wrote. He relied on the notion of *fiducia,* the Latin antecedent of *fiduciary* (literally meaning "trust") in his *Large Catechism.*[35]

About three years before he died, Luther wrote a will leaving all of his estate to his wife Katy, knowing that it had no legal validity. At the time, traditional devises of property at death would be to a son, who then had sole power over its use and management. A married woman typically would be made a ward of her eldest son at the death of the husband.[36] Luther said that he hoped the governing prince would nevertheless enforce his will in the interests of equity, because he could not have accomplished all that he had without Katy's support, skill, and labor.

In other words, Luther trusted the equitable power of the governing authority to provide a sensible legal outcome not yet recognized by the established law. This is precisely the manner in which the modern law of fiduciary duty became recognized; first in equitable forums and later by adoption into formal legal rules and remedies. Contrary to established law and tradition, Luther sought recognition of a bequest to his wife that the established law could not give. He sought to escape doctrinal certainty in the letter of the law to address what he viewed as his own unique equitable circumstances.

The Roots of Modern Fiduciary Obligation

Modern notions of fiduciary obligation began with the first Anglo-Norman kings in 1066 but often are traced to the second half of the seventeenth century in England.[37] Lawyers and judges (who were clerics) refined concepts of *fides* and *fiducia,* giving expression to moral values very similar to those

---

35. In explaining the First Commandment, Luther said: "That now, I say, upon which you set your heart and put your *trust* is properly your god. Therefore it is the intent of this commandment to require true faith and *trust* of the heart which settles upon the only true God and clings to Him alone" (emphasis added). *The Large Catechism by Dr. Martin Luther,* trans. F. Bente and W. H. T. Dau (Electronic Classics Series). Available at: http://www2.hn .psu.edu/faculty/jmanis/m~luther/mllc.pdf.

36. Kittelson, *Luther the Reformer,* p. 283.

37. G. B. Adams, "The Continuity of English Equity," *Yale Law Journal* (1916-17): 557.

Luther relied on, because they saw them as inherent in the notion of justice in courts of equity.[38]

The seminal case illustrating the fiduciary principle is *Keech v. Sandford,* where Lord Chancellor King held that a trustee could not personally profit from his position.[39] The ruling required no showing of wrongdoing by the trustee, but instead focused on the incentives a fiduciary must have to remain loyal to the beneficiary.[40] The trustee who knows he cannot profit will renew efforts on the beneficiary's behalf. Neither heightened legal standards nor payment of damages were enough to accomplish this result. Instead of placing the forbidden fruit on a higher shelf, it removed it entirely with an array of legal remedies that restored all gain to the beneficiary.[41]

The fundamental premise behind fiduciary duty established here was that "in certain relationships where one person possesses power over the interests of another which carries with it the potential for abuse, the courts will jealously guard those interests and impose harsh sanctions for any deviation from them."[42] The fiduciary's ability to act even unwittingly in a self-interested or opportunistic manner at the expense of the beneficiary is so great that fiduciary law supplies both high standards and substantial penalties to ensure undivided loyalty to the interest of another and to prevent trust from being misplaced.[43] Fiduciary law seeks to ensure the integrity of

38. Rotman, *Fiduciary Law,* pp. 163-64.

39. *Keech v. Sandford,* Sel. Cas. Ch 61, 25 E.R. 223 (Eng. Ch. Div. 1726). The trustee profited by taking personal title to trust property (when a lessor refused to renew a lease for the beneficiary) and then by collecting profits gained from the personal title.

40. "If a trustee, on the refusal of [a lessor] to renew, might have a lease to himself, few trust-estates would be renewed *cestui que use* [for the beneficiary]." *Keech v. Sandford.*

41. Getzler, "Rumford Market and the Genesis of Fiduciary Obligations," p. 582; Rotman, *Fiduciary Law,* p. 64.

42. Rotman, *Fiduciary Law,* p. 61, quoting *Story on Equity Jurisprudence* (1856); Paul B. Miller, "The Fiduciary Relationship," in *Philosophical Foundations of Fiduciary Law,* ed. Andrew S. Gold and Paul B. Miller (New York: Oxford University Press, 2014), pp. 63-90.

43. Andrew S. Gold, "The Loyalties of Fiduciary Law," in Gold and Miller, eds., *Philosophical Foundations of Fiduciary Law,* pp. 176-96; Deborah A. DeMott, "Beyond Metaphor: An Analysis of Fiduciary Obligation," *Duke Law Journal* (1988): 879. See, for example, *Birnbaum v. Birnbaum,* 539 N.E. 2d 574 (N.Y. 1989), p. 576: "it is elemental that a fiduciary owes a duty of undivided and undiluted loyalty to those whose interests the fiduciary is to protect. This is a sensitive and 'inflexible' rule of fidelity . . . requiring avoidance of situations in which a fiduciary's personal interest possibly conflicts with the interest of those owed a fiduciary duty. . . . A fiduciary . . . is bound to single-mindedly pursue the interest of those to whom a duty of loyalty is owed."

certain forms of human interaction and to deter parties who may be tempted to act in self-interest.[44]

Clients, Lawyers, and Fiduciary Duty Today

The law that governs the relationship between client and lawyer offers us a specific lens through which to observe the details of this modern fiduciary responsibility. This law has been developed and articulated since the beginning of the American experience.

In addressing the conduct and motives of lawyers, the Supreme Court said in 1850:

> There are few of the business relations of life involving a higher trust and confidence than those of attorney and client or, generally speaking, one more honorably and faithfully discharged; few more anxiously guarded by the law, or governed by sterner principles of morality and justice; and it is the duty of the court to administer them in a corresponding spirit, and to be watchful and industrious, to see that confidence thus reposed shall not be used to the detriment or prejudice of the rights of the party bestowing it.[45]

Commentators relied on this common law to articulate the fiduciary duty lawyers owed clients in lectures and state ethics codes.[46] In the past one hundred years, these codes of ethics have become the basis for professional discipline. Today, nearly every jurisdiction has adopted some version of the current ABA template, called the Model Rules of Professional Conduct. In 2000, the American Law Institute promulgated the Restatement (Third) of the Law Governing Lawyers, which restated all the common law of lawyer

---

44. Rotman, *Fiduciary Law*, p. 142.

45. *Stockton v. Ford*, 52 U.S. 232, 247 (1850). See also *Williams v. Reed*, 29 F. Cas. 1386, 1390 (D. Maine 1824): "When a client employs an attorney, he has a right to presume, if the latter be silent on the point, that he has no engagements, which interfere, in any degree, with his exclusive devotion to the cause confided to him."

46. Samuel A. Alito Jr., "Introduction," in *A Century of Legal Ethics: Trial Lawyers and the ABA Canons of Professional Ethics*, ed. Lawrence J. Fox, Susan R. Martyn, and Andrew S. Pollis (Chicago: American Bar Association, 2009), at p. xxx. See also Susan R. Martyn, "Back to the Future: Fiduciary Duty Then and Now," in *A Century of Legal Ethics*, p. 4.

obligation that governs lawyer behavior. Today, the common law and Rules of Professional Conduct consciously mirror each other and provide significant content to a lawyer's obligations.

These common law and rule of professional conduct developments reflect a slow and steady articulation of the current content of lawyer fiduciary duty, what I label as the "Five C's," or the lawyer's obligations to:

1. Respect client *control* of the matter,
2. Initiate *communication* with the client,
3. Remain loyal, that is, resolve *conflicts of interest,*
4. Keep client *confidences,* and
5. Provide *competent* legal services.[47]

All of these fiduciary obligations originate in the reality that lawyers represent some interest other than their own. The 5 C's recognize that it is humanly impossible for lawyers to have perfect knowledge about whether they are articulating their client's interests, their own, or the interests of some third party. The legal imposition of fiduciary duty on lawyers keeps them focused on the client's interests as articulated by the client.

Control

The first fiduciary duty, control, emphasizes the obvious point that a lawyer represents the client's interests and therefore the client has the right to assume that the lawyer understands what the client wants and will pursue the client's goals.[48]

Twentieth-century lawyer ethics codes articulate this basic fiduciary duty as requiring, for example, that a lawyer "should represent a client zealously within the bounds of the law."[49] Today, the Model Rules of Professional Conduct provide that a lawyer "shall abide by client's decisions concerning the goals of the representation . . . but shall not counsel or assist criminal or

47. See Susan R. Martyn and Lawrence J. Fox, *Traversing the Ethical Minefield: Problems, Law, and Professional Responsibility,* 3rd ed. (New York: Aspen Publishers, 2013), p. 55 and chapters 3-11.

48. Frankel, *Fiduciary Law,* p. 121; Deborah A. DeMott, "The Fiduciary Character of Agency and the Interpretation of Instructions," in Gold and Miller, eds., *Philosophical Foundations of Fiduciary Law,* pp. 321-38.

49. This was the title of the 1969 ABA Code of Professional Responsibility Canon 7.

fraudulent conduct."[50] Controlling the goals of the representation further specifically requires that the lawyer abide by the client's decision whether to settle a matter, and in criminal cases, whether to plead guilty, waive a jury trial, or testify.[51]

A recent case illustrates the crucial significance of this obligation. In *Machado v. Statewide Grievance Committee,* an incarcerated client instructed his lawyer to communicate through a business partner to obtain a bankruptcy.[52] The partner redirected the lawyer's efforts to settle a different matter, which depleted the client's money and left him without the bankruptcy. The lawyer erred by failing to follow his client's instructions and failing to inform his client that the business partner changed the scope of the representation. Protecting the public against lawyers who fail to obey lawful client instructions required a disciplinary sanction despite the lawyer's lack of bad faith motive.

Communication

The fiduciary duty of communication is the foundation for maintaining the client's trust and control. Both nineteenth-century cases and twentieth-century lawyer ethics codes articulate this requirement.[53] Today, it is enshrined in the common law and detailed in ABA's Model Rules of Professional Conduct.[54]

---

50. Model Rules 1.2(a) and (d).

51. Model Rule 1.2(a); RLGL §21.

52. *Machado v. Statewide Grievance Committee,* 890 A.2d 622 (Conn. App. 2006).

53. For nineteenth-century cases, see, e.g., *Baker v. Humphrey,* 101 U.S. 494, 500 (1880) (a lawyer has a duty "to advise the client promptly whenever he has any information to give which it is important the client should receive"); *Williams v. Reed,* 29 Fed. Cas. 1386, 1390 (D. Maine 1824) [Story, J.] ("I agree to the doctrine [as to the delicacy of the relation of client and attorney, and the duty of full, frank, and free disclosure] by the latter of every circumstance, which may be presumed to be material, not merely to the interests, but to the fair exercise of the judgment, of the client.")

54. Model Rule 1.4; RLGL §20. These rules detail six discrete circumstances that require lawyer communication: to obtain the client's informed consent, to consult about the means by which the client's goals will be accomplished, to keep the client reasonably informed about the representation, to promptly comply with reasonable client requests for information, to consult about limitations on the lawyer's conduct, and "to explain a matter to the extent reasonably necessary to permit the client to make informed decisions regarding the representation."

A recent case illustrates the problem when communication does not occur. In *dePape v. Trinity Health Systems, Inc.,* a law firm took on the joint representation of a clinic and a Canadian physician whom the clinic hired for the purpose of obtaining the physician's visa to practice medicine in the United States.[55] Although the physician's immigration status depended on the physician's intentions, during the entire one-year representation, the lawyers communicated only with the clinic client.[56]

At the end of this year, a law firm representative met the physician at the U.S.-Canadian border to instruct him in a "story" he should tell immigration authorities, based on factual assumptions the physician knew were false. When the physician truthfully told border agents about his intention to practice medicine in the U.S., he was denied entry because he had not met the necessary immigration prerequisites. The physician was forced to return to Canada and "restart his life."

In the context of a legal malpractice suit, the court found the law firm's complete lack of communication not a "close call."[57] In fact, it constituted negligence "so obvious" that a layperson could recognize it.[58] The law firm's lack of communication placed the physician in "harm's way" at the border, caused the INS official to closely examine the physician, call him a liar at one point, and lead to the INS official's decision to deny him entry. All this caused the physician both financial and severe emotional harm, resulting in money damages.[59]

Conflicts of Interest

Loyalty requires that conflicts of interest be addressed and remedied. "When a client employs an attorney, he has a right to presume that he has no inter-

55. *dePape v. Trinity Health Systems, Inc.,* 242 F. Supp. 2d 585 (N.D. Iowa 2003).
56. In fact, the physician was unaware of any of his immigration options until years later, when he sued the law firm for malpractice. Just before trial he discovered his options outlined in an engagement letter the firm addressed to both the clients but sent only to the clinic. *dePape v. Trinity Health Systems, Inc.,* 611.
57. *dePape v. Trinity Health Systems, Inc.,* 611.
58. Ironically, the law firm's website advertised the firm as recognizing "the importance of personal contact with clients as an integral part of being a responsive firm." *dePape v. Trinity Health Systems, Inc.,* 589.
59. The court noted that the evidence of "egregious breach of duty and willful and wanton disregard for Dr. dePape's rights" also would have qualified him for a punitive damages award if his lawyers had requested such a remedy. *dePape v. Trinity Health Systems, Inc.,* 617 n. 13.

est, which may betray his judgment, or endanger his fidelity." To ensure this presumption, "[a]n attorney is bound to disclose to client every adverse retainer and every prior retainer which may affect the attorney's discretion."[60]

The twentieth-century Rules of Professional Conduct all include this loyalty obligation, explaining it as essential for the lawyer to "exercise independent professional judgment on behalf of a client."[61] Lawyers have obligations to disclose personal, third-person, and other-client conflicts of interest and obtain informed consent from affected clients before proceeding with a client representation. Even then, they may only ask for consent if the lawyer reasonably believes he or she will be able to provide competent and diligent representation to each affected client.[62]

Another recent case highlights the difficulty caused by conflicted loyalty obligations. In *Anderson v. O'Brien,* a couple befriended a widow, convincing her to sell them her house, and arranging for their lawyer to represent all of the parties to the transaction.[63] Although reluctant to sell, the widow agreed if the couple would build her a cottage in which to live out her days "as part of the family" on the property. Once this was accomplished, the couple then rushed to close the deal a month ahead of schedule, on a day the widow was ill. At the closing, the widow was assured that she did not need her own lawyer, after which the lawyer for all failed to properly preserve her rights in closing documents. The couple then turned hostile, building her a minimal barn-like structure instead of the promised cottage.

The court had no problem finding that all of these events would establish something more than mere negligence on the lawyer's part, perhaps entitling the widow to punitive damages because his conduct was more akin to "highly unreasonable conduct, involving an extreme departure from ordinary care."[64] Such aggravated negligence could result in damages under multiple legal theories, including breach of the lawyer's fiduciary duty of loyalty and trust.[65]

---

60. *Williams v. Reed,* 29 Fed. Cas. 1386, 1390 (D. Maine 1824) (Story, J.). The Supreme Court applied this idea to a lawyer's personal conflicts of interest in *Baker v. Humphrey,* 101 U.S. 494, 501 (1880), laying down as a general rule of numerous cases "that an attorney can in no case, without the client's consent, buy and hold otherwise than in trust, any adverse title or interest touching the thing to which his employment relates."

61. Canon 5 Model Code (1969); Rule 1.7 comment [1] (2013).

62. Model Rules 1.7-1.10, RLGL §§121-35.

63. *Anderson v. O'Brien,* 2005 Conn. Super. Lexis 3365.

64. *Anderson v. O'Brien,* 2005 Conn. Super. Lexis 3365 [*11].

65. The court also upheld a statutory cause of action rarely applied to lawyers for vio-

Confidentiality

The nineteenth-century common law also articulated confidentiality obligations in both agency and evidentiary law.[66] Modern law prohibits lawyers from revealing or using client confidences or secrets without informed client consent.[67]

For example, in *Perez v. Kirk & Carrigan,* a former client sued his lawyers for breach of fiduciary duty because they disclosed the client-truck driver's confidential statement made shortly after a terrible accident to the local prosecutor.[68] The client was driving a company truck when its brakes failed, causing a crash with a school bus that resulted in the death of twenty-one children. The unconsented-to disclosure caused the client's indictment on twenty-one counts for involuntary manslaughter. Although the client subsequently was acquitted by a jury on all counts, it took several years for this to happen, causing the client extreme emotional distress.

The court described the relation between client and lawyer as "highly fiduciary in nature" and explained that "[t]he existence of this relationship encouraged Mr. Perez to trust his lawyers" and "gave rise to a corresponding duty on the part of the attorneys not to violate this position of trust."[69]

They held that Mr. Perez had an obvious claim against his lawyers for breach of fiduciary duty (including emotional distress damages) because the "absolute and perfect candor" required of lawyers flows directly from the attorney-client relationship itself, which the court characterized as "one of

---

lation of the state unfair trade practices act, based on an "immoral, unethical, oppressive or unscrupulous" practice that causes substantial injury to a consumer. *Anderson v. O'Brien,* 2005 Conn. Super. Lexis 3365 [*12-*16].

66. For example, *Taylor v. Blacklow,* 3 Bing. N.C. 235 (1836) (client entitled to recover against his lawyer for improperly disclosing defects in the client's property title to another person); *Hager v. Shindler,* 29 Cal. 47, 64 (1865) (prima facie obligation of lawyers to regard all communications with a client in the professional relationship as confidential and therefore privileged against testimony in adjudicatory proceedings).

67. Model Rule 1.6, 1.8(b); RLGL §§59-60 (fiduciary duty); §§68-77 (attorney-client privilege).

68. *Perez v. Kirk & Carrigan,* 822 S.W.2d 261 (Tex. App. 1991).

69. *Perez v. Kirk & Carrigan,* p. 265. In fact, had the client's former lawyers asked whether they were free to disclose the client's statement to the prosecutor, the client's new lawyer opined that as an experienced criminal law practitioner he would have been able to explain the client's original inculpatory statement as the result of the employer's failure to instruct Mr. Perez about proper use of the truck's brakes, and that such an explanation would have prevented Mr. Perez's indictment. *Perez v. Kirk & Carrigan,* p. 264 n. 3.

uberrima fides, which means 'most abundant good faith,' requiring absolute and perfect candor, openness and honesty, and the absence of any concealment or deception."[70]

Competence

Professionals possess and use expertise, and have long been held accountable for the lack of it.[71] Today, the common law and the Rules of Professional Conduct articulate much the same requirement: "A lawyer shall provide competent and diligent representation to a client, including legal knowledge, skill, thoroughness and preparation reasonably necessary for the representation."[72]

Modern cases adopt these obligations, labeling a failure to meet a filing duty as a breach of a duty of "care" or "competence." Any deception, including failure to disclose the error to the client or more active cover-ups to "hide the lapse," often is labeled as a breach of the fiduciary duty of loyalty, or "failure to act in good faith solely for the benefit of the [client]."[73] Deception also opens the door to additional remedies, including punitive damages, and where relevant, fee forfeiture, disqualification, and constructive trust.

Fiduciary Duty, Luther, and the Function or Use of the Law

Law often embodies the moral values of a society. Modern commentators seem to agree that fiduciary law serves important social purposes in an increasingly interdependent post-industrial society, where we need to depend on specialized expertise in webs of trusting relationships. Trust requires reliance and some degree of vulnerability to the specialist's knowledge and power, which creates the potential for opportunism and abuse.[74] Commentators strongly disagree, however, about the need for stronger or weaker incentives to promote trust and honesty.

70. *Perez v. Kirk & Carrigan,* p. 265.

71. *Williams v. Reed,* 29 F. Cas. at 1389. ("A suit at law will lie for a lawyer's unskillfulness and negligence and the remedy is plain, complete and adequate.")

72. Model Rules 1.1 and 1.3; RLGL §§48-52.

73. For example, *Bayview Loan Servicing, LLC v. Law Firm of Richard M. Squire & Associates, LLD,* 2010 U.S. Dist. LEXIS 132108 (E.D. Pa.).

74. Rotman, *Fiduciary Law,* p. 240.

The contractarians, who favor a cost-benefit analysis, argue that fiduciary principles should be muted or scuttled in favor of reliance on individual autonomy promoted through self-reliance. That is, trust (in the fiduciary's own moral restraint) and verify (by the entrustor's contractual bargaining) should prevail.[75] Society should depend more on the self-interest of individuals who promote their goals (usually wealth maximization) through contract.[76] Some also see broadly applied or overly rigorous fiduciary obligations as capable of inviting disobedience to what are perceived as unduly burdensome legal requirements, and promoting lack of respect for the role of law in organized society.[77]

Others worry that watered-down fiduciary principles can fail to protect social, economic, and political stability. They argue that the complexity and interdependence of modern society require more rigorous legal incentives to promote trust and honesty in important human relationships and to suppress opportunism.[78] For example, in the midst of the Great Depression, Mr. Justice Stone referred to fiduciary duty in an address that considered the cause of that social crisis.

> I venture to assert that when the history of the financial era which has just drawn to a close comes to be written, most of its mistakes and its major faults will be ascribed to the failure to observe the fiduciary principle, the precept as old as holy writ, that "a man cannot serve two masters." . . . No thinking man can believe that an economy built upon a business foundation can permanently endure without some loyalty to that principle.[79]

Henry Drinker, in his 1953 treatise, *Legal Ethics,* similarly opines that a major motivation in developing lawyer rules of lawyer professional conduct was "the imperative necessity of taking a firm stand against the rising

75. Frankel, *Fiduciary Law,* p. 101.

76. Frank H. Easterbrook and Daniel R. Fischel, "Contract and Fiduciary Duty," *Journal of Law and Economics* 36 (1993): 425.

77. Peter Birks, "The Content of Fiduciary Obligation," *Israel Law Review* 34 (2000): 31.

78. Tamar Frankel, *Trust and Honesty: America's Business Culture at a Crossroad* (New York: Oxford University Press, 2006); DeMott, "Beyond Metaphor," p. 879. Henry E. Smith, "Why Fiduciary Law Is Equitable," in Gold and Miller, eds., *Philosophical Foundations of Fiduciary Law,* pp. 261-86; John C. Coffee Jr., "The Mandatory/Enabling Balance in Corporate Law: An Essay on the Judicial Role," *Columbia Law Review* 89 (1989): 1618.

79. Harlan F. Stone, "The Public Influence of the Bar," *Harvard Law Review* 48, no. 1 (1934): 8.

tide of commercialism and the growing influence of those who would turn the profession from a 'branch in the administration of justice' into a mere 'money getting trade.' "[80]

Luther's insights about the uses or functions of secular law seem to mirror the modern debate about the purpose of fiduciary law.

Commentators agree that fiduciary law first functions to protect voluntary agreements to act on behalf of another as a "fiduciary," whether as lawyer, employee, company director, trustee, or guardian. This is similar to Luther's first or political use of the law as an external force to promote social order.

Fiduciary law recognizes these promises to act in the same manner that contract law rests on the foundation of protecting individual human agreements to benefit or encumber.[81] Here, the law promotes the notion that individuals know best what to seek and are entitled to benefit themselves.[82] It also assumes that outcomes should be controlled by the party's manifest intentions.[83] Fiduciary law promotes individual choice by recognizing certain important relationships in the secular world in an effort to enhance trust and individual decision-making.

Fiduciary law's second clear purpose is remedial and prescriptive. It punishes breaches of fiduciary duty by imposing remedies designed to hold agents to their obligations to benefit others and to prevent opportunism in the relationship. This second purpose of fiduciary law also mirrors Luther's first use of the law as preventing harm.[84]

This remedial purpose of the law borrows from the purpose of injury law in general. Both tort and criminal law assume that clear standards must be set to avoid harm and promote security in a complex society. Most of these standards are set to signal minimal standards to the selfish Holmesian "Bad Man," the archetype who seeks his or her own interests without considering potential harm to others. The law articulates boundaries to this selfish human action to promote safety and security.[85]

---

80. Henry S. Drinker, *Legal Ethics* (New York: Columbia University Press, 1953), p. 20.

81. Scott, "The Fiduciary Principle," p. 540; Tamar Frankel, "Fiduciary Duties as Default Rules," *Oregon Law Review* 74 (1995): 1209.

82. Tamar Frankel, "Fiduciary Law," *California Law Review* 71 (1983): 830.

83. DeMott, "Beyond Metaphor," p. 887.

84. The remedial purpose of fiduciary law also serves Luther's second evaluating use of the law, at least to the extent that a fiduciary facing remedial payback might rethink fiduciary behavior.

85. "The bad man . . . cares only for the material consequences which such knowledge

Contract and tort law both presume self-interested human behavior. They build on the assumption that human action and decision-making is motivated by the need to benefit the self, and either encourage (contract) or limit (tort and criminal) this self-motivation to enable a society to function and flourish. Both bodies of law regulate self-interest by providing relief in the form of monetary damages after the fact to parties wronged by breach of contract or injured by tortious (wrongful) conduct.[86]

Fiduciary law assumes not just self-interested motivation or voluntarily assumed obligation.[87] Its distinction rests in its third purpose, roughly similar to Luther's insistence on the use of *epieikeia* or equity to provide clarity about the legal standard and flexible remedies to ensure human reliance on agents. The "aura of morality" in fiduciary law necessary to equitably apply it to a myriad of circumstances assumes that humans are capable of altruistic behavior and the law should impose it for social purposes.[88]

This equitable function does not just protect promise and abstention from harm, but also requires disinterestedness by the fiduciary to properly perform his or her promise, avoid harm, and serve the other's interests.[89] Fiduciary law goes farther than after-the-fact legal remedies provided in tort and contract law by offering measures to prevent harm before it occurs, and by offering remedies for opportunistic behavior even when the fiduciary otherwise serves the entrustor's interests.[90] In the interest of providing proper incentives to fiduciaries generally, it imposes duties of honesty, loyalty, integrity, selflessness, and the utmost good faith.[91]

Fiduciary law acknowledges the reality of self-interested behavior, but also assumes that aspirational modes of behavior can be expected when a person undertakes certain social interactions.[92] Legal duties of undivided loyalty (at times accompanied by moral stigma if not met) convey the

---

enables him to predict, not as a good one, who finds his reason for conduct, whether inside the law or outside of it, in the vaguer sanctions of conscience." Oliver Wendell Holmes Jr., "The Path of Law," *Harvard Law Review* 10 (1897): 171.

86. Frankel, *Fiduciary Law,* p. 108; Rotman, *Fiduciary Law,* p. 240.

87. Frankel, "Fiduciary Law," p. 887.

88. Frankel, *Fiduciary Law,* pp. 104, 272-78.

89. Birks, "The Content of Fiduciary Obligation," pp. 31, 14-17. See Frankel, *Fiduciary Law,* pp. 272-78.

90. Frankel, *Fiduciary Law,* p. 108.

91. Birks, "The Content of Fiduciary Obligation," pp. 10-12; Frankel, *Fiduciary Law,* p. 108; Rotman, *Fiduciary Law,* p. 239.

92. Frankel, *Fiduciary Law,* p. 104.

requirement that fiduciaries must subordinate self-interest to serve the beneficiary.[93]

Fiduciary law's wide expanse of legal remedies also signals fiduciaries how to anticipate, avoid, monitor, and remediate breaches of loyalty.[94] Harsh sanctions follow disapproved behavior, which encourage fiduciaries to engage in altruistic conduct that fosters human interdependence.[95] The combined overall message of this body of law is: "You can do it, here's how, and if you don't, you will suffer serious consequences that make it worth your efforts to comply."[96]

This equitable purpose of fiduciary law acknowledges the social need for specialization in an age of interdependence.[97] As one author puts it, "[A] dialectic is at work: the fiduciary can only serve the beneficiary if armed with extensive powers, and the beneficiary can only hold the fiduciary to account if the fiduciary is hemmed in by potent duties and remedies."[98] The beneficiary's vulnerability to misuse of this power stems from the necessary entrustment to the fiduciary of power that enables her to perform her function.[99] In other words, instead of limiting the fiduciary's power, which would harm the entrustor's flexibility, fiduciary law grants full discretion combined with high obligations intended to guide fiduciary conduct.[100]

In economic terms, fiduciary law imposes an expectation of concern for the other to reduce transaction costs, or the extensive costs of monitoring the fiduciary's actions to ensure fidelity to the entrustor's wishes.[101]

93. Gregory Alexander, "A Cognitive Theory of Fiduciary Relationships," *Cornell Law Review* 85 (2000): 776.

94. Frankel, *Fiduciary Law*, p. 104; Rotman, *Fiduciary Law*, p. 141. For example, *Maritrans v. Pepper, Hamilton & Scheez*, 602 A. 2d 127 (Pa. 1992) (loyalty breach/conflict of interest prevented by injunction that required law firm to cease representation of conflicting clients' cases; former client should not have to wait until harm occurs to seek relief).

95. Rotman, *Fiduciary Law*, pp. 261, 264.

96. Of course, all of these functions of fiduciary law also might cause one to evaluate or self-accuse, consistent with Luther's second use of the law.

97. Frankel, "Fiduciary Law," p. 804.

98. Getzler, "Rumford Market and the Genesis of Fiduciary Obligations," p. 581.

99. Robert Flannigan, "The Fiduciary Obligation," *Oxford Journal of Legal Studies* 9 (1989): 306; Frankel, "Fiduciary Law," p. 809.

100. Robert H. Sitkoff, "An Interdisciplinary View of Fiduciary Law: The Economic Structure of Fiduciary Law," *Boston University Law Review* 91 (2011): 1039.

101. Getzler, "Rumford Market and the Genesis of Fiduciary Obligations," p. 586; Robert Cooter and Bradley J. Freedman, "The Fiduciary Relationship: Its Economic Character and Legal Consequences," *New York University Law Review* 66 (1991): 1045.

Conclusion

Morally, it is wrong to harm anyone, but it is even worse to harm a person who cannot protect himself.[102] The legal requirements of the fiduciary obligation are those necessary to protect the integrity of the particular fiduciary relationship, and to promote it in an interdependent society.[103] They reflect assumptions about the function of law to promote voluntary trust-based relationships, to remediate breaches of trust, and to equitably apply fiduciary law to a wide range of social relationships that serve others.

Although writing in far different historical, political, and social times, modern commentators and Luther each raise similar issues: the law should promote social well-being, provide for remedies when one causes harm to another, and equitably apply to citizens who take on the business of others. Luther's ideas about the uses of the law are reflected in the current debate, and may prove helpful to modern lawyers in articulating and understanding the scope of fiduciary law's protections.

102. Frankel, "Fiduciary Law," p. 832; DeMott, "Beyond Metaphor," p. 891.
103. Flannigan, "The Fiduciary Obligation," p. 311.

PART IV

Lutherans in Their Role as Citizens

CHAPTER 11

The Legal Framework of Lutheran Churches — A Historical European Perspective

Svend Andersen and Morten Kjaer

In 2012, as part of its gender equality policy, the Danish parliament passed a revision of the marriage law, which expands the intimate partnerships eligible for marriage: "This law applies to marriage between two persons of different sexes and between two persons of the same sex." Section 15 of this law also made clear that "[m]arriage can be contracted in a church or a civil wedding." Among several legal paragraphs about the role of the Evangelical Lutheran Church in the marriage law, we find a regulation that states, "The Minister of Ecclesiastical Affairs prescribes rules about which pastors in the Church of Denmark can perform weddings and in which cases they are obliged to do so" (§17).[1] This rule mirrors the fact that some members of the clergy — particularly from the conservative wing of the church — opposed the revision and were granted the right to refuse involvement.

The Danish marriage law is a good expression of the relationship between church and state in Denmark: the political authority, here through one of its government ministries, is the supreme ruler of the Evangelical Lutheran Church. Therefore, one can correctly claim that the Lutheran Church in Denmark has kept the original prince-church structure forged in the Reformation to a greater degree than any other Lutheran church body in the world. We think that the Danish case is a good starting point for discussing and evaluating the legal framework of European Lutheran churches from a historical perspective.

In this chapter, we consider Denmark as a model of the original European Lutheran Church organization, which was closely connected to the

---

1. The text of the Danish marriage law is not available in English yet. The original version can be found here: https://www.retsinformation.dk/Forms/r0710.aspx?id=140525.

territorial state. We describe the development of the legal framework for the state church, from the Church Ordinance of 1539 conceived by Martin Luther's collaborator Johannes Bugenhagen, through the laws of the Danish absolutist period, the semi-democratic constitution of 1849 that defined the Evangelical-Lutheran Church as the "Danish People's Church," into the modern era, when the church is still "supported" by the state. One peculiarity of Danish church history compared with other Lutheran countries is the fact that the People's Church has never obtained its own constitution, but has remained under political rule throughout, thus maintaining a model more faithful to the original than any other, though the church has recently been promised a constitution of its own. By contrast, in other predominantly Lutheran European countries, democratization has resulted in the separation of the church from the state and hence church autonomy, as we will demonstrate, in Germany and some Nordic countries. Finally, we will report on the current Danish discussion about updating the legal regulation of the church to resemble a more separatist model.

The Reformation in Denmark and Its Impact on Denmark's Church Model

At the time of the Reformation, Denmark was an electorate monarchy, in which the Council of the Realm, consisting of the leading members of the nobility together with the Catholic bishops, appointed the monarch. At each election of a new king, he was required to sign a coronation charter, in which he promised to rule the country together with the Council of the Realm and to secure the rights and privileges of existing persons and institutions, most especially the church and the nobility.[2]

This political structure came about because of the chaos at the end of the Union of Kalmar, which had tied the three Nordic countries, Denmark, Norway, and Sweden, together in a dynastic union under Danish leadership between 1397 and 1523. In that year, Sweden finally broke away from the

2. On the Reformation in Denmark, see Martin Schwarz Lausten, *Reformationen i Danmark* (Copenhagen: Forlaget Anis, 2011). In the following, primarily Danish literature will be used, but among the literature available in English or German are: Ole Peter Grell, ed., *The Scandinavian Reformation — From Evangelical Movement to Institutionalization of Reform* (Cambridge: Cambridge University Press, 1995); and Leif Grane and Kai Hørby, eds., *Die dänische Reformation vor ihrem internationalen Hintergrund (The Danish Reformation against Its International Background)* (Göttingen: Vandenhoeck & Ruprecht, 1990).

union, after the unpopular King Christian II failed in keeping the union together. Ultimately he was also deposed in Denmark, and his uncle Frederik I was named king. In 1532 Christian II was imprisoned after his failed attack on Norway in order to regain the throne, and he spent the rest of his life in prison, until he died in 1559.

The union between Denmark and Norway was kept under Frederik's leadership and endured until 1814. Although he had promised in his coronation charter to protect the Catholic Church and fight heretics including Luther's disciples, Frederik I actively but cautiously supported the Reformation by protecting Lutheran priests and severing the ties between the church in Denmark and Rome.[3] The Reformation was, however, not complete when Frederik I died in 1533. After his death, the council chose to postpone the election of a new king, perhaps because his oldest son, the later-named Christian III, who was the most likely candidate, was known as a devout Lutheran and had already completed a Reformation in his principality in southern Denmark, Haderslev. Without a royal successor, a civil war broke out led by the peasants and the townsmen — especially in the great cities of Malmö and Copenhagen, and supported by Lübeck — in order to reinstate Christian II. Reacting to this rebellion, the council chose to appoint Christian III as king in 1534, and he had crushed the rebellion by 1536.

The Legal Implementation of the Reformation in Denmark

Christian III used the defeat of the forces supporting Christian II as an opportunity to implement the Reformation, creating a legal structure for a Lutheran Church in Denmark through the enactment of three important pieces of legislation: *The Recess of 1536* (hereafter, the Recess), *The Coronation Charter of Christian III* (the Coronation Charter), and *The Church Ordinance 1537/1539* (the Church Ordinance).[4] The Recess and the Coronation

---

3. Thorkild C. Lyby, *Vi Evangeliske, Studier over samspillet mellem udenrigspolitik og kirkepolitik på Frederik I's tid* (Aarhus: Aarhus Universitetsforlag, 1993), pp. 423-49.

4. *The Recess of 1536* is found in J. L. A. Kolderup-Rosenvinge, ed., *Samling af gamle danske Love, Fjerde Deel, Danske Recesser og Ordinantser af kongerne af den Oldenborgske Stamme* (Copenhagen: Gyldendalske Boghandlings Forlag, 1824), pp. 157-71. *The Coronation Charter* is found in Selskabet for Udgivelse af Kilder til dansk Historie, *Samling af Danske Kongers Haandfæstninger og andre lignende Acter, 1856-1858* (1856-58; reprint, Copenhagen: Geheimearchivets Aarsberetninger, 1974), pp. 82-89, and *The Church Ordinance* is found in

Charter were both issued on October 30, 1536, at the end of a parliament held in Copenhagen.[5] Together, they implemented the Reformation in Denmark at a constitutional level. Article 1 of the Coronation Charter dealt with the religious responsibilities of the king and stated that he must "above all love and worship the almighty God" and protect and strengthen "his holy word" to "the honour of God and the enhancement of the holy Christian faith."[6] While this statement seems relatively innocent, it is worth recalling that the corresponding article in the earlier coronation charters stressed that the king should "above all love the heavenly God and justly strengthen and protect the holy Church and her servants, and all its privileges, freedoms, statutes and good old customs, which previously have been granted from the holy Roman Church and holy fathers, Christian kings, princes, princesses and principals, in all its articles as confirmed by us."[7]

In addition to this change in emphasis from institutional protection to theological affirmation, the Coronation Charter makes no provision suggesting that the church would have its own jurisdiction, that it would be exempt from taxes, or that it would retain all the other privileges that the earlier coronation charters secured for the Catholic Church as an independent institution with its own legal system, through canon law. Nor are such church rights or privileges found in any of the following coronation charters through 1660, when the last charter was annulled.[8] Thus, the meaning of this

---

Holger Fr. Rørdam, ed., *Danske Kirkelove samt Udvalg af andre Bestemmelser vedrørende Kirken, Skolen og de Fattiges Forsørgelse fra Reformationen indtil Christian V's Danske Lov, 1536-1683 1* (Copenhagen: Selskabet til Udgivelse af Kilder til dansk Kirkehistorie, 1883), pp. 40-133.

5. Parliaments or Assemblies of the Estates of the Realm were assemblies of representatives from the nobility, townsmen, clergy, and peasants, which discussed and sometimes approved/legislated in important matters concerning the realm. For a description of the role and development of parliaments see Poul Johannes Jørgensen, *Dansk Retshistorie. Retskildernes og Forfatningsrettens Historie indtil sidste Halvdel af det 17. Aarhundrede* (Copenhagen: G. E. C. Fads Forlag, 1971), pp. 500-501.

6. Selskabet for Udgivelse af Kilder til dansk Historie, *Samling af Danske Kongers,* p. 83. All translations are made by the authors.

7. Art. 1 in *The Coronation Charter of Frederik I,* Selskabet for Udgivelse af Kilder til dansk Historie, *Samling af Danske Kongers,* p. 71. Cf. the similar articles in earlier coronation charters of Christian I, Hans, and Christian II, pp. 45, 47-48, and 57.

8. Henning Matzen, *Danske Kongers Haandfæstninger. Indledende Undersøgelser* (Copenhagen: University of Copenhagen, 1889), pp. 156-57. The later charters, however, include an obligation to provide the churches and schools with pious, learned Christians and to finance them, if that hadn't already been done, and *The Coronation Charter of Frederik III* further adds that people with a different religion were not allowed to enter the realm.

paragraph of the Coronation Charter is obvious: instead of an obligation towards the church as an independent institution, a privilege the Catholic Church had enjoyed, the king is now only obliged to make personal theological commitments to honor God and the holy Christian faith. To what extent the obligation must be understood to be an obligation to Lutheran Christendom is however more uncertain, but having the background of the Charter in mind, it should be understood as legitimizing the Lutheran Reformation by a Lutheran king. This becomes clearer when the Charter is read together with the Recess of 1536.

The Recess, issued at the conclusion of the parliament called in that year,[9] describes itself as a "constitution of the realm" that should be observed for "eternity."[10] The foreword to the Recess begins by describing the cause and effects of the civil war:

> That because the almighty, benevolent, merciful God, after the death of King Frederik, of blessed memory, because of our great sins, wicked life and government, and especially that the bishops in this realm not at the appropriate time would choose and appoint a king, has severely and harshly let his punishment and wrath fall over us and this realm.[11]

After this statement allocating guilt to the bishops, the Recess describes all of the calamities that were the result of the civil war in Denmark:

> War with fire, murder, plunder, the ruin and destruction of places, castles, and houses, violation and abuse of women and virgins, many sorrowful widows and poor fatherless children. . . .[12]

It goes on to argue that the new king, Christian III, has saved the country from all these calamities and will now secure "peace and order" and a "lasting Christian government."[13]

The substance and effect of this legislation was as profound as the foreword: the Catholic bishops, who had opposed "the word and gospel of God," were removed from office, their estates were forfeited to the king, and they were prevented from ever taking part in the government in the fu-

9. Kolderup-Rosenvinge, ed., *Samling af gamle danske Love*, p. 161.
10. Kolderup-Rosenvinge, ed., *Samling af gamle danske Love*, pp. 161 and 162.
11. Kolderup-Rosenvinge, ed., *Samling af gamle danske Love*, p. 160.
12. Kolderup-Rosenvinge, ed., *Samling af gamle danske Love*, p. 160.
13. Kolderup-Rosenvinge, ed., *Samling af gamle danske Love*, p. 161.

ture.[14] In the service of preaching the true and holy word of God, these bishops were replaced with other "Christian bishops and superintendents,"[15] a
new title originating from Germany that replaced the controversial title of
bishop. (In practice, however, it was not long before people went back to
using "bishop" as the title of the superintendents.)[16]

The Coronation Charter and the Recess contain almost no provisions
concerning the doctrines, organization, or framework of the church. Those
details were supplied in the Church Ordinance, a Danish law issued by the
king and the Council of the Realm, which was sent to and, according to the
royal letter at the beginning of the Ordinance, approved by Luther.[17] At the
request of the king, the reformer Johannes Bugenhagen went to Denmark in
1537 to aid in the implementation of the Reformation and lead the revision of
the draft through to promulgation, in Latin, in December 1537. The Church
Ordinance was translated into Danish in 1539, and became the official version
of the law in 1542.

The Church Ordinance begins with a royal letter from Christian III explaining the background for the ordinance, with special emphasis on Luther's approval and the assistance from Bugenhagen. Their advice and approval are emphasized so that no one would think the king was self-willed or
impetuous in imposing its theological directives.[18] The king then describes
the content of the Church Ordinance, presents his Lutheran beliefs, and
condemns the "party of Antichrist" and the "teachings of the Devil," listing
many grave abuses and wrongdoings of the Catholic Church.[19] At the end
of the letter, the king threatens to punish any violations of the Church Ordinance. The new church has thus become a church governed by and protected
by the Lutheran king.

After the royal letter, a preamble written by the king and the Council
of the Realm describes in more moderate terms the events that led to the
promulgation of the Church Ordinance and expresses hope that it will secure
peace in religious matters in the realm.[20]

---

14. Kolderup-Rosenvinge, ed., *Samling af gamle danske Love*, p. 164, meaning: they
were not Lutheran.

15. Kolderup-Rosenvinge, ed., *Samling af gamle danske Love*, p. 163.

16. Lausten, *Reformationen*, p. 149.

17. Rørdam, *Danske Kirkelove 1*, p. 41. It is, however, not certain that he explicitly gave
his approval. On the origin of the Church Ordinance, see Lausten, *Reformationen*, pp. 135-38.

18. Rørdam, *Danske Kirkelove 1*, p. 41.

19. Rørdam, *Danske Kirkelove 1*, p. 44.

20. Rørdam, *Danske Kirkelove 1*, pp. 47-48.

As is evident from the process of passing the Church Ordinance, legal responsibility for regulating the church and spiritual matters was left to the king and the Council of the Realm, the secular authority (*"Obrigkeit"* in German), but the king and council took great care in consulting the theologians before taking action under it. This consultative procedure became standard in regulating the church or religious matters after the Reformation, and in fact, this is the process explicitly prescribed at the end of the Ordinance to amend it, subject to the caveat that nothing could be changed that violates the word of God and his true doctrine.[21]

In the following we will focus on three aspects of the legal framework of the first Danish Lutheran Church as it is described in the Ordinance: the doctrines of the church, the appointment and removal of priests and the new Lutheran superintendents, and the relationship between church and state.

Church Doctrines

The Church Ordinance contained no explicit obligation for members or clergy to make a particular theological confession.[22] The theological foundation in the works of Luther and Melanchthon is, however, clear when one reads the royal letter and the Church Ordinance. It is especially clear from the list of books that the Ordinance prescribed that all priests should possess: "Doctor Morten Luthers Postille," "Apologiam Philippi" — meaning both *Confessio Augustana* and the apology by Melanchthon,[23] "Locos Communes Philippi," Luther's Small Catechism, and "Instructio-

21. Rørdam, *Danske Kirkelove 1*, p. 132. Cf. Jørgen Stenbæk, "Den danske kirkeordinans af 1537/39 — Teologi og funktion," in *Reformationen i Norden. Kontinuitet och förnyelse*, ed. Carl-Gustaf Andrén (Lund: GWK Gleerup Bokförlag, 1973), pp. 130-55, 135, and 137.

22. Stenbæk, "Den danske kirkeordinans," pp. 139-43; Lausten, *Reformationen*, pp. 178-80. In 1569 it was, however, prescribed that all foreigners should adhere to a list of articles on the faith before they were allowed to enter the country. This list could be viewed as a confession for Denmark after the Reformation. See Holger Fr. Rørdam, ed., *Danske Kirkelove samt udvalg af andre bestemmelser vedrørende Kirken, Skolen og de Fattiges Forsørgelse fra Reformationen indtil Christian V's Danske Lov, 1536-1683 2* (Copenhagen: Selskabet til Udgivelse af Kilder til dansk Kirkehistorie, 1886), pp. 126-34.

23. Lausten, *Reformationen*, p. 178. In contrast, Stenbæk believes it is only a reference to *Confessio Augustana* (Stenbæk, "Den danske kirkeordinans," p. 141), but this corresponds very poorly to the wording of the Ordinance.

nem Visitationis Saxonicæ" among others.[24] Beyond these, new books were banned, unless theologians at the University of Copenhagen and the superintendents had approved them.[25] Perhaps ironically, in listing books written by both Luther and Melanchthon, the Church Ordinance does not appear to contemplate the possibility that Luther and Melanchthon did not agree on everything.[26]

In terms of doctrine, in accordance with the Lutheran attack on the Catholic Church's teaching on the seven sacraments, the Church Ordinance recognized only three sacraments: Baptism, the Eucharist, and the sacrament of penance.[27] The Ordinance also provided the priests with a list of topics they ought to include in their sermons with special emphasis on justification.[28] In it, the priests were warned against talking about God's providence and Christian liberty or similar subjects that are well beyond human understanding, and about which humans are easily offended.[29] Among the detailed rules on the sermon, the priests were forbidden to preach longer than one hour.[30]

24. Stenbæk, "Den danske kirkeordinans," pp. 118-20.

25. The University of Copenhagen, founded in 1479, was reopened after the Reformation as a Lutheran university, the main task of which was to educate priests for the church. On the influence of the Reformation on the university and universities in general, see Leif Grane, ed., *University and Reformation: Lectures from the University of Copenhagen Symposium* (Leiden: Brill, 1981).

26. Stenbæk, "Den danske kirkeordinans," p. 142, and Lausten, *Reformationen,* p. 179. The differences between Luther and Melanchthon resulted later in the theological conflict between followers of Melanchthon and Luther especially concerning the Eucharist. For a short introduction to this controversy and the legacy of Melanchthon see J. A. O. Preus, "Translator's Preface to the First Edition," in Philip Melanchthon, *The Chief Theological Topics, Loci Praecipui Theologici 1559,* 2nd ed. (St. Louis: Concordia, 2011), pp. xxiii-xxxviii.

27. The status of the sacrament of penance was disputed, but its inclusion among the sacraments was in accordance with *Apologia Confessionis Augustanae.* Cf. *Die Bekenntnisschriften der evangelisch-lutherischen Kirche,* 7th ed. (Göttingen: Vandenhoeck & Ruprecht, 1976), 259.41 and 292.4.

28. Rørdam, *Danske Kirkelove,* pp. 50-51.

29. Rørdam, *Danske Kirkelove,* p. 51. This had been at the center of the debate between Erasmus and Luther concerning free will, a subject perhaps both difficult to grasp for non-theologians and also a subject that could provoke debate and conflict among theologians.

30. Rørdam, *Danske Kirkelove,* p. 60.

Appointment and Removal of Priests and Superintendents

The Church Ordinance contains detailed rules about the appointment and removal of priests and superintendents.[31] It states that the priests and superintendent from each district must appoint a rural dean, whose work was to nominate new priests for appointment together with a group of the most prominent lay members from the parish.[32] Before ordination, a priest candidate would be examined by the superintendent, inquiring about his wisdom and faith. If he was approved by the superintendent, he was sent to the local sheriff to be approved by the king and to swear an oath,[33] beginning with a declaration of loyalty to the king and the priest's obligation to promote the king's honor, reputation, and peace, followed by a promise to faithfully perform his service as a priest.[34] The Church Ordinance prescribed that if a priest violated his obligations under this oath, he should first be reminded of them, then corrected, and ultimately, if he persisted, after the assessment of the rural dean and the superintendent, he would be judged and removed by the authorities — probably the local sheriff.[35]

For the appointment of a new superintendent (later referred to as a bishop) to a vacant diocese, all the priests from the diocese were required to gather at an assembly and nominate four priests who would appoint the new superintendent. The candidate was then examined by the nearest sitting superintendent. If the candidate passed the examination, he was sent to the king for the final approval and also to swear an oath of allegiance to the king (promoting his honor, well-being, peace, order, and obedience) and to carry out his obligations to the church, the gospel, and God.[36]

The order of recitation of these obligations is telling. While the king in his charter first makes a promise to God, then to the obligations of his office, the priest and superintendents first make a commitment to the king,

31. The rules for appointing priests can be found in Rørdam, *Danske Kirkelove,* pp. 74-70. The rules regarding superintendents can be found in Rørdam, *Danske Kirkelove,* pp. 116-17.

32. This was the ordinary way of appointing new priests; the Ordinance also contained other procedures.

33. In Danish *lensmanden.* Administratively, Denmark was divided into fiefs, *len* (not to be confused with feudal estates), which were governed by the local sheriff.

34. Rørdam, *Danske Kirkelove,* pp. 75-76.

35. Rørdam, *Danske Kirkelove,* p. 80. The Danish word used is *Herskabbet*; a more direct translation is "the master or ruler," but it is translated as "authority" here, which reflects the meaning more correctly.

36. Rørdam, *Danske Kirkelove,* pp. 126-27.

then to the obligations of their religious offices! Not only are the superintendents directly approved by the king, but the king also pays their salaries,[37]
so the superintendents are government officials.[38] To remove a misbehaving
superintendent, the Ordinance prescribed that he must be brought before
the king, who in the presence of two or three other superintendents must
examine him, with the king having the ultimate power to remove him from
office.[39] It is important to note that after the Reformation, no archbishop
position existed in Denmark: the superintendents were in principle equal,
and instead of higher clerical authority, it was the king who exercised the
ultimate control over the church.[40]

The Relationship between State and Church

After the Reformation, canon law — which among other things had regulated the affairs of the church, marriage, and various criminal offenses,
especially crimes against the church, usury, and the various sexual offenses
— was abolished.[41] The Church Ordinance itself was clear about the role
of the church: it could still excommunicate, but in accordance with the
Lutheran view, that only meant banning miscreants from the Eucharist
(excommunicatio minor).[42] "[E]verything else belongs to the [secular] authority," according to the Church Ordinance, which conversely states that
"the sword" must serve and protect the church.[43] Thus, the church could
no longer exercise jurisdiction over crimes such as adultery, fornication,

---

37. Rørdam, *Danske Kirkelove,* p. 109. The salaries of the priests were paid through the
tithes, one-third of which was to go to the priests; cf. pp. 98-104 and Kolderup-Rosenvinge,
Samling af gamle danske Love, pp. 165-66.

38. Stenbæk, "Den danske kirkeordinans," p. 150; and Lausten, *Reformationen,* p. 147.

39. Rørdam, *Danske Kirkelove,* pp. 115-16. The Ordinance directly explains the use of
the other superintendents as required by 1 Timothy 5.

40. Lausten, *Reformationen,* p. 147.

41. Lausten, *Reformationen,* pp. 219-24; and Jørgensen, *Dansk Retshistorie,* p. 95.

42. Cf. *Die Schmalkadischen Artikel 1537,* in *D. Martin Luthers Werke: Kritische Gesamtausgabe,* vol. 50 (Weimar: H. Böhlau, 1914), p. 247.

43. Rørdam, *Danske Kirkelove,* pp. 80-81. The Danish word used is *Herskabbet;* as
before, we translate as "authority" here, which reflects the meaning more correctly. Cf.
Stenbæk, "Den danske kirkeordinans," pp. 143-44. *Excommunicatio major* was, however,
reintroduced in 1629 in an effort to strengthen church discipline and avoid God's wrath —
it was closely associated with the Danish defeats during the Thirty Years' War. Jørgensen,
Dansk Retshistorie, p. 531.

and usury, following the Lutheran view on the separation of spiritual and secular authority.[44]

Instead, the Ordinance stated that the servants of God had nothing to do with marriage except performing the marriage ceremony and guiding the worried consciences of the people on marital problems. As it noted again, "everything else belongs to the secular authority."[45] Other than rules prohibiting relatives within certain degrees of consanguinity to marry and banning secret engagements, the Ordinance decreed that the marriage ceremony should follow Luther's ritual in his Small Catechism. Furthermore, the new superintendents were directly warned against participating in any marriage disputes or adjudicating any "secular case" such as a divorce.[46] These rules thus follow the Lutheran view that marriage is a worldly matter that must be governed by the secular authority.[47] However, this rule separating the church from marital disputes did not exist for long because there arose too many difficulties in leaving adjudication of marriage and adultery cases to the local sheriffs or the mayor and council in the cities as prescribed by the Ordinance. As early as 1542, the Ordinance was amended to take these cases before a mixed court consisting of the local sheriff and theologians from the cathedral chapters.

The Reformation was thus a turning point in Danish legal history. It brought an end to canon law and to the church as an independent legal institution with its own courts. The process of finding a way of efficiently regulating the matters previously dealt with in canon law was, however, a long and painful one — revolutions such as the Danish Reformation are not always kind toward the legal system.[48]

44. See especially Luther's *Von weltlicher Obrigkeit, wie weit man ihr Gehorsam schuldig sei,* in *D. Martin Luthers Werke. Kritische Gesamtausgabe,* vol. 11 (Weimar: H. Böhlau, 1900), pp. 245-82. Cf. p. 265 for his criticism of the bishops who "sind weltliche Fürsten worden und regirn mit gesessen, die nur Leyb unnd gütt betreffen" and furthermore "regirn sie außwendig schlösser, stedt, land und leutt und martern die seelen mit unseglicher mörderey." In the Church Ordinance, there is, however, a sole and unique exception to the principle that fines now should be paid to the secular authority. See Lausten, *Reformationen,* p. 222.

45. Rørdam, *Danske Kirkelove,* p. 74.

46. Rørdam, *Danske Kirkelove,* p. 108.

47. "Dem nach weil die hochzeit und ehestand ein weltlich geshhefft ist, gebürt uns geistlichen odder kirckendienern nichst darynn zu ordenen odder regirn." *Ein Traubücklein für die einfältigen Pharrherr 1529,* in *D. Martin Luthers Werke: Kritische Gesamtausgabe,* vol. 30, book 3 (Weimar: H. Böhlau, 1910), p. 74. Cf. Stenbæk, "Den danske kirkeordinans," p. 145.

48. On the impact of the Lutheran Reformation on law, see in particular Harold J.

While the Ordinance certainly reflected Luther's thought on the distinction between the two kingdoms in that the exercise of political government belonged to the secular authority, it did not conform to the second part of his thought, his rejection of the right of the secular authority to intervene in religious affairs. Confronted with the practical problem of reforming the church, Luther, however, acknowledged that the secular authority, e.g., the prince or king, as an emergency solution, could step in and help with the organization of the church. What for Luther was an emergency solution quickly became the permanent solution in practice. And in his theology Melanchthon went even further, arguing that the secular authority was the guardian of the two tables of the Decalogue; and as the guardian of the first three commandments, he was responsible for establishing a Lutheran Church.[49]

As the first legal framework for the Danish Lutheran Church, the Church Ordinance 1537/39 was in force for about 150 years in Denmark until it was replaced with the church regulations in the National Law of Denmark 1683. It was also in force in Norway until Norway finally got its own Church Ordinance in 1607. In both countries, the church had now become regulated by the king and council, with the king at the top of the hierarchy. It was now integrated into the apparatus of, and controlled by, the state, which in turn had become a Lutheran state.

The Period of Political Absolutism and the Church

In 1660, a significant political shift occurred in Denmark, resembling the shifts in many other European nations: the king became the absolute legal authority, not answerable to any other; or, to use the terminology from the time, the king became sovereign. As with the political changes in 1536, this

Berman, *Law and Revolution II: The Impact of the Protestant Reformations on the Western Legal Tradition* (Cambridge, MA: Harvard University Press, 2003); and John Witte Jr., *Law and Protestantism: The Legal Teachings of the Lutheran Reformation* (New York: Cambridge University Press, 2002). See the former for the use of "revolution" on the Reformation.

49. Cf. Svend Andersen, "Law in Nordic Lutheranism," in *Law and Religion in the 21st Century: Nordic Perspectives,* ed. Lisbet Christoffersen, Kjell Å Modéer, and Svend Andersen (Copenhagen: DJØF Publishing, 2010), pp. 393-411, here 397-99. On the general development of the Lutheran churches and the theological legitimization thereof, see Witte, *Law and Protestantism,* pp. 131-32.

change occurred after a crisis. After a disastrous war with Sweden, where Sweden came close to annexing Denmark, the king used the opportunity at hand, ordered the army to close the gates of Copenhagen, and through an alliance with the townsmen and clergy forced the Council, trapped in the city, to cancel the last Coronation Charter and accept the king as a hereditary monarch — in order to prevent any future election of monarchs or coronation charters.[50] As a consequence, the Council of the Realm lost its rights and privileges in favor of, instead, a lone supreme ruler. Unlike absolutism in other European countries, Danish absolutism was expressed in a constitution: *Kongeloven* (King's Law) of 1665, or, as it was called in Latin, *Lex regia.* This constitution contained three important articles concerning the regulation of the church.[51] As was the practice in the Coronation Charters, the first article dealt with the king's duties toward God in directives such as: "The best beginning for everything is to begin with God";[52] the king must "serve and worship the one right and true God" according to his "holy and true word" and dictated by "our Christian Faith and confession" in the "form and way, as it pure and genuine has been set forth and presented in confession from Augsburg the year one thousand five hundred and thirty"; and the king must keep his subjects adhering to the same faith and protect his realms from all heretics. The commitment to *Confessio Augustana* was bound together with the requirement that the king should keep the realm together and not renounce his absolute power, with the only restraint on the exercise of his absolute power being found in *Lex regia.* An article in *Lex regia* binds the king's "ancestors, children and grandchildren a thousand degrees paternal and maternal," explicitly mirroring the biblical language that God had commanded the keeping of his covenant to a thousand generations.[53]

Article Two of the *Lex regia* reinforced the absolutist nature of the king's power, describing the king as the "highest and supreme head on earth, above

50. On the origin of the Danish absolutism and the events in 1660 see Thomas Lyngby, Søren Mentz, and Sebastian Olden-Jørgensen, *Magt & Pragt. Enevælde 1660-1848* (Copenhagen: Gads Forlag, 2010), pp. 13-72.

51. A. D. Jørgensen, *Kongeloven og dens Forhistorie. Aktstykker udgivne af de under Kirke- og Undervisningsministeriet samlede Arkiver* (1866; reprint, Copenhagen: Selskabet til Udgivelse af Kilder til Danmarks Historie, 1973), pp. 38-67.

52. Art. 1, *Kongeloven*, p. 43.

53. Psalm 105:8, and likewise the promise of vengeance or rewards to a thousand generations found elsewhere in the Bible in the Ten Commandments, Exod. 20:6, and, e.g., Exod. 34:7 and Deut. 5:20 and 7:9.

all human laws, and with no other head or judge above either in spiritual or secular cases, except God alone."[54] Article Six explicitly carried this principle forth to the governance of the church, stating that the king alone had the "highest power over all the clergy" and that he could arrange and prescribe "all church and church service, meetings, gatherings and assemblies regarding religious cases" when he found it convenient.[55] *Lex regia* thus conferred on the king ultimate authority over the church, leaving no doubt about the ultimate outcome of the Danish Reformation on the relationship between church and state: the king had become the supreme head of the church.[56] At the beginning of absolutism, legislation was codified in the National Law of Denmark *(Danske Lov)* of 1683, one of the six parts of which dealt with "religion and clergy." Some of these very detailed rules about church activities still govern the Danish church today. Indeed, the very definition of the confessional foundation of the state church even today is enshrined in the National Law: Holy Scripture, the three early symbols of faith, the Augsburg Confession, and Luther's Little Catechism.

The Danish Lutheran Church in Light of the European Move toward Democratization

With the beginning of European democratization in the nineteenth century, one might have expected that the Danish state-church model would be replaced by one reflecting church autonomy, given that the Danish state-church model contradicts a core tenet of Lutheran Christianity: the independence of the spiritual realm from secular dominance. Or, to put it differently, with democratization, it became very difficult to regard governmental rule over the church as equal to church autonomy as recognized by Lutheran doctrine, even though government rule had been theoretically consistent

54. Art. 1, *Kongeloven*, p. 44.
55. Art. 1, *Kongeloven*, p. 45.
56. For a discussion of whether article 6 presupposed that the internal affairs of the church were left to the church, see Knud Fabricius, *Kongeloven. Dens tilblivelse og Plads i Samtidens Natur- og Arveretlige Udvikling. En Historisk Undersøgelse* (1920; reprint, Copenhagen: H. Hagerups Forlag, 1971), pp. 317-18. See the discussion in Inger Dübeck, "Den kirkelige retshistorie. Confessio Augustana og prærogativanordninger," in *Bekendelse og Kirkeordnniger. Kirkeretsantalogi 2010*, ed. Zacharias Balslev-Blausen, Peter Christensen, Lisbet Christoffersen, Peter Garde, Anders Jørgensen, and Kirsten Busch Nielsen (Copenhagen and Aarhus: Selskabet for Kirkeret, 2010), pp. 17-44, 34-36.

with Lutheran theology as long as the notion of *"praecipua membra ecclesiae"* — the king is the highest bishop — made some sense.

However, the development in Denmark shows that it was possible to abolish absolutism as a political system and yet keep the essence of the Lutheran prince-church: the political rule of the church. The Danish Constitution of 1849 (hereafter Constitution) marked the end of absolutism, replacing it not with democracy proper but rather with a constitutional monarchy. Whereas previous Danish law was founded on a classical Lutheran theory about political and legislative legitimacy of the monarch, the new constitution was rooted in modern ideas about the sovereignty of the people, though infused with natural law theory linking back to Lutheran theory.

As to the existing relation between the state and the Lutheran Church, there are some paradoxes in the modern democratic constitution. The Evangelical Lutheran Church is declared to be "the Danish People's Church" *(den danske folkekirke)* and "as such," it is to be supported by the state (Constitution §4).[57] Freedom of religion is secured. But the Lutheran Church is obviously privileged, which is also clear from the fact that the monarch is required to be a member of that church (§6). And, as indicated initially, a crucial paragraph states that "the constitution of the People's Church is to be arranged by law" (§66).[58] This statement clearly intends to proclaim that the Lutheran Church should rule itself, hence that the prince-state model should be abandoned.

However, strangely, this paragraph of the constitution has never been implemented, even if several attempts have been made, one argument being that political rule actually guarantees internal freedom. And so Denmark still has the absolutist model for church-state relations, only now the role of the king is taken over by parliament and government. This situation explains the peculiar 2012 marriage law revisions described at the beginning of this chapter: generally speaking, all regulation of church matters continues to have the status of governmental legislation.

The Danish model stands in stark contrast to the legal church-state situation in the motherland of the Reformation, Germany, as well as other Nor-

57. The official translation has been "the Established Church of Denmark," which is not the literal translation of "den Danske Folkekirke." According to the "fathers" of the constitution, the "People's Church" is defined as the church of which the predominant part of the Danish population are members.

58. The official translation has been as follows: "The constitution of the Established Church shall be laid down by statute."

dic countries. In Germany, the Lutheran prince-state model was abrogated with the end of World War I with the termination of the German monarchy. The democratic constitution of the Weimar Republic states that "there is no state church"; rather, it secures freedom of religion and attributes to some religious communities the status of "corporations of public law." This is also true of the Lutheran churches that have signed contracts with the individual states of the German federation, e.g., about theology as a course of study at state public universities. The paragraphs on religion in the Weimar Constitution were later integrated into the constitution of the Federal Republic of Germany promulgated in 1949, one hundred years after the Danish constitution.[59] Thus in Germany, the Lutheran Church is separate from the state, but has retained a semi-official status as a cooperating partner to the state for such matters as religious education in public schools. Ecclesial legislation is autonomously promulgated and enforced by the Lutheran churches themselves. Civil law is enacted by the secular government, while the churches contribute by participating as nongovernmental organizations in public political debate and in hearings.

In the Nordic region, all countries other than Denmark have, in one way or another, changed their national law in order to erect some kind of "wall of separation" between church and state. In *Sweden,* the crucial step from a state-church model to church autonomy was taken through a law passed by the Swedish parliament in 1998. The law defines the Swedish church as an Evangelical Lutheran religious society along with other denominations, but also recognizes it as an "open people's church," having a kind of prominent status. The church enjoys self-determination: all regulation of church matters is enacted by the church's own bodies, and the supreme ecclesial body is the church assembly.[60] The formal separation of the Swedish Evangelical Lutheran Church from the state took place on January 1, 2000.

Finland obtained its national independence only in 1917, when it ceased being a principality in the Russian Empire. However, under Russian rule, the Evangelical-Lutheran Church of Finland was given extensive autonomy by a law passed in 1869. According to the Finnish church law, regulation of

59. The reunification in 1990 meant that the German Democratic Republic was incorporated into the Federal Republic of Germany, and the united Germany was covered by the constitution of 1949.

60. The church assembly *(Kyrkomötet)* is the body with highest authority within the Church of Sweden. The assembly that meets twice every fall consists of 251 members, the vast majority of whom are elected among church members over the age of sixteen — pastors and laypeople alike.

church matters is formally enacted by the parliament and the government, but the church's own bodies actually draw up the regulations. The political authorities do not have the possibility of overruling the church's own ruling.

Norway promulgated its democratic constitution in 1814, when it was separated from Denmark after the Napoleonic wars. In that constitution, the Evangelical Lutheran Church was given the status of a state church, but in a revision of the constitution in 2012, the state-church model was abolished, even though the Evangelical Lutheran Church remains the People's Church of Norway and as such is supported by the state.[61] Unlike its Danish counterpart, the Norwegian church now has wide autonomy, an issue that was settled in a church law passed in 1996. Similarly, the Evangelical Lutheran Church of *Iceland* obtained extensive independence from the state owing to a law of 1998.

Thus, the pattern of the development in most Nordic countries shows a transition from the original Lutheran prince-church model to a largely independent and autonomous status given by state law, though the ties between church and state have not been totally cut, a fact that is manifested in the legal designation of these church bodies as the "People's Church" (*folkekirke*) in these nations. As to legal matters, the situation in these Nordic countries — as in Germany — is such, basically speaking, that there is a clear separation between, on the one hand, regulation that concerns the church and is passed by the church's own legislative bodies, and, on the other hand, civil law, in the creation of which the churches may participate on the same terms as other agents in civil society.

As noted, the one exception is Denmark, where until now the Evangelical Lutheran Church continues to be comprehensively under state rule. As mentioned, since the adoption of the constitution in 1849, several attempts have been made to fulfill the constitution's promise of church independence. However, none of the attempts has succeeded. In 2011 the new government announced a plan to modernize church law and appointed a commission for this purpose. In its report, the majority of the commission recommends the establishment of a separate national church body, but without any real legislative authority in church matters. The commission proposes that the final legal authority over church governance should still lie with the Minister of Ecclesiastical Affairs and in some cases even with the queen.[62]

---

61. *Constitution of the Kingdom of Norway*, §16.

62. Cf. *Folkekirkens styre. Betænkning fra udvalget om en mere sammenhængende og moderne styringsstruktur for folkekirken. Betænkning 1544.* Kirkeministeriet April 2014.

It would be remiss not to end with the church-state story, less well known, of *Greenland,* the world's largest island. A colony for centuries, since 2009 Greenland has had its own home rule government, but it is still part of the kingdom of Denmark, together with the Faroe Islands. As such, the Danish constitution still governs Greenland, though legislative and administrative power has been delegated to the Greenlandic parliament *(Inatsisartut).* In 2010, this parliament passed a church law that gave the Lutheran Church of Greenland a good deal of autonomy. In the first paragraph of this law, the Evangelical Lutheran Church is identified as "the Greenlandic People's Church." The next paragraph states that the Evangelical Lutheran Church "is part of the People's Church of the Danish Commonwealth [or realm], subjected to Greenland's Home Rule Government, and as such supported by the same." This clause is remarkable in that it regards the Lutheran Church of Greenland as part of the People's Church of Denmark, based on the fact that the Danish constitution — which defines the Evangelical Church as the People's Church — is also valid in Greenland.

Thus far, the Lutheran Church in Greenland still appears as connected to the secular political authority as its mother church on the Denmark mainland. This impression is confirmed by the next paragraph in the Greenland church law, which states that the main responsibility for the church lies with the Home Rule Government, and Section 4 extends this to such "inner church" matters as liturgy, rituals, and hymnbooks. However, both of these paragraphs state that the government's regulation of these church matters has to take place "after negotiations with the bishop." The role of the bishop is made clear in §6: "The bishop over the diocese of Greenland manages the central administration of the church and conducts inspection of [the clergy]." All in all, one can say that the Greenlandic church law takes a crucial legal step toward church autonomy. Whereas the link to the state is kept, church autonomy in the sense of §66 of the Danish constitution is realized by making the bishop the real head of the church. In Greenland, the *summus episcopus* belongs to the spiritual realm — and the *summus episcopus,* it may surprise our Lutheran forebears to know, is a woman!

Conclusion

One feature of the Lutheran Reformation in Europe was that all legislative authority resided with the secular government, so that not only laws on marriage, schools, crimes, paupers, etc., but also church laws were passed by kings or princes. But as these worldly rulers were heads of their national churches, their legislation was of course influenced by Lutheran faith.

However, as a result of a gradual development since the end of World War I, Lutheran churches in Germany and the Nordic countries have obtained autonomy in various degrees, the one exception being Denmark. As a consequence of church autonomy and the loosening of the ties to the state, secular and civil legislation have been separated. The churches state the rules for their own affairs, and their influence on civil law is based on their being agents in civil society.

The peculiar situation in Denmark means that this legislative separation has not taken place in our country; hence the state is still legislator in all matters, including ecclesial ones. The People's Church has no formal authority to participate in legislation, not even in matters pertaining to its own internal affairs. This is true, even if church representatives of course are heard when church-related laws are changed, as was the case with the marriage law.

In Denmark, Lutheran impact on civil legislation can therefore, principally speaking, only have the character of Lutheran citizens participating in the public political debate and seeking to make their influence count that way. On the other hand, there is no obstacle to Lutheran pastors being members of the Danish parliament, the *Folketing,* and actually some are members right now.

Unlike the development in the other Nordic countries, there is no indication that the status of the Evangelical Lutheran Church in Denmark will change within a foreseeable future. For the proposal of the commission mentioned above was not able to gain support from the needed number of members. All in all, then, in Denmark the legislative situation is almost the same as at the time of the Reformation, the main difference being that the state has — in spite of its remaining ties to the church — become largely secular.

CHAPTER 12

Military Chaplains and the Law

James M. Childs Jr.

The First Amendment to the United States Constitution provides that "Congress shall make no law respecting an establishment of religion, or prohibiting the free exercise thereof. . . ." The former phrase is usually referred to as the "Establishment Clause" and the latter as the "Free Exercise Clause." The chaplaincy exists as a carefully structured legal accommodation to the Establishment Clause. The military has chosen to establish and sustain the chaplaincy in order to provide for the free exercise of religion for members of the military and their families who, due to the special nature of life in the military, would not otherwise have access to religious services. As will be clear, the design of the accommodation to the Establishment Clause and the mandates placed upon chaplains for the provision of free exercise, taken together, seek to maintain the intention of the Constitution while serving the well-being of service members and their families.[1]

1. Ira C. Lupu and Robert W. Tuttle, "Instruments of Accommodation: The Military Chaplaincy and the Constitution," *West Virginia Law Review* 110 (February 2008): 90-166. Lupu and Tuttle have reviewed some sixty years of Supreme Court decisions involving challenges to governmental accommodations to the Establishment Clause. From this history they have delineated four principles of religious accommodation by government entities: accommodation must (1) relieve a significant government-imposed burden on the private exercise of religious freedom; (2) facilitate private and voluntary religious practices; (3) be available on a denominationally neutral basis; (4) not impose significant burdens on third parties. The authors go on to apply these criteria to the military chaplaincy as an accommodation. The ways in which the military has operated with these criteria should be evident as the discussion progresses. I am grateful to Robert Tuttle for his counsel in the preparation of this essay and for his generosity in sharing some of his work on this subject. I am also grateful to my colleague, the Rev. Dr. Wollom Jensen, Executive Director in the Office of the Episcopal Bishop Suffragan for Federal Ministries in Washington, D.C., with whom I have

In order to comply with the constitutional requirements as stated within
the First Amendment, the Department of Defense (DoD) provides oversight
and guidance through the implementation of directives and instructions addressing the religious practices within the armed services. Key provisions of
Department of Defense Directive (DoDD) 1304.19 read as follows:

It is DoD policy that Chaplaincies of the Military Departments:

4.1 Are established to advise and assist commanders in the discharge
of their responsibilities to provide for the free exercise of religion in the
context of military service as guaranteed by the Constitution, to assist
commanders in managing Religious Affairs (DoD Directive 5100.73 [ref-
erence (e)]), and to serve as the principal advisors to commanders for all
issues regarding the impact of religion on military operations.

4.2 Shall serve a religiously diverse population. Within the military
commanders are required to provide comprehensive religious support to
all authorized individuals within their areas of responsibility. Religious
Organizations that choose to participate in the Chaplaincies recognize this
command imperative and express willingness for their Religious Ministry
Professionals (RMPs) to perform their professional duties as chaplains in
cooperation with RMPs from other religious traditions.[2]

Defense Department Instruction (DoDI) 1304.28 sets forth the military's
professional requirements for RMPs.[3] The provisions require candidates to
receive the endorsement of a qualified religious organization. RMPs must be
educationally qualified, possessing both a baccalaureate degree with not less
than 120 semester hours from a qualifying educational institution and a graduate degree of no fewer than seventy-two semester hours of theological or
related study from a qualifying educational institution. Related studies could
include topics in general religion, world religions, the practice of religion,
theology, religious philosophy, religious ethics, and/or the foundational

---

been working on a project in military ethics. Dr. Jensen is a retired captain in the chaplaincy
of the U.S. Navy. He has been my main personal source for these matters, and provided the
quotations noted in this chapter.

2. DoD Instruction 1304.19, Appointment of Chaplains for the Military Departments
(June 11, 2004), http://www.dtic.mil/whs/directives/corres/pdf/130419p.pdf (accessed
October 16, 2014).

3. DoD Instruction 1308.28, Guidance for the Appointment of Chaplains for the Military Departments (June 11, 2010), available at http://www.dtic.mil/whs/directives/corres/
pdf/130428_2004_ch3.pdf (accessed October 16, 2014).

writings from the applicants' religious tradition. Provision is also made for consideration of candidates from unaccredited educational institutions.[4]

A candidate must be "willing to function in a pluralistic environment, as defined in this Instruction, and [be] willing to support directly and indirectly the free exercise of religion by all members of the Military Services, their family members, and other persons authorized to be served by the military chaplaincies."[5]

DoDD 1304.19 and DoDI 1304.28, each in their own way, speak to the commitment to provide for free exercise. In the interest of free exercise, both state the need to minister in a situation of diversity, in a pluralistic setting. The insistence on good professional credentials serves the effectiveness of the chaplain's ministry. At the same time, it is clear that the military does not attempt to dictate the content of that preparation, for that would violate the Establishment Clause. The military also does not dictate what faith communities may participate in the chaplaincy as long as the chaplain candidates possess the above-mentioned endorsement and have met the other criteria set forth in DoDI 1304.28. The ecclesiastical endorsement and the role of religious institutions in the preparation of candidates make it clear that government cedes the matter of eligibility for authorized ministries to the faith communities. Chaplains are affirmed in their functioning in accord with the theology and practices of their own faith communities while yet being ready to minister in what is now a growing phenomenon of pluralism. We will need to say more later on the matter of pluralism and the integrity of the Establishment Clause in the practice of the chaplaincy.

Further indication of the military's interest in meeting the religious needs of its service members is found in the newly revised DoDI 1300.17, which became effective January 22, 2014. Many consider this to be a more accommodating approach than heretofore:

In accordance with section 533(a) (1) of Public Law 112-239 (Reference [d]), as amended, unless it could have an adverse impact on military readiness, unit cohesion, and good order and discipline, Military Departments will accommodate individual expressions of sincerely held beliefs (conscience, moral principles, or religious beliefs) of Service members in accordance with the policies and procedures in this instruction. This does not preclude disciplinary or administrative action for conduct by a

4. DoD Instruction 1308.28, Sections 6.1, 6.1.4, 6.2.2, pp. 3-4.
5. DoD Instruction 1308.28, 6.1.2, p. 3.

Service member requesting religious accommodation that is proscribed by Chapter 47 of Title 10, United States Code (the Uniform Code of Military Justice), including actions and speech that threaten good order and discipline.[6]

The instruction is clear that accommodation and the behavior of those seeking accommodation should not compromise military readiness, good order, discipline, health, and safety. Chaplains too are subject to discipline under the various prohibitions set forth in the Uniform Code of Military Justice. At the same time, 1300.17 seeks to comply with section 533 of 112-239, The National Defense Authorization Act (2013), which requires the Armed Forces to

> accommodate the conscience, moral principles, or religious beliefs of its members, and in so far as practicable, may not use such beliefs as the basis of any adverse personnel action, discrimination, or denial of promotion, schooling, training, or assignment.[7]

In addition, the law prohibits any member of the Armed Forces from requiring a chaplain to perform any rite, ritual, or ceremony that is contrary to his or her beliefs, and prohibits discrimination or adverse personnel action against a chaplain for a refusal to comply with a directive that is against his or her beliefs.[8]

Freedom for grooming and apparel that have religious significance (e.g., Sikhs' beards, Jews' yarmulkes) are involved in the discussion of DoDI 1300.17. It seems clear that chaplains who would have problems with gay marriage are delivered from the duty to preside by virtue of section 533 above. However, though these policy changes are welcome in many respects, there is predictable concern among some that this may give too wide a berth to some who are overly zealous in pressing their own faith on others. In any case, interpretation on a case-by-case basis will doubtless continue to raise issues from time to time.

The chaplaincy has been established by the government in the interest of

6. DoD 1300.17, Accommodation of Religious Practices within the Military Services, available at http://www.dtic.mil/whs/directives/corres/pdf/130017p.pdf (accessed October 16, 2014).

7. U.S.C. 553(a)(1) (2014), available at https://www.govtrack.us/congress/bills/112/hr4310/text (accessed October 16, 2014).

8. U.S.C. 553(b) available at https://www.govtrack.us/congress/bills/112/hr4310/text (accessed October 16, 2014).

the Free Exercise Clause and with respect for the integrity of the Establishment Clause. As such, the military chaplaincy embodies the healthy tension between church and state within a legally delineated military community in which both live together in day-to-day intimacy. With accommodations come corollary tensions: a duty to the theology and practice of one's faith community and, at the same time, a duty to a religiously diverse population; a duty to conscience and, at the same time, a duty to the well-being of the military mission. We shall explore and expand upon these tensions further as we move forward.

Lutheran Tradition on the Secular Government and Just War

Lutheran tradition on the status of civil government and its related embrace of just war thinking provide the basis for Christian military service in general and the chaplaincy in particular. The *Augsburg Confession (AC)*, Article XVI states the following:

> Concerning public order and secular government it is taught that all political authority, orderly government, laws, and good order in the world are created and instituted by God and that Christians may without sin exercise political authority; be princes and judges; pass sentences and administer justice according to imperial and other existing laws; punish evildoers with the sword; wage just wars; serve as soldiers; buy and sell; take required oaths; possess property; be married, etc.[9]

This affirmation of God's institution of civil government and Christian participation in its affairs is a rebuke to both the Anabaptist refusal to serve in civil government or take oaths and to claims of perfection through monastic withdrawal from worldly activities.

Article XVI of the *Apology of the Augsburg Confession (Apology)* notes that the confessors' opponents have no disagreement with the position taken in *AC* XVI, indicating a point of continuity with existing church tradition. It goes on to advocate use of "legitimate political ordinances" as an avenue

9. All citations from the Lutheran Confessions are taken from *The Book of Concord: The Confessions of the Evangelical Lutheran Church,* ed. Robert Kolb and Timothy J. Wengert, trans. Charles Arand, Eric Gritsch, Robert Kolb, William Russell, James Schaaf, Jane Strohl, and Timothy J. Wengert (Minneapolis: Fortress Press, 2000). The quotation from the *Augsburg Confession,* article XVI, is from the translation of the German text, p. 48.

for the practice of love. "For the gospel does not destroy the state or the household but rather approves them, and it orders us to obey them as divine ordinances not only on account of the punishment but also 'because of conscience' [Rom. 13:5, NIV]."[10] We are directed to Luther's distinction between the two modes of God's governance (centuries later to become known as the two kingdoms doctrine) as the *Apology* speaks of Christ's kingdom as spiritual in contrast to the civil order; the gospel thus is not the source of new civil laws. In "Temporal Authority: To What Extent It Should Be Obeyed" (1522), Luther, having noted at length the wickedness of the world and the scarcity of true Christians(!), says that "for this reason God has ordained two governments: the spiritual by which the Holy Spirit produces Christians and righteous people under Christ; and the temporal, which restrains the un-Christian and wicked."[11] The two must be distinguished and both must remain. Christians operate in life under both modes of governance. This includes obedience to civil authorities and even bearing of the sword for the sake of the common good, which Luther grounds in Romans 13:3 and 1 Peter 2:14. Thus for the Christian's calling, he says, "at one and the same time you satisfy God's kingdom inwardly and the kingdom of the world outwardly. You suffer evil and injustice, and yet at the same time you punish evil and injustice."[12]

The twofold citizenship of Christians under both modes of divine governance and its inherent tensions in some respects look much like a theological corollary of the tension between the Establishment Clause and the Free Exercise Clause in the institution of the military chaplaincy. It also means that, as *AC* XVI states it, Christians may participate in just wars. At the same time, they do so as persons of faith committed to the neighbor love Jesus commands, even love of the enemy (Matt. 5:44, NIV). From this perspective, the ministry of the chaplain stands at the crossroads of this twofold vocation. It is a ministry that seeks to sustain faithful service members in the throes of the tension inherent in the admixture of love and war, a tension the chaplains also feel.

The Confessions don't discuss what that means in detail, but it is clear that they and Luther himself stand in the tradition of just war thinking that

10. This biblical text is quoted in the *Augsburg Confession,* in Kolb and Wengert, eds., *The Book of Concord,* p. 231.

11. Martin Luther, "Temporal Authority: To What Extent It Should Be Obeyed," in *Luther's Works,* vol. 45, *The Christian in Society II,* ed. Walther I. Brandt, trans. J. J. Schindel and Walther I. Brandt (St. Louis and Philadelphia: Fortress Press, 1962), p. 91.

12. Luther, "Temporal Authority," p. 96.

goes back to Ambrose of Milan in the fourth century, and found expression in the writings of Augustine and Thomas Aquinas.

Luther maintains that you should first offer your antagonist justice and peace. If this fails, the prince may have to defend his territory by force. However, it should be clear that such defense is not on behalf of his own gain but for the protection and welfare of his people. Here we have the rudiments of the just war provision of last resort and just cause. Luther then goes on to argue that victory must be followed by expressions of mercy and peace for the defeated *(jus post bellum).*[13] Just wars for Luther are wars of "necessity," not of choice; they cannot be avoided even though they are not desired.[14]

Luther then lays the groundwork for what we might construe as selective conscientious objection. "What if a prince is in the wrong?" he asks. "Are his people to follow him then too?" Luther says that the answer is "No," for one must obey God who desires the right rather than human leaders (Acts 5:29, NIV).[15] Luther also recognizes that one may not be certain if the prince is right or wrong. In such cases if, after due diligence, the subject is still unable to know for sure, then that person is free to obey the prince without peril to their soul.[16]

Regardless of how one might interpret the relevance of Luther's counsel for today, Lutherans in America have been on record in support of selective conscientious objection, a public position prompted by the public turmoil over the Vietnam War. The following is from the 1973 study document produced by the former Lutheran Council in the U.S.A. subsequent to testimony before the Senate Armed Services in February of 1971 on behalf of selective conscientious objection:

> U.S. Lutherans of the three churches participating in the Lutheran Council [the American Lutheran Church, the Lutheran Church in America, and the Lutheran Church–Missouri Synod] have expressed as their official policy the position of support for selective conscientious objection — the individual's right to refuse participation in a particular war when such participation, to him, would clearly be wrong. The churches have asked the government to change the law so that selective objection is legal; they

13. Luther, "Temporal Authority," p. 125.
14. Martin Luther, "Whether Soldiers Too Can Be Saved" (1526), trans. Charles M. Jacobs and Robert C. Schultz, in *Luther's Works,* American Edition, vol. 46, ed. Robert C. Schultz (Philadelphia: Fortress Press, 1967), p. 121.
15. Luther, "Whether Soldiers Too Can Be Saved," p. 130.
16. Luther, "Temporal Authority," pp. 125-26.

have also committed themselves to pastoral support of those who find themselves in conflict with law for reasons of conscience.[17]

Lutherans were and are among a number of Christian denominations and Christian ethicists that have taken such a stance. On October 21, 1971, the United States Conference of Catholic Bishops issued their Declaration on Conscientious Objection and Selective Conscientious Objection. Having stated their respect for the consciences of those who serve in the armed forces and for those who are conscientious objectors or selective conscientious objectors, the bishops acknowledge the procedural complications of selective conscientious objection but still call on moralists, lawyers, and civil servants to work for a policy change that "can reconcile the demands of the moral and civil orders concerning this issue."[18] They reaffirm the recommendation made in their 1968 pastoral letter, *Human Life in Our Day,* calling for

[a] modification of the Selective Service Act making it possible for selective conscientious objectors to refuse to serve in wars they consider unjust, without fear of imprisonment or loss of citizenship, provided they perform some other service to the human community.[19]

However, the law has not been changed to accommodate such a choice. DoDI 1300.6 clearly states that conscientious objection, to be recognized by the military, must be objection to "war in any form." Thus, Section 3.5.1 of 1300.6 states: "An individual who desires to choose the war in which he or she will participate is not a Conscientious Objector under the law. The individual's objection must be to all wars rather than a specific war."[20]

17. *The Witness of U.S. Lutherans on Peace, War, and Conscience:* A Social Document from the Lutheran Council in the U.S.A. (1973), available from http://download.elca.org/ELCA%20Resource%20Repository/Peace_War_ConscienceLCU.pdf (accessed October 17, 2014). This document remains available through the website of the ELCA.

18. United States Conference of Catholic Bishops, "Declaration on Conscientious Objection and Selective Conscientious Objection" (1971), available at http://www.usccb.org/issues-and-action/human-life-and-dignity/war-and-peace/declaration-on-conscientious-objection-and-selective-conscientious-objections-1971-10-21.cfm (accessed October 17, 2014).

19. United States Conference of Catholic Bishops, "Human Life in Our Day," statement issued November 15, 1968, paragraph 152, available from http://www.priestsforlife.org/magisterium/bishops/68-11-15humanlifeinourdaynccb.htm (accessed October 17, 2014); "Declaration on Conscientious Objection and Selective Conscientious Objection."

20. Christopher J. Eberle, in a lengthy article arising from his experience teaching at

Here it seems we have another example of how the respect for conscience in the free exercise of religion, however generous, must still operate within the constraints of what the military considers essential to its mission. While this law against selective conscientious objection in today's voluntary armed services for the most part impacts service members who are potential combatants, chaplains again stand at the crossroads. They need to support the military's mission by their loyalty and their pledged service to military personnel and their families. However, in that very capacity they may well be called upon to provide pastoral care for a potential selective conscientious objector (SCO) with whose position they may feel some sympathy, especially given the fact that many Christian chaplains come from faith communities who have been on record in favor of selective conscientious objection and have even lobbied for changing the law prohibiting it. Whatever the case, the chaplain will of course minister to those who struggle with concerns of conscience over a given war or may have been court-martialed for refusal on grounds of conscience to participate in a specific war.

Pluralism and Proselytizing

While increasing numbers of clergy and their church bodies are open to ecumenical cooperation and even interfaith conversation, their call usually does not entail an intentional ecumenical theology or even a clear understanding of other faiths, as desirable as these may be. Indeed, some faith communities and their theological schools discourage ecumenical and interfaith engagement as contrary to their theological convictions.[21] Military chaplains do not

---

the United States Naval Academy, has argued that "theists," people of religious faith, cannot commit to indiscriminate obedience, including obedience to legal orders in an unjust cause since obedience to God always transcends obedience to government. Officer candidates who hold such belief should not take the Oath of Commissioning unless they can somehow understand that oath to be valid only for just causes. Be that as it may, Eberle's concern is the moral validity of a faith-based or "theistic" argument in a context of public service. He claims no knowledge of the legal entailments. "God, War, and Conscience," *Journal of Religious Ethics* 35, no. 3 (2007): 479-507.

21. Sang-Ehil Han, Paul Lewis Metzger, and Terry C. Muck have offered particular curricular recommendations for better preparing evangelical students for a pluralistic world. They seek to inculcate a greater measure of hospitality in dealing with those of other faiths than has been the practice of evangelical exclusivism. Their laudable effect illustrates the problem. "Christian Hospitality and Pastoral Practices from an Evangelical Perspective," *Theological Education* 47, no. 1 (2012): 11-13.

and should not have this option; they need to have a clear understanding of how their own theological commitments relate to those of other traditions with whom they will be intimately involved under often stressful circumstances. Military chaplains must, as we have seen, be prepared to minister in a pluralistic setting, including the need to serve those outside one's own faith community when it is necessary to do so and to cooperate fully with chaplains of other faiths for the purpose of guaranteeing free exercise.[22]

Lutheran theologian Ted Peters has identified three different approaches that theologians and church bodies have taken to interacting with other faiths. The first of these is called "confessional universalism." Those who take this approach clearly affirm the authentic claims of their faith but remain open to the insights of others. This stands on contrast to what Peters terms "confessional exclusivism." As the label suggests, this position brooks no alternative to its own faith tradition. The third type is named "supra-confessional universalism." Simply stated, adherents of this view believe all religions point to the same transcendent reality and all have a partial share of its revelation.[23] It hardly needs arguing that Lutheran theology, being strongly confessional in faith and practice, would find the third type a bad fit, notwithstanding contemporary readiness for interfaith conversation and cooperation in the cause of the common good.

Confessional exclusivism is also at odds with the theological substance and sensibilities of the Lutheran tradition. Luther's theology of the cross, made famous by his attack on the "theology of glory" in the *Heidelberg Disputation* of 1518,[24] requires a measure of humility in the encounter with those of other faiths. Luther's target in the ecclesiastical context of his day was the arrogant presumption of an authoritarian church leadership that claimed

22. Peter French, a philosophy professor, was engaged by the Navy during the Iraq conflict to provide ethics training for chaplains. Commenting on the wide range of academic preparation from rigorous theological schools to Bible colleges and conservative seminaries with narrow curricula, French observed, "In my early years as a college philosophy professor, I taught large undergraduate courses in which the academic abilities of students varied dramatically, but I could not recall teaching such a radically diverse group in terms of academic preparation as those chaplains." Peter A. French, *War and Moral Dissonance* (Cambridge: Cambridge University Press, 2011), p. 7.

23. Ted Peters, *God — The World's Future: Systematic Theology for a New Era,* 2nd ed. (Minneapolis: Fortress Press, 2000), pp. 353-54. Peters is addressing interfaith relations, but in the context of our discussion of pluralism in the military his categories also apply readily to interdenominational relations within Christianity.

24. Martin Luther, *Heidelberg Disputation* (1518), *Luther's Works,* vol. 31, *Career of the Reformer I,* trans. and ed. Harold J. Grimm (Philadelphia: Fortress Press, 1957), pp. 36-70.

absolute truth for its teachings. Moreover, these theologians of glory, Luther believed, were distorting the gospel by prescribing burdensome and false works needed for salvation. For theologians of the cross who have seen the truth of their own brokenness in the brutal reality of the crucified, there could be no such pretense regarding one's infallibility or ability to contribute to one's salvation. The corollary of the theology of the cross is the central theme of the Reformation: justification by grace through faith. Even as we grow in faith and love by the ministry of the Spirit through the gospel, we know that sin remains *(simul justus et peccator!)* and with it the judgment of the law that continually draws us back to the promises of the gospel in which alone we have hope.

The theology of the cross as a consequence conveys a spirituality of humility. Douglas John Hall has captured this nicely:

> The *theologia gloria* confuses and distorts because it presents divine revelation in a straightforward, undialectical, and authoritarian manner that silences doubt — silences therefore real humanity. It overwhelms the human with its brilliance, its incontestability, its certitude. Yet just in this it confuses and distorts, because God's object in the divine self-manifestation is precisely not to overwhelm but to befriend.[25]

The spirituality of the cross is incumbent on all faithful Christian leaders, but for military chaplains, there is a special urgency to cultivate a genuine sense of humility and the primacy of servanthood in openness to warriors of other faiths who need their ministry.

The missional fervor often characteristic of exclusivism is illustrated by the following account. From 2003 to 2005 the Rev. Kristen J. Leslie, a professor of pastoral care at the Yale University Divinity School, was engaged as a consultant to the chaplains at the United States Air Force Academy. The report of her work there led to her testimony before the House Armed Services Committee in June of 2005 as part of the congressional investigation of allegations of religious intolerance and Christian proselytizing at the Academy. Her discoveries were stunning. "[T]he majority of the Christian chaplains understood their pastoral role to be that of Christian evangelist."[26]

25. Douglas John Hall, *The Cross in Our Context: Jesus and the Suffering World* (Minneapolis: Fortress Press, 2003), p. 20.

26. Kristen J. Leslie, "Pastoral Care in a New Public: Lessons Learned in the Public Square," *Journal of Pastoral Theology* 18, no. 2 (Winter 2008): 87.

One of the chaplains returning from deployment in Iraq told of conducting baptisms of service members in Saddam's pool. "The triumph of Christianity over Islam was lost on no one."[27]

> During a general Protestant worship service, a chaplain admonished 600 cadets in attendance to return to their tents and proselytize their bunk-mates, reminding them that those who were not "born again will burn in the fires of hell."[28]

There is, by contrast, a strong historical tradition in the military chaplaincy that has been described as "cooperative pluralism," in which chaplains understand themselves to be

> pastor to some, chaplain to all. That is, they are pastors or religious professionals using their liturgical, sacramental, and historical authority . . . to serve the dietary, communal and spiritual needs of their particular faith group. And they are chaplains to any member of the community, regardless of religious confession, who wants the spiritual and institutional support offered by a religious professional.[29]

The description of "cooperative pluralism" just given is a practice that fits nicely with the confessional universalist perspective and which also seems best to fit the demands chaplains have to serve in a pluralistic setting. Confessional universalism seems to me to preserve the integrity of one's theological tradition — the theological teaching one swore to uphold at ordination or its equivalent — while yet displaying openness to the faith and needs of others.

This brief definition of cooperative pluralism seems to align rather nicely with the explanation of "pragmatic pluralism" developed by Ira C. Lupu and Robert W. Tuttle. Lupu and Tuttle take up the case of a former chaplain in the Navy, the Rev. Veitch, an ordained minister of the Reformed Episcopal Church, who, subsequent to his departure from the Navy, filed suit claiming religious discrimination on the part of his supervisor, a Chaplain (Captain) Buchmiller, a Roman Catholic priest. Veitch charged that his supervisor was hostile to evangelical Protestants and criticized the content of

27. Leslie, "Pastoral Care in a New Public," p. 87.
28. Leslie, "Pastoral Care in a New Public," pp. 87-88.
29. Leslie, "Pastoral Care in a New Public," p. 92.

his sermons and his strong doctrine of *sola scriptura*. Buchmiller in return said his critiques were not of the doctrinal content of Veitch's preaching but of his manner of denigrating other chaplains by giving the clear impression that they were all wrong, if not unregenerate; his theology alone was valid. Veitch filed an employment discrimination complaint with the Navy but was unsuccessful when the investigating officer cited his failure to "preach pluralism." Veitch was relieved of his duties and charged with insubordination but resigned before the court martial could proceed (in accord with the Uniform Code of Military Justice incumbent upon chaplains as well). His subsequent lawsuit was also dismissed for a different reason: the court judged that he had not been coerced into resignation as he claimed.[30]

In relation to Veitch's sort of behavior, Lupu and Tuttle clearly see that "[a] chaplain that denigrates other faiths and undermines the ministry of fellow chaplains acts in direct contradiction to the basic justification for the chaplaincy itself."[31] Moreover, "[s]uch disparagement could reasonably be seen as a threat to the cohesion of military units and also an obstacle to service members' access to religious services, especially if the chaplain's disrespectful attitude leads service members to avoid seeking his or her assistance, or the assistance of other chaplains."[32]

That said, Lupu and Tuttle also express concern over the constitutional implications of the charging officer's finding that Veitch "was removed for failure to preach pluralism among religions." That statement creates the danger that the government in the form of the military is prescribing a doctrinal norm and, consequently, vulnerable to critique from the standpoint of both the Establishment Clause and the Free Exercise Clause. This sort of duty, "to preach pluralism," is what they call "maximal pluralism." By contrast, they advocate a "minimal pluralism" that they refer to as "pragmatic pluralism" for which they provide a convincing legal defense. In sum, pragmatic pluralism calls upon chaplains to be true to the theology and practice of their own respective traditions while yet showing respect for other faiths and a readiness to facilitate free access for all through cooperative efforts within the chaplain corps and a readiness to serve all if called upon in a situation of necessity. Freedom of speech for chaplains does not extend to practices that undermine the purpose of the chaplaincy itself and its role in the military.[33]

---

30. Lupu and Tuttle, "Instruments of Accommodation," pp. 134-35.
31. Lupu and Tuttle, "Instruments of Accommodation," p. 140.
32. Lupu and Tuttle, "Instruments of Accommodation," p. 141.
33. Lupu and Tuttle, "Instruments of Accommodation," pp. 136-42.

A close relative to the failure to respect the pluralistic context of the military is the problem of proselytizing already briefly mentioned. Lupu and Tuttle also take this up. While observing that proselytizing, such as in the context of a chaplain's nonreligious services, is strictly forbidden, they note that existing regulations neither permit nor prohibit proselytizing. The chaplain who believes proselytizing is an essential element of his or her theology and practice of ministry may conceivably seek protection under one of several religious liberty provisions of law, such as the Religious Freedom Restoration Act. However, Lupu and Tuttle argue that such a free exercise claim would be weaker than the government's liability under the Establishment Clause if it were to give free rein to proselytizing. Given the clear understanding that chaplains are to minister in a pluralistic environment in support of the free exercise of all, Lupu and Tuttle conclude that "[a] court would accord quite significant deference to a judgment by the military that proselytizing may cause tension in the ranks, and may interfere with the chaplain's primary obligation to facilitate the free religious exercise of service members."[34]

In addition to my previous remarks about the implications of the theology of the cross for servanthood in a pluralistic setting, the position of the Evangelical Lutheran Church in America (ELCA) on religious liberty would seem to clearly support opposition to proselytizing by military chaplains. The social statement *Religious Liberty in the United States* was adopted at the Fourth Biennial Convention of the Lutheran Church in America, July 19-27, 1968. As a social statement of a predecessor body of the ELCA, it remains as counsel to the ELCA until and unless a new statement is adopted. The statement is a broader discussion than our present focus but nonetheless relevant. The statement recognizes that religious liberty is constitutionally guaranteed in the United States; and in true Lutheran fashion, it upholds the civil authority of government to ensure this liberty and the equal status of all religions under the law. The document makes clear that the statement

---

34. Lupu and Tuttle, "Instruments of Accommodation," pp. 123-25. The authors also give an account of a court case in which a former chaplain at a VA hospital filed suit claiming employment discrimination. He argued that his dismissal was because of his refusal to adhere to the CPE model endorsed by the VA in which pastoral care is geared to the faith of the patient not that of the chaplain. He was prohibited in this policy from explicit evangelical outreach. The court concluded in favor of the VA: "[The] VA must ensure that the existence of the chaplaincy does not create establishment clause problems. Unleashing a government-paid chaplain who sees his primary role as proselytizing upon a captive audience of patients could do exactly that" (pp. 160-61).

should not be taken to mean all religions are equally valid from a theological standpoint, which suggests to me a view compatible with the position of confessional universalism discussed above. More to the point are these statements of theological foundation:

> Christian faith asserts that religious liberty is rooted in our creation in the image of God and in God's continuing activity in the created world. . . . We are all creatures to whom God speaks and from whom God expects response. To deny religious liberty and other civil liberties, therefore, threatens to dehumanize us all.
>
> Christian faith asserts that God will not force anyone into communion with God. If then, God refuses to impose divine will on humanity, then persons exceed their prerogatives if they try to use coercion of any kind on one another to obtain religious conformity. Religious liberty for all is thus not only a demand of civil justice but also an aid to our response to the Christian gospel.[35]

The affirmations that follow in the document uphold persons' right to freedom from religious coercion and a corollary freedom to follow their own belief whether religious or nonreligious.

"Two Collar Conflict" and Confusion

Peter French has described what is termed the "two collar" conflict facing military chaplains:

> On the right collar is the insignia of military rank. On the left collar is the insignia of the chaplain's faith — a cross, tablet, a crescent, or a Dharmacakra. At virtually every PDTC [professional development training course] at least one chaplain would point to his two collars during the discussion of an ethical issue related to some military situation that struck very near to home. That action was the universal symbol in the Corps that expressed the schizophrenic nature of their jobs.[36]

35. Lutheran Church in America, "Religious Liberty in the United States," Social Statement adopted by the Fourth Biennial Convention, Atlanta, Georgia, June 19-27, 1968, p. 1, available from: http://download.elca.org/ELCA%20Resource%20Repository/Religious _LibertyLCA68.pdf (accessed October 17, 2014).

36. French, *War and Moral Dissonance*, p. 10.

One of the chaplains, he reports, expressed it this way, "I preach love and forgiveness and mercy and respect for other people while I work for an organization that sees itself as having only two jobs: to kill people and destroy property."[37] French goes on to discuss situations of troubling moral conflict that chaplains face but to which they sometimes feel unable to adequately respond.

The chaplain's vocation in a real sense embodies in the person and the corps the relation of church and state in the taut interplay of ministry and military. While we have seen that Lutheran chaplains and others with a similar theological perspective seem well suited to enter into this situation, it does not mean that legal constraints they voluntarily accept for the sake of ministry will not be the source of moral and spiritual tension that is the experience of other chaplains, particularly those who have seen combat.

However, while the experiences of combat can be a source of "two collar conflict," for some it can be a source of two collar confusion. I refer to the problem of the chaplain taking up arms in the heat of battle.

As is well known, the Geneva Conventions (III of 1949) classify chaplains as noncombatants who, if taken prisoner, are not considered prisoners of war and should be free to carry on their ministry (Articles 33-37). While this document may not entail a strict prohibition, the armed services of the United States regard it as such in the formulation of their own policy. The U.S. Army Field Manual 16-1 *Religious Support* states that the "[p]olicy of the Chief of Chaplains forbids chaplains from bearing arms." This prohibition is further stated in the documents of both the Navy and the Marine Corps. The Department of the Navy's policy adds this with respect to the immunity from being treated as prisoners of war that chaplains have as noncombatants under the Geneva Conventions: "An individual chaplain who violates this policy endangers the noncombatant status of other chaplains."[38]

Notwithstanding these strict regulations, there have been reports of chaplains taking up arms in defense of their comrades under extreme conditions. Donald Sensing, a former artillery man and now an ordained Methodist minister, related on his blog one such incident that took place in Iraq and was reported in the Toronto press. The chaplain was said by an MSNBC cameraman to have manned a .50 caliber machine gun. The explanation offered was that he was compelled to fight in order to protect himself and his

---

37. French, *War and Moral Dissonance*, p. 10.

38. Quoted in Donald Sensing's April 16, 2003, blog post, "Sense of Events," http://senseofevents.blogspot.com/2003/04/Chaplains.

soldiers. In reflecting on this event, Sensing struggles with the dilemma that may face chaplains in extreme situations. What is the greater good, protecting the sanctity of the office or coming to the aid of those in mortal peril? Sensing believes that the prohibition must remain for the integrity and effectiveness of the ministry of the chaplains and what they represent. However, he concludes that he would personally not like to be a chaplain in such a dilemma.

My colleague in a project on military ethics, Rev. Dr. Wollom Jensen, a Vietnam combat veteran as a young soldier and a retired Navy chaplain, has shared this observation:

> There are stories of chaplains picking up weapons in the heat of battle to fight off the enemy. These actions are often justified by asserting that it was a last defense by the chaplain to his comrades if not him or herself. While this may appear honorable at first blush, those same soldiers reported that in those instances when their chaplain picked up a weapon they lost hope. . . . The chaplain is no longer able to represent Christ as the one who gave himself up for the sake of all others. This is a very heavy burden and one which requires courage, commitment, honor and obedience that can only arise out of a deep and abiding sense of call to the life of *agape* in loving service to others.[39]

Regardless of how one might respond to Jensen's assessment of the theological and spiritual consequences, his judgment drives right to the point of the integrity of the chaplain's vocation, not only as embodied in the acts of ministry, but as very presence of divine mercy in a merciless context. Whatever else the framers of the Geneva Conventions and the authors of the policies of the military services may have had in mind, these "laws" not only provide for free exercise but can also serve as protection for the spiritual integrity of the chaplaincy.

Summing Up

Members of the armed services and their families are often in situations in which the normal access to religious services is not possible. Thus, as we have seen, the military chaplaincy has been established by the govern-

39. See note 1, above.

ment to ensure the First Amendment rights of the Free Exercise Clause for those service members and their families. At the same time, the United Sates Constitution that provides for free exercise also prohibits the establishment of religion. Through various regulations adopted by the Department of Defense, the appropriate balance in the legal structure of the chaplaincy is sought to protect the integrity of both the Free Exercise Clause and the Establishment Clause.

The Establishment Clause is honored by the fact that the military neither places restrictions on which religious traditions may participate in the chaplaincy nor does it seek to regulate doctrinal content. Furthermore, the military leaves the criteria and process of authorization of candidates for ministry to the judicatories of each religious community. These policies serve the Free Exercise Clause concerns as well. In addition, both clauses are served by the insistence that chaplains be ready to serve willingly in a pluralistic setting. This does not require that chaplains compromise their own theological convictions but it does mean that they must be open to cooperation with the leaders of other traditions and ready to serve service members of all faiths as extenuating circumstances require.

As we have also seen, the demand for willing service in a pluralistic context and corollary concerns with proselytizing is a window to the reality that the military chaplaincy exists in the tension of service to both church and state. The violation of respect for the military's pluralistic religious context and the questionable practices of proselytizing are not only a problem for free exercise; they are also a threat to the cohesion of military units and therefore to the mission and the effectiveness of the chaplaincy. This is particularly acute when parochial impulses on the part of chaplains lead to the denigration of other faiths. Thus, in this case and in other respects we have seen that the freedom granted the chaplaincy in the free exercise of religion does not extend to behavior that can potentially compromise the military's mission and the role of the chaplaincy in that mission.

The Lutheran tradition affirms the role of the state and distinguishes but does not separate that civil government as of the left-hand mode of God's rule from God's right-hand rule through the gospel. This "two kingdoms" theology is well suited as a basis for participation in the military chaplaincy when paired with Lutheran acceptance of just war thinking. Moreover, Luther's theology of the cross grounds a humility of openness to others in a pluralistic setting as does Lutheran affirmation of religious liberty with respect for conscience and the belief that God does not coerce faith. Congenial as these theological perspectives are for service in the military chaplaincy, they do not deliver chaplains and the service members they serve from conflicts of conscience endemic to life at the crossroads of church and state. Thus, the just war thinking that enables Christians to participate in war efforts when "just" can also give rise to the problematic issue of selective conscientious objection. Other deep moral conflicts play themselves out when chaplains, forbidden to bear arms, find themselves in dire situations where self-defense seems the lesser evil. Here, as in the Department of Defense policies we reviewed, the Geneva Conventions and the policies of the services forbidding chaplains to bear arms serve to protect the integrity of the chaplaincy.

CHAPTER 13

The Right to Freedom of Association: Organizing in Rwanda after Genocide

Victor Thasiah

The right to freedom of association, often tied to the right to freedom of assembly, entitles people to form, join, and participate in groups that take collective action based on common views, values, interests, and/or objectives. Some stress its importance to individual liberty, while others focus on its connection to democratic government.[1] Watchdog organizations claim that this right — enshrined in the Universal Declaration of Human Rights; the International Covenant of Civil and Political Rights; the International Covenant on Economic, Social, and Cultural Rights; and the African Charter of Human and People's Rights — is under threat in the Republic of Rwanda.[2]

1. See Ellen Frankel Paul, Fred D. Miller Jr., and Jeffrey Paul, eds., *Freedom of Association* (Cambridge: Cambridge University Press, 2009).

2. See Human Rights Watch, "Rwanda," *World Report 2014,* available at http://www.hrw .org/world-report/2014/country-chapters/rwanda (accessed September 25, 2014); Amnesty International, "Rwanda," *Annual Report,* 2014, http://www.amnesty.org/en/region/rwanda/ report-2013 (accessed September 25, 2014); and Scott Straus and Lars Waldorf, eds., *Remaking Rwanda: State Building and Human Rights after Mass Violence* (Madison: University of Wisconsin Press, 2011). "Everyone has the right to freedom of peaceful assembly and association. No one may be compelled to belong to an association": The Universal Declaration of Human Rights, Article 20, http://www.un.org/en/documents/udhr/ (accessed September 25, 2014). "Everyone shall have the right to freedom of association with others, including the right to form and join trade unions for the protection of his interests": International Covenant on Civil and Political Rights, Article 22, http://www.ohchr.org/en/professionalinterest/pages/ccpr .aspx (accessed September 25, 2014). On organizing, joining, and participating in trade unions,

I would like to thank John Baumann, Innocent Rugaragu, John Rutsindintwarane, Ron Snyder, Robert Tuttle, and Kate Warn for their helpful comments on earlier versions of this chapter.

On their view, certain authoritarian acts of governance — however justified for security, stability, recovery, and development after the country's total undoing during the 1994 Rwanda genocide — restrict too many legitimate acts of association.

After examining these complex criticisms, I set out how Rwandan Lutheran organizer John Rutsindintwarane unlocks and expands the exercise of the right to freedom of association by building Rwandan community organizations, sourced and supported by local churches, that effectively pursue sustainable development and participatory democracy without tripping state repression.[3] His work also prudently avoids the impasse of predictable human rights criticism and Rwandan government denial. I argue that Rutsindintwarane's organizing practices — interpreted as group responses to God's call to service and justice, and civic forms of love; and enabling ordinary Rwandans to stand up to religious leaders and public officials — enact a theology perceptive to the needs of the nation. Paul Hawken describes comparable work as "a reimagination of public governance emerging from place, culture, and people."[4] My approach, based on ethnographic research conducted across Rwanda in 2013 and 2014, is that of a critical, participant observer of the theological and political dimensions of Rutsindintwarane's efforts. We begin by considering the criticisms of the Rwandan government related to the right to freedom of association.

---

see International Covenant on Economic, Social and Cultural Rights, Article 8, http://www .ohchr.org/en/professionalinterest/pages/cescr.aspx (accessed October 27, 2014). "Every individual shall have the right to free association provided that he abides by the law": African Charter on Human and Peoples' Rights, Article 10, http://www.achpr.org/files/instruments/ achpr/banjul_charter.pdf (accessed September 25, 2014).

3. I conducted ethnographic research, extensively accompanying Rutsindintwarane, the founding executive director of PICO (People Improving Communities through Organizing) Rwanda, as he did his work in Rwanda in 2013 and 2014. I observed adults and youth involved in organizing in rural and urban settings; attended meetings with PICO Rwanda staff, organizers, clergy, community leaders, various constituencies, and public officials; and participated in two training sessions led by Rutsindintwarane. I also read PICO Rwanda project reports and grant proposals from 2006 to the present; and interviewed either formally or informally an estimated fifty people associated with one or more of PICO Rwanda's projects. The interviews included people participating in and/or related to Rutsindintwarane's organizing: local, regional, and national-level public officials; field staff and executives of local, national, and global faith-based, nongovernmental organizations (NGOs) working in development; and lay, clergy, and regional and national leaders from several different Christian denominations.

4. Paul Hawken, *Blessed Unrest: How the Largest Social Movement in History Is Restoring Grace, Justice, and Beauty to the World* (New York: Penguin, 2007), p. 18.

Rwanda and the Right to Freedom of Association

The Constitution of the Republic of Rwanda guarantees the right to freedom of association, generally understood as the assembling of individuals into groups such as religious communities, civil society organizations, political parties, trade unions, or clubs to "express, promote, pursue or defend a field of common interests."[5] Rwanda has also ratified two core international human rights instruments — the International Covenant on Civil and Political Rights and the International Covenant on Economic, Social, and Cultural Rights — which include the right to freedom of association.[6] While restrictions on the right to free speech in countries usually result in more global media attention and public concern, the right to freedom of association is equally important for some corresponding reasons.

The social practices constituting association make for much of our personal and political life. "By associating with one another," Amy Gutman observes, "we engage in camaraderie, cooperation, dialogue, deliberation, negotiation, competition, creativity, and the kinds of self-expression and self-sacrifice that are possible only in association with others."[7] Effective public dissent is one form of such self-expression. "Without access to an association that is willing and able to speak up for our views and values," Gutman continues, "we have a very limited ability to be heard by many other people or to influence the political process, unless we happen to be rich or famous."[8] Crucial to the protection of individual liberties, establishment of community organizations, and legitimacy of democratic governments, the right to freedom of association relates to many civil, political, economic, social, and cultural rights.

Maina Kai, the United Nations Special Rapporteur on the rights to freedom of peaceful assembly and of association, assessed the protection and promotion of these rights in Rwanda in January 2014.[9] His findings are

5. Maina Kai, "Statement by the United Nations Special Rapporteur on the Rights to Freedom of Peaceful Assembly and of Association at the Conclusion of His Visit to the Republic of Rwanda," January 27, 2014, available at http://freeassembly.net/rapporteurpress news/rwanda-visit-statement/ (accessed September 25, 2014).

6. Rwanda ratified both covenants without reservation on April 16, 1975.

7. Amy Gutman, "Freedom of Association: An Introductory Essay," in *Freedom of Association,* ed. Amy Gutman (Princeton: Princeton University Press, 1998), p. 4.

8. Gutman, "Freedom of Association," p. 3.

9. The assessment took place January 20-27, 2014. See Maina Kai, "Statement by the United Nations Special Rapporteur." For the Rwandan government's reaction to his

consistent with those of Human Rights Watch, Amnesty International, and many other human rights experts on the region.[10] The UN representative, in his report filed with the Human Rights Council on June 10, 2014, starts with recognition of "the vibrancy of Rwanda's economy and its remarkable progress in developing infrastructure, building institutions and ensuring stability and security" — conditions arguably necessary for democracy. Then, after an explanation of the meaning and significance of the rights falling within its purview, especially sensitive to Rwanda's postgenocide context, the report turns to criticism.

> The rights to freedom of peaceful assembly and of association are essential for democracy and sustainable peace. They are all the more important in a society deeply traumatized by genocide still seeking to heal and reconcile. These rights accommodate and foster pluralistic views, help ensure that dissent is peaceful, and strengthen democracy's ability to prevent social unrest. While acknowledging the progress that Rwanda has achieved, the Special Rapporteur expresses concern about the prevailing opposition to vigorous debate and free expression of opinions, which make the current social reconciliation process unstable.[11]

An incongruity is immediately apparent in Kai's account of the situation in Rwanda. In pursuit of reconciliation, unification, and healing after the wounds of genocide, the Rwandan state suppresses public disagreement, debate, and dissent. Given the associations in Rwandan minds, for example, between opposition parties, ethnic violence, and civil war in the early 1990s, some consider such state actions reasonable and appropriate,

---

report, see "Mission to Rwanda: Preliminary Comments by the Government on the Report of the Special Rapporteur," Advance Version, Human Rights Council, Twenty-Sixth Session, Agenda Item 3, June 10, 2014. The following summarizes the official preliminary response: "The information provided to the Special Rapporteur regarding the political order in Rwanda is false and entirely misleading. Constructive public criticism and dissent is a feature of the Rwandan political order and exercised by all without fear or favour. The boundary between ordinary dissent and genocide ideology is very clear. Genocide ideology in Rwanda is clearly defined by law in Rwanda and anyone engaging in it cannot then claim to be exercising their right to dissent."

10. Again, see Human Rights Watch, "Rwanda," *World Report 2014;* Amnesty International, "Rwanda," *Report 2013;* Straus and Waldorf, eds., *Remaking Rwanda.*

11. "Report of the Special Rapporteur on the Rights to Freedom of Peaceful Assembly and of Association," Advance Unedited Version, Human Rights Council, Twenty-Sixth Session, Agenda Item 3, June 10, 2014, 8.82.

at least for now, while the nation recovers. A narrower, normative human rights perspective, though, sees such suppression as a violation of rights, and therefore, by definition, incompatible with peace. The UN representative, accordingly, "believes that attempts at reconstruction, reconciliation and the realization of human rights can only succeed if Rwanda calls for an honest, robust and civil debate, hence the need for an active and unfettered civil society."[12] Determining how exactly unfettered civil society should be, and what is acceptable or tolerable after genocide, requires ongoing consultation between public officials and civil society, broad-based social discernment.

While attentive to challenges connected to freedom of association in Rwanda, the Special Rapporteur argues that development, like peace, depends on the greater exercise of this right, on more political latitude and less social control. Associations that are relatively autonomous, independent in deliberation and judgment, and free to act — even when collaborating with the government — have their own important role to play. The report concludes that state policies limit that role too much.

> [T]he development partnerships between the Government and local and international NGOs are of a compulsory nature. This is evidenced by the necessity of aforementioned collaboration letters, action plans that must align with the development objectives of the district, down to the level of activities, and in some cases demands for performance contracts to be concluded between local authorities and NGOs. In fact, the perception of some in Government, but also in the civil society sector, appears to be that NGOs are implementers of governmental policies, or merely service providers that should act at the behest of the Government. . . . NGOs should be able to determine and operate within their priority areas of concern without interference or direction by authorities, including working on issues that authorities do not consider to be priorities. The power of innovation is enhanced through openness. A multiplicity of interventions and approaches will serve to strengthen the capacity of the sector to respond to the needs of beneficiaries and ultimately, to all Rwandans.[13]

Again, some consider these kinds of state policies as matters of coordination, efficiency, effectiveness, and, perhaps most importantly, accountability.

12. *Report of the Special Rapporteur*, 2.11.
13. *Report of the Special Rapporteur*, 5.68–5.69.

Others, though, argue that such top-down control violates rights, disempowering individuals and communities in the process. They view the above limits on self-determination and self-governance, amid state-sponsored decentralization, as detrimental to sustainable development.

Less diplomatically, other human rights experts make similar claims about the situation on the ground in Rwanda. Susan Thompson explains,

> Postgenocide Rwanda represents a context where political power is firmly held by the state in a system where sociopolitical domination is commonplace and accepted by ruler and ruled alike. When the power of the state is exercised at the local level, it takes the form of directives from "on high" (the regime in Kigali) and of strict monitoring of the ability and willingness of local officials to "implement government orders effectively and efficiently."[14]

Timothy Longman's observations are comparable: "The RPF [Rwanda Patriotic Front] regime has systematically intimidated, co-opted, and suppressed civil society, so that Rwanda today lacks independent social organizations capable of articulating most public interests. The regime tolerates very little public criticism, strictly limiting freedoms of speech, press, and association."[15] Further, both Longman's account of the governmental logic and his prognosis matches that of the UN representative's report:

> Defenders of the RPF regime . . . claim that restrictions on freedoms are necessary for national unity, given the history of genocide, and that benign authoritarian rule is necessary for economic development, their top priority. Rwanda's persistent authoritarian rule may ultimately prove disastrous for the country's long-term stability, as it prevents the public from expressing its interests through productive, peaceful political means and also prevents the regime from benefiting from the contributions of much of the population.[16]

Paul Gready summarizes this line of criticism well: "The current regime's preferred modus operandi for civil society remains service-delivery and gap

---

14. Susan Thompson, *Whispering Truth to Power: Everyday Resistance to Reconciliation in Postgenocide Rwanda* (Madison: University of Wisconsin Press, 2013), p. 8.

15. Timothy Longman, *Christianity and Genocide in Rwanda* (Cambridge: Cambridge University Press, 2010), pp. 26-27.

16. Longman, *Christianity and Genocide in Rwanda*, p. 27.

filling. A 'you're with us or against us' rationale prevails."[17] Rights advocates continue to call the Rwandan government — ethical, competent, and progressive in significant ways — to allow more space for critical, civic participation in governance. While vigilant state monitoring for NGO corruption, incompetence, and negligence remains necessary, civil society should be able to monitor the same propensities in government.[18]

The right to freedom of association includes the right to participate in public, open-ended political processes that consider and determine the problems, interests, priorities, and responses of one's own community. This fundamental entitlement also entails the right to contribute collectively to the development and governance of one's own community and country through association. Nations that repress or fail to secure this freedom jeopardize themselves politically. "A government that begins to oppose the organs of civil society," John de Gruchy warns, "has begun to attack one of the pillars of democracy. It is therefore in danger of undermining both its own legitimacy and the future of democratic rule."[19] Rights advocates contend that peace, development, and democracy in Rwanda are dependent on the exercise of this freedom. Rwandans should, of course, determine for themselves what the scope and extent of such freedom should be, factoring in conditions specifically connected to their postgenocide context. Before turning to Rutsindintwarane's related efforts, a biographical sketch and background material on his approach to organizing are in order.[20]

John Rutsindintwarane and People Improving Communities through Organizing (PICO)

John Rutsindintwarane grew up among Rwandans at the Nkwenda/Kimuli Refugee Camp in Karagwe, Tanzania. Christian faith, refugee life, and resis-

17. Paul Gready, "Beyond 'You're with Us or against Us': Civil Society and Policymaking in Post-Genocide Rwanda," in Straus and Waldorf, eds., *Remaking Rwanda,* p. 89.

18. On problems associated with NGOs in Rwanda, see Peter Uvin, *Aiding Violence: The Development Enterprise in Rwanda* (West Hartford, CT: Kumarian Press, 1998).

19. John W. de Gruchy, "Democracy," in *The Blackwell Companion to Political Theology,* ed. Peter Scott and William T. Cavanaugh (Oxford: Blackwell, 2004), p. 441.

20. For more biographical information, see Victor Thasiah, "Reconfiguring Church-State Relations: Toward a Rwandan Political Theology," in *Lutheran Identity and Political Theology,* ed. Carl Henric-Grenholm and Goran Gunner (Eugene, OR: Wipf & Stock, forthcoming).

tance to internalized oppression shaped his political consciousness, manifest in the intensity, commitment, and effectiveness of his work over the past two decades in Rwandan repatriation, resettlement, reconciliation, and reconstruction. Immediately after his ordination in the Evangelical Lutheran Church in Tanzania (ELCT) and appointment near the Rwanda border in Ngara, Tanzania, in 1994, Rutsindintwarane faced the fallout of genocide: hundreds of thousands of survivors and perpetrators streaming across the border toward his church, desperate and traumatized. By late 1995, after having worked in emergency assistance services at the Benaco Refugee Camp in Ngara for nearly a year, the new pastor had relocated to Rwanda, joined the recovery efforts of the Lutheran World Federation (LWF) there, and, with four other Rwandan returnees, established the Lutheran Church of Rwanda (LCR).

Rutsindintwarane was a thought leader for the emerging Lutheran Church of Rwanda as it developed its vision, mission, and operations. Midway through a long tenure as the LCR's General Secretary, serving multiple terms from 1995 to 2011, he completed two master's degrees abroad in the United States: the first in peace and conflict transformation at Eastern Mennonite University and the second in theology, development, and evangelism at Wartburg Theological Seminary. An internship in community organizing and leadership development at the PICO National Network, based in Oakland, California, rounded out his education.[21] Upon return to Rwanda, Rutsindintwarane founded the organization Congregations Rebuilding Communities in Rwanda (CRCR) in 2006, transposing and adapting PICO's approach to organizing from the urban centers of the United States to the rural villages of East Africa. In 2011, he was elected bishop of the Lutheran Church of Rwanda but declined, opting instead to further dedicate himself to community organizing and leadership development

21. Originally the Pacific Institute of Community Organizing, PICO changed its name to the PICO National Network in 2004 to reflect the national scope of its work. See "History," *PICO National Network,* http://www.piconetwork.org/about/history. See also John Rutsindintwarane, "A Strategy for Empowering Communities," in *"So the Poor Have Hope, and Injustice Shuts Its Mouth": Poverty and the Mission of the Church in Africa,* ed. Karen L. Bloomquist and Musa Panti Filibus (Geneva: Lutheran World Federation Studies, 2007), pp. 141-44. For a critical analysis of PICO's work, see Richard L. Wood, *Faith in Action: Religion, Race, and Democratic Organizing in America* (Chicago: University of Chicago Press, 2002). On a similar approach to community organizing in the United States and for comparison, see Mark R. Warren, *Dry Bones Rattling: Community Building to Revitalize American Democracy* (Princeton: Princeton University Press, 2001).

as the executive director of PICO Rwanda, newly founded by Rutsindint-warane and replacing CRCR.

His current projects include working with a remote community completing a major medical center; another rural community launching a roof-tiling collaborative; urban women collectively transitioning from prostitution to legal, business ownership; two youth groups organizing for employment; a church building a school; sustainable reforestation efforts; and various congregational development plans.[22] The barriers many of these projects encounter are formidable, compounded by the related, but distinct, needs and concerns of a postgenocide people. They are often matched by a comparable community determination to respond. For example, in one project, over half of the 110 women have left illegal street work to establish cooperatives selling produce, cleaning markets, and styling hair. These women have no formal education. They have on average three children, each of whom faces risks ranging from disease to malnutrition to developmental issues. Rutsindintwarane's organizing in relation to the building of a major medical center in Mumeya, Rwanda, now serves as a model for his projects elsewhere in the country and East Africa. Dozens of churches and communities use variations of his organizing practices. We will examine what happened in Mumeya after taking a closer look at where Rutsindintwarane learned to organize.

The Pacific Institute for Community Organizations (PICO), founded by a Jesuit priest named John Baumann in 1972, began as a regional training institute to support neighborhood organizations in California.[23] Jose Carrasco and Scott Reed helped PICO develop its "congregation-community model," in which religious congregations serve as the institutional bases for community organizations. PICO was renamed PICO National Network in 2004 to reflect its evolution into a sprawling set of faith-based, nonpartisan, multicultural community organizations, which today boasts of fifty-five affiliated federations and eight statewide networks working in 150 cities and towns in twenty states. The national network claims, "More than one million families and one thousand congregations from 40 different denominations and faiths participate in its work." PICO organizers en-

22. See "PICO International," http://www.picointernational.org (accessed October 29, 2014); "PICO Rwanda," http://www.picointernational.org/rwanda (accessed October 29, 2014).

23. See "PICO National Network," http://www.piconetwork.org (accessed October 29, 2014). The quotations in this paragraph and the one that follows are from the PICO National Network website.

gage problems facing urban, suburban, and rural communities across the country, working with ordinary people, public officials, and other power brokers to "increase access to health care, improve public schools, make neighborhoods safer, build affordable housing, redevelop communities and revitalize democracy."[24]

To enact a "vision . . . that unites people across region, race, class, and religion," PICO organizing mobilizes members of religious congregations to address problems in their communities by building broad-based, nonpartisan, multicultural organizations, which, in turn, can strengthen or regenerate the respective congregations of participating members. The approach "involves teaching people of faith how to build and exercise their own power to address the root causes of the problems they face" and hold public officials accountable to the communities they represent. Both PICO Founder John Baumann and PICO Director of International Projects Ron Snyder (previously the executive director of Oakland Community Organizations) mentored Rutsindintwarane during his internship in Oakland, California, in 2006, and they continue to consult with their former intern today as he leads PICO Rwanda.

Rooted in religious culture, in the beliefs and practices of mostly Christian congregations, and relying on established commitments to family, friends, and neighbors, PICO Rwanda mobilizes Rwandans to organize, deliberate, and act to improve their communities. Richard Wood's account of PICO organizing in the United States further clarifies Rutsindintwarane's approach: "In the language of democratic theory each organization strives to empower its constituents to articulate their public concerns in the political arena in order to redirect governmental policy to better meet the needs of less privileged members of society. In the process, they seek to transform the relationship between citizens and public institutions."[25] The transformation that Rwanda needs today to complement its economic and infrastructural transformation has to do with advancing democracy and deepening development.

Rutsindintwarane's organizing practices, as forms of rights-based development, implicitly begin by calling Rwandans to exercise the right to freedom of association. He does not refer to the various problems linked to poverty that communities face as rights violations though. He prefers framing these problems politically, for example, in terms of a lack of independence,

24. See "PICO National Network."
25. Wood, *Faith in Action*, p. 8.

when people no longer living under colonial rule do not take responsibility for themselves and their country, and a lack of accountability, when they do not use their own capabilities for development. Thus, Rutsindintwarane often sums up his agenda as "helping people to think for themselves."

PICO and the Mumeya Medical Center

While training pastors, bishops, lay leaders, and public officials in community organizing and leadership development in 2006 at a Lutheran World Federation field office in Kibungo, Rutsindintwarane met Cyrus Nzajibwami, a pastor from the remote rural villages of Mumeya, Rwanda.[26] Finding organizing extremely challenging there, Nzajibwami acted shrewdly; he invited the new trainer to meet with residents in the area. Rutsindintwarane remembered that he had traveled for hours across the steep, rocky terrain to Mumeya once before, while doing field research for his master's thesis. He also recalled that he had offered a ride to a twelve-year-old boy in the area whose leg was badly injured. The boy refused to be taken to the hospital, however, because it was too far away; it would not be easy to get home from there. Rutsindintwarane decided to go back to Mumeya, set near the borders of both Burundi and Tanzania and isolated from outside contact and public services, to see if he could help Nzajibwami organize the Mumeyans.

Near Rwantonde in the Gatore Sector of the Kirehe District, Mumeya is home to 30,000 residents, 13,000 of whom are children. A reporter for *The New Times,* a Rwanda English-language newspaper, describes reality in Mumeya:

This close proximity to those borders therefore means that most of the area inhabitants are returnee refugees who are struggling to cope with the serious business of survival, and so their existence is mostly characterized by a frustrated sense of hopelessness. The nearest hospital, [in] Kirehe, is 30 kilometers away. There was no school in a radius of 10 kilometers by 2006. The place itself is inaccessible, with only a rugged track serving for the road that they use to take in some supplies. They have to trudge five kilometers to the Akagera River to get a jerrycan of water for home use. What this actually translates into is a life of extreme hardship for the

26. See John Baumann, S.J., "PICO International Organizing in Central America and Rwanda, Africa," *Social Policy* 41, no. 3 (Fall 2011): 33-35.

people living it; deaths, be they maternal or children, are a common occurrence, when most of them would have been preventable.[27]

On June 26, 2006, Rutsindintwarane met with Ezra Nkubana, a local community leader, to discuss the possibility of organizing there. Nkubana laughed at Rutsindintwarane, well aware of the many others who had come to help, including development organizations, government representatives, and Christian missionaries, all making promises that would never be fulfilled. The community leader, though, noticed an important difference. This visitor promised nothing, other than his "heart and mind." Nkubana was skeptical, yet open enough to agree to gather people for further conversation.

Dozens of members from various local churches — Catholic, Lutheran, Anglican, Baptist, and Adventist — assembled around a tree, now called "the Jesus tree," amid dirt and rocks, to meet with Rutsindintwarane. He started by talking about his birth in exile, life as a refugee, and the need to rebuild faith, families, communities, and the country after genocide. He then dealt with the church's failures. Instead of peace, justice, and reconciliation, Rutsindintwarane explained how Rwandan Christians practiced hatred, division, and scapegoating. The church had long lost its "prophetic message," and had lacked a critical posture toward the state. Public officials and military leaders had sowed ethnic division and political violence without the church's rebuke and resistance. Taking responsibility for this failure as a church leader himself — although as a refugee he had never been to Rwanda before the genocide — Rutsindintwarane confessed to those present that his own faith needed to be restored. His testimony resonated with many Mumeyans, though many also wondered whether this Lutheran pastor-organizer was out to steal members from other congregations. It would take a year for them to trust that he had no such intentions.

Rutsindintwarane went on to play many roles as an organizer in Mumeya, including communicator, agitator, recruiter, group builder, researcher, strategist, tactician, political educator, mediator, fundraiser, and transporter of people and materials.[28] As we examine what was done, we must keep in mind the context. Exercising the right to freedom of association involved more than just gathering Mumeyans around a possible community

27. D. Gusongoirye, "Kirehe: Building and Healing Together as a Community," *The New Times* (November 1, 2009), available at http://www.piconetwork.org/news-media/coverage/2009/0323.

28. Eric Mann provides a comprehensive list of roles effective organizers should play in his *Playbook for Progressives: 16 Qualities of the Successful Organizer* (Boston: Beacon, 2011).

development project. Genocide-related difficulties such as the coexistence of victims, perpetrators, and, more generally, survivors and returnees, constantly required personal risk, establishing trust, and repairing severely damaged relationships.

Rutsindintwarane's training began with practice on how to conduct one-to-one conversations that expose problems in the community connected to development. The assignment was to ask the following questions: (1) How long have you lived here, and what development have you seen since the genocide? (2) What kind of development would you like to see here? (3) What would be your role in the desired development? and (4) Do you think that other people share your views; and if so, would you be willing to bring them to the next training session? Over the course of the next few months, an estimated 2,000 of these conversations took place in Mumeya.

The practice of one-to-ones and broader community discussions contributed to the formation of a local organizing committee and a relational infrastructure primed to pursue development. In one-to-ones, Mumeyans welcomed and listened to neighbors; established a sense of trust and hospitality; discerned values, interests, motivations, and goals; discussed common problems, how people are affected, and possible responses; identified potential leaders, attempting to reflect the diversity of the community; and increased the number of people feeling a collective responsibility for improving their community. Commenting later on this phase of organizing, one Mumeyan remarked, "These one-to-ones could have prevented the genocide."[29] Now, at least, the ongoing use of one-to-ones on local issues can contribute to conditions conducive to the range of approaches Rwandans take to reconciliation.

After collecting the insights and concerns of the community, Rutsindintwarane and the Mumeyans elected by the community to serve on a local organizing committee formed an association, researched commonly identified problems, prioritized resolvable issues, considered alternative perspectives, and determined what authority and which resources were necessary for the development possibilities. Through these structured, organizing practices, a Rwandan form of grassroots, deliberative democracy emerged. Easily the most pressing issue, according to the one-to-ones, was access to healthcare, especially maternal and neonatal care. Other urgent matters were the lack of nearby water sources and primary schools. One community leader, speaking to a Catholic bishop, communicated the frustration and painful

29. Field notes, 2013, on file with author.

memories of many: "We have been asking the Rwandan government to build a clinic in this area since 1973. . . . [W]hen we get sick, the nearest hospital is Murgwanza in Tanzania or Muyinga in Burundi. We break immigration rules and cross the river Akagera at night when members of our families are sick. An average of 15 expectant mothers and children die per year on the way to hospital."[30]

With a local organizing committee in charge and Rutsindintwarane organizing and training, the Mumeyans considered plans to build a major medical center in the area, including a laboratory, pharmacy, training facilities, and a mobile health clinic. During the research phase, they held meetings with influential church leaders, public officials, and health professionals. Reflecting on Rutsindintwarane's approach, one Mumeyan woman explained,

[The] training exercises my critical thinking because it makes me look and think in a different perspective than I ever did before, like political and faith ways. That's where I get to exercise my critical thinking more, like in strategizing for research meetings, thinking about targets of self-interest, all these things that I did not understand before. I have learned skills that have built my confidence, which allows me to deal with new situations, deepen my knowledge of how to fix the problems facing us.[31]

After estimating both the cost of building and operations, committee leaders formed construction and environmental task forces to oversee the development, with each group taking study trips outside the region to increase their knowledge of technical issues and generate planning ideas.

Between 2007 and 2008, regional leaders — in response to consultations with Nkubana and other Mumeyans — donated six acres of land for the medical center. Residents quickly cleared it, broke tons of rock, laid the foundation, and started construction. Rutsindintwarane used his Land Cruiser to carry 600 tons of material to the site. While one-to-one conversations and research continued, Rutsindintwarane attended PICO training events in the United States, receiving individual consultancy from Baumann and Snyder, and met with many donors for further financial support. Today, the medical center, an impressive (especially given the surrounding rugged topography) thirty eight-room clinic with laboratory and pharmacy, is staffed and operational. Another building on site houses a store, restaurant, meeting space,

30. "PICO Rwanda," http://www.picointernational.org/rwanda.
31. "PICO Rwanda."

and crop storage facilities. The center is linked to the nearest city, Kirehe, by road, increasing access to medical supplies. Protais Murayire, the mayor of Kirehe, tasked people sentenced by community-based Gacaca courts for genocide-related crimes to build the road and make bricks for the center. They worked alongside the residents of Mumeya. Efforts continue to get clean piped water and electricity to the broader area.

Since 2006, Rutsindintwarane has trained and mentored over 100 people in Mumeya in organizing and leadership. Over 30,000 area people now have access to healthcare services (70 percent of the daily patients at the medical center are children), and women in labor no longer have to be carried across mountains and rivers by stretcher (the multiple accounts I heard of this were harrowing) to reach a hospital or fear death while giving birth.[32] Throughout the process, many Mumeyans gained experience in both reflecting and deliberating on community needs, interests, and priorities, and in effectively communicating with religious leaders and public officials. They met with all levels of government, from the Mayor of Kirehe to the current President of the Rwanda Senate in Parliament, former Minister of Health Jean Damascene Ntawukuriryayo. The local organizing committee pushed public officials for financial and technical support for construction, public services, nursing and other staff, medical equipment, and medicine. Pressuring them through calls, meetings, and petitions, Mumeyans gained inclusion of the medical center in the regional budget and national health plans. They also enrolled nearly all area residents in the national health insurance program to increase coverage for healthcare services.

As the minds of Mumeyans changed concerning their own capabilities and potential, the minds of religious leaders and public officials also changed as they realized that ordinary people can take action, do research, deliberate, exert political power, and develop their own communities.[33] Mumeyans now have clout. "Taking action," according to Rutsindintwarane, involves typical organizing practices such as setting agendas for and meeting with public officials; presenting the community's testimonies, research, and proposals; listening to and judging the adequacy of the officials' stated response; confronting what is considered unacceptable; establishing commitments for resolving the problem; and holding officials responsible. While opposition party politics remains fraught with danger — real or perceived — after civil war, genocide, and Rwandan intervention in the Democratic Republic of

32. Field notes, 2013.
33. Field notes, 2013.

the Congo (DRC), Rutsindintwarane's organizing practices peacefully and effectively enact a form of political accountability when instrumental to the community's own development agenda.

The practice of self-evaluation, normed by the local organizing committee's vision, mission, and religious culture, and especially important for critical postures, follows action. As a rule, criticism without self-criticism is not accepted. In a setting where rights advocates warn of state control, co-optation, and instrumentalization of civil society, honest and penetrating self-evaluation can contribute to independence in thought and action. Rwandan civil society organizations involved in development, Paul Gready suggests, should "learn to balance and shift between collaboration on the one hand, and monitoring, lobbying, critique, and outright confrontation on the other."[34] In pursuit of community empowerment and leadership development, Rutsindintwarane's organizing practices respond to the United Nations Special Rapporteur's call for more critical engagement with the Rwandan government and public policy. His efforts include democratic reasoning concerning the allocation and distribution of resources connected to development, and grassroots resistance to governance unresponsive to public needs, interests, and priorities.

Exercising their right to freedom of association, Mumeyans learned to hold themselves accountable to their religious beliefs, commitment to serve others, and capacity and potential for development.[35] They also learned how to hold others, especially area religious leaders and public officials, accountable to their respective responsibilities. Working together across gender, class, denomination, and, most importantly, ethnic lines, Mumeyans established a strong, broad-based, democratic organization. Further opportunities have transformed these trainees into trainers themselves, who travel across the country and East Africa to share stories of creating a sustainable alternative to government-run poverty eradication efforts that lack strong community participation. Presentations of their work across Europe, the United States, Central America, and Haiti through the organization PICO International confirm that they have become a legitimate global model for organizing.[36]

34. Paul Gready, "Beyond 'You're with Us or against Us,'" p. 87.
35. Field notes, 2013.
36. See "PICO International," http://www.picointernational.org, for reports on comparable work in Central America and Haiti.

Love Exercises the Right to Freedom of Association

Rutsindintwarane unlocks and expands the exercise of the right to freedom
of association — necessary for peace, development, and democracy, according to human rights advocates — as he helps ordinary Rwandans to assemble,
deliberate, and build organizations that improve their communities. These
associations, often sourced and supported by local churches, can strengthen
or regenerate the multiple respective congregations of participants, while
those same congregations inspire and sustain the participants through
worship, prayer, and other relational and theological provisions. As these
organization-congregation connections become symbiotic, blurring the
distinction between association and church, it can be difficult to determine
where one stops and the other starts. The associations spring from churches
as individual members respond, establish organizations across other congregations, and participate in the development of their own communities.
Meanwhile, they can also function as modest anticipatory communities
themselves, partially prefiguring the desired systemic structural change as
they work toward it more broadly.[37]

Rutsindintwarane's organizing practices, which I interpret as group responses to God's call to service and justice and as civic forms of love, enact
a theology especially perceptive to the needs of the nation. They facilitate
both democratization from below and a dilution of concentrated power
from above, reducing vulnerability to the state's totalizing tendencies. In
the face of Rwandan fears — some of which are valid, others of which are
not — concerning the existence of opposition parties, Rutsindintwarane
trains ordinary Rwandans in grassroots democratic action, to be used when
needed in service of development. Finally, by enabling the exercise of the
right to freedom of association, his practical approach prudently avoids the
impasse between predictable human rights criticism and Rwandan government denial.

Many Rwandans are now taking charge of their local communities and
futures through organizing. "A community organization is a means," explains
Luke Bretherton, "by which the economically poor and politically marginalized can address their situation rather than be made dependent on either
state welfare or private charity, for such an organization enables them to
forge a place from which to act in the political arena rather than simply be

37. See Larry Rasmussen, *Earth-Honoring Faith: Religious Ethics in a New Key* (Oxford:
Oxford University Press, 2012), p. 121.

acted upon by state technocrats and paternalistic elites."[38] Rwandan community organizing, like comparable civil society organizations, offers people the possibilities of taking responsibility for the social, economic, and political arrangements affecting their communities and country as a whole, and can increase their capabilities of resisting state domination and aid dependency. This organizing serves as a means for the consultation with and consent of the governed, with the potential to check the arbitrary exercise of power.

Participants' respective congregations, from which these associations spring, support PICO Rwanda's community organizing and leadership development work. The ritualized communication of the self-giving love of Christ through the Spirit's material media of language and sacraments creates associations called churches, according to Lutheran theological perspective. The communication calls people to love God and others as themselves, to work for peace, justice, and reconciliation, and to care for the earth. This human vocation, again in terms resonant with Rutsindintwarane's own Lutheran theological views, corresponds to the state's calling, apart from the latter's authorization to use coercive force in certain contexts. Svend Andersen observes, "Christian love has the same aim as the institution of government, namely to meet the needs of people; love as beneficence is (also) political neighbor love."[39] Thus, I argue that the human vocation to love others as one loves oneself should include critical and constructive, civic participation in governance. "A Christian," Martin Luther maintains, "honors those in authority, serves, helps, and does all he can to assist the governing authority, that it may continue to function and be held in honor and fear."[40] Community organizing — as a set of practices responding to God's call to service and justice, and reminding the state of its God-given calling — on my interpretation, enacts this human and Christian vocation in its civic mode.

---

38. Luke Bretherton, *Christianity and Contemporary Politics* (Oxford: Wiley-Blackwell, 2009), p. 104.

39. Svend Andersen, "Can We Still Do Lutheran Political Theology?" *Studia Theologica* 67, no. 2 (2013): 115. Andersen links this view to Martin Luther. "According to Luther, Christian political ethics is a way of acting by Christians that realizes governance in such a way that other people profit from it and created human life flourishes. There is a congeniality between Christian neighborly love and the function of political authority." Andersen, "Can We Still Do Lutheran Political Theology?" p. 115. See also Svend Andersen, "Democracy and Modernity: A Lutheran Perspective," *Religion and Normativity*, vol. 3, *Religion, Politics, and Law*, ed. Peter Lodberg (Aarhus: Aarhus Universitetsforlag, 2009), pp. 14-29.

40. Martin Luther, "Temporal Authority: To What Extent It Should Be Obeyed," in *Martin Luther's Basic Theological Writings*, ed. Timothy F. Lull (Minneapolis: Fortress Press, 1989), p. 668.

The four central, structured, organizing practices of one-to-one conversations, conducting research, taking action, and self-evaluation offer new possibilities for Rwandans to exercise the right to freedom of association and express civic forms of love. They are paths to serve one's community and country, both directly through sustainable development and indirectly through policy formation. Organizing has the potential to facilitate maximal, critical public assistance to the state as it carries out its responsibilities. As public officials in Rwanda face the complex challenges of governing in a post-genocide context, they could use all the consultation they can get. Through organizing, ordinary Rwandans can build trust across ethnic identities and strengthen relationships; deliberate on the allocation and distribution of public resources; improve critical thinking and educate their judgment; and exercise wise and effective leadership in their communities. This is deep development, the capacitation and empowerment of associations for civic or political neighbor love.

To help us envision such multi-church–based associations, we turn again to the Lutheran tradition. Imagining the church as a community of moral deliberation, Gary Simpson refers to doctrines such as:

> the priesthood of all believers and an expansively understood "mutual consolation and conversation of sisters and brothers," as well as the — oft overlooked — magisterium of all believers together and the churchly communion of bearing one another's burdens in and with a complex world of diverse neighbors and global neighborhoods. Such bearing surely includes bearing one another's ethical discernment, deliberation, discussion, disagreements and agreements, and — sometimes — decision-making.[41]

41. Gary Simpson, "Church as Community of Moral Deliberation," *Journal of Lutheran Ethics* 14, no. 4 (April 2014), www.elca.org/jle. For a variation on churches as communities of moral deliberation, see Gary M. Simpson, "Civil Society and Congregations as Public Moral Companions," *Word & World* 15, no. 4 (Fall 1995): 420-27. There Simpson proposes the following marks of the church as a public moral companion: "As public moral companions, congregations acknowledge a *conviction* that they participate in God's ongoing creative work. In a communicative civil society, congregations exhibit a *compassionate commitment* to other institutions and their moral predicaments. The commitment of moral companions always yields a *critical* and *self-critical,* and thus fully *communicative,* procedure and practice of moral engagement. Finally, as public moral companions, congregations participate with other institutions of communicative civil society to *create* and *strengthen* the moral fabrics that fashion a life-giving and life-accountable contemporary society." Simpson, "Civil Society," pp. 426-27.

As lay rural and urban Rwandan Christians take up these vocations and become more powerful through associations, their enhanced capabilities threaten dominant religious leaders just as much as public officials. While human rights criticism raises awareness of the challenges people face working with the latter, lay Rwandan Christians I talked with noted the challenges they face working with the former. Thus, Rutsindintwarane seeks to facilitate the dismantling of the domination of churches by religious leaders while he does the same to the domination of development by public officials.

In his treatise "Temporal Authority: To What Extent It Should Be Obeyed," Martin Luther attempts to "learn how far its arm extends and how widely its hand stretches, lest it extend too far and encroach upon God's kingdom and government." He warns, "It is essential for us to know this, for where it is given too wide a scope, intolerable and terrible injury follow."[42] This perennial, universal concern calls for political vigilance. The UN Special Rapporteur and others monitoring human rights globally contend that the Rwandan government is overextending itself, threatening the right to freedom of association. Rutsindintwarane's organizing practices present new possibilities for Rwandan Christians across congregations and others to assemble, deliberate, and contribute to the peace, development, and democratization of Rwanda. Structured, disciplined responses to God's call to service and justice and civic forms of love, these practices enact a theology that advances democracy and deepens development. Part of the process of "reimagining public governance emerging from place, culture, and people," they enable Rwandans to find their own ways of confronting and counteracting, when necessary, the overextension Luther names.

42. Luther, "Temporal Authority," p. 678.

CHAPTER 14

Disturbing Unjust Peace in Nigeria through the Church and Legal Reforms: The Contribution of Luther's Critical Public Theology

Ibrahim Bitrus

Nigeria is not currently at war with any country, nor fighting a civil war, but the relative peace that the country currently enjoys is an "unjust peace." Just as just peace is not only an absence of armed battles but also the presence of justice, an unjust peace is the ungodly peace in which systemic evils are perpetrated by those in power for their own benefit while their victims do little or nothing to disturb these evils. Even though some courageous individuals have made attempts to disturb this unjust peace through lawful, nonviolent resistance — to destabilize the oppressive "peace" that oppresses the majority — their attempts are condemned as "disturbance of public peace" and suppressed by the perpetrators under the pretense of maintaining law and order. Those who resist the people in power hope to establish just peace in which the rule of law and equity prevail at all times and places in Nigeria. Thus, by disturbing unjust peace, I mean the use of lawful and nonviolent means to resist and destabilize the deadly peace that oppresses the majority of the people and benefits the privileged few.

The trouble with Nigerian society is not that there is no recognition of the rule of law that could guarantee just peace, but rather that the rule of law has been poorly enforced, if not shamelessly undermined, by those in power. Therefore, a mere revision of existing laws, or even promulgation of new ones, without a corresponding resolute political will by those in authority to obey the laws, and a truly independent and incorruptible judiciary that will enforce them, will not disturb the unjust peace in Nigeria. Unsettling unjust peace demands both faithful adherence to the rule of law enshrined in the Nigerian constitution, and also effective implementation of existing laws to change the dysfunctional behavior of the people. This requires sustained anticorruption efforts to detect, arrest, and prosecute perpetrators of corruption and deter the economic and financial crimes that are the intractable causes of unjust peace in Nigeria. Similarly, disturbing unjust peace in Nigeria demands more than just audacious public rebuke by the church of corrupt leaders; it requires that the church use the *whole law and gospel* in the public sphere both by exposing systemic injustice and corruption and by participating in public protest against it. Hence, Luther's vision of the triune God ruling the world through the gospel and the secular law is a potential contribution of his critical public theology to the enterprise of dismantling the unjust peace in Nigeria through the church and legal reforms.

This essay consists of four parts. In the first and second parts, I will outline the context for Nigeria's unjust peace, including the current abuses of the rule of law in Nigeria. In the third part, I will describe how Luther's critical public theology provides the basis for disturbing the unjust peace in Nigeria. In the last two sections, I will describe concrete tactics that Nigerian churches (not just Lutheran churches) and legal reformers (when informed by Luther's public theology) might use to dismantle the unjust peace in the country.

Unjust Peace: The Church in the Nigerian Context

With an estimated membership of over eighty million, the Christian churches in Nigeria are indeed experiencing phenomenal growth, which one would ordinarily expect might translate into building of a just peace in the country.[1] But the scale of injustice perpetrated in Nigeria amid such rapid growth is beyond imagination. Public resources and positions are unequally distributed to favor the privileged few at the expense of the poor majority. For example, while an average Nigerian lives on less than a dollar per day, Nigerian lawmakers are the world's highest-paid legislators, with an annual salary of about $189,000, surpassing their counterparts in Britain and the United States.[2] About seven hundred billion dollars of public funds have been stolen by corrupt officials since Nigeria's independence in 1960.[3] Though Nigeria

---

1. John Thomas Didymus, "Images of Indigenous Nigerian Churches — Christianity in Africa," *Digital Journal Reports* (April 21, 2012), http://digitaljournal.com/article/323394 (accessed December 26, 2013).

2. Alaba Johnson, "Economist Magazine: Nigerian Legislators World's Highest Paid," *Naija Pundit* (July 22, 2013), http://www.naijapundit.com/news/economist-magazine -nigerian-legislators-world-s-highest-paid (accessed December 7, 2013).

3. Omololu Ogunmade, "Nigeria: U.S. $600 Billion Stolen by Nigerian Elite Since

is the sixth largest oil exporter in the world, one hundred million Nigerians out of a population of one hundred fifty million live in destitution.[4] Such pervasive economic injustice and massive political corruption are the major causes of the personal insecurity of most Nigerians as well as the insecurity of the country. These conditions contribute to attracting many unemployed young people to commit violent crimes, and also to being hired by desperate, power-hungry defeated and even currently serving politicians as thugs or assassins of their perceived or real political enemies.[5] This world of political violence in part accounts for Boko Haram's Islamist insurgency, the booming kidnapping "business" in Nigeria, and lingering ethno-religious conflict in various parts of the country.

Those who govern refuse, with gross impunity, to deal squarely with corruption, and economic and financial crimes that are responsible for injustice in Nigeria in spite of the establishment of anticorruption commissions such as the Code of Conduct Bureau (CCB) which was established in 1999, the Independent Corrupt Practices and Other Related Offences Commission (ICPC) in 2000, and the Economic and Financial Crimes Commission (EFCC) in 2004.[6] Therefore, in Nigeria, where people who loot the public treasury not only receive lighter jail terms than those who steal a cell phone but also live in affluence and luxury while the majority languishes in absolute poverty, it is safe to say that there is no just peace.[7] Such an unjust peace

Independence," *This Day* (June 19, 2013), available from http://allafrica.com/stories/ 201306190182.html (accessed February 15, 2014); Toyosi Ogunseye, Allwell Okpi, and Leke Baiyewu, "$31 Billion Stolen under President Jonathan of Nigeria," *Sahara Reporters* (November 24, 2012), available from http://saharareporters.com/news-page/31-billion -stolen-under-president-jonathan-nigeria-%E2%80%93punch (accessed November 24, 2012).

4. Everest Amaefule, "100 Million Nigerians Live in Destitution — World Bank," *Punch* (November 12, 2013). Available from: http://www.punchng.com/news/100-million -nigerians-live-in-destitution-world-bank/ (accessed December 7, 2013).

5. Eme Okechukwu Innocent and Anthony Onyishi, "The Challenges of Insecurity in Nigeria: A Thematic Exposition," *Interdisciplinary Journal of Contemporary Research in Business* 3, no. 8 (2011): 172-85.

6. Human Rights, "Corruption on Trial? The Record of Nigeria's Economic and Financial Crimes Commission" (2011). Available from: http://www.hrw.org/sites/default/files/ reports/nigeria0811WebPostR.pdf (accessed February 16, 2014).

7. "Director Jailed 2 yrs for Stealing N33bn Pension Fund Freed on N250,000 Fine," *Premium Times* (January 28, 2013). Available from: http://premiumtimesng.com/news/117599 -director-jailed-2yrs-for-stealing-n33bn-pension-fund-freed-on-n250000-fine.html (accessed December 9, 2013); Tunde Odesola, "Man Jailed 45 Years for Stealing Nigerian Governor Aregbesola's Phone — *Punch Newspaper*," *Sahara Reporters* (April 30, 2013), available from

is more heinous than actual war, seriously harming millions of Nigerians silently through poverty, corruption, and crime on a scale greater than even modern sophisticated warfare probably would. As Dr. Kunle Olajide sees it, Nigeria is in "an undeclared state of war."[8]

The Current Abuses of the Rule of Law in Nigeria

One of the authentic pillars of true democracy and good governance is the rule of law. Because Nigeria is at least on paper a democratic country, the rule of law — the absolute supremacy or predominance of the law over the organs of the government, groups, and individuals — is explicitly enshrined in the Nigerian constitution. Chapter 1, section 1 of the 1999 Nigerian constitution, which brought the present democratic government into existence, states: "This constitution is supreme and its provisions shall have binding force on all authorities and persons throughout the Federal Republic of Nigeria."[9] The Constitution not only demands unqualified respect for law from the government and the governed, which precludes arbitrary policies, actions, or inactions of the government that undermine the provisions of the law. According to the famous Nigerian Justice Chukwudifu Oputa,

> The rule of law presupposes that the state is subject to the law, that the judiciary is a necessary agency of the rule of law, that the Government should respect the right of individual citizens under the rule of law and that to the judiciary, is assigned both by the rule of law and by our constitution the determination of all actions and proceedings relating to matters in disputes between persons, Governments or authority.[10]

http://saharareporters.com/2013/04/30/man-jailed-45-years-stealing-nigerian-governor -aregbesola%E2%80%99s-phone-punch-newspaper (accessed January 14, 2014).

8. Kunle Olajide, "Nigeria Is in an Undeclared State of War," *Nigerian Tribune* (2013). Available from: http://www.tribune.com.ng/news2013/index.php/en/politics/item/28366 -nigeria-is-in-an-undeclared-war-yuf-scribe.html (accessed December 11, 2013).

9. Constitution of the Federal Republic of Nigeria, chapter I, part I, sec. 1 (1999), available from: http://www.nigeria-law.org/ConstitutionOfTheFederalRepublicOfNigeria.htm (accessed December 12, 2013).

10. As quoted in Ifedayo Timothy Akomolede, "Good Governance, Rule of Law and Constitutionalism in Nigeria," *European Journal of Business and Social Sciences* 1, no. 6 (2012): 69-85, 73. Available from: http://www.ejbss.com/Data/Sites/1/septemberissue/ ejbss-12-1150-goodgovernance.pdf (accessed December 12, 2013).

The Nigerian Constitution, which also provides for human rights in chapter 4, encompasses civil, political, economic, social, and cultural rights. The Constitution requires the government to respect and safeguard these inalienable human rights through establishment of an independent judiciary saddled with the responsibility of delivering unbiased judgment in accordance with provision of the law. Appreciating the crucial role of an independent judiciary both in upholding the rule of law and checking the excesses of other arms of government as regards abuse of office, human rights, and corruption, section 17(1) (e) of the 1999 Constitution, states that "the independence, impartiality and integrity of courts of law, and easy accessibility thereto shall be secured and maintained."[11]

It is one thing to enshrine the idea of the rule of law in the Constitution; it is another thing, however, to practice it. Nigeria's situation bears an eloquent testimony to this truism, as there has been a consistent discrepancy between the constitutional provisions requiring the rule of law and its practice in Nigeria. If there is anything that Nigeria's successive governments have been consistent about, it has been the gross violation of this constitutional provision. The military governments that ruled Nigeria for more than three decades laid the foundation for such violations. As the epitome of tyranny, the military governments suspended the Constitution and consequently the rule of law, replacing civil courts with military tribunals whose members even lacked expertise in the law. The execution of Ken Saro Wiwa and eight other Ogoni human rights activists by the military government at the time, in defiance of national and international appeals, was the most awful expression of this military tyranny.[12] Since 1999, that kind of impunity practiced in military rule has found its way consciously or unconsciously into the contemporary democratic rule. Nigeria continued to experience abuses of the rule of law with the arbitrary arrest and unlawful detention of suspects, extra-judicial killings, harassment of civil rights groups, and repressive crackdowns on political enemies under former President Jonathan's administration.[13] The hopes and expectations of the Constitution's

11. Constitution of the Federal Republic of Nigeria, chapter II, sec. 17(2)(e) (1999), available from: http://www.nigeria-law.org/ConstitutionOfTheFederalRepublicOfNigeria.htm.

12. Alka Jauhari, "Colonial and Post-Colonial Human Rights Violations in Nigeria," *International Journal of Humanities and Social Science* 1, no. 5 (2011): 53-57. Available from: http://www.ijhssnet.com/journals/Vol._1_No._5;_May_2011/7.pdf (accessed December 12, 2013).

13. "Civil Rights Group Lists 17 Worsening Human Rights Violations under President Jonathan," *iReports-ng* (November 4, 2013). Available from: http://ireports-ng

framers that restoration of democracy would translate into the enthrone-
ment of the rule of law have been dashed.

The democratic government is no better than the military was. As Dr.
Elijah Okon John suggests, "Civilian regimes in Nigeria have not fared better
... with respect to the rule of law. In fact, civilian administrators seem to sur-
pass the military in their open disrespect to the rule of law."[14] All three arms
of the government are guilty of this appalling misconduct. In the thirteen
years that it has been a democratic country, Nigeria's executive arm has consistently behaved as if it is above the law, if it is not the law itself, shamelessly
disobeying with impunity the judgments of the courts of the land.[15] One of
the clear-cut cases of such executive lawlessness was the arrogant refusal of
former President Olusegun Obasanjo to remit the local government funds
that he unlawfully withheld to the Lagos State Government in 2004, despite
the Supreme Court's ruling that his action was unconstitutional and its order
to release these funds.[16] For example, Dr. John reports that when journalists
criticized Obasanjo's unwarranted and expensive foreign trips and *Mid-Day
News* attempted to expose them on July 6, 2002, "Obasanjo against all advice
resorted to executive lawlessness — a crackdown on journalists."[17]

This executive lawlessness is exacerbated by the abuse of the "immunity
clause" enshrined in Section 308 of the 1999 Constitution. That provision
shields elected executive political leaders from having any civil or criminal
proceedings instituted against their persons during their period in office.[18]
Though the immunity is intended to provide political leaders with security
of tenure so they can deliver the dividends of democracy to the people, it
has been misused by too many of them as absolute power, emboldening

---

.com/2013/11/04/civil-rights-group-lists-17-worsening-human-rights-violations-under
-president-jonathan/ (accessed December 13, 2013).

14. Elijah Okon John, "The Rule of Law in Nigeria: Myth or Reality?" *Journal of Politics
and Law* 4, no. 1 (2011): 211-14, 212.

15. R. A. Lawal-Rabana, "The Nigerian Bar Association and the Protection of Rule of Law
in Nigeria" (unpublished paper), p. 2. Available from: http://www.ibanet.org/barassociations/
bar_associations_Zagreb_conference_materials.aspx (accessed December 13, 2013).

16. Attorney-General of Lagos State v. Attorney-General of the Federation, S.C.
70/2004 (Supreme Court of Nigeria 2004). Available from: http://www.nigeria-law.org/
Attorney-General%20of%20Lagos%20State%20V%20Attorney-General%20of%20the
%20Federation.htm (accessed December 13, 2013).

17. John, "The Rule of Law in Nigeria: Myth or Reality?" p. 213.

18. Constitution of the Federal Republic of Nigeria, chapter VIII, part II, sec. 308
(1999), available from http://www.nigeria-law.org/ConstitutionOfTheFederalRepublicOf
Nigeria.htm.

them to disobey court judgments and to perpetrate and get away with all kinds of graft and even violent atrocities while they are in office. Even the constitutional provision permitting trial of such political leaders after they are out of office, or impeachment by the National Assembly or their State Houses of Assembly for local politicians, has proved impossible to enforce. This makes it extremely difficult, if not impossible, to bring them to justice. Political absolutism, which common sense requires should be denounced, is what the Nigerian Constitution seems to approve with the immunity clause.

Similarly, the amended Nigerian Constitution (2010) requires every public officer to submit to the Code of Conduct Bureau and to make a written declaration of all his or her properties, assets, and liabilities immediately after assumption of office and at the end of his or her term. But this provision has not been followed by many public officials, including former President Goodluck Jonathan. When he was severely castigated for not declaring his assets, he dismissed the entire idea of assets declaration as a matter of personal principle rather than rule of law. President Jonathan said, "The issue of asset declaration is a matter of principle. I don't give a damn about it, if you want to criticize me from heaven."[19]

Moreover, the legislative branch of the government that is responsible for checking such executive lawlessness through impeachment and legislation is ineffective and corrupt. It has only succeeded in investigating the grossest executive abuses of office through various investigatory committees, but the recommendations that it has made to eliminate these abuses have been either neglected or abandoned. Sadly, Drs. Mojeed Olujinmi A. Alabi and Joseph 'Yinka Fashagba have argued that "investigations undertaken by various committees of the central legislature were often meant to arm twist government ministries or agencies into giving money to members of the assembly. Lack of sincerity has, in most cases, affected the extent to which the various committees of the house could provide effective check against abuse of executive power."[20]

---

19. Laolu Akande, "President Jonathan's Refusal to Declare His Assets Violates Agreement between Nigeria and United States-Empowered Newswire," *Sahara Reporters* (June 30, 2012). Available from: http://saharareporters.com/2012/06/30/president-jonathan'-refusal-declare-his-assets-violates-agreement-between-nigeria-and-unite (accessed December 13, 2013).

20. Mojeed Olujinmi A. Alabi and Joseph 'Yinka Fashagba, "The Legislature and Anticorruption Crusade under the Fourth Republic of Nigeria: Constitutional Imperatives and Practical Realities," *International Journal of Politics and Good Governance* 1, nos. 1-2 (2010): 31-32.

Undoubtedly, leaders of many ad-hoc committees of the National Assembly have been embroiled in bribery and corruption scandals, giving the National Assembly the reputation of accepting bribes for budget approval and confirmation of ministerial nominees.[21] Former President Obasanjo wonders, "What sort of laws will they make?" Continuing, the former president said, "The judiciary is also corrupt. . . . If the judiciary becomes corrupt, where is the hope for the nation? Justice, no doubt, will go to the highest bidder. The judiciary did not see anything wrong with a former governor but the same set of evidence was used to sentence him in the United Kingdom."[22]

Finally, there is no branch of government that has been more marginalized and incapacitated in upholding the principle of rule of law than the judiciary, which now is effectively either an extension or an appendage of the executive branch. Despite the unambiguous declaration that it should be an independent branch of government in the Nigerian Constitution, the judiciary lacks the autonomy with which to administer bold and neutral justice. According to Professor A. A. Olowofoyeku, the judiciary's "institutional independence and a substantial part of the judges' individual independence is generally undermined by the other arms of government. The judges themselves effectively undermine, through the deficiency in integrity or impartiality *of some* of them, their own individual independence."[23] Unlike the executive and legislative branches, which enjoy relative institutional and financial independence, the judiciary today depends on the executive for the appointment of its superior judges and funding, in clear contravention of Section 81(3) of the 1999 Constitution, which states that the judiciary shall be funded from the Consolidated Revenue Fund through the National Judicial Council.[24]

---

21. On the bribery and corruption scandals in the National Assembly, see George Agba et al., "Nigeria: U.S. $620,000 Bribery Scandal — Police Detain Faruk Farouk Lawan Overnight," *Allafrica.* Available from: http://allafrica.com/stories/201206150333.html (accessed February 17, 2014); John Bulus, "Any End on the Corruption Infested House Reps," *Vanguard,* available from: http://www.vanguardngr.com/2012/06/any-end-on-the-corruption-infested-house-reps/ (accessed February 17, 2014); Emma Chukwuemeka et al., "Curbing Corruption in Nigeria: The Imperatives of Good Leadership," *African Research Review* 6 (3), no. 26 (2012): 338-58, available from: http://www.ajol.info/index.php/afrrev/article/viewFile/80255/70515 (accessed December 14, 2013).

22. Simon Utebor, "Rogues, Armed Robbers in N'Assembly," *Punch* (May 23, 2012). Available from: http://www.punchng.com/news/rogues-armed-robbers-in-assembly-obasanjo/ (accessed May 23, 2012).

23. A. A. Olowofoyeku, "The Beleaguered Fortress: Reflections of the Independence of Nigeria's Judiciary," *Journal of African Law* 33, no. 1 (1989): 70. Italics in original.

24. Constitution of the Federal Republic of Nigeria, Chapter V, Part I, sec. 87 (3) (1999),

This dependency syndrome is not only responsible for the appointment of incompetent and unethical judges to the bench, but also the underfunding of the judiciary. The root cause of corruption in the judicial system, this funding scheme subverts its autonomy and results in the lack of personal integrity and corrupt practices of these "bad elements" within the judiciary, compromising its independence. As the Senior Advocate of Nigeria (SAN), Femi Falana, has lamented, "Some highly placed judges have betrayed their oath of office by engaging in wanton corruption. . . . Under the current democratic dispensation, some of the heads of the judiciary do not believe in the independence of the judiciary."[25] Falana states that in Nigeria, where judicial corruption has become virtually institutionalized, it is not surprising the judiciary has either freed the wealthy and powerful charged with theft of billions of dollars from the Nigerian people, or imposed absurdly low fines if they are convicted.[26]

This story of lawlessness is also true of the police force. Dr. Emmanuel C. Onyeozili claims that "the police are [a] constituent part of police ineffectiveness."[27] Police corruption in Nigeria has perverted the noble mission of the police: instead of protecting citizens' life and property, they instead appear to aid and abet crimes. Onyeozili claims that police corruption takes "various forms: extortion from motorists at illegally mounted road blocks, [and] collection of monetary gratification (bribery) in order to alter justice in favor of the highest bidder."[28] Research has shown that the Nigerian police force is a highly corrupt security body whose members, for a bribe as low as $1, will not only let a criminal go, but will intentionally cause a bus accident that kills a passenger.[29] As a premeditated crime, some police help to arm

---

available from http://www.nigeria-law.org/ConstitutionOfTheFederalRepublicOfNigeria.htm.

25. Femi Falana, "The Rot in the Judiciary," *Premium Times* (May 27, 2013). Available from: http://premiumtimesng.com/opinion/136274-by-femi-falana.html (accessed December 14, 2013).

26. Falana, "The Rot in the Judiciary."

27. Emmanuel C. Onyeozili, "Obstacles to Effective Policing in Nigeria," *African Journal of Criminology and Justice Studies* 1, no. 1 (2005): 45. Available from: http://www.umes.edu/cms300uploadedFiles/AJCJS/acjavol1no1onyeozili.pdf (accessed December 12, 2013).

28. Onyeozili, "Obstacles to Effective Policing in Nigeria," p. 42.

29. See "Bribery and Corruption Survey: Nigeria Police Rank Number One in Fed Govt Agencies," *Stitch,* available from: http://www.snitchngr.com/bribery-and-corruption-survey-nigeria-police-rank-number-one-in-fed-govt-agencies/#sthash.Js2p5DFQ.dpuf (accessed February 17, 2014); "N50 Bribe: Irresponsible Policemen Cause Bus Accident in Ogun State, Waiting Passenger Killed," *Sahara Reporters* (November 18, 2013), available

criminals by renting out or selling their rifles, and others are themselves armed robbers. Onyeozili reports that in one case, an Inspector General of Police (IG) opened fictitious bank accounts through which bribe money and police service money were laundered, including N1.4 billion which the Independent National Electoral Commission (INEC) paid to the police for security during the 2003 general elections. When the head of the police force is lawless, it is difficult to expect anything else of the rank and file.

In summary, while the rule of law is unambiguously embedded in the Constitution, and could guarantee justice in Nigeria, those who are entrusted with the duty to make, interpret, and enforce the law are virtually lawless. They have blatantly suspended, subverted, ignored, or even violated the rule of law with impunity in favor of the rich and the powerful, while the poor and less privileged are harassed daily in the name of enforcing the law. Such harassment targets every attempt by civil society groups and human rights organizations to challenge such an unjust social order, leading to an unjust peace, a total breakdown of the rule of law![30] Before discussing the church's role and what legal reforms are needed to unsettle this unjust peace in Nigeria, I will first explore Martin Luther's critical public theology, which gives a theological justification for the enterprise of establishing a just peace in Nigeria.

Luther's Critical Public Theology

Luther's critical public theology speaks emphatically about the crucial significance of government as an effective instrument in making and enforcing laws that maintain a just public peace. Luther's public theology sets very high moral political standards for those in political authority for delivering good government to the people, but also spells out explicitly the pastoral obligations of ecclesiastical leaders, should they fail to live up to these stan-

---

from: http://saharareporters.com/news-page/n50-bribe-irresponsible-policemen-cause-bus-accident-ogun-state-waiting-passenger-killed (accessed February 17, 2014).

30. See "Soldiers Shoot to Disperse 'Occupy' Protesters in Lagos as Nigerian Secret Police Raids CNN Office," *Sahara Reports* (January 16, 2012). Available from: http://sahara reporters.com/2012/01/16/soldiers-shoot-disperse-occupy-protesters-lagos-nigerian-secret-police-raids-cnns-office (accessed February 17, 2014). Ayo Okulaja, "Police Fire Tear Gas at Peaceful Protesters in Lagos," *Radio Netherlands Worldwide Africa* (July 19, 2012). Available from: http://www.rnw.nl/africa/article/police-fire-tear-gas-peaceful-protestors-lagos (accessed February 17, 2014).

dards. In his 1523 treatise, "Temporal Authority: To What Extent It Can Be Obeyed," Luther explains the basis and task of worldly government. Luther believes that temporal authority is not of human, but of divine origin.[31] He affirms this divine foundation to assure citizens that temporal government was instituted in the world from the beginning by God's will and ordinance. Even Christ's injunction that one should not resist evil does not abolish, but rather confirms, the divine ordination of public authority. What Jesus prohibits by that injunction, according to Luther, is the inherent human tendency of individual persons to exercise coercive power by wielding the sword in their own interest rather than letting the temporal authority exercise that power: "No Christian shall wield or invoke the sword for himself and his cause," says Luther. "In behalf of another, however, he may and should wield it and invoke it to restrain wickedness and to defend godliness."[32]

Thus, Luther claims that God ordained the secular government with "temporal sword and law," entrusting the prince with punishing the wicked and protecting the upright.[33] The worldly government is then a good work of God for preserving worldly peace. Luther suggests that a wise prince, though he may be a "rare bird," has the duty to maintain the worldly peace and "must have the law as firmly in hand as the sword, and determine in his own mind when and where the law is to be applied strictly or with moderation, so that law may prevail at all times and in all cases, and reason may be the highest law and the master of all administration of law."[34] Recognizing how destructive the misapplication or perversion of retributive justice might be for the people, Luther cautions the prince against pedantic reliance on the "letter of the law" in adjudicating legal cases. According to Luther, there is more to sound justice than what is embedded in the writ-

---

31. Luther's claims about the divine origin of temporal authority will certainly sound odd to contemporary political scientists and legal practitioners who believe that temporal authority derives its legitimacy from the people and the constitution. As a theologian, Luther thinks that temporal authority derives its ultimate legitimacy from divine, i.e., natural law rather than from any human-made law or constitution, i.e., positive law. This is significant because the existence of temporal government precedes any human law. The constitution is developed later to simply confirm and guarantee its divine legitimacy and to make it democratic!

32. Martin Luther, "Temporal Authority: To What Extent It Should Be Obeyed" (1523), in *Luther's Works*, vol. 45, *The Christian in Society II,* ed. Walther I. Brandt and Helmut T. Lehmann (Philadelphia: Muhlenberg Press, 1962), p. 103.

33. Luther, "Temporal Authority," p. 87.

34. Luther, "Temporal Authority," p. 119.

ten law and jurists' opinions. To decide legal matters in a way that pleases God and does justice to the neighbor, Luther admonishes the prince not to neglect love and natural law. He argues, "A good and just decision must not and cannot be pronounced out of books, but must come from a free mind, as though there were no books. Such a free decision is given, however, by love and natural law, with which all reason is filled; out of the books come extravagant and untenable judgments."[35] He thus advises that a "magistrate should stand on his own feet and not rashly give ear to accusations made by flatterers and courtiers. If a magistrate listens to one flatterer here and to another one there, and lets himself be led around by the nose, he will never be a good ruler."[36]

Luther claims that there would ordinarily be no temporal authority if the whole of the world were populated by Christians, but since even genuine Christians themselves are sinners and saints at the same time, Luther insists that the institution of secular authority is necessary in the world to restrain evil and to promote temporal peace through administration of retributive justice. In his 1530 commentary on Psalm 82, Luther argues that earthly peace is essential, for without it, first and foremost, life and property will be jeopardized by crime, violence, and wickedness, and second, children cannot be taught and brought up in the fear and discipline of God. As one with a double mandate to bear the sword and administer the law, the virtue of the political leader is therefore to "guard against violence and force," which "is called peacemaking."[37] The prince is to procure justice for those who fear God and suppress those who are godless.

For Luther, God did not institute the worldly government to maintain public peace and order purely through retributive justice. To read Luther only from this perspective is to misinterpret his entire public theology. Rather, Luther believes that God instituted the temporal government for the prince to also administer distributive justice. Luther argues that political leaders must fear God and love their subjects. In this spirit, they ought to trust God, earnestly praying for wisdom to deal thoughtfully with their needs. Like Christ, they should empty themselves of their power and authority, not just putting on the needs of their subjects, but dealing with them as they would deal with their own needs. Thus, the concern of secular leaders,

35. Luther, "Temporal Authority," p. 128.

36. Martin Luther, *Luther's Works*, vol. 8, *Lectures on Genesis: Chapters 45–50*, ed. Jaroslav Pelikan (St. Louis: Concordia, 1966), p. 212.

37. Martin Luther, "Commentary on Psalm 82," in *Luther's Works*, vol. 13, *Selected Psalms II*, ed. Jaroslav Pelikan (Saint Louis: Concordia, 1968), p. 55.

according to Luther, should not be "how to lord it over them and dominate them, but how to protect and maintain them in peace and *plenty*."[38]
Convinced that political leaders must maintain their people in material
abundance, Luther suggests in his commentary on the fourth petition of
the Lord's Prayer, in his Large Catechism, that it would be appropriate "if
the coat of arms of every upright prince were emblazoned with a loaf of
bread instead of a lion or a wreath of rue, or if a loaf of bread were stamped
on coins."[39] Gary Simpson rightly claims, "Luther tethered power tightly to
distributive justice — the bread loaf — for the common good and especially
for the well-being of the vulnerable. Within this, power was also tied to
retributive justice — the sword. . . . [Thus] the majesty or prestige of the ruler
then is doubly dependent on connecting power and justice."[40] Undoubtedly,
while condemning the economic injustices meted out against the peasants
by their princes and lords, Luther argues that secular leaders have been appointed not to exploit their subjects for their own profit and advantage, but
rather to promote their well-being.[41]

Therefore, for Luther, the commandment against killing proscribes
more than just the physical murdering of a person. If we — including the
prince — have the means to help our needy neighbors, but refuse to do
so, we have killed them. Luther expresses this in his discussion of the Fifth
Commandment:

> This commandment is violated not only when we do evil, but also when
> we have the opportunity to do good to our neighbors and to prevent,
> protect, and save them from suffering bodily harm or injury, but fail to do
> so. If you send a naked person away when you could clothe him, you have
> let him freeze to death. If you see anyone who is suffering from hunger
> and do not feed her, you have let her starve.[42]

---

38. Luther, "Temporal Authority," p. 120. Emphasis added.

39. Martin Luther, "The Large Catechism," in *The Book of Concord: The Confessions of the Evangelical Lutheran Church,* ed. Robert Kolb and Timothy Wengert (Minneapolis: Fortress Press, 2000), p. 450.

40. Gary Simpson, "Retrieving Martin Luther's Critical Public Theology of Political Authority for Global Civil Society Today," in *Theological Practices That Matter,* ed. Karen L. Bloomquist (Minneapolis: Lutheran University Press, 2009), p. 160.

41. Martin Luther, "Admonition to Peace: A Reply to the Twelve Articles of the Peasants in Swabia," in *Luther's Works,* vol. 46, *The Christian in Society III,* ed. Robert C. Schultz and Helmut T. Lehmann (Philadelphia: Fortress Press, 1967), pp. 17-43.

42. Luther, "Large Catechism," p. 412.

In his commentary on Psalm 82, Luther similarly argued that "[t]he second virtue of a prince is to help the poor, the orphans, and the widows to justice, and to further their cause. . . . This virtue includes all the works of righteousness."[43] Such works of righteousness include not only enforcing good laws and customs, but orderly conduct resulting from spontaneous obedience to order by all people.

Luther argues that where good laws are not promulgated and maintained, oppression and exploitation of the poor and the marginalized by the powerful are bound to occur. Expressing firm faith in the power of just laws and godly political leaders to forestall these evils and deliver the commonwealth to the people in the earthly kingdom, Luther admonishes civil leaders to make and enforce just laws, for "if the law were not kept . . . all would have to become beggars together and be ruined and destroyed."[44] He argues that after the gospel or the ministry, there is nothing of greater value in this world "than a ruler who makes and preserves just laws. Such men are rightly called gods. These are the virtues, the profit, the fruits, and the good works that God appointed to this rank in life."[45]

Pursuing a distributive justice theme, Luther also suggests that a prince should transform his entire kingdom into a hospital where curative and preventative medicine would be provided for everyone so that the poor are empowered and others are prevented from retreating into poverty. As Luther accurately expresses,

> See now what a hospital such a prince can build! He needs no stone, no wood, no builders; and he need give neither endowment nor income. To endow hospitals and help poor people is, indeed, a precious good work in itself. But when such a hospital becomes so great that a whole land, and especially the really poor people of that land, enjoy it, then it is a general, true, princely, indeed, a heavenly and divine hospital. For only a few enjoy the first kind of hospital, and sometimes they are false knaves masquerading as beggars. But the second kind of hospital comes to the aid only of the really poor, widows, orphans, travelers, and other forlorn folk. Besides, it preserves rich or poor, his living and his goods for everyone, so that he does not have to become a beggar or a poor man. . . . However, there are many who are not beggars and do not become beggars. For

43. Luther, "Commentary on Psalm 82," p. 53.
44. Luther, "Commentary on Psalm 82," pp. 53-54.
45. Luther, "Commentary on Psalm 82," p. 54.

them the overlord is providing in this hospital. For so to help a man that he does not need to become a beggar is just as much of a good work and a virtue and an alms as to give to a man and to help a man who has already become a beggar.[46]

Luther warns rulers against laziness and the egocentric use of their office driven only by unbridled craving for honor, power, luxury, selfish profit, and pride. Luther claims that God endows political leaders, as partakers of the divine majesty, with immeasurable good works with which to assist God in executing retributive and distributive justice in the earthly city for the gospel to thrive.

Drawing on Psalm 82:1-2, 4 and 6, where civil leaders are described as "gods" and the "children of the Most High" who should rule with justice and equity, Luther reiterates that secular government, by virtue of its divine origin, commands the unimpeachable obedience of all its subjects. But in making this assertion, Luther does not absolutize either the power of the earthly leaders or the duty of loyalty of the people to the government. Secular leaders are accountable to God who "keeps down the rulers, so that they do not abuse his majesty and power according to their own self-will but use them for that peace for which he has appointed and preserves them."[47] As one who rejects political tyranny, Luther argues that God has not placed political leaders over his own congregation (by which he does not mean the church but the worldly kingdom — including the heathen city of Nineveh) to do whatever they please: "Not so! God Himself is there [*to hold them accountable*]. He will judge, punish and correct them; and if they do not obey, they will not escape. 'He stands in His congregation,' for the congregation is also His; and 'judges the gods,' for the rulers, too are His. And because both are His, it is right for Him to take the part of both."[48]

Because they are ultimately accountable to God, Luther warns self-willed secular rulers that they are not rulers over their own personal property, but over God's own congregation which God constantly creates, supports, and protects so that in the fear of God and humility the earthly city may live in peace. God and the congregation are inseparable, for where the congregation is, there is God also. As the stewards of God's own congregation, temporal rulers must fear God and act justly in caring for his

---

46. Luther, "Commentary on Psalm 82," pp. 53-54.
47. Luther, "Commentary on Psalm 82," p. 45.
48. Luther, "Commentary on Psalm 82," pp. 45-46. Emphasis added.

congregation, harkening to his warnings. Thus, Luther argues that secular leaders who tend to misconstrue public criticism as sedition so that they can "do whatever they wish, without hindrance or rebuke, without shame or fear" are subject to scrutiny by the same word of God that establishes the legitimacy of their authority. He chides arrogant princes who resist anyone rebuking their self-will and wickedness that "'God stands in His congregation and judges the gods'; that is, He rebukes them."[49] "Therefore," Luther argues, "they are not to despise [God's Word], for it is their institutor and appointer; but they are to be subject to it and allow themselves to judged, rebuked, made and corrected by it."[50]

Despite God's rule over the earth, in the case of secular law, God's critical engagement with rulers must be done by human beings, and particularly, ministers of the Word. As Simpson claims, "[Luther] was convinced that, while publicity's rebuke comes from God, God does not work immediately, but rather through earthly means. God rebukes 'mediatedly.' In this sense, publicity is the vehicle that instills the fear of the Lord, which is the beginning of wisdom and wise politics."[51] Luther suggests that God "has His appointed priests and preachers [from among the congregation], to whom He has committed the duty of teaching, exhorting, rebuking, comforting, in a word, of preaching the Word of God."[52] If ministers of the Word in their official capacity admonish secular rulers to fear God and keep his commandments, they are not interfering in the political affairs of secular government, but rather rendering service and obedience to the supreme authority, God. This is crucial because the minister of the Word, whose office and authority are independent of the secular government, owes his allegiance to God rather than humans, and thus "is neither a courtier nor a hired hand."[53]

To restrain secular leaders from becoming despots, Luther admonishes the ministers of the Word to publicly and honestly rebuke them, contending that it would be more disastrous to the secular government if ministers of the Word should be silent and permit political tyrants to provoke the masses to violence and lawlessness. Luther implores bishops and preachers who are lackadaisical about rebuking secular rulers to "observe, however, that a preacher by whom God rebukes the gods is to 'stand in the congregation.' He is to 'stand'; that is, he is to be firm and confident and deal uprightly and

49. Luther, "Commentary on Psalm 82," p. 58.
50. Luther, "Commentary on Psalm 82," p. 48.
51. Simpson, "Retrieving Martin Luther's Critical Public Theology," p. 163.
52. Luther, "Commentary on Psalm 82," p. 49.
53. Luther, "Commentary on Psalm 82," p. 51.

honestly with it; and 'in the congregation,' that is, openly and boldly before God and people."[54] However, to rebuke these "gods" is not to "slander or backbite" them. Luther suggests that any minister of the Word unwilling to take the trouble of rebuking secular leaders openly and boldly should either stop speaking behind their backs or go and hang himself (!) to prevent those sins of unfaithfulness and backbiting from destroying the moral fabric of government ordained for the common good.[55]

In effect, for Luther, if church leaders were consistently faithful in rebuking temporal leaders for their structural sins, political oppression might be checked, if not entirely eradicated, and hence there would be durable, just peace. Even if political tyrants do not totally disappear with clergy rebuking them, their political excesses might certainly be contained. Regrettably, church leaders have defaulted on their pastoral obligation of critical political publicity as we can see by the ubiquity of political tyrants around the world today. Therefore, the significance of Luther's public theology for achieving just peace through the church and legal reforms in Nigeria cannot be overemphasized. The Nigerian church will play a crucial role in identifying and implementing pragmatic tactics necessary to unsettle unjust peace.

The Church's Role in Creating Just Peace in Nigeria

Undeniably, the Nigerian Christian church commands one of the largest church memberships in the world, but its role in upsetting unjust peace in the Nigerian society leaves much to be desired. This is partly due to the unwarranted and singular focus of the church with the spiritual aspects of salvation to the detriment of its critical public prophetic role.[56] While Luther recognizes the distinction between the kingdom of God and the kingdom of the world, he is only intending to affirm the institutional and functional separation of the church from the state, not prescribing a double standard that requires Christians to live by faith in the church, while accepting a lawless state.[57] Nor does he mean that the church should restrict its activity entirely to the spiritual sphere, a realm that floats beyond everyday life. Rather, Luther intends that Christians who live by faith in the church should act justly

---

54. Luther, "Commentary on Psalm 82," p. 49.
55. Luther, "Commentary on Psalm 82," p. 50.
56. See Ibrahim Bitrus, "An 'Absence of God' from Public Life? The Disconnect between Faith and Life in the Church in Nigeria," *Word & World* 33, no. 3 (2013): 248-56.
57. Luther, "Temporal Authority," p. 92.

and mercifully in the state. Therefore, Nigerian church leaders need their prophetic imagination to be liberated from the captivity, and to heed Luther's call to go beyond their commission to proclaim the Word to save souls. We are embodied creatures: the soul of humankind can never be salvaged apart from the body.[58] What is required of the Nigerian church now is to publicly rebuke evils committed in high places that impede the liberation of the people from the pervasive subversion of the rule of law perpetrated by Nigerian public officials in all branches and levels of government. Church leaders should speak the truth that will unsettle the powers that inflict oppression and injustice on the Nigerian people. Rather than focusing endlessly on asking church members for money for the church's cause or preaching obsequious messages that appease corrupt leaders' guilty consciences over their massive looting of public wealth, church leaders should preach messages that disturb their guilty consciences unto repentance. It is only when public leaders are rebuked in love and humility to die to sin and be raised to new life by the Word that they will be capable of serving the people rather than themselves.[59]

Disturbing this unjust peace goes beyond open and honest reprimanding of unjust public leaders: it requires the church leadership to employ whatever lawful methods and resources are at their disposal within and outside the church to challenge institutionalized corruption and injustice. First, church leaders must live out the message they preach to the ruling class if they are to succeed in the critical enterprise of establishing just peace in Nigeria. Church leaders who condemn corruption and injustice are obliged by law to not only expose and report clear cases of corrupt practices and financial and economic crimes to anticorruption agencies, but also to reject any illegal monies donated to the church. To this end, the churches should meticulously investigate the source of any huge donations made by their members before they are accepted. Dr. Ahmed Olayinka Sule has suggested this very boldly, stating that

> [s]ince the church is a tax-exempt organisation, it owes the government a responsibility to ensure that anybody who places ill-gotten money through the church system is exposed and reported to the authorities. There have been instances in the past whereby people have stolen funds

58. Luther, "Large Catechism," p. 474.
59. See Ibrahim Bitrus, "The Theology of the Cross: A Stumbling Block to the Neo-Pentecostal Gospel," *TCNN Research Bulletin* 58 (2013): 16-28.

running into tens of millions of Naira and placed these criminal proceeds in the church to fund church capital expenditures. The church should arise and reject these illegal funds. Furthermore, the church should institute anti–money laundering procedures to mitigate and prevent a recurrence of the placement of criminal proceeds in the church.[60]

Church leaders should also reject whatever support a corrupt government gives to the church under the pretext of promoting religious piety. One of these forms of support is the millions of dollars of taxpayer money that governments at all levels spend annually to sponsor privileged church leaders and members to lead pilgrimages to Jerusalem. Though the government does this under the guise of supporting religious piety, it is often intended to "buy" the vote of the church during elections or to silence the critical public voice of church leaders.

An equally important strategy is that church leaders should not only advocate justice for the victims of injustice and corruption, but also push for the prosecution of the perpetrators. Today, some prominent church leaders help corrupt public officials to evade justice, which is unacceptable.[61] Therefore, Nigerian churches must cultivate an uncompromising attitude to corruption and injustice just as they do with other moral issues like polygamy and divorce, for example.[62] The current situation in which Nigerian churches rigidly deal with these moral issues, forbidding them under almost all circumstances, including banning whoever is involved in them from communion, while welcoming to the table those who perpetrate structural evils of corruption and injustice, is unscriptural. Thus, there is an urgent need for the Nigerian churches to rethink whether or not the "sins" of polygamy and divorce are deadlier than systemic corruption and injustice.

Finally, when an unjust and corrupt government refuses to harken to the aforesaid measures and uphold the rule of law and justice, the church

60. Ahmed Olayinka Sule, "An Open Letter to the Nigerian Church" (unpublished letter). Available from: http://www.nigeriavillagesquare.com/articles/an-open-letter-to -the-nigerian-church.html (accessed December 27, 2013).

61. "CBN Governor Sanusi Accuses Pastor Adeboye of Aiding Corrupt Rogue Banker Akingbola to Evade Justice," *Sahara Reporters* (January 12, 2014). Available from: http:// nairaland1.rssing.com/chan-13289095/all_p286.html accessed (January 12, 2014).

62. Cf. Matt. 23:23, RSV, where Jesus said, "Woe to you, scribes and Pharisees, hypocrites! for you tithe mint and dill and cumin, and have neglected the weightier matters of the law, justice and mercy and faith; these you ought to have done, without neglecting the others."

should call for a boycott of all government functions and visibly identify with and participate in peaceful public resistance against the government. As a way to "jam a spoke in the wheel" of the government, they should mobilize their large membership base to embark on public nonviolent mass demonstrations and rallies along with the organizations of civil society.[63] Simpson beautifully describes civil society not only as "God's most creative work" but also as "God's preferential option" for just peacemaking and publicity about justice.[64] Governor Rotimi Amaechi, who believes that such a public outrage against corrupt political leaders is long overdue, claims that the reason they keep looting the government's funds is because Nigerians have never bothered to stone them.[65] Indeed, now is the time for church leaders and civil society organizations to take the destiny of their dear nation in their hands, including pushing for legal reforms.

Disturbing Unjust Peace through Legal Reforms

Since the basic cause of unjust peace in Nigeria is the endemic corrupt practices that undermine the principle of the rule of law enshrined in the Constitution, Nigeria's first need is the president's and governors' strict and meticulous obedience to the rule of law, without which all credible legal reforms are doomed to failure. As Ibraheem Ojo Tajudeen argues, "We can make the best laws but if the implementation is suspect, nothing would come out of it. The provisions of the constitution, if properly implemented, are enough to check our corrupt leaders."[66] In particular, strict and meticulous adherence to the rule of law requires that the principles of equality before the law, respect for human rights, and the separate functions of the arms of government should be enforced according to the law.

63. The phraseology of jamming a spoke in the wheel of government is from Dietrich Bonhoeffer, *A Testament to Freedom: The Essential Writings of Dietrich Bonhoeffer*, ed. Geffrey B. Kelly and F. Burton Nelson (New York: HarperCollins, 1990), p. 132.

64. Gary M. Simpson, *War, Peace and God: Rethinking the Just-War Tradition* (Minneapolis: Augsburg Fortress, 2007), p. 89.

65. Anonimi Villager, "We Steal Because You Never Stoned Us — Amaechi," *Village Square* (December 15, 2013). Available from: http://nigeriavillagesquare.com/forum/main-square/80489-we-steal-because-you-never-stoned-us-amaechi.html (accessed January 10, 2014).

66. Ibraheem Ojo Tajudeen, "Executive Immunity in Nigeria: Putting Off Old Garments," *Journal of Politics and Law* 6, no. 3 (2013): 195. Available from: http://dx.doi.org/10.5539/jpl.v6n3p189 (accessed December 23, 2013).

The Constitution provides for strict enforcement of the rule of law against executives who violate it. According to Section 143 (11) of the 1999 Constitution, the president and vice president are to be impeached if found guilty of "gross misconduct" — a "grave violation or breach of the provisions of this Constitution or a misconduct of such nature as amounts in the opinion of the National Assembly to gross misconduct."[67] To restore just peace in Nigeria, the National Assembly and other legislative arms of the government at all levels should view any obvious act of disrespect to the rule of law by the executives, including deliberate noncompliance with court judgment and abuse of citizens' rights, as gross misconduct and therefore an impeachable offense. In fact, any executive who is guilty of such misconduct should not only be removed but also arrested and tried for treason. This dramatic response is necessary because where political rulers do not maintain just laws that they make to protect the public good, as Luther claims, "the poor, the widows and the orphans are oppressed."[68]

Second, legislators need to eliminate the immunity conferred on executive political leaders as enshrined in the 1999 Constitution. Removing immunity will not just reduce the naked abuse of power and looting of public accounts by political leaders, it will stop them from behaving if as they are above the law while in office, and it will enthrone transparency, justice, equity, and rule of law. This reform will empower anticorruption agencies — the ICPC and the EFCC — to arrest, prosecute, and convict political leaders who engage in corruption and financial crimes while in office. The House of Representatives Ad-hoc Committee on the Review of the 1999 Constitution rightly proposed to remove the immunity clause, but even if it were passed, Nigeria needs a stricter retributive justice system that stipulates punitive penalties for corruption, financial, and economic crimes. The removal of legislative immunity, even if achieved, cannot be effective unless the Nigerian retributive justice system, which deals with corruption, economic, and financial crimes, is also reformed. The existing penalties for such crimes are too lenient and thus out of tune with the magnitude of these crimes in Nigeria. For instance, while the penalties for the various corrupt practices in the section "Offences and Penalties" of the ICPC Act 2000, No. 5, range from one year to not more than seven years' imprisonment, the penalty provided for economic and fi-

---

67. Constitution of the Federal Republic of Nigeria, Chapter VI, Part I, sec. 143 (11) (1999), available from http://www.nigeria-law.org/ConstitutionOfTheFederalRepublicOf Nigeria.htm.

68. Luther, "Commentary on Psalm 82," p. 53.

nancial crimes in Section 18 (2) of the EFCC Establishment Act 2004 is mere "imprisonment for a term not less than two years and not exceeding three years."[69] In Nigeria, where corruption and impunity reign, unless the crimes in question carry a sentence between life imprisonment or capital punishment, the penalties cannot serve as a deterrent to the "would-be" plunderers of the public treasury. Those officials found guilty of these crimes should also forfeit whatever money and property they have plundered from the government purse by law. Legislators must remove the current powers conferred on the Attorney General by Section 174 of the 1999 Constitution to withdraw corruption-related cases from prosecution or to fetter the powers of the anti-corruption agencies if these agencies are to perform their functions with little or no interference from the executive arm of the government.

As a final point, this reform is also bound to fail without an independent and incorruptible judicial system. For the judiciary to be genuinely independent and dispense justice according to law without executive interference, the judicial branch should not be dependent on the executive branch of the government for the human, material, and financial resources it needs to function. This means, first, that the appointment and discipline of superior judicial officers should be conducted by the National Judicial Council subject to the approval of the legislature. Moreover, not only should funds be allocated to the judiciary through the Consolidated Revenue Fund by the legislature, but such funds should be solely under the control of the judiciary.[70] Because the judiciary is a fully-fledged and co-equal arm of government, the salary and other remunerations of judicial officers should not be less than that of their counterparts in other branches of the government. This reform will institutionalize a much-needed vibrant justice system that will not only deliver unhindered retributive justice but also promote unproblematic access to fair judgment and a fair share of the national wealth in Nigeria.

Conclusion

In this essay, I have demonstrated that an unjust peace in Nigeria is "nonviolent" crime that too many Nigerian leaders commit against the people by

69. Establishment Act of the Economic and Financial Crimes Commission, Statute of Nigeria (2004). Available from: http://efccnigeria.org/establishment_act.html (accessed December 26, 2013).

70. See A. Ademola, *Independence of the Judiciary: Problems and Prospects in Nigeria* (Nigeria: The Faculty of Law University of Nigeria, Enugu Campus, 1987), pp. 21-23.

overtly robbing the country's public resources for their personal aggrandizement. I have argued that the rule of law explicitly embedded in the Constitution to safeguard just peace has in many ways been ignored, if not brazenly contravened, by those in authority. If Nigerian lawmakers can take the rule of law seriously in enforcement, repealing the immunity clause and ensuring a truly free and incorruptible judiciary that can impose severe penalties against corruption, economic, and financial crimes in collaboration with anticorruption commissions, they might unsettle the unjust peace in Nigeria. When I argue that the Nigerian church and its leadership should publicly and audaciously denounce, expose, and report institutionalized injustice and corruption to anticorruption commissions and initiate nonviolent public demonstrations with civil society organizations against these structural sins, I am by no means intending to politicize the church. Rather, my proposal will Christianize the church's public existence and make real its obligation as a critical public community of faith that promotes and maintains just peace — an ongoing and eschatological reality — bound up with the triune God.

CHAPTER 15

How Should Modern Lutherans
Try to Shape Secular Law?

Robert Benne

Our Checkered History — The Fruit Has Not Always Been Great

Lutheranism has had a bad reputation when it comes to its public role in
shaping just secular law. A good deal of this negative assessment has to do
with Ernst Troeltsch's verdict on Lutheranism in his magisterial *The Social
Teachings of the Christian Church.* After a very lengthy analysis of Lutheranism, he makes the following points: "The yielding spirit of its wholly interior
spirituality adapted itself to the dominant authority of the day. This passivity
involved the habit of falling back on whatever power happens to be dominant
at the time." From the very beginning, according to Troeltsch, Lutheranism
has, unlike Calvinism and Catholicism, lacked a "capacity to penetrate the
political, legal, and economic movements of Western nations. . . . Its tendency is to alleviate but not re-create."[1] With regard to shaping law, Troeltsch
argues, it has been pervasively quietistic.

Unfortunately, H. Richard Niebuhr, the great Yale professor, fatefully
and fully imbibed Troeltsch's teaching. Though he gets much about Lutheranism right in his account in *Christ and Culture,* he follows Troeltsch
in his assessment of Lutheranism's relation to the public square.[2] He sees
Lutheranism as essentiality dualist, tempted toward both antinomianism in
personal ethics and quietism in social and political ethics.[3] For Niebuhr, Lutheranism's profound grasp of the wonder and transcendence of God's grace

---

1. Ernst Troeltsch, *The Social Teachings of the Christian Churches* (New York: Harper
Torchbooks, 1960), pp. 574-75.

2. I will use "public square" to denote "shaping of secular law" at times.

3. H. Richard Niebuhr, *Christ and Culture* (New York: Harper & Row, 1951), pp. 186-89.

in Christ makes its theological ethics indifferent to the relative distinctions that are so important in earthly life, especially to the political task of shaping law. So it adapts to whatever is, preferring order over the chaos that might accompany constructive change.

Richard Niebuhr's more politically active brother, Reinhold, followed both Troeltsch and his brother in their assessment.

> By thus transposing an "inner ethic of spontaneous love" into a private one, and making the "outer" or "earthly" ethic authoritative for government, Luther achieves a curiously perverse social morality. He places a perfectionist private ethic in juxtaposition to a realistic, not to say, cynical, official ethic. . . . This has led to an absolute distinction between the "heavenly" or "spiritual" kingdom and the "earthly" one, which destroys the tension between the final demands of God upon the conscience, and all the relative possibilities of realizing the good in history.[4]

Reinhold Niebuhr did later allow that there may be exceptions to this dismal analysis. In a footnote in volume 2 of his *Nature and Destiny of Man* he says that this pervasive Lutheran quietism may have a possible exception in the Scandinavian countries with their "impressive development of constitutional democracy." But, he says, he has not found any authoritative analysis of how this development happened in countries where the Lutheran religion was dominant.[5]

As a young, self-consciously Lutheran graduate student at the University of Chicago Divinity School, I decided that I would provide Niebuhr with that authoritative analysis by doing my dissertation on the Scandinavian Lutheran contribution to their democracies and their welfare states. However, the wind was taken out of my sails when I consulted a number of Swedish theologians. It seems that the Lutheran Church fought those democratic advancements tooth and nail. Secular socialism was the real source. So I had to find another topic for my dissertation.

In spite of the efforts of American Lutheran scholars such as George Forell and William Lazareth to show that Lutheranism need not be quietistic and dualistic, the Troeltschian/Niebuhrian analysis has continuing influence. Lutheran political and legal ethics are reactive, not constructive.

---

4. Reinhold Niebuhr, *The Nature and Destiny of Man*, vol. 2 (New York: Charles Scribner's Sons, 1949), pp. 194-95.

5. Reinhold Niebuhr, *Nature and Destiny*, 2:278.

Moreover, Lutheranism's historical record seemed to bear witness to its bad rap. Luther and his cohorts carried out a Reformation of the church without touching the medieval trappings of an authoritarian society. When the authority of the prince was challenged by the peasants, he called for their total annihilation. Sadly, during the American Civil War, Lutherans split according to the governments they lived under. Northern and Southern Lutherans didn't reunite until 1918. But, even more disturbing, Lutheranism remained quiescent — except for a few heroic souls in the Confessing Church — amidst the rise of Nazism and its perverse legal regime in Germany.[6] Lutherans also reflected this quietism in the face of authoritarian and unjust governments and their laws in Soviet satellite countries, Chile, and South Africa.

Given this record, perhaps we should just junk the whole theological apparatus that has led to such abysmal historical results. The Americanist Lutherans led by Samuel Simon Schmucker did just that amid the Second Great Awakening of the first half of the nineteenth century. Schmucker explicitly denied a number of Lutheran distinctives — including the two kingdoms doctrine — in his headlong commitment to the evangelical effort to "Christianize" the new republic.[7] Fueled by post-millennial expectations, Schmucker jettisoned the quietism of traditional Lutheranism for an activist involvement in evangelical revivals and voluntary societies.[8] The Americanist movement in Lutheranism was a robust attempt to build the kingdom of God in America, much like that of the Puritans in the First Great Awakening. It aimed at many legal changes, including the banning of slavery, alcohol consumption, and Sabbath-breaking. The cost for this participation was giving up some Lutheran distinctives that were deemed not only nonessential but unbiblical. (Schmucker's battle cry, by the way, was *sola scriptura!*) Schmucker's enthusiastic move to evangelicalism was magnified by

6. My colleague Paul Hinlicky has recently published a book on Lutheran theologians' response to the rise of Nazism; *Before Auschwitz — What Christian Theology Must Learn from the Rise of Nazism* (Eugene, OR: Cascade, 2013). He points out that several major Lutheran theologians — Werner Elert and Paul Althaus — were so enthused about Hitler early in the 1930s that they theologically legitimated him as a leader of near-messianic qualities. They overcame Lutheran quietism in precisely the wrong way.

7. Sydney Ahlstrom, *A Religious History of the American People* (New Haven: Yale University Press, 1972), pp. 520-26.

8. One of the most important voluntary societies was the Christian college. Three classmates — David Bittle, Theopholis Storck, and Ezra Keller — who attended Schmucker's Gettysburg Lutheran seminary went on to found Roanoke College, Newberry College, and Wittenberg College as instruments of this "Christianization" of America. See William Eisenberg, *The First Hundred Years: Roanoke College* (Strasburg: Shenandoah, 1942).

his worry that newly arrived Lutherans — especially those of the Lutheran Church–Missouri Synod (LCMS) — would retreat into rigidly confessional, "sectarian," ethnic enclaves and diminish the Lutheran contribution to the exciting evangelical project of providing virtuous citizens and laws for the new republic.

Less dramatically, we could relinquish the traditional Lutheran reticence about intervening in the public square by joining the liberal Protestant activism that has been so pronounced in America since the 1960s, an activism that connects with the earlier Second Great Awakening through the Social Gospel.[9] This has been the option chosen by the Evangelical Lutheran Church in America (ELCA). Here the assumption seems to be that church officials have a peculiarly accurate reading of what God is doing in history and therefore can prescribe exactly what public policies will be consistent with God's action and therefore should be supported by the church. They take positions on many, many policies. They seem to believe there is a straight line from the ethic of the gospel to specific policies and laws, and, by unerring discernment, they have perceived and followed that straight line. Oddly enough, the agenda dictated by the gospel generally leads to the liberal agenda of constant expansion of the welfare and regulatory state. To be fair, straight-line thinking can also be evidenced in support for rightwing Republican policies by some evangelical and fundamentalist churches that lead to opposite policies, but there seem to be no Lutheran churches among them.

So, I ask, has our history shown only negative results from our adherence to Lutheran theological ethics? Are our choices traditional Lutheran quietism or Americanist/liberal Protestant activism? Happily, the record indicates better options. Indeed, the condemnation heaped upon Lutheranism by the Troeltsch/Niebuhr analysis has been sharply revised by John Witte, a Reformed scholar trained in both theology and law. He has written a marvelous book titled *Law and Protestantism* in which he argues that early Lutheranism was a species of "constructive Protestantism." It built a Lutheran version of Christendom. After the volcanic first years of the Reformation, Lutheran theologians had to cooperate with Lutheran secular authorities, especially jurists, to rebuild a new society out of the chaos of the old. Lu-

---

9. A foreshadowing of this move toward liberal Protestantism emerged in the Augustana Synod in the teaching and writing of A. D. Mattson, who was a strong devotee of the Social Gospel movement in America. His teaching career at Augustana Seminary from the 1930s to the 1960s influenced many students toward both liberal theology and ethics.

theran theologians, employing the two kingdoms doctrine, worked hand-in-hand with secular agents to reform law, politics, and society. (Fatefully, I might add, the Lutherans gave over to the princes the care and control of the churches, which led in time to passive state churches.)

Witte does a careful analysis of how Melanchthon worked with the great Lutheran jurists, Eisermann and Oldendorp, to shape a Lutheran society. They all began their work "with a basic understanding of Luther's two-kingdoms framework. While Luther tended to emphasize the distinctions between the two kingdoms, Lutheran jurists tended to emphasize their co-operation."[10] For example, Witte argues that Melanchthon and the jurists tended more than Luther to view the Bible as an essential source of earthly law and to apply the three uses of the law to the governance of the earthly kingdom. In short, they built bridges between the two kingdoms.[11] Witte concludes the book with the bold claim that "a good deal of our modern Western law of marriage, education, and social welfare, for example, still bears the unmistakable marks of Lutheran Reformation theology."[12]

Even though we might delight in Witte's revised history — as I emphatically do — we still must seek modern examples of how Lutheran churches might properly relate to the public sphere and its laws. After all, it wasn't long before the sixteenth-century Lutheran synthesis of Christ and culture broke down and the Lutheran Church necessarily had to seek a new role in a changed society. The Lutheran Church soon found itself as one voice among many, and soon more or less passively adapted to the status quo.

Moreover, neither the Americanist Lutheran approach of Schmucker nor the liberal Protestant approach of the ELCA has much persuasive power, partly because both have sloughed off Lutheran distinctives. I would propose, though, that we have two contemporary models that do better. One emerged in the public witness of the Lutheran Church in America (LCA) from the mid-1960s to the mid-1980s. A postwar generation of young theologians had gone off to Union Seminary in New York

10. John Witte Jr., *Law and Protestantism: The Legal Teachings of the Lutheran Reformation* (Cambridge: Cambridge University Press, 2002), p. 168.

11. Witte, *Law and Protestantism*, p. 170, shows how Melanchthon applied the three uses of the law to criminal law and punishment; the civil use corresponded with deterrence; the theological use with retribution; and the educational use with rehabilitation.

12. Witte, *Law and Protestantism*, p. 295. Witte followed that book up with the marvelous *From Sacrament to Contract — Marriage, Religion and Law in the Western Tradition* (Louisville: Westminster John Knox, 2012), where he traces how the Christian vision of marriage became embedded in the laws of almost all Western countries.

to study with Reinhold Niebuhr. Chastened by the Niebuhrian criticism of Lutheranism but yet maintaining their commitment to Lutheran theological ethics, theologians such as George Forell, William Lazareth, and Richard Niebanck proceeded to guide the formation of a number of important social statements. They employed a more dynamic interpretation of the Lutheran two kingdoms doctrine with impressive results, including important statements on church and state as well as on nuclear deterrence, which stood against the pacifist-tinged witness of both liberal Protestantism and the Catholic bishops.[13] The LCA also maintained an office in Washington that carried on a bona fide ministry to political actors. By honoring the lay vocation of politicians as well as the social statements of the church, the office had both pastoral and prophetic dimensions. That office did very little direct advocacy work. No doubt the ELCA Division of Church and Society and the LCA offered too many statements on too many issues, but nevertheless, it provides a positive model for Lutheran witness in the public sphere. That was soon replaced with a highly politicized approach to public advocacy that simply imitated that of the liberal Protestant churches. Instead of a ministry to those in the public sphere, the ELCA became a center of advocacy for liberal causes.

The other positive example I might mention is that of the Lutheran Church–Missouri Synod. In recent years its Commission on Theology and Church Relations has developed excellent reports and opinions on a number of important issues of a church and society nature, particularly those having to do with abortion and religious freedom. The reports are directed internally for the edification of pastors and laypeople from a clear Lutheran theological perspective. It has not engaged in frequent direct advocacy. When it has engaged in public witness, however, it has been strong and forceful, especially on issues of religious freedom and respect for nascent life. It has successfully gone all the way to the Supreme Court in the *Hosanna-Tabor* case, protecting its right freely to appoint and dismiss teachers in its school system. The LCMS has even organized its own voluntary association — Life Ministries — to engage in pro-life advocacy.

13. The rather admirable history of LCA public witness, especially the composition of social statements, is told in *Politics and Policy* (Minneapolis: Fortress Press, 1989), by Christa Klein and Christian von Dehsen. The American Lutheran Church had a similar history, though less developed theologically than the LCA. See Charles P. Lutz, *Public Voice: Social Policy Development in the American Lutheran Church, 1960-1987* (Minneapolis: American Lutheran Church, 1987).

On What Theological Basis Might We Move Forward?

On what solid theological basis might we go forward, we who seek to maintain a genuinely Lutheran approach to involvement in the public square, including the shaping of its laws?[14] What might we learn from these genuine public witnesses by our churches? We perhaps have again an opportunity to offer a genuinely Lutheran view of the gospel's relation to the public sphere.[15] In the following I want to articulate such a view.

We aim to operate from a distinctively Lutheran theological ethics, with the full realization that we are part of a much larger Christian witness. This means that we believe that the Lutheran teaching about the two ways God reigns in the world is of continuing truth and relevance. We want to maintain a sharp distinction between what God does in Christ with his right hand for our salvation — in which we are wholly receptive — and what humans can do in cooperation with his left hand in the historical realm. Such a distinction protects the radicality, transcendence, and universality of the gospel from all efforts to reduce it to human work or to submit it to human divisions. (It also helps to define and protect the central mission of the church — the proclamation of the gospel, not the transformation of society.) That distinction preserves Lutheran theological ethics from religionizing politics or from politicizing religion, faults that have had horrific effects in human history. Only the God-man saves, not the man-god.[16] The man-gods of both

14. The "we" I am talking about is the common witness of the Lutheran Church–Missouri Synod and the North American Lutheran Church (NALC). Of course what I am suggesting is simply that — a suggestion from one Lutheran theological ethicist. It has no official standing.

15. In a remarkable article titled "The Lutheran Difference," *First Things* (February 1992): 31-40, Mark Noll calls for Lutherans to make a badly needed contribution to American thinking and acting with regard to religion and politics. Such a contribution would mitigate the heavily Reformed perspective — now secularized — that dominates American attitudes as it applies personal transformation (sanctification) too easily to the public/political sphere. Alas, he says, Lutherans have generally failed in this important task. I wrote my book, *The Paradoxical Vision — A Public Theology for the Twenty-First Century* (Minneapolis: Fortress Press, 1995), in response to Noll's challenge, but that book has not altered the theological landscape.

16. After the bloodiest of centuries (the twentieth), we tend to think we are free of ideologies with the capacity to claim redemptive power. My nomination for such a contemporary ideology is militant environmentalism, with its tendency to shut down debate and enlist the enormous coercive powers of the state to dominate economic, social, and political life to realize its vision.

Nazism and Communism, both of which promised heaven on earth, made the twentieth century a chamber of horrors.

Further, we agree that what happens in the earthly realm is not autonomous, neither ontologically nor epistemologically. God is sovereign in history. In spite of the Fall, he has not abandoned his world. The left-hand kingdom is under the reign of God's Law, and politics and law are beholden to that standard. Moreover, the two ways of God's reign are not sealed off from each other. They are not on two parallel tracks that do not interact. Rather, they intersect in Christian vocation and witness. Further, the work of the Law is not only negative — a dike to sin — but also positive in working toward a more just and wholesome society.

We further believe that politics is not beholden only to reason and natural law, but also to critique from the gospel in its larger sense, the whole Trinitarian faith. The biblical revelation of God as Father, Son, and Holy Spirit — and the reflection on that revelation for several millennia — has built a Christian intellectual and moral tradition that comes into play as we engage the public sphere, including its laws.[17]

Such a perspective demands that the church — and its individual members — participate critically in the political sphere and its formation of law. Informed critical participation will enable Lutherans to make the relative distinctions that are so important in human history, neither accommodating fully to the politics and legal order of the day, nor rejecting them as completely given over to coercion and violence, as the neo-sectarians so popular today have it.[18] Further, we hold the solid Lutheran conviction running through the two kingdoms doctrine that humans will never be able to construct the kingdom of God on earth. The persistence of Satan's work in history — and the human sin that enables it — will prevent any full realization in this aeon. Lutheran thinking is realistic, thoroughly non-utopian. Rather, we look for small steps forward and hope there will not be big steps

17. In Christian higher education it has become evident how important it is to employ the Christian intellectual and moral tradition in engaging the claims of the various secular fields. If a college relies only on reason and experience to engage secular claims, little engagement takes place. Secular claims go on, unchallenged by Christian claims. This is a formula for the secularization of schools, which has pervasively affected ELCA colleges since they have proudly claimed themselves to be "First Article" colleges.

18. One of the major challenges to Christian witness in political and legal affairs is the neo-sectarian agenda of Stanley Hauerwas and his followers, who in principle seem unable to participate in shaping the laws of a society, since laws by definition involve coercion and the threat of violence to enforce them.

backward. As Lutherans take their vocation as citizens seriously, they will become leaven and salt in that quest for those small steps. We are not to lose hope.

We are committed to a theologically grounded preference for indirect modes of affecting the public sphere. We believe in Christian vocation. All Christians are called to be citizens, some even to become politicians, judges, and legal philosophers. The church is called to proclaim the gospel and form its participants in the moral and intellectual capacities that will enable them to participate critically and energetically in the public sphere. The church is not primarily a political actor. When churches take on that role, they tend to push to the margins their main mission as proclaimers of the gospel. We have seen the damage that such displacement can do when we look at the leadership of the mainline Protestant denominations. Few engage in serious evangelism at home and abroad. Many find political involvement more exciting than their religious task. Evidence abounds in the shrinkage of church membership at home and the diminishing numbers of evangelists abroad.

However, Christian citizens *are* public actors in their role as citizens and as members of voluntary associations, some of which are cause-oriented. Voluntary organizations can be more focused and vigorous in their promotion of, for example, the pro-life cause than a church can be. Further, the associations do not claim to be the church, which avoids the temptation to fuse the church's message with a secular agenda.

On the individual level, one serious Christian legal philosopher or judge is worth far more than ten thousand church social statements. Christian discipleship in the political and legal spheres can be a powerful thing. One would hope that, in his providence, God would raise up influential legal philosophers who would supply a more fulsome base in the natural law tradition for positive law than has been regnant in recent decades.

When the church is really the church, it cooperates with the Spirit in forming the hearts and minds of its members in profound ways. They then shape the guidance system of the society — its culture — which in turn affects public life. Many historical studies have shown the profound effect that the Christian mission in the West has had on its laws, institutions, culture, and politics.[19]

19. For example, Glenn Tinder has shown how core Christian convictions about the worth of each individual as created in the image of God have influenced Western politics; see *The Political Meaning of Christianity* (Baton Rouge: Louisiana State Press, 1989). Right now, Christian values seem to be both in decline and increasingly unwelcomed in a public sphere dominated by a secular progressive elite. But American religion is a brawling and

We might take a further step. Both churches — the LCMS and the North American Lutheran Church (NALC) — have excellent reports and advisements that will edify their members if they read them and internalize them.[20] As mentioned earlier, the LCMS has fine statements on church and state, religious freedom, and on biomedical issues. The NALC, much younger, has "letters of counsel" on the protection of nascent life and Christian concern for the poor. Laity do need instruction, and churches should provide that with regard to issues in society that need addressing from a Christian point of view. Both churches can provide that.

Yet, we believe that the church must speak at crucial times. While we rely mostly on indirect modes of bearing public witness, there are times when the church as church must speak. The church is entrusted with the Word of God — both law and gospel — and one of the important callings of the church is to hold the laws and policies of the state accountable to the Law of God, both negatively and positively. Individual witness alone is not sufficient.

Negatively, when the policies or laws of the state clearly violate the core moral and religious convictions of the faith, the church must say "no," and, if necessary, refuse to obey such laws. In extreme cases, which we hope and pray will be rare, the church calls for *status confessionis* for its members, i.e., they cannot remain Christians and follow those laws. They directly violate what is essential in church teaching. The church resists and calls upon its members to do the same.

We have some excellent historical examples of such a "no." When the Nazi Quisling state in Norway demanded that pastors read Nazi proclamations from their pulpits, Bishop Bergrav called upon them to disobey, which they did.[21] Currently, we have examples of church resistance to some of the

---

vigorous affair, and has often provided the occasion for national awakenings. Such unlikely happenings are not beyond belief, given the cultural confusion and unraveling that are on the increase.

20. The North American Lutheran Church was formed in 2010 in Columbus, Ohio. It broke from the Evangelical Lutheran Church in America after the ELCA voted to allow gay and lesbian unions to be blessed and gays and lesbians in such unions to become ordained pastors and bishops. Though those votes were the occasion for separation, they are viewed by the NALC as symptomatic of a larger disagreement about the authority of the Bible and the Lutheran Confessions. The NALC has around 450 congregations and is forging its approach to public witness. The set of commendations in this essay are contributions to how that approach will take shape.

21. Unfortunately, we have many examples in which the church should have said "no" but didn't. Again, from the Nazi time: when the Nazis first came to power in 1933, they legislated the Aryan Paragraph, which dismissed non-Aryans from participation in public

provisions of the Affordable Care Act, which require that institutions of the church provide contraceptive and abortion services in their insurance plans. There may be many more similar cases in the future in which the church simply has to say "no" and disobey. It is possible that some nation-states will require churches to marry gays and lesbians, as is already happening in the Scandinavian countries. Then it will be time for the church to withdraw as an agent of the state so far as enacting marriage goes and let the state carry out its legal actions while the church carries out its religious responsibilities.

How is the church to speak positively? One of the best ways to speak positively is to *call attention publicly* to serious problems of justice in society. As a start, the church should speak prophetically about the needs of the poor and working poor members of our society. For example, it is clear that certain segments of the population — the working poor, for example — do not have adequate access to affordable health insurance. Our churches must be more restrained in the number and kind of policies we recommend. There are few straight lines from core to public policy. In addition, there is a constellation of Christian convictions that move in relatively straight lines toward policy for which we should advocate. These convictions compel us in a general direction, though they don't dictate specific policies.

First, we should support policies and court decisions that protect the exercise of religious freedom, including the freedom to express our religiously based moral values in our church-related institutions. (The LCMS has been a staunch defender of religious freedom for many years, partly in remembrance of the threat of governmental pressure to become a Union church in Germany, as well as its remembrance of nativist pressure to close private schools in this country in the early twentieth century.) The challenges to the free exercise of religion may be the most threatening we will have to face in the future.

A second core conviction that moves in a relatively straight line toward public policy is support for those laws that protect life at its beginning and end. There seems nothing more morally clear than the need to protect the intrinsic dignity of every human life, including those yet unborn, and those at a vulnerable end. The American temptation toward an unreflective utilitarianism will present an increasing threat to this Christian value. With re-

---

institutions, including the church. Even Jews who had converted to Christianity generations ago were dismissed. Bonhoeffer immediately protested this, partly because it affected his brother-in-law, who was a Lutheran pastor. The Confessional Church finally said "no" to this policy, but the larger church never did, to its everlasting shame. See Hinlicky, *Before Auschwitz*, p. 72.

gard to this challenge, alliances with the Roman Catholic Church will be utterly necessary. Its natural law teachings will be a moral bulwark before the looming juggernaut.

The third is support for traditional marriage and the natural family. Throughout the ages, Christians have seen the one-flesh union of man and woman within the permanent covenant of marriage — and the family that naturally ensues from that union — as the building block of both church and society. They have embedded that vision in the laws of all Western countries, as Witte has so convincingly shown. These laws are now being thinned out by a secular contractual view of marriage. We are now living with the disastrous results of such social experimentation. Marriage and family life have fallen into disarray, especially among the poor and working classes. It is for the good of society that we press for laws that again honor and protect marriage and the natural family.

This approach is particular relevant to the poor and working poor members of our society. For example, we have thousands of young children born into squalor and poverty in this country. They cannot be held morally accountable for their status in life; we as fellow citizens owe them a decent chance at life. Another: we have millions of undocumented people — especially those born in America — who have contributed much to our society but yet are legally vulnerable in many ways.

In these cases I do not think the church has any special gift for crafting legislation or for discerning which legislation is best and therefore worthy of the church's support. It is best to call attention to the problem and call for government or citizen action. But crafting legislation is probably best left up to the laity who are called into political life as citizens, legal advisors, and politicians.

Nevertheless, we have to make up our minds as citizens. We know, however, that making up our minds about specific public policies is a complex process. The movement from core moral principles to a specific public policy — and to the laws it enacts — involves a number of steps: how core moral convictions are expressed in more concrete principles, how they engage new challenges, how they relate to our considered political philosophies, how we read the empirical situation, how we assess incentives and disincentives, how we foresee unintended consequences, how our own social location affects us, how legislation may be compromised in the political process, etc. Yet we make our judgments. We "sin boldly," knowing full well that other Christians may reach different conclusions.

The church may have to sin boldly, but not too often. The church as church is wise not to opt for too many specific public policies in light of the complexity of the process. Christians of good will and intelligence take different paths to public policy with every step in the process. There are few obviously "Christian" policies and/or laws, though my email box is almost daily the recipient of exhortations by the ELCA Washington Office to support a plethora of policies, including the expansion of the EPA rules, measures to impede global climate change, the Farm Bill, pressure on Israel, and to resist any cuts in the current food stamp program as well as any attempt to defend the Defense of Marriage Act. Most of the policies the ELCA wants me to support are those with which I disagree. Such unreflective activism leads people to ask whether the movement from core to policy is more a product of the political bias of church bureaucrats than of careful Christian argument. This liberal Protestant activism has led to the depletion of whatever moral capital those churches and their ecumenical organizations had. The politicization of their main ecumenical agency, the National Council of Churches, has made it a shadow of its former self; witness its move from a magnificent Riverside Drive building in New York City to a modest set of rooms in Washington.

Where Do We Go from Here?

I believe we are at a historic moment when we Lutherans can demonstrate how public witness should really be done. My dream is that both churches continue to develop their reports and advisements as theological rationales for public witness. They can be used both internally and externally. Our leaders can be given room to speak publicly on the basis of those theological rationales. The NALC can participate in the programs of Life Ministries. Our legal counsels can be alert for threats to religious liberty. Perhaps in time a joint office can be opened in Washington to offer a genuine pastoral ministry to Lutheran government personnel and elected and appointed officials, one that can offer both comfort to the afflicted and affliction to the comfortable. An authentic Lutheran voice of public witness needs to be heard.

Table of Cases

Index of Names and Subjects

Lutheran Church in America (LCA), 332-33; Lutheran Church in Germany, 262; Lutheran Church–Missouri Synod (LC-MS), 331, 333; military chaplaincy and, 270, 274-84; Henry Melchior Muhlenberg and American Lutheran church, 44-45; in Nigeria, 306, 321-24, 327; ordering of scripture and tradition by, 11-12; People's Church of Norway, 263; "religion" vs., 41-42; in Rwanda, 292, 296, 298, 301-4; secular worldview and, 51; Swedish Evangelical Lutheran Church, 262; Charles Taylor on, 32n.11; unresolved Lutheran questions about, 38; Roger Williams's "Wall of Separation" metaphor and, 43

Church, political and public role of: American Lutheran Church (ALC) Social Statement, "Church-State Relations in the USA," 59, 59n.118; Robert Benne's view of political participation by, 334-40; as a community of moral deliberation, 303; critical participation in public life by, 58, 335; critical political publicity of, 321; as critical public community of faith, 327; errors about relation of God, secular law, and, 210-20; Gregory VII's opposition to secular appointments of bishops, 34; hospitality to strangers and immigration for, 182-84, 199; human trafficking, responsibilities of, 148-49, 179; Martin Luther King Jr. on public role of, 72; liberal Protestant church and Social Gospel movement, 331; Luther on government and God-human relationship for, 34, 36; Luther's criticism of public role of, 36; Luther's *Temporal Authority: To What Extent It Should Be Obeyed* and, 36-37; Luther's two-kingdoms theory and, 166; modern state and, 39; political participation of Americanist Lutheran church, 330-31; political participation

of, brackets around, 57; post-Reformation Protestant jurisdictions of, 35, 37; relation to state of, 30-31, 31n.10, 32, 206; tension for politically engaged Christians within, 168; Vatican II "Declaration on Religious Freedom" and, 58

Citizens and citizenship, 4; American, 59; Christian responsibility as, 149, 271; conscientious objection of, 273; equal, 64; groups, role of, 134; immigration and, 173, 182, 183, 185, 187, 188, 189, 190, 192, 193, 194, 196, 197, 201, 271; Luther's view of, 134, 148, 167, 169; path to citizenship, 197, 198, 199, 201; and race, 72

Civil society: church-state relations, 39, 44; as community of moral deliberation, 26, 303, 324, 237; Nordic countries, 263, 265; in Rwanda, 287, 289, 290, 291, 300, 302, 314, 324; third use of law for, 211, 220, 221; trafficking and, 163

Climate change: economic impact of, 125; equity under, 136n.140; harm from, 105, 137, 138; political lobbying and, 340; water policy and law for, 116, 124, 126, 127, 128, 129, 131, 132

Colorado, state of: membership in Colorado River Compact, 117; membership in Rio Grande Compact, 119n.70; in Southwestern U.S., 104; *State of Texas v. State of New Mexico and State of Colorado*, 118-19; State-wide Water Resources Initiative, 134; water transfers from 1988 to 2009, 129n.114

Colorado River: *Arizona v. California* and, 102, 129n.11; Central Arizona Project and, 122, 123, 129; Colorado River Basin Water Supply and Demand Study, 124, 129, 132, 134; Colorado River Compact, 105, 117, 131; Colorado River Governance Initiative, 131, 132; water delivery from, 124n.86, 125

in, 230; as *finitum capax infiniti*, 3, 82, 108; First Commandment of, 230n.21; fitting human response to the law of, 221; forgiveness of, 226; Fourth Commandment of, 217; gift of faith in, 13, 34, 46, 111; grace of, 12, 13, 108, 138; Douglas John Hall's view of, 276; heaven-earth dualism and, 12n.17; Hosea 4 on knowledge of, 107; identification with creation by, 84; as jealous, 79; Jesus as God-man, 81, 334; law of, 12, 13, 15, 37, 74, 110, 206-7, 216, 220, 337; "masks of," 85, 101, 108, 108n.26, 109, 202; natural or created grace of, 108, 138; nature of, 222; as ordering universe through law and gospel, 9n.1, 12; power of, 31; preferred human future of, 216, 220; presence of, 85, 95; presence of as warning and promise, 81; promise of, 13; reign of, 12; relation to creation of, 106, 106n.13, 106n.14, 149; salvation by, 90, 217; saving activity of, 13; spiritual governance by, 29; story of, 14, 24, 27; talk about, 29-30; twofold rule of, 12, 29, 30, 34, 36, 39, 41, 50, 57, 186; voice of, 220; will of, 94, 221; Word of (God's word), 11, 12, 13, 14, 36, 36n.25, 36n.28, 57, 90, 91, 100, 200n.49, 214, 219, 220, 221, 320, 337; works of, 34, 57, 67, 105, 221; world infused with, 80-83, 93

God and humanity: agency, human and divine, 100; community participation and God's law at work, 220; God's gift of reason to humanity, 221; human nature and God, 40n.41, 100; human obedience to God, 37; human participation in history and kingdom of God, 335; human responsibilities and God, 91, 94; human theonomous self and God, 81n.5, 99-101; image of God in humans, 13, 29, 31, 32n.11, 34, 58, 67, 79, 85, 91, 95, 99-101, 105-7, 109, 149, 213, 220; justification and human law, 13; Martin Luther King

Jr.'s view of humanity's relation to God, 72-75; LCA statement, *Religious Liberty in the United States,* on relation of humanity and God, 280; Lutheran view of humanity's relation to God, 80, 82-85, 101, 149; Paul Tillich's view of secular worldview of God-human relationship, 57; work of God in the world, human discernment of, 213-14, 219-20

God and the secular worldview, 51-52; First Amendment and, 51-52; secular jurisprudence assumptions about God-human relationship, 51; Supreme Court and the secular worldview, 48-52; U.S. Constitution and God-human relationship, 47-48

Gospel, 29, 36, 38, 38n.34, 166, 167, 183, 184n.4, 187n.11, 190, 208, 221, 251, 271, 276, 283, 336; law-gospel distinction, 9, 12, 12n.14, 13, 337; in LCA Statement, *Religious Liberty in the United States,* 280; Luther's views on, 90, 145, 170, 224n.3, 318, 319; and the public sphere, 306, 331, 334, 335; Romans 13 and, 271

Government, 16; ALC *Declaration on Religious Freedom* on, 59; and bureaucracy, 221; church, Reformation-era Protestant relation to, 35; church, relation to, 31, 36, 41n.48, 42, 44, 47; civil, 12; citizens' rights and, 210; civic participation and, 302; of colonial America, 44, 48; constitutional originalism and powers of American, 21; contemporary religion and, 48-49; corruption in, 175; in *Dandridge v. Williams,* 210; Danish church-state relations, 260-62; Danish Evangelical Lutheran Church, rule of, 247, 256; democratic self-rule and, 16, 18, 21, 42; *Dignitatis humanae* on, 58; in early modern Europe, 35; and East African poverty, 300; federal, 18, 52, 117, 118, 120, 130n.118, 158; First Amendment and, 46, 51, 266n.1; and

quoted, 204; recent discussion of "daily bread" metaphor in, 109n.30

Love: Augustine on, 39; of Christ, 302; of Christians, 302; Paul VI on love of God, 58-59

Love, and its civic forms, 301, 304; civic participation and, 301, 302, 304; and civic participation of Rwandans, 303; and political authority, 302n.39

Love, and the Christian church, 221; commandment to, 31, 169, 182, 185, 198, 302; and right to freedom of association, 301

Love, in Luther's thought: faith active in love, 169; for God and others, 214-15; God's love, 167, 215; justice as experience of God's love in secular realm, 167; justification frees one to love neighbor, 167; Lutheran Immigration and Refugee Service (LIRS) principles for immigration reform and love of neighbor, 197, 199; Peter Meilaender on prioritized love of fellow citizens and strangers, 187, 189; on neighbor-love, 91-92, 101, 148, 168-70, 181, 182-83, 185, 271; Reinhold Niebuhr's critique of Luther on love, 329; by princes and secular authorities, 316; priorities of love for neighbor, 192; rebuke of public leaders' sin, and love, 322; of strangers and immigrants, 186, 187n.11, 198, 202; Ten Commandments and, 110, 217-18; theology of the cross and love, 276; and well-being of all creatures, 167; and work of military chaplains, 271

Love of enemies, 170n.21; in Danish church documents, 250; in Exodus 20:4, 79; and human respect, 75; Jesus', 225; Martin Luther King Jr. on, 72, 75; King on justice and, 75

Loyalty: African American paradoxical posture of loyalty to and critique or protest toward law, 64, 72; of African Americans to Constitution, 64; Danish Church Ordinance's requirement

of oath of, to king, 255; fiduciary law and, 224, 226, 231, 231n.43, 235, 236, 238, 239, 241, 242, 242n.94; Hugo Heclo on Christian loyalty, 32n.11; in Hosea 4, 107; Martin Luther King Jr. on, 75; Luther on, to secular authorities, 319; of military chaplains to military mission, 274; and religious freedom, 53

Luther, Martin: on children, 143-44, 144n.8; on Christian freedom, 167; on Christian moral life, 63; on Christian vocation, 168, 200, 302, 304; concept of God of, 109, 138; cosmic drama, view of, 100; and distributive justice, 316-18; Fifth Commandment, explanation of, 317; on first use of the law, 209, 219, 223, 240; Brian Gerrish on, 93n.47; God's law, 194; God's law vs. civil law, 9n.1; God's panentheistic presence and, 81; on grace alone, 13; Douglas John Hall on Luther's theology of glory, 276; justification by faith, view of, 13, 167, 190, 276; law-gospel distinction by, 9, 12, 12n.14, 13; *sola scriptura* principle of, 11; on spirituality of the cross and humility, 276, 283; on Ten Commandments, 110, 147-48, 217; on theology of glory, 275; on theology of the cross, 275; third use of the law and, 208; on two kingdoms, 29, 45, 66-67, 168, 182, 202, 220, 271, 283, 304, 321, 330, 334; on two uses of the law, 206-8

Luther on government, 166, 314; Christian vocation and, 214n.25; on God's governance, 304, 315, 315n.31; love commandment and, 168, 202; medieval theology, Luther's use of, and, 166; natural law and, 316; obedience to authority, 272, 273-74n.20; obligation of obedience to, 319; preachers' and bishops' duty to call to account, 320-21; priesthood of all believers, 17; Psalm 82 and, 316-21; public theol-

105, 111, 131; Sixth Commandment, Luther's explanation of in *Small Catechism*, 218; trafficking of children and, 146

Texas: El Paso Irrigation District No. 1, 118-19, 119n.70; and one hundredth meridian, 103n.4; Rio Grande Compact, 119n.70; Rio Grande Project, 119-20; and Southwestern U.S., 104n.11; *State of Texas v. State of New Mexico and State of Colorado*, 118; and U.S. Bureau of Reclamation, 120; and water transfers to City of El Paso and between Texas and other Southwestern states, 122, 129

Theology. *See* Public theology

Tort law: distinguished from criminal law, 240; presumption of self-interested behavior, 241; relation to fiduciary law, 241

Transformational (transformative) economy: assumptions about human beings in concept of, 99; and climate change, 125, 138; and decision of *Lucas v. South Carolina Coastal Council*, 99; defined, 103; distinguished from an economy of nature, 90, 98; effects of on Southwestern Native Americans, 127; El Paso authorities and, 122; implications of for property rights, 86; and mindset in the Southwest, 117; Larry Rasmussen and Christiana Peppard on water transfers and, 133; Joseph L. Sax on economies of nature and, 98-100; and water rights, 115

Troeltsch, Ernst: dissent from view of on Lutheranism by George Forell, William Lazareth, Richard Niebanck, and John Witte Jr., 329-32; influence of on H. R. Niebuhr's and Reinhold Niebuhr's views, 329; and H. Richard Niebuhr's views of Lutheranism, 328; Samuel Schmucker's Americanist movement in relation to, 329-30; Second Great Awakening and Social

Gospel influence on Lutherans' activism and, 331; view of Lutheranism, 328

T visa: burden of proof for, 174; and cooperation with law enforcement, 175; protection of human trafficking survivors holding a, 174-75, 177

Two kingdoms, doctrine of: and Christian social engagement, 168; complementary modes of God's governance through law and, 167, 214, 271; contemporary protection of children and, 145; and Danish Church Ordinance, 258; human laws and, 149; and immigration issues, 199; and justice and justification before God, 186; Martin Luther King Jr.'s theology and, 64; late twentieth-century dynamic interpretation of, 333; Luther's views of parenting and, 145; and military chaplaincy, 283; post-Reformation period's understanding of, 332; and reality of sin, 149; Samuel Schmucker's denial of, 330; secular contemporary jurisprudence and, 57; the sword and God's Word in, 166; and temporal and spiritual kingdoms, 166-68

Uniform Code of Military Justice: and religious expression by military personnel, 268-69; Veitch case, 277-78

United States Congress: in *Arizona v. Colorado*, 117; Boulder Canyon Project Act of 1928 by, 102; Colorado River Compact and authority of, 117; First Amendment and, 11, 46, 266; investigation of religious intolerance by, 276; Lutheran Immigration and Refugee Service (LIRS) assessments of immigration legislation by, 200; ratification of interstate river compacts by, 117; refusal of to ratify International Covenant on Economic, Cultural, and Social Rights, 205, 205n.4; RICO reports to, on

Wingren, Gustav: on discernment and
freedom in Luther's theology of
vocation, 110n.38; on human responsibility to God, 109; on Luther's two
kingdoms theory and social responsibility, 168
Witness. *See* Public witness
Women: commodification of persons
and, 161, 164; M. Shawn Copeland
and African American women's experience, 67-68; effect of Danish civil
war on, 251; Enlightenment influence
on subjugation of African American women, 71; factors influencing
trafficking victim cooperation with
law enforcement, 162, 180; feminist
critique of trafficking of, 155; inadequacy of criminal trafficking laws and
enforcement for, 154, 161; Senator
Ted Kennedy on Robert Bork's views
on, 20; methods of trafficking of, 162;
non-legal ways to address trafficking
of, 172, 180-81; perspectives of on
New Mexican water issues, 134n.133;
reform of trafficking laws and gender
equality, 154, 171; John Rutsindintwarane and women in Mumeya, 299;
Rutsindintwarane's work with urban
Rwandan women in prostitution,
293; Safe Harbor Act's aims, 157; sex

trafficking of, 163, 164-65; sexuality
of, 158; social disagreement on rights
of, 143; structuralist approach to
explaining the sex trade of, 152-53;
Trafficking Victims Protection
Reauthorization Act of 2013, 178; and
the U.S. Constitution, 16; as victims
of sex trafficking, 150-51; Violence
Against Women Act, 178; vulnerability of to trafficking, 165; World Bank
role in combatting trafficking of, 174
Word of God: and amending the Danish
Church Ordinance, 253; arguing from
Scripture and the human conscience,
219; and church's public responsibility on law and policies, 337; and
divine will, 215; fundamentalist
identification of the Bible with, 11;
Brian Gerrish on reason and, in Luther's thought, 93-94n.37; and human
behavior, 90-91; human response
to, 221; Luther on distinguishing
scripture and the, 11; Luther on
preaching of the, under scrutiny of
princes, 35-36n.25, 320; as narrative
of God's dealings with humanity,
13; and removal of Danish Catholic
bishops during Reformation, 251-52;
and third use of the law, 221